Once a King

Once a King

The Lost Memoir of Edward VIII

Jane Marguerite Tippett

HODDER &
STOUGHTON

First published in Great Britain in 2023 by Hodder & Stoughton
An Hachette UK company

3

Copyright © Jane Marguerite Tippett 2023

The right of Jane Marguerite Tippett to be identified as the Author
of the Work has been asserted by her in accordance with the
Copyright, Designs and Patents Act 1988.

A CIP catalogue record for this title is available from the British Library

Hardback ISBN 9781399723930
Trade Paperback ISBN 9781399723947
ebook ISBN 9781399723954

Typeset in Sabon LT Std by Palimpsest Book Production Limited,
Falkirk, Stirlingshire

Printed and bound in Great Britain by Clays Ltd, Elcograf S.p.A.

Hodder & Stoughton policy is to use papers that are natural,
renewable and recyclable products and made from wood grown in
sustainable forests. The logging and manufacturing processes are
expected to conform to the environmental regulations
of the country of origin.

Hodder & Stoughton Ltd
Carmelite House
50 Victoria Embankment
London EC4Y 0DZ

www.hodder.co.uk

To M and B – love for always

Contents

Cast of Characters

King Edward VIII, later The Duke of Windsor, 'Edward' (1894–1972).
First son of George V and Queen Mary, he succeeded to the title of
Prince of Wales in 1910. He was King Edward VIII for only ten
months before abdicating on 11 December 1936. He lived in exile in
France until his death on 28 May 1972.

Wallis, Duchess of Windsor, 'Wallis' (1896–1986). Born Bessie Wallis
Warfield, she grew up in Baltimore, Maryland, and moved to London
after her second marriage to Ernest Simpson. Her romance with
Edward and his determination to marry her precipitated his abdication.

Lt Colonel Sir John Aird (1898–1973). Equerry to Edward from 1929
to 1936; the two men met in France during the First World War.

Sir Ulick Alexander (1899–1973). Appointed Keeper of the Privy
Purse by Edward in 1936.

Sir Albert George 'A.G.' Allen (1888–1956). Solicitor to Edward and
one of his principal advisers during the abdication crisis of 1936.

Cleveland Amory (1917–1998). American author, journalist and
noted chronicler of international café society, Amory briefly served
as Wallis's ghostwriter in 1955.

Sir Max Aitken (1910–1985). Lord Beaverbrook's son, and eventual
Chairman of Beaverbrook Newspapers Ltd.

Stanley Baldwin, 1st Earl Baldwin of Bewdley (1867–1947).
Conservative Prime Minister in 1936.

Charles Bedaux (1886–1944). Franco-American millionaire who lent
his Loire valley home, the Château de Candé, to Edward and Wallis
for their wedding.

Alfred Duff Cooper, 1st Viscount Norwich (1890–1954). Secretary of State for War in 1936.

Peregrine 'Perry' Cust, 6th Baron Brownlow (1899–1978). Appointed as a Lord-in-Waiting to Edward in 1936, he accompanied Wallis as she fled from England to France in December 1936.

William Maxwell 'Max' Aitken, 1st Baron Beaverbrook, 'Lord Beaverbrook' (1879–1964). Canadian press baron, political insider and founder of the *Daily Express*.

Sir Winston Churchill (1874–1965). Conservative politician, statesman and Prime Minister during the Second World War.

Queen Elizabeth The Queen Mother (1900–2002). Born Elizabeth Bowes-Lyon, she married Edward's brother, Albert (later George VI), in 1923.

King George V (1865–1936). Edward's father, who reigned as George V, 1910–1936.

King George VI (1895–1952). Edward's younger brother, the second son of George V and Queen Mary, he succeeded to the throne upon Edward's abdication.

Prince George, Duke of Kent (1902–1942). Fourth son of George V and Queen Mary, he was Edward's favourite brother.

Walter Graebner (1909–unknown). American journalist, author and Time Inc. executive based in London.

Alexander 'Alec' Hardinge, 2nd Baron Hardinge of Penshurst (1894–1960). Assistant Private Secretary to George V, Private Secretary to Edward VIII and George VI.

Prince Henry, Duke of Gloucester (1900–1974). Third son of George V and Queen Mary.

Samuel Hoare, 1st Viscount Templewood (1880–1959). Conservative politician and diplomat, he was First Lord of the Admiralty in 1936 and later served as British Ambassador to Spain (1940–1944).

Rt Hon. Sir Alan 'Tommy' Lascelles (1887–1981). Private Secretary to Edward 1920–1929, later Assistant Private Secretary to George V, Edward VIII, George VI and Elizabeth II.

Cosmo Gordon Lang, Archbishop of Canterbury (1864–1945). Archbishop of Canterbury in 1936.

Daniel Longwell (1899–1968). Co-founder and editor of *Life*, he later served as the Chairman of the Board of Editors from 1946 until his retirement in 1954.

Henry Luce (1898–1967). Founder of the Time Inc. media empire, which included the magazines *Time, Fortune, Life* and *Sports Illustrated*.

Queen Mary (1867–1953). Wife of George V and Edward's mother.

HRH The Princess Mary, Princess Royal, Countess of Harewood (1897–1965). Only daughter of George V and Queen Mary, sister of Edward.

Bessie Merryman (1864-1964). Wallis Simpson's aunt.

Walter Monckton, 1st Viscount Monckton of Brenchley (1891–1965). Lawyer, politician and adviser to Edward during the abdication crisis and later in exile.

Charles J. V. Murphy (1904–1987). Time Inc. journalist and noted ghostwriter, Murphy collaborated with the Windsors on their successive memoirs published between 1947 and 1956.

Sir Edward Peacock (1871–1962). Canadian-born banker, he was Edward's principal financial adviser and helped negotiate his financial settlement during the abdication crisis.

Kenneth 'Ken' Rawson (1911–1992). Book publisher and editor, Rawson met Murphy in 1934 when both were members of Admiral Richard Byrd's second Arctic expedition.

Bernard Rickatson-Hatt (1898–1966). Editor-in-Chief of Reuters News. Friend of Ernest Simpson.

Herman (1891–1957) and Katherine Rogers (d.1949). Wealthy American expatriates and long-standing friends of Wallis Simpson.

Sir Walford Selby (1881–1965). British diplomat, envoy to Austria (1933–1937) and Ambassador to Portugal (1937–1940).

Ernest Aldrich Simpson (1897–1958). British-American shipbroker, who was Wallis's second husband (1928–1937).

John Simon, 1st Viscount Simon (1873–1954). Home Secretary in 1936.

Sir Godfrey Thomas (1889–1968). Edward's Private Secretary from 1919 until 1936.

Henry 'Hank' G. Walter (1910–2000). Edward's American lawyer, based in New York, who oversaw the financial negotiations with *Life*.

Freda Dudley Ward (1894–1983). English socialite and Edward's mistress for much of the 1920s.

Monica Wyatt (1922–2005). Charles J. V. Murphy's long-time secretary at Time Inc., and his principal assistant during the writing of Edward's memoirs.

Philip Ziegler (1929–2023). Historian, and Edward's official biographer.

Introduction

This is not the book I intended to write. In the summer of 2022, I was in the second year of writing what was to be an in-depth examination of the personal and political consequences of the thirteen crucial months in the life of Edward VIII following his abdication on 11 December 1936 to marry the twice-divorced American, Wallis Simpson. From the outset, I considered Edward's memoir, *A King's Story* (1951), and Wallis's autobiography, *The Heart Has Its Reasons* (1956), to be key sources in understanding the controversial actions that now dominate the public's perception of their lives.

Disregarding the inevitable questions of self-censorship and self-mythologising that surround any autobiography, there were, however, in the Windsors' case further risks for an author relying too heavily on their words. Published in an age less used to the celebrity tell-all, the memoirs were highly controversial. The wisdom of an ex-king choosing to subject himself to public scrutiny was hotly debated, and conventional British voices were even more shocked by Edward's decision to precede his book's publication with seven feature articles in the American picture magazine, *Life*. Aside from Queen Victoria's benign autobiographical account of life in Scotland with her consort, Prince Albert, *Leaves from the Journal of Our Life in the Highlands* (1864), no British monarch had ever published a record of royal life. But, then, no British monarch had ever voluntarily abdicated the throne. Edward, always a catalyst for controversy, by choosing to publish had in the eyes of his critics wilfully violated the mores of constitutional monarchy in exchange for personal satisfaction and financial gain. Wallis's memoir, published five years later, was viewed largely as an afterthought. Clearly, then, the circumstances surrounding these texts argue for a cautious approach. Nevertheless they are the only lengthy public pronouncements the Windsors ever made on the major events of their lives – lives they felt had been subject to much public misinformation. Hence, I regarded their published memoirs as an essential part of the foundation on which I had to build. I was soon to learn there was much more to be found.

In the early stages of my research, I hadn't penetrated far beyond the published editions, both of which had been prepared with the help of Charles J. V. Murphy – an American journalist and long-standing correspondent for *Life*. Murphy's assistance was acknowledged at the time of each book's publication, but his presence in the Windsors' lives has remained little more than a footnote. Like others, I had been content to rely on Murphy's own published account, *The Windsor Story* (1979), as his exhaustive and final word on the couple. In fact, the book had been predominantly written at the urging of and by Murphy's collaborator Joe Bryan, a former editor of the *Saturday Evening Post*, who had social and professional connections with the Windsors.

It was not until I came across a source note in Andrew Morton's 2018 biography of the Duchess of Windsor, *Wallis in Love*, that I began to think more seriously about Murphy's role as their 'ghostwriter'. Morton boasted of having uncovered 'the biographical equivalent of Aladdin's cave' [1] in finding the uncatalogued archive of Cleveland Amory, who in 1955 had briefly replaced Murphy as Wallis's collaborator. Thanks to the age of digitisation, I was able to receive overnight most of the files Morton had accessed. They included more than five hours of recorded interviews with the Duke and Duchess of Windsor discussing topics that ranged from the abdication, the denial to Wallis of the style 'Her Royal Highness', and their escape from France in June 1940. I was confused, however, by the discrepancy of Wallis referring to their interviewer as 'Charlie', and Edward recalling his mother's sympathetic final words at Royal Lodge, 'Remember . . . because then we put it in the book . . .' [2] – until I realised that these were not Amory's interviews with the Windsors but Charles Murphy's.

My eyes were now fully open to Murphy. If the relatively small amount of material in the hands of a fleeting hired scribe had been so revelatory, what might the papers of the man who had spent a decade in and out of the Windsors' orbit be like? It took only a quick search to find that Murphy's papers were on deposit at Boston University's Howard Gotlieb Research Center, publicly accessible since their arrival in the mid-1990s. All seventeen boxes of Murphy's papers had been painstakingly itemised, and four were devoted entirely to the Windsors. The excitement was intense, and I headed for Boston.

There is always hesitation on these trips. Will they yield results, or will it be a slog that was worth neither the time nor the expense? As I sat down in the reading room on an extremely warm June morning, I soon knew that this trip would be more than worthwhile. It was an archival feast, and I found myself wading through an exhaustive record of Murphy's relationship with the Windsors – with a particularly rich concentration of material relating to time he spent working with Edward. Unedited first drafts of *A King's Story* were preserved alongside hundreds of pages of Murphy's own notes, many of which were records of conversations with Edward or the multitude of others he had spoken with to gain insight into the Duke's life – including Edward's advisers George Allen and Walter Monckton as well as his former Private Secretary Godfrey Thomas and the newspaper tycoon Max Beaverbrook. Picking up a folder labelled 'Diary', I discovered two small slips of Waldorf Astoria memo paper – a bullet-point list in the Duke's hand-writing, 'very proud . . . independent . . . chic . . . exacting',[3] clipped to another paper and labelled by Murphy as 'HRH's Description of Duchess'. Immediately following it were more than thirty pages of Murphy's typed diary entries. An excerpt from one dated January 1950 read: 'Today for the first time the Duke and Duchess faced up to the issues involved in the abdication. It was a weird experience . . .'[4] The archive also included at least two hundred pages of transcripts from his interviews with Wallis and Edward made in late 1954 as he began to prepare *The Heart Has Its Reasons* – a small part of which mirrored the tapes in the Amory interviews – proving that it had been Murphy's gentle yet subtly penetrating approach that elicited from the Windsors their expansive and extremely uninhibited answers. As I would learn over the coming months, it was the Windsors' trust in Murphy and the Duke's affection for him that allowed the couple to feel so at ease with the American journalist.

Over two days I tried, without much success, to remain focused on the original subject of my research, 1937, but it became impossible not to veer off topic and peruse the wide-ranging content of the archive, which also included Murphy's extensive correspondence over the years he spent with the Windsors. His letters captured in almost minute detail the trials, tribulations and enjoyment that went into producing, in particular, Edward's memoir. The role of *Life* in this process became more and more apparent as men such as the magazine's Chairman, Daniel Longwell, emerged as central players in the story of Edward's writing. Like so many others, I had ignored Edward's journalistic endeavours and overlooked the story around his brief tenure as an American magazine writer.

It took me less than forty-eight hours to discover I had a brand-new book to write. Over the next year, along with return visits to Boston, I made a series of further research trips expanding the collection of primary material that makes up the narrative that follows. Once alerted to the almost forgotten collaboration between Edward and Murphy, I quickly found, in otherwise well-mined archives, material that had also been ignored. Lord Beaverbrook's papers contained chapters, not in Murphy's archive, written by Edward in 1949 about the abdication. They bore little resemblance to the published material in either *Life* or *A King's Story*. Daniel Longwell's archive documented, with greater precision than Murphy's, the diplomatic tightrope that the men at Time Inc. had walked not only to secure Edward's memoir but to sustain his momentum over more than four years. And buried within a box of uncatalogued papers in the Royal Archives were Edward's handwritten first drafts – still tied together with his signature 'India string', the short red cords with toggles at the end that had first been used by Queen Victoria as a form of nineteenth-century paperclip. Having worked off the assumption that Murphy had been the primary author behind Edward's published material, I was intrigued to discover that many of Edward's words, particularly regarding his childhood, were in fact reproduced verbatim in the published account. With even greater delight, I realised that many more personal reflections had not made it into the public domain. Now, not only had I discovered the story of how Edward's memoir had been created, I had uncovered that, with Murphy's help, Edward had become a writer.

The Duke of Windsor first met Time Inc. journalist Charles J. V. Murphy over lunch at the Waldorf Astoria in New York City during the summer of 1945. Both men were at a crossroads. Edward was heading back to an uncertain future in France after five years as Governor General of the Bahamas, and Murphy was on his way to China, where he was to research a story on Chiang Kai-shek. Just days after arriving in New York from the Bahamas, Murphy's recently published three-part series on Winston Churchill in *Life* caught Edward's eye. Murphy had crafted, featuring Yousuf Karsh's imposing portrait of the wartime hero on its cover, an elegiac but heroic homage to 'the last truly great man of the Western world',[5] lavishly illustrated from Churchill's private photograph album.

Life was founded in 1936 by Time Inc.'s Chairman, Henry Luce, as a current-events picture magazine; its feature stories were by 1945 increasingly focused on profiles of exceptional men and women – actors, royalty and statesmen – individuals whose stories embodied the aspirational enthusiasm of American culture. Edward was by no means a stranger to *Life*. A profile of Fort Belvedere, his residence in Windsor Great Park, was featured in its debut issue on 23 November 1936, and in June 1941 he and Wallis, titled as 'The Windsor Team', had posed for the magazine's cover in what was billed as an intimate portrait of their life at home in the Bahamas. But Edward was particularly impressed by *Life*'s handling of Churchill. He liked the story's historic but humanising tone and immediately appreciated how Murphy's style, shaped specifically for the American reader, might be successfully applied to his own narrative.

Through his New York attorney Hank Walter, who knew Murphy socially, Edward arranged to meet the author. The two men had what Murphy later described to Henry Luce as a 'long and pleasant talk' as Edward discussed 'the idea of publishing some part of the story of his life'. Yet the afternoon produced no immediate result. 'Well,' Murphy told Luce, 'I was on my way to the Pacific – the idea at the time didn't stimulate me particularly – there was a war going on – and the matter was dropped.'[6]

Though Charles Murphy is today an almost unknown figure, when Edward encountered him in 1945, he was one of Time Inc.'s pre-eminent journalists. Born on 11 October 1904 in a suburb of Boston, Massachusetts, to Irish-Canadian parents, Murphy's childhood was shaped by his mother's death in 1915 and his father's immediate remarriage to the family's housekeeper with whom he had a further four children. A mediocre student, Murphy dropped out of Harvard University in September 1924 after only two years when chance offered him a job as a rewrite man in the New York City office of Associated Press. He spent the next decade climbing the ladder of American journalism with roles at the United Press, New York's *Evening Post* and the *New York World*. His nose for a story led him to report on the American admiral and explorer Richard Byrd, who quickly noticed Murphy's skills as a storyteller and commissioned him to write a series of autobiographical accounts of his adventures as well as a full-length memoir published in 1928, *Struggle: The Life of Commander Richard Byrd*. Their success helped transform Byrd into an all-American hero, and along the way Murphy became one of his closest advisers and friends. Byrd eventually persuaded the now freelance journalist to accompany him on his second Antarctic expedition, tasked with writing the weekly CBS broadcasts that Byrd and others on the mission delivered from their base, Little America. Murphy eventually took on the outsized role of Byrd's chief-of-staff and oversaw the explorer's daring winter rescue from the meteorological station he had spent five months operating alone. To preserve Byrd's heroic appeal, which he had spent the previous six years crafting, Murphy concealed the fact that Byrd had himself radioed for help and knowingly risked the lives of the men he called to his aid. The lightly censored adventure produced two bestsellers, which Murphy wrote on behalf of the explorer over the next four years, cementing his career as ghostwriter *par excellence*.

In 1935, while still working with Byrd, Murphy landed a job at *Fortune*,

Time Inc.'s monthly business magazine, which had been founded in 1929. 'It was the magazine I wanted to write for,'[7] he later told a friend. But as an employee of Time Inc., he quickly found himself assigned to writing for the organisation's other major publications, all of which remained under founder Henry Luce's direct managerial control. Murphy was often frustrated with Luce's editorial decisions, and his relationship with his boss was frequently fractious. 'Both men were intelligent and forceful personalities,' Murphy's son-in-law and private biographer John Holbrook remembered.

> Although they shared a conservative political outlook, they marched to different drums – the demands of a good story versus the demands of a profitable journalistic empire. They often argued about what would stay in and what would be taken out of Murphy's articles, and the arguments often became quite heated . . . . Murphy was a thorn in Luce's side, but Luce kept Murphy on the staff because of his unusual intellect, his unparalleled network of friends and acquaintances, his uncanny nose for a story, his sheer competence in crafting a story, his elegant prose, and his wit – the importance of which cannot be underestimated.'[8]

Murphy's career at Time Inc. flourished, and for the next decade he found himself at the forefront of America's most influential media empire. His narrative flair was particularly effective for the dramatic wartime features he wrote between 1941 and 1945 when on assignment overseas for *Life*. In April 1941 he and fellow Time Inc. photographer David Scherman (who a few months later would photograph the Windsors in the Bahamas) were on board the Egyptian cargo ship *Zamzam* when it was sunk by the Germans. Murphy captivated *Life*'s readers with a stirring account of their rescue, and the several weeks he and the other two hundred (largely American) passengers spent on the German freighter *Dresden* before being deposited in France. For the remainder of the war, Murphy covered Allied offensives in Europe and the Pacific, returning to Britain in early 1945 to write his heroic portrayal of Churchill. The success of the three articles, eventually published in book form as *The Lives of Winston Churchill*, convinced Luce that Murphy was the right man to produce a similarly inspirational story about Chiang Kai-shek's stand against Mao Tse-tung. Luce viewed Chiang as the final bulwark against a Communist takeover of Asia. Murphy spent five months in China writing his story, but the article went unpublished. Almost immediately upon his return to New York City, he faced a backlash from *Life* executives who feared that such overt political support for Chiang Kai-shek, an increasingly unpopular figure in the United States, could jeopardise the magazine's standing among its American readers. Despite this setback, Murphy emerged from the wartime years as one of the leading journalists at Time Inc., whose publications then reached more than a quarter of the adult population of the United States.

In the eighteen months that passed between Edward and Murphy's first and second meeting, the Duke's approach to the writing of his life story had altered dramatically. His interest in the summer of 1945 had been one of tentative curiosity, and he was by no means sold on the idea of writing a memoir, which he knew would be controversial. Having spent the last six years as Major General to the British Military Mission in France and then as Governor of the Bahamas, Edward was anxious to secure an official position from the British government. He settled his hopes on a diplomatic post in the United States aimed at fostering Anglo-American relations. From October 1945 to March 1946, he did his best to persuade his brother, King George VI, of the value of this idea. But faced with the implacable hostility of the King's principal courtiers and the government's cautious concern about the potential hazards of two competing British diplomats in Washington D.C., George VI refused Edward's request. 'I have no intention of remaining idle,' Edward told his brother, on 10 April 1946, after he was informed of the decision. 'I must look for a job in whatever sphere and country I can find one suitable to my qualification.'[9]

Rebuffed by the old world, Edward's mind returned to the meeting with Murphy and the idea of trying to bring together the threads of his life in some publishable format. Less than a month after his rejection by the British government, Edward floated the idea of a memoir to his long-time counsellor Sir Walter Monckton, a clear indication that he was now seriously considering the prospect of publication. He wrote to Monckton on 31 May 1946:

> It has been suggested to me from not uninteresting quarters that the time has come for me to write my side of the abdication story. It seems considerable conjecture still lives in the minds of many thinking people – both in Great Britain and America – concerning that episode. This is a project I would naturally wish to discuss with you, and it is a subject of such historical and political interest that the lone hand I had to play throughout the negotiations with the politicians both of church and state, could not be accurately chronicled without the advice and assistance of my liaison officer.[10]

As events would later reveal, Monckton was horrified by the news. But with his characteristic diplomacy, he sent Edward a cautious reply noting merely he was 'very interested in your idea' and willing to 'help'[11] when he finally got started. This tacit approval from one of the most trusted voices in his life left Edward free to ruminate further about the future. By the time he arrived in New York on 11 November 1946, he was ready to resume the conversation with Murphy.

Murphy greeted Edward's second approach with far more enthusiasm than he had when they last met. With the excitement of wartime reporting now over and eager for the next big assignment, Murphy was in a far more receptive mood for a collaboration with the ex-King. 'I have been thinking over the possibilities of a book,' Murphy told Hank Walter shortly before he and Edward met on

14 November 1946, 'and they are truly fascinating. Some years ago, I swore I would never do another ghost job, but this could be a wonderful thing.'[12]

In contrast to the tepid reception Edward had received from Buckingham Palace, Murphy and his colleagues at *Life* were exhilarated by the prospect of his potential authorship. Despite his outsider status in Britain, Edward remained an admired and highly romanticised figure in the United States. His matinee-idol good looks had charmed North America in the early 1920s, and the abdication, precipitated by his love for an American woman, had caught the country's popular imagination as it indulged in the fairy-tale elements of a story that seemed straight out of a Hollywood script. The Windsors' geographic proximity to the United States during the war years and their highly publicised visit to New York City in 1941 had kept them at the centre of American celebrity culture – and thus ideally suited for the pages of *Life* magazine.

Though the formal overtures were made by Henry Luce, it was Daniel Longwell, Chairman of the Board of Editors, who took charge of Edward and, through a diplomatic deft hand, secured his trust and the commitment to publish in *Life*. Acutely aware that financial incentives* alone were not enough to induce Edward to publish, Longwell went to great lengths to encourage his at times hesitant author, assuring him of the project's lasting historical value and reminding him that he, as a *Life* contributor, was in the company of other notable men who were also committing their memoirs to the magazine – including Winston Churchill. Removed from the immediacy of the daily working frustrations that eventually developed, Longwell was a sustaining presence for both Edward and Murphy. 'I was the hand-holder, the slave driver, the mean guy, the patcher-up of quarrels, and the entertainer,'[13] as Longwell later described it. And though he gave Murphy the 'credit for Windsor . . . and a magnificent job it was, too',[14] Longwell's role was vital. His support was particularly essential in overcoming the

---

* Edward received $75,000 for the three articles, which were published in 1947. He received $106,000 for the four published in 1950 – equivalent to $1,334,293 or £1,065,232 in today's currency.

stinging criticism that emerged from Edward's two principal advisers in Britain, Walter Monckton and Edward's solicitor, Sir George Allen, both of whom had been central players in the abdication crisis. Neither supported his decision to write his memoir, though both breathed a sigh of relief at the news that it would end in 1936, and each tried to prevent its publication. But backed by the men of Time Inc. Edward made it through to the finish, and he left behind his memoirs: those published successively in 1947, 1950 and 1951, and those unpublished, which form the core of this book.

From July 1947 until January 1951, Edward and Murphy were in each other's company on an almost daily basis, constant partners in their work and leisure hours. Murphy discovered almost immediately that Edward needed to 'learn the habits of work'[15] and their languid schedule, which for the first two years was set against the backdrop of the Windsors' home, La Croë, on Cap d'Antibes, proved a highly unorthodox office environment for a forty-two-year-old journalist used to an action-packed scene and quick turnarounds. Murphy also faced the unexpected challenge of teaching Edward the art of reminiscing, as his perspective on his multitude of exceptional experiences was, as Murphy told Longwell, 'less than penetrating'.[16] Though constantly mindful of the grievances that had characterised his now eleven-year exile, it was an entirely new experience for Edward to recall his life before the abdication. Yet judging him 'willing' and 'sincere',[17] Murphy was not disheartened. His task, he realised, was to help Edward find a voice – both figuratively and literally – with which he could articulate his past.

Deciding not to conduct direct interviews (a technique he would later use with skill when it came time to write Wallis's memoir), Murphy determined that the best way of compiling the necessary material for the memoir was to suggest topics and invite Edward to talk about them – much like a schoolmaster encouraging a recalcitrant child. Edward, either alone or in concert with others who were induced to

participate in the project, explored his assigned subjects through mono-
logues, characterised by a mixture of humour, candour, objectivity and
reticence, that were recorded in shorthand by a secretary. Edward was
eased into the art of reminiscing through Murphy's careful strategy.
Though their preliminary forays were noticeably stilted, as the process
continued Edward became more comfortable and his observations
more astute. He began to take control of his narration, which finally
enabled him to write about more sensitive themes that were pivotal
to the presentation of his story. Along the way, Murphy captured
Edward's often ad-hoc observations, which were probably the result
of casual conversation. Always mindful that Edward was his subject
rather than his friend, Murphy would hastily note down these remarks,
which were then typed out and filed according to their subject matter
or their relevance to a particular article or chapter.

Murphy's secretary, Monica Wyatt, who was present during many
of their meetings and would take down in shorthand Edward's words,
described the routine that developed at La Croë: 'He [Murphy] dines
with the Windsors at least four nights a week, plays golf with the Duke
every afternoon . . . and then from 6 to 8:30 each evening . . . [he's]
with the Duke going over what's been done'.[18] Murphy, a noted racon-
teur who loved nothing more than to hold court among a group of
cultivated listeners, soon became an indispensable element in Edward's
milieu, offering him the constant stimulation of an interesting and
informed companion. The friendly rapport the two men established
was the essential first step in creating an environment conducive to
Edward feeling able to discuss his life with someone who, at least on
paper, had very little in common with him. Yet Edward responded
positively to Murphy's intelligence, his easy manner, his Americanness
and his determination. Edward, as he later told Murphy, always admired
self-made men who did 'things' and abhorred the company of people
whose conversations were dominated by their own 'undue sense . . .
of rank'.[19]

The two men's intimacy was reinforced when Murphy's family joined
him in France and the domestic routines of the Murphy household
became intertwined with those of Edward and Wallis. Murphy's wife

Jane joined him at the Windsors' dinner table, and his two youngest children, Edythe ('Edie') and Charles, became enlivening fixtures of life at La Cröe. Always fond of children, Edward delighted in them – particularly Edie, whom he taught archery and who frequently accompanied him on long afternoon walks around the rocky coastline of Cap d'Antibes. The rambunctious nature of the Murphy adolescents was a source of consternation to Wallis but of sheer amusement to Edward, who found their playfulness charming. When childish exuberance led to a beautifully laid picnic table set up on the beach near La Croë being pushed out into the sea, Edward was captivated – in marked contrast to Wallis's anger and Murphy's parental horror. The family also shared Edward's love of dogs, and when a particularly naughty cairn terrier arrived, which Wallis decided was unmanageable, Edward gifted it to Edie.

Murphy's strategy laid the groundwork for Edward to begin writing the first drafts of his memoir. Using the conversations and notes that were compiled, Edward began preparing material in what was his distinctive pencil printed style. At what was, for Murphy, a sometimes agonisingly slow pace, Edward covered the pages of his yellow legal pads with narrative passages that he did not, frustratingly, always tackle in chronological order. Murphy was there to edit and suggest but not to be the initial draughtsman. Typed up by an awaiting secretary who meticulously noted the date of Edward's text, the pages were then passed on to Murphy for his revision before being recirculated to Edward, who would often rewrite entire sections before adding 'OK' at the bottom of a page.

Most of Edward's writing never made it into either the *Life* articles in 1950 or *A King's Story*, which was published by G. P. Putnam's in the United States and by Cassell & Co in Great Britain in 1951. But that was not unexpected. Edward had approached the memoir with the unorthodox aim of first creating an 'unexpurgated book', one that would 'omit nothing however secret and personal'[20] and from which selected material could be extracted for publication. Though the commercial imperatives of Time Inc. interrupted the completion of that project, Edward began by creating content he had no intention of publishing. Written freely, these drafts were his attempt to make sense of a life characterised, in public and private, by controversial choices. His uncensored words built a portrait of his role as Prince of Wales and his reinvention of that role for a twentieth-century audience. They also offer insight into his views on his family, his education and his relationship with Wallis, as well as describing the challenges he faced before and during the abdication. And though his vision of kingship failed to resonate within his own time, his perspective, outlined in this never-before-seen material, proved prescient in the way it anticipates the style of Britain's Royal Family today. His writing also captures with subtle poignancy the personal experiences of a man struggling to come to terms with obligations that, because of a chance of birth, he was forced to fulfil. His reflections and observations reveal that he thought more deeply about his life, its failures and successes, than popular opinion recognises.

While some of these handwritten drafts survived in his own papers, most were saved by Murphy, who recognised the value that Edward's reflections would hold for future historians. They appear in this book for the first time. As the reader will discover, Edward was no great stylist, but he nevertheless offers penetrating accounts of an extraordinary life that alternate between nuanced observations and frustratingly minimal descriptions. But having honed his skills over the course of two years, when it was time in mid-1949 to write about the abdication in chapter form, Edward was ready to be the architect of his own story. He tackled the defining event of his life with verve and drama, but his account was impossible to publish in his own lifetime.

The reconstruction of Edward's memoirs that follows does not aim to be a comprehensive biography or an exhaustive chronicle of the abdication. It is also not a portrait of the Windsors' marriage. Instead, it is a record of perceptions of and about Edward by himself and the people, including Wallis, who helped craft the story of his life. Murphy is a central figure in this chronicle, guiding and narrating a process that, in less agile hands, could have failed. Despite the frustrations that eventually surfaced, Murphy refused to give up on Edward and he readily returned to the Windsors' milieu in 1954 to assist Wallis on her autobiography. The subsequent collaboration supplied none of the subtle enjoyment of his work with Edward, but he soldiered through to its completion and in the end came to regard her book as an important postscript to *A King's Story*. But it is perhaps Murphy's sporadic diary entries, made between 1947 and 1956, that afford us the most insight into the Windsors as he knew them. Humorous at times, poignant at others, these recollections capture an enigmatic couple at their most unguarded. Through the perspicacity of their ghost, we gain an entirely fresh perspective on their lives – and for the first time we can hear from the Windsors directly.

It was the desire to give the Windsors back their voice that convinced me this was the book I was meant to write, at least for now. The Duke and Duchess occupy an almost legendary status in the popular history of the twentieth century, yet they remain elusive figures – in part because we have never been able thoroughly to understand what they did and why. Sweeping generalisations and critical stereotypes now dominate our perception of them. Rumour and gossip about their lives has been gradually transformed into fact, and, without any heirs to shepherd their legacy, they have been easy targets for the sensationalist headlines of modern media culture. The Duke of Windsor has essentially been erased from the canon of twentieth-century British royal history even though he was a senior member of the dynasty for over forty years and an integral asset to its survival in the period immediately following the end of the First World War. My work on 1937 had aimed to tackle a small chapter in his controversial history and challenge existing categorisations, most notably that he was an unequivocal Nazi sympathiser. I had hoped to rescue Edward from the one-dimensional stereotypes that now exist of him, produced in part by such contemporary efforts as the television series *The Crown*. But 1937 was just one snapshot from the seventy-two years that filled the most unconventional royal life of the twentieth century. Whatever work I did, however meaningful, could have been easily overwhelmed by the handful of anecdotes and hearsay comments that circulate out of context and continue to sustain an almost universally negative view of Britain's last-to-perish king-emperor. This book offers a far more ambitious rescue: it liberates Edward (and Wallis, who suffers perhaps even more egregiously from biographical misinformation) from the caricature-like status to which popular culture has reduced him. The candour and vitality of his words, which Murphy captured and preserved, bring him to life again, restoring his humanity and opening a new window into his character.

This book is a chronicle of the writing of a memoir that, in turn, becomes a frame for the unpublished and illuminating material omitted from the final editions. It tells Edward's story as he saw it, lived it and remembered it. His failures, weaknesses, naivety and flaws are on full display, but so, too, are his intelligence, his loyalty, his love and his resolve. It is not a perfect story – royal or otherwise – but it is, for the first time, Edward's story.

Editorial Note

This book has been created primarily from material held within the archive of Charles J. V. Murphy (Howard Gotlieb Research Center, Boston University). Murphy's archive is the repository for the majority of Edward's first and unpublished drafts of *A King's Story* as well as other interviews, notes and diaries that were created during the writing of both his and Wallis's memoirs. Further material not preserved in Murphy's papers was subsequently located in the Beaverbrook Papers (Parliamentary Archives) and finally the Royal Archives (Windsor Castle), which hold Edward's handwritten first drafts. It was in locating Edward's original manuscripts at the Royal Archives that I was able to confirm his authorship of the typewritten drafts that survive in both Murphy's and Beaverbrook's papers, which were produced between 1947 and 1949. Much of this material was scrupulously dated (day, month and year) by either Edward or the secretary who typed it, and thus it appears in this text chronologically according to the date it was written. Where no date was recorded, I have done my best to approximate a time frame and inserted it accordingly. The exception to this is my treatment of the abdication (Beaverbrook Papers), which has been reproduced according to the chronology of 1936.

The guiding editorial principle behind this book was to select material by Edward that had not been published in either the articles for *Life* or *A King's Story*. As with any editorial enterprise, much has been omitted from the pages that follow. Edward left behind voluminous early drafts, which cover a range of topics and experiences. Without being able to include them in full, my aim has been to publish material that offers us the most insight into the momentous events of his life and his character as expressed in his writing. In selecting only unpublished material, I have therefore been forced to exclude certain parts of Edward's life that too closely resemble his published words. For example, Edward's handwritten drafts about his childhood (pre-1912) were reproduced almost verbatim in *A King's Story*, as were other recollections, including his description of his only State Opening of Parliament in 1936.

As Charles Murphy noted in July 1947, Edward was 'quite thoroughly Americanized' and his writing, which employed both American spelling and punctuation, is a testament to a cultural metamorphosis that began in 1919 with his first visit to the United States. His adoption of American vernacular has been preserved in this publication. The only corrections that have been made to his original words are to spelling errors.

Finally, a note on the two different typefaces used in the book. The text interweaves lengthy passages quoted from original sources inter-mittently with my own narrative and personal analysis. To assist the reader in distinguishing my voice from the voices of the various indi-viduals who lived the story I tell, their words are printed in a larger and different font.

I

A Self-Made Monarch

On 9 May 1947, a chillier than usual May morning in New York City, His Royal Highness Prince Edward, Duke of Windsor – formerly King Edward VIII of Great Britain, Northern Ireland and the British Dominions Beyond the Seas, Emperor of India – stepped out from the entrance of the Waldorf Towers onto a blustery Park Avenue pavement where his chauffeur-driven black Cadillac, 'The Duchess', was waiting. Climbing in through the 'W.E.' monogrammed rear passenger door, Edward sat down on the plush, rose-coloured broadcloth back seat set against an interior of rich walnut. Gifted to Edward and Wallis for their 1941 visit to New York by the Chairman of General Motors, Alfred P. Sloan, the bespoke hand-crafted automobile included power windows, white satin privacy curtains, four brushed stainless-steel jewellery cases and even a humidor for Edward's prized cigars. In this epitome of new-world luxury, Edward travelled the two long blocks from 50th and Park Avenue to the Time & Life Building at 9 Rockefeller Plaza. Arriving at the thirty-six-storey tower, Edward would have needed to look only slightly upwards to see *Progress*, the artist Lee Lawrie's ornate art-deco bas relief that had been carved above the entrance. A voluptuous rendering of Columbia – the female personification of America leading the Greek symbol of inspiration, her horse Pegasus – the relief was a hopeful metaphor for the ex-King as he strode through to the elegant first-floor reception room. The assistant of *Life*'s Chairman of the Board of Editors Daniel Longwell was on hand to escort him up to the main office floor where Longwell and other leading *Life* executives were waiting to greet Edward. The visit was the culmination of several months of wooing on the part of Longwell, Henry Luce, the founder and CEO of Time Inc., and their pre-eminent writer Charles J. V. Murphy, who were all eager to secure a journalistic coup and convince Edward that the time was right for him to speak.

'The editors,' Luce had written to Edward on 19 March 1947, 'do not want a long, involved, detailed and possibly contentious biography. What they have in mind is much more simple . . . your own account of your boyhood in England . . . in brief, the career and upbringing of the Prince of Wales.' He assured Edward there was no intention of straying close to the political edge. Instead the 'charming' story would aim to evoke 'an England rather different from the England of today, full of great comings and goings, famous men and women, wonderful ideas; an England securely placed in a world which itself seemed absolutely certain and good'. Luce suggested he should write a total of three articles, which 'in our experience is the ideal number; it whets the appetite without sating it – an important distinction if you should ever decide to go ahead with an autobiography'.[1]

Despite these reassuring words, which Murphy drafted, Edward remained uncertain. 'While the idea of writing three articles with such a title as "The Education of a King" certainly interests me,' Edward replied to Luce, on 24 March, 'I will have to consider it from other angles than that of actually writing them.'[2] The unmentioned impediment was Edward's family. 'There are many obstacles to his doing this,' Longwell had advised Luce, on 14 February, before Edward was formally approached, 'the Royal Family's objections for one thing.'[3] Murphy, who had met with Edward twice since the beginning of 1947, was even more sensitive to the effect their reaction posed for him. 'Will the Duke agree to such a book?' he mused, in a memo to Luce on 20 February. 'Two years ago the Duke was eager for it; now he is wavering.' Murphy blamed this hesitation entirely on the 'cool reception' Edward had supposedly received on a recent visit to Queen Mary in October 1946, which had left him 'a little flustered and unsure of his position'. 'But,' Murphy concluded optimistically, 'he needs dollar exchange and, I suppose, a little attention. He would like to be remembered as something more than the man who wasn't allowed to remain King of England.'[4]

'A little attention' was exactly what Longwell hoped to give Edward during their morning together in May 1947, and by all accounts he succeeded. Edward cabled his thanks and 'good wishes'[5] to Longwell from on board the *Queen Elizabeth* the next day. Arriving in London to see his mother, who was shortly to celebrate her eightieth birthday, Edward quickly discovered that he would not be included in the official family celebration at Buckingham Palace on 27 May. 'Thirty-one members of the Royal Family celebrated her birthday at a luncheon with the King . . . The Duke of Windsor spent three quarters of an hour with his mother,'[6] was how one newspaper reported the situation. The exclusion was another painful reminder that the doors to his old world were still firmly closed.

The opposite was true of the men at *Life*, who welcomed him with heartening enthusiasm. Perhaps eager to find the acceptance that had eluded him in Britain, Edward turned himself over to the auspices of Time Inc., and, by the end of June, he had given the go-ahead for Murphy to join him and Wallis at La Croë. They still had not agreed on either a formal contract or a publication date, but Longwell was willing to take the risk. In a letter to the Duke's New York lawyer, Hank Walter, on 3 June 1947, Longwell set out his generous proposition. Murphy would be dispatched to La Croë, where he would spend the remainder of the summer working with Edward to write three articles on his youth. Longwell agreed that once completed, they would only move forward with publication after Edward had given final confirmation – which necessitated the approval of 'the Court'.[7] For his efforts, Edward would receive $75,000 and the option to sell the articles' British rights. Writing to Longwell on 19 June, Edward signalled his approval to all that had been proposed but reminded his editor that there would be 'no question of drawing up a contract . . . until the three articles are written and I find myself able and willing to publish them'.[8]

Situated on the tip of Cap d'Antibes, La Croë was an idyllic setting in which to write. A three-storey white classically designed villa, 'it gave the impression,' Murphy later wrote, 'of a noble white vessel afloat on a calm sea'.[9] Rented in 1938, it had been the Windsors' base in the two years leading up to their flight from France in June 1940, and despite the upheavals it had endured during the war, when it was used as a billet for Italian troops, La Croë remained the closest thing Edward and Wallis had to a home. Restored to its former glamour after their return in 1945, it provided an appropriate showcase for the material trappings of Edward's former life, including the imposing Order of the Garter banner that greeted guests as they arrived in the marble-floored entry hall. Yet in spite of its grandeur there was, observers remarked, a 'freshness of the seascape' that permeated the villa's interiors,[10] which led seamlessly towards the outside terraces and poolside cocktail lounge. 'You can't imagine the sense of luxury at La Croë in that first summer after the war,'[11] the Baroness de Cabrol told the writer Suzy Menkes. The Windsors' guests were a who's who of international café society, and included the writer Somerset Maugham, who lived at La Mauresque on Cap Ferrat, ex-King Leopold of the Belgians, his wife, Princess Lilian, and the Aga Khan, to name just a few.

Murphy arrived on 1 July and installed himself at the nearby Hôtel du Cap, itself a notable watering-hole for the Riviera's most fashionable visitors. The scene, as Murphy later described it in an article for *Life*, was a 'veritable sliver of lotus land, a realm composed entirely . . . of theatrical mountains, a blue sea, gleaming white villas, pastel villages, irrigated by champagne and a vin du pays rosé, and inhabited by people whose pockets are stuffed with 5,000-franc notes, who subsist on steaks, soufflés and mille feuilles, and whose only occupations are the unflagging pursuit of trifles and the slow burning of the body back to the aboriginal brown.'[12]

Despite the seductive nature of the setting, Murphy was eager to begin. But a week into the assignment, as he reported back to Longwell on 13 July, there was 'little to show in the way of actual writing'. Edward, Murphy quickly realised, had first to 'learn the habits of work'. 'Our friend,' he continued, with an air of disappointment, 'has anything but a brilliant mind . . . His point of view concerning the vast affairs in which he was both a spectator and an actor is less than penetrating.' Yet, Murphy concluded, 'his story on that account will be all the more characteristic of the kind of life in which he was raised. He is an extremely sincere, intelligent and willing person; on this score, we could not ask for anything better.'[13]

In order to 'cover the ground fairly fast',[14] as Murphy described it, the two men agreed to meet twice daily, from 10 a.m. until 12.45 p.m. and again from 5.30 p.m. to 7.30 p.m. Their sessions were invariably set against the backdrop of Edward's oak-panelled study, one of a series of rooms in the penthouse-style suite he occupied on the top floor of La Croë, which he tellingly nicknamed 'Fort Belvedere', after his former home in Windsor Great Park. Inspired by his father and his early years at the Royal Naval College, Dartmouth, the 'flavor of the décor', Murphy remembered, was decidedly 'nautical; deep-blue curtains, chairs and a sofa with white slip-covers'[15] in the adjacent sitting room. The thick shag-pile rugs scattered throughout completed a scheme that was designed to be simple yet comfortable. Mementos and photographs of his life as Prince of Wales were dotted everywhere, including on the wall that overlooked his desk. Sheltered from the comings and goings of the world below, it was the perfect setting for Murphy and Edward to immerse themselves in Edward's past.

As a routine of sorts developed, Murphy began to teach Edward, as he told Longwell, 'how to organize his ideas'.[16] During the remaining weeks of July, despite the 'steady procession of guests . . . dinner parties, cocktail parties at Cannes or in local villas',[17] as Murphy described it, the two men progressed over the part of Edward's life that was to be covered by the three articles: his boyhood and youth up to the end of the First World War.

Though not dated clearly enough for us to be certain that they were Edward's opening lines, Murphy's notes labelled 'Summer 1947' nonetheless offer a penetrating opening insight into the ex-King and what he hoped his articles might convey.

La Croë, Summer 1947

This is the simple story of a man who was raised to be a King, and whose thoughts and aspirations were shaped toward that end. Story of my life – or, if you wish, career.

I was a simple youth. I had too many inhibitions; at the same time I was never a bluffer; I was shy, diffident: a bad speaker.

In that sense I differed greatly from my father who had a

natural flair for kingly role . . . However, I learned, teaching myself; a self-made monarch . . .

Today I am only 53 . . .

Yet in a sense I speak from a great distance; as a man who was trained to be a King. The circumstances that caused me to give up that profession [are] not [the] subject of these articles. Here I am interested only in the education; a life which, considered wholly apart from personal aspects, was a wonderful thing. It was not an important life. It gave rise, I'm sorry to say, to no book, or scientific invention, or any important ideas. But as a life it was a wonderful thing . . .

In the first surviving drafts of 1947, Edward wrote about his time as a student at Magdalen College, Oxford, where he studied from 1912 to 1914.

La Croë, 16 July 1947

. . . Although I worked hard, I knew it wouldn't wreck my 'career' if I did not graduate, so I would learn rather spasmodically. I liked German and French, but German best. I liked political economy . . .

It is terrifying to think how little I learned at Oxford – I suppose because I never wanted to go there – my heart was in travel. I was no longer hankering for the Navy, but had this desire for travel. My next brother, now King George VI, was in the Navy and by that time he had gone to sea and was making trips around the world. That irritated me very much because I wanted to be traveling too. I couldn't think why he should be so lucky to do these things and not me. So I thought Oxford was an awful waste of time; not that it wasn't good, but it didn't suit me . . .

I had not been raised in a very scholastic environment at home, for my family were not always surrounded by a very bookish atmosphere . . .

I was not taught bookkeeping or value investments or monetary subjects or taxation . . .

Father and mother used to write to me – my mother visited me often and she loved the historical side of Oxford. We would have lunch in my room and then take a drive around . . . I had a 1912 Daimler car then which I used to take on trips. It was my own car and I was very proud of it. It was given to me when I went to Oxford . . .

I had a fairly gay life, too . . .

There were some tough people at college, too. There was a little group of men who started gambling in their rooms . . . and someone was always posted to watch the door. The stakes were very high, and I played quite a bit. Of course all this was a big offence at college . . .

There were several clubs, and one college would invite another – all were feats of drinking . . .

I never spent much time in clubs after college and never to one for the sake of sitting around. I like to spend my evenings with my wife after a busy day and exchange views with her. Those who play cards, probably enjoy clubs. I prefer home . . .

One of those clubs, he later told Murphy, was the infamous Bullingdon Club. 'I belonged . . . but did not care for it as it seemed to be rather snobbish and there was a great deal of drinking . . .'[18]

In a later undated draft, Edward ruminated further on his second year at Oxford and his emotional development during this period.

My second year at Oxford slipped by outwardly as uneventful as the first. But from my diary I can detect the seeds of new ideas that were taking root and influencing the character-building process. Some people develop early, others later. I believe I was in the second category. The inhibitions from which I had suffered during my first year began to disappear and I gained a confidence in myself. I became less shy – less scared of people – less self conscious. In short I was for the first time at last beginning to grow up. These changes in my thinking were unimportant at the time and because of the war not to find expression until some years later.

In the summer of 1914 Edward left Oxford and turned his attention to what became the formative experience of his young adulthood: the First World War. Beginning his army life as a member of the Oxford Battalion of the Officers' Training Corps, he spent two weeks training at Aldershot, returning to London shortly before the outbreak of hostilities. Though he was still cosseted within the walls of the palace it was impossible, Edward wrote, to overlook the 'vague indefinable feeling then that war was coming'.[19]

La Croë, 17 July 1947

I was at Buckingham Palace when War was declared, doing absolutely nothing and terribly worried because I wasn't . . .

I recall seeing the Second Battalion of Grenadier Guards going [on] a route march when I went to view them with my father. I was in plain clothes and felt awful. On my return I went to one of the old Courtiers, Colonel Sir William Carrington [Keeper of the King's Privy Purse] . . . I said I was in a desperate state, a war was on . . . would he help to get me attached to a Regiment . . . Quite soon afterwards . . . [he] told me he had seen the King who had given permission . . . for me to go in the Grenadier Guards [1st Battalion of Grenadier Guards]. So we went across the road and saw the man in charge. He told me to go to a tailor to measure for clothes, and then to report to Wellington Barracks. I was thrilled. I joined in a funny khaki uniform that I had used at Oxford, for I had to report in uniform. Finally I received my Grenadier's uniform . . . I still have this uniform.

After a period of training at Warley Barracks in Brentwood, the battalion was transferred to Wellington Barracks in London ahead of deployment to France. On 8 September 1914, a week before their departure, Edward learned that he would not be going with them.

I went to my father at once and said, 'We have had wonderful news, and we are off.' But he would not let me go . . . So off they went, and I was transferred to the 3rd Guards. But it was all a blow to me and I never felt the same in the 3rd as I did when in the 1st Battalion.

Edward remained with the 3rd Battalion of the Grenadier Guards in London until 16 November, when he joined the staff of Field Marshal Sir John French, then Commander-in-Chief of the British Expeditionary Force in France (later 1st Earl of Ypres). Though hardly the frontline post he hankered after, it brought him closer to the fighting.

. . . I was anxious to go to the front . . . I said I wanted a combat job. However, I was sent to join Lord French's staff instead . . . All his staff was older, and I had a pretty unhappy time. I was given little commissions to do – it was all purely camouflage to satisfy me . . .

By this time almost a third of the men who had been with me had been killed. The whole of my generation was eventually almost decimated. I am now talking only of the first four months of war. About fifty of my closer friends were killed; the Oxford Honor Roll has the names of many of them . . . a big hole was drilled in my generation.

After a time I felt I couldn't stand the staff job any longer – it was too far back of the lines and too inactive. We lived in a very little house on the street of an old French town . . . St Omer. Shortly after I had gone there, my father paid a visit to French's headquarters in early December 1914 . . . he told me about a conversation he had with French. French had told him of some of his plans and said, 'By Christmas it will all be over!' My father said he thought French had been a bit optimistic. It showed the calibre of leaders then – they were old campaigners and had no idea of the war that was being fought – the kind of war it was. In their time war was a simpler matter and a question of how to use the cavalry and infantry. These were the kind of men who were fighting now against trained Germans, and they got nowhere. It was the younger men, who had to forget everything they had been taught, that had to apply themselves to a newer science of warfare. So I would sit about in the evening and there was good food and wine, but one had the feeling those 'leaders' did not go up to the front very often, and felt they were completely out of touch and it was better 'not to see too much'. Of course, our army was very small then . . . They had a ghastly time and not enough ammunition, and from the chaos all about, the calm of headquarters was bunk . . .

In the First World War the casualties were terrible – it was a mass slaughter. Men who would be called up for the army and, without exception of being taught to shoot in a superficial manner or some bayonet fighting, they had little training because there was not much time for it. There was a course in France for them in bayonet fighting, trench mortar training, bomb throwing, but the men were not in the highly trained and physical shape the soldiers were in World War II.

In September 1915, shortly before the start of the Battle of Loos, Edward was transferred to the staff of Major General, later Field Marshal, Lord Cavan (Rudolph Lambart, 10th Earl of Cavan), who was in command of the newly formed Guards Division. The battle, which lasted from 25 September to 8 October, ended in a British and French defeat. Though kept safely away from the fighting lines, Edward was still on hand to observe the full horror of conditions.

La Croë, 18 July 1947

. . . As a rule when there was an actual attack, we were kept terribly busy at headquarters with sending and receiving reports – there was never time for 'sightseeing' . . . If no attack . . . we would visit brigades and ask a brigade captain how things were going. It was a ride of about two miles along bad road . . . Bicycles would be clogged with mud . . .

The Germans were lying about four miles away opposite the Guards Division . . . The Guards Division being newly formed . . . were put in at first . . . It takes a lot of experience for seeing that supplies alone were available, and also one of the big headaches was to prevent traffic jams so supplies could be brought up . . .

. . . I remember spending one night in the rain to direct traffic. There was one bad bottleneck going up to the front. The zero hour had gone and after two days of terrible casualties we decided to put in the 'K' Army Division – new volunteers and badly trained. These men had not had any meals for two days before, and were starving. And there was rain, rain, steady rain and mud, and they were thoroughly demoralized. When talking with some of them we learned they had not been put into any billets, and they were soaked, cold and had marched I forget how far. So I said I did not see how they could make any kind of showing. But they were sent on their way, and when they encountered terrific shelling and were shot at, they slipped off their equipment and bolted before they reached the hill . . . The Guards division was waiting in reserve, and . . . the order came . . . These battalions marched forward in brigades and we knew which would go into action first. Two or three would relieve the first that were sent into action, and we were at headquarters arranging for which brigades would go next. There were terrible casualties . . .

We never got [captured] the ridge. It was just carnage. There was noise of wheels; gun fire crescendoing [sic] all night. The rain and mud were the awful part; there were no lights except flashlight; the weather was terrible and cold. Of course the gunfire and rockets would light up the sky . . . .We were getting

pretty cynical about these battles, and one never had an opportunity of asking the where and why of orders . . .

When the battle failed, we had to go down with someone
from the Brigade to see how things were. They were given
time to bury the dead and clear the place. There were piles
and piles of horses . . . There was only this one road, and
by the time ten wagons passed, it got bogged. Then when
they got to a certain place the men and horses were slaugh-
tered by enemy fire. Whenever transports came into view,
the Germans shelled them . . . the dead men and dead horses
that were lying about were appalling. The Germans had
the high ground and had ours spotted so well that our poor
devils had to attack the hill knowing they would be killed.

. . . We remained six weeks after the battle, counting the
dead . . .

After an 'uneventful winter in 1916', Edward was sent to Egypt and
spent six weeks stationed near the Suez Canal, where he was given
more 'fictitious jobs'. In May 1916 he returned to France and joined
Lord Cavan's staff in the 14th Army Corps. Cavan, as Edward described
him, was a 'fat little man, great personality, very brilliant and popular
with troops'. His empathetic and 'human' approach to battle created
'a wonderful spirit among his men'.[20] It was sorely needed when two
months later the Corps went south to the Somme.

La Croë, 18 July 1947

. . . The Guards division came down with us. Many went
through our hands; the attacks were desperate . . .

We took our part in it, and were told what sector would
have another attack . . . There would be a zero hour for
attacking, or a zero-minus-30, or one hour before, and we
would start to pound the first line trenches, then the barrage
would be static for a while and then creep on again . . .

We built camps at headquarters because the terrain as we

advanced was all destroyed by shellfire and there was no house in which to live. So [Cavan] thought it best to remain in our hut instead of establishing headquarters as the troops went ahead . . . Bombardment went on all day and all night long . . .

I used to make regular tours to the Divisions and Brigades, but there was no elation connected with anything – it was all grim, and friends were killed every day . . .

Occasionally I was used as an interpreter, so was helpful in that way. Some German officers and prisoners would come to HQ, I would be sent for to ask questions we wanted to know. One German officer recognized me immediately from having been in Germany in 1913 [Edward had made a tour of Germany in that year] . . .

And I made rounds of the camp. One evening I found a sentry asleep, and as everyone knows, nothing could be worse in wartime. He was a Welsh Guardsman, and a nice boy. I had to call the Sergeant and tell him the boy was asleep. The boy was sent for and it was decided to send him back to his unit. Two days later he was killed. I always felt I was the cause, but I had to report him for in times like that it was a terribly serious crime for a sentry to fall asleep – serious for all . . .

One day was like another – blood, death, destruction. We had to take turns to sleep in the office and listen for telephone calls all night. We had some pretty close escapes, and if shells were coming, one would lie down quickly and hope fervently one could escape . . . Every day there were changes – wounded, killed; or men were given other jobs. One received the casualty lists very quickly so had the news at once.

We didn't talk about the grimness of it much among ourselves. We tried to talk about other things; soldiers generally do. There was so much death and destruction around us that we didn't particularly want anyone coming up and asking about it – preferred that someone bring good news. We would talk about life at home, or families or last leaves. Leave was always a popular subject. And a great fatalism would develop.

One used to attend funerals. Once a wooden cross was raised to some 100 Grenadier Guardsmen that were killed around September 20th, 1916. Before the winter set in we had a ceremony pretty close to the line, and the chaplain read a prayer. The saddest thing of all in the Battle of the Somme was the human sacrifice . . .

Edward's experiences on the Somme also brought him into close contact with the French Army.

. . . A lot of the high French Generals didn't worry much about their men – wanted their soup and wine – and there was a big separation in France between the French officers and their men compared to the British officers and their men. The British officers and their men really became comrades. The French never did.

It was something that one would definitely notice after various experiences of talking with French officers when visiting them. We would ask the location of their ration dump and how their men received their supplies, but they didn't know. If we asked about washing facilities, they said, 'Wash? Why need water?'

The French soldiers had good discipline and were scared of their officers . . .

In November 1917 Edward and the 14th Army Corps, still under Cavan's command, were sent to Italy. He remained there, except for a brief return to England, until September 1918. His observations included meetings with King Victor Emmanuel III of Italy and his wife Princess Elena of Montenegro, Pope Benedict XV and his impressions of the Italian troops.

La Croë, 21 July 1947

I saw the King of Italy at his wartime headquarters. It was there the Italians were fighting up the Zanzo at the Austrian frontier.

The King had very short legs, abnormal, for he had had an accident at birth. He led a very simple life, and married a Montenegrin Princess . . . she was also very simple in her manner and tastes. The Montenegrins are really peasants. The Queen of Italy was so down to earth that all she wanted to know was how many children anyone had.

. . . In this War [Second World War] he was labeled a Fascist and everything else, but I hope that was more force of circumstance than anything – he more or less had to be, for Mussolini was in control and the King had little opportunity to choose. But I certainly saw no traits of fascism even with Mussolini there and I didn't think the King's character could have been influenced to the extent that he could have been readily swayed. He remained on the throne when Mussolini marched on Rome in 1922 . . .

One of the things that impressed me about the Italian troops was the fact they didn't seem to have a rotation of troops in the line . . . I had just completed the battle of Loos and then the winter with the Guards Division, and everything was so well organized one never left the men under shell-fire longer than two months without bringing them back for a rest, for war was a degrading and dreadful life, and we wanted our men to have a chance of recovering a more normal atmosphere. But the Italians never did that, and it impressed me very much.

The human suffering Edward witnessed forged in him a lasting distaste for warfare. He became, in all but name, a pacifist, determined to prevent another similar conflict whatever the cost. It also brought him, for the first time, into contact with ordinary men and opened his eyes to a range of human experiences that he had hitherto never imagined within his cloistered royal existence.

In the early days of the war, the line was very thin and the troops were not very well organized. But later – after a year of war – every man was entitled to ten days leave. They were taken across on Channel steamers organized into leave boats ... I went across on these boats myself, but I was very punctilious about taking leave, and only took the one occasion when I reported to my mother about my father's fall. [George V fell from his horse while visiting troops in France on 28 October 1915.] It would generally be sixteen or eighteen months before I got back to England. I was not in combat duty, and always felt if I took leave it would deprive someone else of having it. The boats were gay going to Britain, but sad coming back. Men were weary, mentally and physically, for all war is a squalid life ...

One of the sad things of war was that some men whose nerves began to go used to take refuge in drink, and of course they could get all the liquor they wanted; start 'knitting' [drinking] at night during shelling. Another serious thing during the War was shell shock. Now there are psychiatrists, but then there was the cruel system of writing off the shell-shocked; it was not kept in mind that men might not be cowards who couldn't take the strain of constant shelling. The officers had a better chance of getting away with it than the men. If an officer absented himself from reach they would say he was shell-shocked and he was treated. But if a man quit from shell shock, he was shot, being termed a deserter. One had to or else most would quit. One saw many cases of shell shock or would see it coming. Some men got shaking and never stopped shaking the rest of their lives. The doctors were very good and if they saw a man couldn't take it any more, they would send him back. One had to be careful of malingering of course.

There was another thing that was prevalent, and finally punishable by court martial, and that was self-inflicted wounds, like cutting off the end of a finger on the left hand.

War is a strain, and humans should not ever be subjected to it.

Despite his earlier impressions of camaraderie among the British troops, Edward became increasingly aware of the unequal treatment between officers and their men. Just as he questioned his own inherent status as a royal prince set apart from others, so too did he begin to see the inherent injustices of a class divide that had tragic human consequences.

La Croë, 22 July 1947

During the First World War there was a bigger gap between the men and their troops because of trench warfare.

On one occasion during the Battle of the Somme, it was raining terribly and we were having our evening meal – I was sitting with the junior officers at one end of the long table, and the General and his staff were grouped at the other end. One of the men near me said it was a helluva night and what must it be like for the poor devils out in the rain. A senior officer overheard him and said, 'How do you mean that? They have their waterproof sheets, don't they? Pass the port wine!' That was the inhumanity of a lot of the staff toward the men in the trenches. The senior officer who spoke was a Grenadier Guardsman, and the brains in the back of Cavan. But it was a terrible thing to say. Cavan would never have said it. The other was a seasoned officer and had excellent staff-knowledge behind him, but lacked humanness.

The social strata between officers and men was far different in the Second World War: they were closer together, and were thrown together more because of the different kind of warfare. In my time, the staff did not talk with men much except to give them a helping hand. But there was much debate and criticism by the junior officers of their superiors . . .

It was the younger generation who worried about the comforts of the troops. But the operations side was the main interest of the Generals and their staffs . . . War seemed endless, and we felt the uselessness of it, especially after it went on and on. When the casualty lists would come in, one would write to the homes of our friends who were on it . . .

Edward spent the final months of the war stationed with a corps of Canadian troops near Mons (France). He was with them when peace was declared on 11 November 1918, though he did not return to England until February 1919. He spent the intervening months visiting the imperial troops that remained in France. He was now approaching his twenty-fifth birthday, and had come of age in an era of total war. Its effects would shape the next phase of his life.

La Croë, 23 July 1947

. . . To me the coming of peace meant helping my father with the business of kingship . . . I did not look forward with great relish to assisting in public affairs – once I started going out in public life my private life was finished.

I spent the spring of 1919 in Great Britain and quite a lot in the way of visiting industrial places . . . So I became very conscious of losing my private life, and it was like a knife – it was even difficult to walk around Piccadilly without having people look at one all the time . . . I was active in the Veterans Association. But it seemed a pity and an incongruous thing that after the War millions had been allocated to take care of graves, but no funds were available to help disabled veterans. At least half of the money should have been appropriated to building houses for them or making extensive medical care possible. I think it is better organized now.

The slums were pretty bad because of the War, and there was a great deal to be done about them. I visited Glasgow, Cardiff, Newcastle, London . . . At the end of the last war, we had riots about veterans' pensions, taxes etc . . . and I then did become conscious of the change that had taken place in my generation. It was not so much what the people thought they could get, but they were not going to have anything taken away from them . . .

At this stage with Murphy, Edward also briefly reflected on political life in Britain, writing about the three most prominent politicians of his early youth: David Lloyd George, Herbert Asquith and, his eventual nemesis, Stanley Baldwin.

. . . Lloyd George played a certain part in my life. He was Prime Minister when I was first traveling around in the British Commonwealth. I was under the spell of his charm, [but] my father disliked him, and never forgave him for an inflammatory speech L.G. made as a young man that was bordering on treason when he said, 'What do we need a King for!' (I was still at school then.) . . .

My father didn't like Baldwin either; few did. But he did like Herbert Asquith – a great intellectual. He was Prime Minister before and during the War; was 100% Liberal but not the reformer L.G. wanted to be . . . He was exceedingly tactful, and handled my father in a tactful and clever manner . . .

The men who were called 'Radicals' in those days are called 'Commies' today.

Lloyd George . . . [had] amazing charm, even if he was a scamp.

At the same time Edward also began to take the first tentative steps towards discussing more personal issues – his father George V and the unique 'position and privilege'[21] he occupied as Prince of Wales.

La Croë, July 1947

We would see my father in his room while he was at breakfast, usually, and remained standing in his presence, as I remember.

One time, my father asked me about my schedule . . . And I said the first week of March I was going to Glasgow. He said, 'Whoever heard of anyone going to Glasgow except in August for grouse?' He didn't say I couldn't go but was astonished why I should have these preferences when I had been raised to follow him. So he would continue, 'When I go to Scotland, you go to France. Why don't you come to Scotland?' I said that I wanted to go to Italy or France.

After his illness in 1928 my father became more tolerant and didn't want to fight the younger generation too much.

I understand perfectly well that at ceremonies or official occasions one might be at the center of things and everyone else had to show me greatest respect. But what I couldn't understand was that when back home, one was different than anyone else. So I set up a curious resistance to it and was always fighting . . . unnecessary privilege.[22]

My next brother [George VI] never had that resistance – he rather liked it. But my youngest brother [Prince George, Duke of Kent] was like me, and we discussed it often.

By the end of July Edward had produced 150 pages of typed material – a 'reconnoitering of the ground',[23] as Murphy described it. In the process of their two intensive weeks together, Murphy had also been given his first intimate glimpse of the Windsors' private lives, which sparked his fascination and formed the basis for his lengthy 'interim report' to Luce's right-hand man and Time Inc. Vice President, Allen Grover.

Charles Murphy to Allen Grover
Cap d'Antibes,[24] 30 July 1947

. . . As he talked and searched his memory I become sorely puzzled. Something was missing, some central ingredient to give vitality and meaning to his growth.

He moved in events without ever being part of them. He made me think of a stone in a lively brook. Then I began to understand what it was that was lacking. It was the element of struggle. There was no risk in his life. Not only was everything settled for him; he himself slipped naturally and unprotestingly into the role prepared for him. Until he became King he had no access to Ministers. The Government might just as well have been on the moon as far as he was concerned. Nobody consulted him, and he was in no position to consult anybody else . . . And the role necessarily preserved him apart from the turmoil of the times as safely as Church dogma cushions a Pope from the secular excitement of his day.

I have not yet come upon the contrasts and surprises, the pervading philosophy . . . He just doesn't seem to remember or think in images, in words. In the gallery of his memory everybody apparently looks the same and nobody said anything brilliant or funny. But, of course, we have only just started, and as I start retracing the ground I am sure that new material will start oozing from the reluctant memory.

A very hopeful sign is that he understands exactly what is wrong and is making a valiant effort to remedy the fault. The Duchess has taken over the job of jogging his memory. I had a talk with her . . . and was pleased by the brisk, businesslike way she set out to teach the Duke the basic requirements of American journalism. In the course of their long acquaintance he has told her various anecdotes and tales of his boyhood, which she remembers. Some are extremely funny and others are a little sad. She began to pull these out of him again, while I sat by listening, and inwardly amused. There's no question but that Wallis is a woman of strong will and determination. She interrupted her husband again and again – in the manner of all self-confident wives – and finally the Duke who had grown restless and a little annoyed, exclaimed, 'But, darling, it is my life, you know, and who is better qualified than I to describe exactly what did happen to me?' His English reserve is, of course, the hidden villain; it is impossible for him to give way to his emotions. And I think also that he is keeping an inner eye on his mother's possible response to whatever he might write . . .

My first impression of him still holds. He's an engaging, intelligent and thoroughly straightforward man. Did I tell you that the phrase that so struck Harry [Henry Luce] – 'When I was King' – occurred several times in our conversation? But no bitterness attached to it. In fact, so far as an emotional significance was concerned, he could just as well have said, 'When I was at Balmoral.' He is wholly natural and at ease in his dealings with all kinds of people . . .

Grover was not the only Time Inc. boss with whom Murphy kept in close touch during the early weeks of his collaboration with Edward. He wrote regularly to Longwell, informing him with military precision of their progress. Included among his reports was an account of a brief visit to London in mid-July where he met Sir Walter Monckton, Edward's adviser, and Sir George Allen, his solicitor, for the first time. Both were deeply suspicious of Edward's plans, and though Monckton expressed his views in an 'urbane and sympathetic' manner, Allen made no effort to conceal his 'melancholy mistrust of the project'.[25] Murphy returned to La Croë justifiably nervous – a feeling exacerbated by Edward, who remained tentative about the suitability of publication, even as he continued to write. Longwell intervened to calm heightened emotions. With gentle prodding and reassurance he urged his hesitant royal author onwards. 'Should you be happy about the results of your summer's work,' he wrote to Edward on 30 July, 'and if the project progresses to the point where you wish to submit it to those personages whose advice you feel proper to take, may I stress to you and to them one of the very important considerations in the whole project over and above our friendliness to you, and that is the possible importance of such a document in Anglo-American relations.'[26]

Longwell's letter provided the reassurance Edward needed. He was confident, he told Longwell on 15 September, that 'certain difficulties that may arise with regard to our project . . . can be overcome . . . Anyway,' he concluded, 'I am all set and r'aring [sic] to go.'[27] These 'difficulties' were undoubtedly Edward's concerns for his family's reaction, and, although he still planned to forewarn his mother and his brother the King when he saw them in October, he was now determined to publish, he told Murphy, even 'in the face of family resistance'.[28] This tenacity marked a shift in Edward's earlier reticence, perhaps reflecting a newfound confidence born of finding, at least temporarily, something meaningful to do.

Buoyed by Edward's enthusiasm, Murphy and the bosses at *Life* were eager to pin down a publication date. Yet Edward's 'peculiar working habits – or more precisely his lack of working habits',[29] as Murphy described them, made that difficult and it soon became clear that he would miss the desired November deadline. Edward was, after all, unused to a formal schedule of 'work'. But there may have been other more fundamental reasons behind his reluctance to finish the articles. Writing had given him his first real occupation since departing from the Bahamas in 1945. Having endured the disappointment of failing to find employment from the British government, he was now invested with a revitalised sense of purpose. Enjoying the daily stimulation of Murphy's urbane company, of which he was increasingly fond, and unconcerned with the demands of any commercial strategy, Edward may simply have seen no need to rush through a process he was so obviously enjoying.

Despite these nagging frustrations, Murphy remained resolute. 'A job like this never proceeds in a straight line,' he told Hank Walter, but rather 'by fits and starts and with many halts and interruptions, and even retreats, because the principal is seldom sure exactly where he is going . . .'[30]

Everyone breathed a sigh of relief when on 8 October Murphy telegraphed to Longwell from London that 'the last obstacle is removed: Mother and brother' have 'both given their blessing'.[31] Longwell was jubilant and replied later that same day. 'That is wonderful news,' he wrote. 'Don't think you realize how close you are to a great coup full of honors . . . Everyone here elated . . .'[32]

In fact, Edward had been less than forthright to Murphy about the 'blessing'. Walter Graebner, who as *Life*'s London Bureau Chief was handling illustrations, was baffled when George Allen advised against contacting 'Buck House' for access to Edward's personal albums, which were stored at Windsor Castle. Those and various paintings *Life* wished to illustrate, including the 1912 portrait of Edward in his Garter robes by Sir Arthur Stockdale Cope, were considered vital to the commercial appeal of the series. 'Allen,' Graebner told Longwell on 1 November, 'believes it would be most unwise to try for these . . . as it would focus . . . attention and perhaps upset the applecart . . . I was somewhat baffled by Allen's caution and when I said, "But surely the family have blessed the project," Allen said not exactly. "The author has told them what he's doing."'[33]

By November 1947, much to everyone's relief at *Life*, the articles were finally nearing completion and were scheduled to appear over the course of three consecutive weeks beginning on 8 December. The dashing 1921 photograph of Edward in the uniform of the Welsh Guards was chosen for the cover of the issue that contained the inaugural chapter on his life. Just two weeks away from publication with all three articles still unfinished, Edward, Wallis and Murphy arrived in New York. The Windsors moved into their usual suite 28A at the Waldorf Towers, the residential wing of the city's most fashionable hotel. With sweeping views of the Manhattan skyline before him, Edward got down to work.

Their arrival filled society gossip columns, with one outlet reporting that they had arrived for 'yet another vacation'.[34] Amused, Edward sent the clipping to Henry Luce with the note, 'Dear Harry: As I was knocking off work at 4 a.m. to get a little sleep before your represen- tatives arrived at 9, this story came to my attention . . .'[35]

The prospect of a busy work-filled few weeks offered a welcome distraction from publicity surrounding the Windsors' conspicuous absence at the wedding of Edward's niece, the future Queen Elizabeth II, which took place in London shortly after their arrival in New York. There was no question of Wallis being included and, emphatic that he would not attend without his wife, Edward's secretary issued a pre-emptive state- ment on 13 October confirming they had not received an invitation and would therefore not be attending. Yet despite the estrangement, strong ties remained between Edward and the monarchy as an institution, if not with his family personally. Edward refused to allow *Life* to announce publication of the articles until after the wedding – a telling reminder that, despite his outsider status, he retained a sense of the royal rulebook. Longwell reported disappointedly to Luce on 28 November that Edward had also refused to allow *Life* to 'use the word King' in any of the titles 'out of consideration for his brother'.[36] And despite their no doubt lukewarm response to news of the articles, Edward gave strict instruc- tions to Walter Graebner in London as to how his family should receive copies of the magazine. 'HRH,' Murphy advised Graebner, 'for reasons which he did not divulge but which I can surmise, does not want the impression given that the copies are being delivered at his request. He suggests . . . that you deliver them to their respective private secretaries with the compliments of Time Inc.'[37]

From across the Atlantic, Allen remained watchful of his principal's sprint to the finish. Despite being down to the wire, drafts were couriered to him for his review, his corrections to be sent hastily back to Murphy via telegraph. Murphy bemoaned the hurried final flourish that had led to this rushed conclusion. 'What a pity that the royal education put so little store by time,' he wrote to Allen, on 2 December, just three days before the first article was set to appear in print. 'Five months have vanished more or less from my life, but I don't think that my dear colleague, if I may use the term, has even noticed it. Occasionally he will peer out of the window at his high apartment and comment on the weather, but otherwise the slow change in the seasons seems to have passed unnoticed.'[38]

If Longwell shared Murphy's frustrations, he did not show it. Instead, he welcomed Edward warmly into his professional and personal circle. He and his wife Mary dined with the Windsors several times, and on 10 December Edward joined the editors of *Life* at their regular Wednesday lunch in the Time Inc. boardroom at Rockefeller Plaza. It was 'most amusing,' Longwell reported to Henry Luce on 19 December. 'We all tried . . . to get him [Edward] to collaborate with us on the story of Charles J. V. Murphy. He offered a number of anecdotes about Charlie and the Riviera. It seems that Charlie arrived there without a dinner jacket, so he proposed having one made. The Duke took a doubtful view of the local skill of such an enterprise, but Charlie went ahead with an Italian tailor who made him a coat with six brass buttons which he finally gave to a waiter as a kind of waiter's coat.'[39]

The lunch was followed by an afternoon meeting of *Life's* staff and, at Longwell's instigation, watching 'the third installment of your articles being put to press'.[40] Free to exercise his undisputed charm to the full, these were moments at which Edward excelled. Longwell wrote enthusiastically to him the next day, 'I was most grateful that you joined our regular Editors' lunch yesterday and inspected our editorial floors and the telephone room. My phone was busy the rest of the afternoon with "Thanks" and "What a nice guy!" A part of Luce's journalism is that everyone works hard for the readers. You joined these folks in their efforts for our readers and they like you for it.'[41] On 12 December, 'The Editors of *Life*' feted Edward at a black-tie dinner at New York's Union Club, the highlight of which was the presentation of a silver plate dedicated to 'H.R.H. The Duke of Windsor: In Honor of His Perseverance and Skill with Pen and Brownie'. 'No token of friendship,' Edward wrote to Luce on 22 December, 'has given me greater pleasure, nor has there been one I valued more.'[42]

As predicted, the articles when at last they appeared were a commercial hit. Titled 'The Story of the Education of a Prince', the three-part series, which debuted on 8 December 1947, was a serene retrospective on Edward's childhood and early adulthood, which omitted the raw and searing descriptions he had written about his wartime experiences. These memoirs, as Murphy wrote in a short introduction, were 'a backward look into yesterday . . . a glance from the tension and disquietude of our tumultuous times in the life of a famous prince who was also a British boy in an age when boyhood seemed utterly secure and good.'[43]

Despite Longwell's belief that the articles constituted 'nothing . . . other than rather charming remembrances of his youth',[44] Edward and the men at *Life* waited expectantly for any hint of royal reaction. On 13 December they received the first inkling of palace gossip.

Walter Graebner to Charles Murphy
London, 13 December 1947[45]

. . . I expect to get a pretty full report from the Duchess of Kent to whom I sent a copy this morning. But in the meantime I thought you might like to have one or two comments we picked up.

The Duchess of Kent told a good friend of mine, who is one of the Queen's best friends, that the King and Queen felt the Duke of Windsor was guilty of 'appallingly bad taste' in writing the story . . .

My friend, who has been talking to one of the Ladies-in-Waiting, also said that 'Royal circles are talking about nothing else except the Windsor stories.'

From another source inside the Palace we have had confirmation that the King and Queen felt it was 'bad taste' for Windsor to write the articles, and that Queen Mary is annoyed and worried. She is worried about what the Duke is going to say in the next articles, especially the section referring to his meeting with Mrs Simpson . . .

The full royal report came just a few days later via the unexpected source of Murphy's friend and correspondent for *Time* magazine, Raimund von Hofmannsthal.

Raimund von Hofmannsthal to Charles Murphy London, 19 December 1947[46]

I hasten to tell you – very privately and confidentially – that the second instalment of the Duke of Windsor's memoirs was placed into the hands of 'brother, Bertie, now the King' yesterday afternoon at 6 o'clock, by your humble servant, during a cocktail party at St James's Palace.

If I had your wonderful photographic memory, plus your talent of description, I would give you a detailed account of what happened. As it is I shall make no such attempt but merely try to give you an accurate report of the part of the conversation that referred to your story.

. . . He then said, 'By the way, that description of Sandringham in my brother's story is really first class' (this is the only time he mentioned the Duke as 'my brother'. For the rest of the conversation he said 'he'). 'That fellow (he made a great effort to remember your name, but I said 'Murphy') has done an extraordinarily good job. I enjoyed reading it very much and I laughed a great deal. Do you know how they worked together?'

As you know, I knew very little about it but I said I thought that the Duke had a great deal of letters, albums and material of all kinds at his disposal and after going through it by himself he would talk to you about it and you would make a draft, which he saw and edited, added, eliminated etc.

The King then asked me, 'There are only three articles like that, aren't there?' I said that I believed this was so for the time being and that I had brought the second one along and explained that he was getting his copy before anybody else, even in America, saw it.

He was very pleased about that gesture of ours and thanked me, and then said, 'Do you know whether the whole idea came from him or whether he was approached to do it?' I replied that to my knowledge we had heard some rumours that he was going to do it and we then approached the Duke. He then asked, 'Did you see him last time he was here in England?' I said, 'No, sir,' and he said, 'Well, I did. And I had heard about this – you know one hears of these things somehow or other – and I asked him point blank about it and he said he had been approached by your people.' He then asked me whether I knew how much the *Express* had paid him. I said I did not but I did not think it was an excessively large sum.

He then frowned a little and murmured something like 'He certainly doesn't need the money' and then said, clearly, 'You know, he is an immensely rich man, he doesn't pay any taxes and that is the reason why he doesn't live in this country. There is nothing else to stop him from coming back.'* At that moment the Queen joined us and the King said to her that I had brought the second instalment along, which seemed to please her and then she said, 'I hear several papers bid for the rights to print the story in this country.' I said, 'Yes, I believe Lord Rothermere also made a bid for it but that Lord Beaverbrook . . .' and before I could finish my sentence, the Queen said 'Is richer,' and smiled . . . After a few minutes, the Queen said to the King, 'We must go now,' and, laughingly to me, 'We see people so rarely these days that we don't know

---

* This was not an entirely accurate position – George VI had written to Queen Mary in 1946, just before Edward's first visit to the war: 'It seems to me that when he does come here . . . we must take the line that he cannot live here. We have told him we are not prepared to meet "her" and they cannot live in this country without ever meeting us.'

any more when to leave.' By then it was five-to-eight
and the 20 odd people, of whom only six or eight had
an opportunity to talk to either the King or the
Queen, bowed and curtsied them out with a sigh of
relief. We all had been standing for two hours . . .

Still, I think this conversation is a great tribute to
your work and I feel my labour was not lost. I hope
you will be pleased by His Majesty's kudos . . .

Murphy shared Hofmannsthal's letter with Edward and, though his
reaction is not recorded, whatever disapproval George VI expressed
did little to dampen his brother's enthusiasm for the finished result or
discourage him from future endeavours. Moreover, he closed 1947 with
a genuine appreciation for Murphy's talents. 'Your assurance,' Edward
wrote on 30 December, 'that the summer you spent away from home
was not too tedious encouraged me in the hope that some day again
we can all spend some pleasant weeks in the sunshine . . . far away
from any disturbing influences to aggravate your analytical mind. But
joking apart, I have greatly enjoyed our association . . . and working
with you. It was a tough undertaking for a novice, but your interest
and patience throughout sustained me at dark moments when a sense
of inadequacy and the deadline loomed very menacingly.'[47] The satisfaction Edward felt at the year's close was evident. As if further proof
that his stock remained high for the bosses at Time Inc. were needed,
Longwell provided it in full on 30 December in the form of an admiring
letter to Edward:

May I be personal with a short recollection? I have
been a book and magazine publisher and editor for a
good many years – too many. I started before most of
my contemporaries, and I've probably got mixed up in
as many publishing ventures and temperaments as
anyone my weight and age. I must say I've never had
a more pleasant experience than your three articles in
LIFE. The innate goodness of the work has come

48

from you. Your humor, your respect for your family, for your countrymen and your readers everywhere was the spirit that made the pieces happy occasions.

A good editor or publisher is a frustrated writer who sublimates his personal ambitions into his author's efforts and quite incidentally gets his pride from his author's success. I don't claim to be a good editor, but I must say I've had – and all of us at LIFE have had – great satisfaction and pride in your success . . . [48]

2

On Tour

The publication of the three *Life* articles ended Edward's first foray into memoir writing. Longwell's praise for the magazine's newest author was effusive and evidently sincere. Even George Allen, who had maintained his scepticism from the beginning, was satisfied with the end product. 'I must congratulate you most sincerely on the result,' he wrote to Murphy. 'Your patience and efforts have been justified and rewarded.'[1] Knowing his misgivings, Murphy was particularly appreciative of Allen's compliment, responding a few days later, 'The work throughout was hard and exhausting, the more so as our friend had to be led carefully and painstakingly up the creative path . . . I promised the Duke at the outset that it could be done without sensationalism . . . This promise was kept.'[2]

But *Life*'s mission was not complete. Longwell, like Murphy, had further ambitions for Edward. Both dreamed of future articles that would cover the only thing they felt the world really wanted to know about him – the story of 1936. But Edward was reticent. It had taken much persuasion and money to convince him to tackle the relatively innocuous subjects covered in this first series. What would it entail to delve into the events of the abdication? Just over eleven years had passed since December 1936. Wounds remained unhealed. Edward's bitterness towards his family, notably in relation to their treatment of his wife, was acute. They in turn viewed him as an institutional delinquent and outcast, his wife a scheming adventuress, not fit to be considered a royal duchess. It was contentious ground. Yet despite the mutual acrimony, the first forty-two years of Edward's life as a royal prince had instilled in him certain inalienable principles of conduct, one being that family warfare waged on the battlefield of public opinion was unthinkable. How could the work Longwell envisaged be undertaken with dignity and without descending into personal recriminations? Edward was clearly uncertain.

The men at *Life* were undeterred by these challenges. Longwell was again on a charm offensive. On 3 January he wrote to Edward, telling him, among other news, that he had begun compiling 'a little library on contemporary England in case we need it',[3] at his *Life* office. A keen hunter, Longwell sent the Windsors a brace of pheasants shot on his estate in upstate New York for their New Year table at Lakeridge, a rented Georgian-colonial-style mansion located on fashionable South Ocean Boulevard in Palm Beach. Edward valued the attention. 'Your thoughts of us in this and other ways is [sic] much appreciated,' he wrote from Palm Beach on 8 January, 'more especially your letter of December 30th. While I hardly feel my first literary efforts are worthy of such compliments, all you say about them has given us both a great deal of pleasure and satisfaction.'[4] But Edward, as Murphy observed, remained 'cautious and careful',[5] and resisted Longwell's attempts to dispatch him to Florida. Yet after discussions with Hank Walter, Edward eventually agreed. 'It is hardly necessary for me to tell you,' Murphy wrote to Edward on 13 February, 'that we are all delighted with the news that you are going forward with this undertaking. That,' he continued, 'is a corporate view. With me the personal meaning is much more important. I am looking forward to resuming our pleasant days together. And now there is the knowledge that we can work together on something which should be and must be a perfect thing.'[6] Murphy rented a small house in Delray, thirty minutes south of Palm Beach, and installed himself there with his wife and children. 'I know the sun and rest will do my wife good,' he wrote to Edward on 8 March, shortly before his arrival. 'I tell you this so that you will know we do not wish you to feel any particular responsibility towards us. We intend to live quietly and tranquilly.'[7]

Murphy arrived in Palm Beach on 13 March 1948. Under the warmth of a late-winter Florida sun, Edward began to reminisce. The 1947 articles had provided only a few lines on his post-First World War career as Prince of Wales. With Edward's secretary, Elsa Blaisdell, taking dictation as he and Murphy conversed, they began with Edward's official debut on the world stage: his 1919 tour of Canada and the United States. Recollections were scattered and the typed drafts of these early conversations were often an assemblage of disjointed thoughts. Yet the process was an effective means of establishing the narrative framework of Edward's story.

On 5 August 1919 Edward had set off from Portsmouth aboard the British cruiser *Renown*. The three-month tour had covered the length of Canada and ended with an unplanned, but triumphant, visit to the United States, where he met an ailing President Woodrow Wilson and an up-and-coming Assistant Secretary of the Navy, Franklin D. Roosevelt. Edward's staff included Admiral Lionel Halsey, Godfrey Thomas and Edward Grigg – a political ally of the Prime Minister, David Lloyd George, who had engineered the tours, believing the presence of the Prince of Wales would strengthen the weakening bonds of Empire.

'I had started forth,' Edward told Murphy, 'as a royal icon . . . a small embodiment of Britain officially provided with the proper thing to say and the right uniform to wear.'[8] Planned along precedents established in his father's and grandfather's day, Edward, emboldened by his experiences in the First World War, immediately realised that a drastic stylistic shift was needed to succeed. Eschewing the formality of what he believed was a bygone era, he embraced an informal and democratic style. It worked. Combined with his charm and good looks, he proved irresistible for the people he encountered and the media that covered him. Pairing perfectly with the burgeoning age of mass photography and newsreel, the effect was to transform his image into that of a matinee film idol. Mobbed wherever he went, the 'vigorous and uncontrolled' public euphoria startled even a prince who, as he later wrote, had been reared with crowds 'almost from my first conscious memories'.[9] Unsettled by the adulation, George V wrote disapprovingly to his son,

'I feel angry at the amount of handshaking and autograph writing you seem compelled to face!'[10] But Edward's formula was an undisputed triumph. Leo Amery (Personal Secretary to the Colonial Secretary Lord Milner), who was instrumental in planning this tour, later recalled, 'The Prince's winning smile, his beautiful speaking voice, his natural gift of saying the right thing, his genuine human interest in all kinds and conditions of men and women and, not least, his very youthfulness, made an irresistible appeal. Here was the living embodiment of the bright hopes of unity and happiness . . .'[11]

The notes taken on 19 March 1948 about his first months back in England after the war and his North American tour formed the basis for a later undated draft written in Edward's hand in pencil on his signature yellow legal notepaper.

I was discharged or retired from active service in the army in April [in fact February] 1919, and found myself, like hundreds and thousands of my generation, out on a limb as far as experience of anything beyond fighting the Germans to fit us for a career. Even if some of us had an objective profession before the war, conditions and circumstances had so materially changed that the process of readjustment was not easy. Furthermore, four years of tough life on the various fronts had changed our thinking too, and the ideas we brought back clashed with those of the older generation.

. . . But my duties as Prince of Wales claimed me immediately . . . My apprenticeship was tough . . . I had hardly ever performed at public functions, had never been taught to speak, or been given more than the vaguest line of what was expected of me . . . After a month or so I began to feel I was not doing too badly, and was pleased with the good impression the less stilted and more democratic technique I was adopting seemed to be making. But a conversation with one of the older members of my father's staff . . . on the subject of how a Prince should deport himself and go about his business took me aback.[12]

This clash involved George V's Assistant Private Secretary Frederick 'Fritz' Ponsonby, whose father Henry had been an éminence grise at the court of Queen Victoria, serving as her Private Secretary from 1870 until his death in 1895. Edward considered the veteran courtier Frederick, in whom had been instilled a reverence for the monarchy as fashioned in the Victorian era, out of sync with the modern world.

I had known Fritz Ponsonby all my life. He was an intelligent and astute courtier. He had offered to supply me with a few standard opening and closing paragraphs for speeches when we got to discussing this business of 'Stunting', as my brothers and I came to call our public appearances and engagements. Ponsonby maintained I was on the wrong track trying to democratize the role of the Royal Family and to bring the monarchy nearer to the people. I countered by saying that, from what I had seen and sensed, the people thought and felt different about it all since the war; that they had lost some of the reverence for the Throne, and that they wanted a closer and less formal touch. Ponsonby concluded . . . the King must remain on a high pinnacle . . . and that the Royal Family, although a few steps lower down, should also remain aloof or else the monarchy would lose its prestige in the eyes of the people.

I did not heed Ponsonby's or my father's injunctions that I always appear in top hat and morning coat in public. I continued to wear war-time uniform until this had been discarded for the conventional peace-time plain clothes. Then I adopted a business suit and bowler hat, often to the chagrin and perhaps displeasure of the mayors and aldermen of another generation, who derived pleasure and smug satisfaction in decking themselves out in their municipal robes and regalia. But I maintained that the crowds preferred the more conventional clothes, which were anyway more practical for the varying kinds of things I was asked to do after the formalities were over.

. . . I welcomed the first opportunity of travel overseas . . .

I was then twenty-five . . . I was very young, and I had no political, economic or literary background whatsoever. My early speeches were mostly naïve, and as I lack confidence in speaking, I instinctively pulled my punches. These circumstances I think account for the fact that I seldom engaged in deep political or economic talk with local statesmen or business men, and they, for their part, may have had their doubts as to whether my youth and lack of experience would enable me to assimilate the wisdom they had stored up.

. . . Any information concerning royal progresses in Canada . . . was out of date . . . Fantastic archaic schedules were prepared along the 1901 lines [the previous tour of Canada by Edward's parents]. Official entries into cities and provinces were to be made in horse-drawn landaus, with mounted cavalry escorts. Pompous ceremonial was to be observed at all public functions. In other words, I was to revert to the cherished top hat and morning coat if the occasion did not demand uniform. But I had spent the last weeks of the war with the Canadian Army Corps, and my meetings with a great number of Canadian veterans had been completely informal. How could I suddenly revert from an army major to an upstage Prince? No – I was developing my own technique, and I was determined not to be put off my stride.

One embarrassing feature of my overseas tours was that my new 'Princing' techniques sometimes clashed with more hidebound lines along which Governor Generals operated . . .

My appearance at each place was an event. A holiday was proclaimed, and unless we stopped off more than one day at any one place, one could not shop, as all the stores were closed. But for me it was monotonous most of the time. Civic receptions, entertainments, lunches and dinners, and always balls; parades of veterans, visits to hospitals, cornerstones, honorary degrees at universities . . . And always the school kids, massed in a park or football stadium singing patriotic songs. I can still hear the strident strains of 'O Canada', The

Maple Leaf' and the inevitable 'God Bless the Prince of Wales', usually sung out of beat with the local band. Sometimes I thought the almighty's generosity was being overtaxed by the supplications on my behalf, but if His response took the form of the goodwill and enthusiasm which the petitioners bestowed on me, then I was more than liberally rewarded, and that above all sustained me in what literally became a test of physical endurance . . .

The visits to the big cities were always the worst beatings. The public engagements were more set and formal, the speeches longer and more important . . .

The small towns were mostly reached by railroad . . . I lived on trains . . . and there was an observation car at the end which, although providing enjoyment of the scenery, also provided an all too convenient platform from which it was impossible to avoid the inevitable call for an impromptu speech. As a matter of fact, I got more information from conversations with crowds gathered back on the observation car, and more wise-cracks, than from the longer stop-offs. Uncontrolled laughter and gibes were the response to some dumb, naïve questions as to the population, the industry and the amenities of the place, particularly after dark, when the local inhabitants may have fortified themselves against my stop-off with mild alcoholic celebrating.

Even some of the small towns prepared set schedules and addresses of welcome. I remember one occasion, when seated with a small-town mayor on a bunting-decorated platform . . . he turned refreshingly to me after a harassingly long pause, and asked, 'Say, Prince, are we in shape for readin' right now?' The tension eased immediately, and the informality made my day . . .

One day Halsey, Grigg and I were discussing the tour on the train on our way back East from British Columbia when I remarked that it did seem fantastic to be visiting on the North American continent without going to the U.S. Both agreed but pointed out that, although so recently our allies, some in London might be hesitant . . . But I would not be put off. I had been attached to General Pershing's Headquarters at Chaumont only a few months before and had made some friends in the American Army and in the Navy . . . After a considerable exchange of cables with London, Grigg was called to Washington by the British Ambassador [Edward Grey] for consultation. It was not many days before he wired that all was arranged and that he was rejoining me in Canada . . . with a draft schedule in his pocket.

Until almost the last minute Edward's visit to the United States had been in doubt. Political tensions around the American government's ratification of the Treaty of Versailles and the ailing health of President Wilson made both sides nervous about an official princely progress. George V was particularly vocal in his disapproval and sent a cable to his son ordering him to cancel the trip. But Edward was determined and, with Lloyd George's ally Grigg's support, refused to acquiesce. His insistence was, as the historian Ted Powell notes, 'a mark of his [Edward's] newfound confidence in the wake of his success in Canada'.[13]

On 10 November Edward crossed the US border by train. After visits to Washington D.C. and the Naval Academy at Annapolis, Maryland, he arrived in New York City on 18 November. Determined to choreograph the most elaborate welcome possible, the reception committee, led by American department-store magnate Rodnam Wanamaker, insisted that Edward enter the city by boat. Accordingly, he disembarked from his train at Jersey City, where he then boarded a barge to take him the short distance to the ferry terminal at Battery Park City in Lower Manhattan. After weeks of coverage of Edward's Canadian progress, New York was poised to welcome him with enthusiastic fanfare. The twelve-day trip that followed was the beginning of a lifelong love affair with all things American.

[I] approached New York with mixed emotions, excited yet apprehensive; and my first view of that enchanted island, looking up the canyon of Lower Broadway, provided one of the most magnificent spectacles of my life . . .

My first impression was of a maelstrom in a tunnel. The outline of the building, the tallest I had ever seen, was obscured by what at first glance appeared to be a driving snowstorm; and there was a roar in the air like the sound of a thousand express trains.

Grover Whalen, the city official responsible for organising the welcome ceremony, informed Edward this 'snowstorm' was in fact a New York invention: the tickertape parade.

As an Englishman, brought up on the decorous and slow-gaited show, this demonstration struck me as feverish and wasteful. But all the same the effects were intoxicating. I found myself lifted and supported by the excitement of the crowd: it went to the head, like champagne. And before the journey was half finished, I found myself bowing and saluting in every direction, like an actor who had scored a personal triumph . . .

All this might have gone to my head had not a wise American, a semi-philosophical Brooklyn detective attached to my staff, advised me not to attach too much importance to these ovations. 'Americans are suckers for anything new . . . Grover Whalen could wow the same crowds with a Ubangi Indian.'

I left the U.S. a changed man. I had gone there imbued with conventional British prejudices. Among well-born Englishmen there was a widespread inclination to look down upon Americans as rather loud, pushing upstarts – a cult of superiority arising in part out of a fear that these strange continental people, speaking the same language, worshipping the same religions, sharing the same culture, were already doing a number of important things better than we were. And I must confess for myself that some of what I saw repelled me. But by and large I was delighted by American ways. If France had enchanted me and Canada had awed me, the United States took my breath away. I felt its movement and power, its boldness and greatness; and more than that I liked it all.

The innovations that made Edward's tour so successful were entirely his own. 'I did not get much of a directive,' he declared to Murphy in July 1947. 'That was left to me pretty much once I started out. Although my father said it was an important mission, he himself did not give me any detailed instructions.'[14] The one piece of advice Edward did receive from George V was the staunchly formal royal pronouncement: 'Remember your position and who you are.'[15] As he wrote in a later undated draft, it did little to ease the uncertainty he felt about the role he was to play in British public life.

This remark of my father's was disturbing to a young man who only so recently had been one among millions of men fighting in the war lost in a vast crowd where position had lost much of its old meaning. That I could not act like other people. In other words, I was different. But except in so far as birth and inheritance were concerned, which it must be admitted were unique – how different was I from other people? Through school, college and the war, I had certainly discovered my shortcomings. Not only was I not better than other people – the fact was I possessed no outstanding qualifications to set me up above my contemporaries. In the competitive struggle of my youth, I found that however hard I tried I was not as good at anything as the average of my contemporaries, be it education, sport or games.

When I looked back and came to think of this question of my position, had I not built up a resistance to seeming to be different from other people? I recalled my resentment during my last year at Dartmouth [Naval College] when my father had directed that half my weekly hours at engineering should be substituted for political study. Not that I liked engineering, on the contrary, it made better sense to me, but the switch made me seem different from other cadets. At Magdalen College, Oxford, my rooms had been made more comfortable and a bath had been specifically put in for me. Not that I didn't enjoy the extra comfort provided but it made me seem <u>different</u> from the other undergraduates. I had not been allowed to take my chance as a regimental officer in the war and my movements in the combat zone had been ridiculously restricted. Not that I wanted to get killed or wounded or taken prisoner or spend four years in the trenches but being denied what I regarded as the proper place in battle for a young man of twenty made me seem <u>different</u> from the millions of other young men being offered up for cannon fodder be they friends or enemies.

Now I was being launched on a career in public life not of my choosing which was going to make me seem more different from other people than ever. OK, I said to myself, I will act differently – when in reality I never had been different at all only in birth and position. So, I decided from the start that I would act as differently from other people as was required of me when on show but that 'off duty' I would work out my own life along the lines of my tastes and inclinations. This occasion of mine at the outset of my public career is responsible for the development of my character through its various phases – unorthodox for a Prince of Wales as it may be regarded by my critics but nevertheless gaining for me a certain measure of popularity and success at the time.

It was all this that made me seek informality – to observe all ceremonial punctiliously but to dispense with it whenever I could and it seemed out of place. To take part and enjoy the pleasures of all sections of the community from foxhunting to playing darts.

Edward returned to Britain in December 1919. Despite his success, the trip had left him 'physically and mentally exhausted'.[16] Though he held back the full psychological impact of his exhaustion from Murphy, he alluded to the strain in a later conversation. 'One incident,' he recalled, 'that remains in my mind . . . is a speech I was working on very hard. I was very tired and was just about to finish . . . when Ned Grigg came in with two more sheets of paper to add . . . I burst into tears and said, "I can't write another page – it is too much to ask for." I was completely exhausted . . .'[17]

In March 1920, having been back in Britain for just a little over three months, Edward left for a seven-month tour of Australia and New Zealand, which also included stops in Barbados, Hawaii, Mexico, Antigua, Bermuda and Panama. Edward found the 'freshness' and 'vitality'[18] of Australia intoxicating. Yet despite the enthusiasm of his reception, he remained at a distance from any real engagement with the places he visited. 'It was all the same,' he declared to Murphy. 'The same boring schedule. The machine would take hold.'[19] This monotony, Edward believed, accounted for how little stood out in his memory of these trips. 'I must confess,' he wrote later, 'that concerning a good deal of my travels my mind is puzzlingly blank. There is, I think, a simple explanation for this. I was not out to get information about others, to learn particularly about them. My mission was to impress my personality upon them, to make a good impression; to be a symbol of a British Prince and of British power and of British stability. And so the nervous strain on me took a peculiar form. I was worried what they should think of me and not about how I should judge them.'[20]

Edward docked at Portsmouth on 10 October and spent the following twelve months in Britain. On 26 October 1921 he departed again, this time for an eight-month tour visiting India, Ceylon, Hong Kong and Japan. It was his third official tour. The free-wheeling and democratic style that had characterised his earlier journeys was replaced with the rigid formality that colonial officials deemed imperative in India. The trip was controversial, and many felt unwise, given the volatility of Indian politics. Edward shared these doubts and up to the point of departure hoped it would be called off. Though his experiences were mitigated by the inevitable barriers of his 'royal progress', 'India,' he told Murphy, 'awed me.'[21] His observations of the experience and the political dynamics in India were characteristic of his generation and class.

Palm Beach, 23 March 1948

. . . There had been some trouble in India and the purpose of my trip was to try to impress the natives with the stability and power of the British Crown. It was all to be pomp and ceremony, and the pattern had been set by earlier state visits. Because it was all so stiff and formal the whole business was less exacting from my viewpoint. The British role was based on pomp . . . The Orientals loved solemnity and I suppose that our subsequent difficulties grew out of the failure of the British Raj to realize that along with the splendor the Indians were also interested in more explosive matters . . .

I landed at Bombay . . . [the Marquess of] Reading was Viceroy, a great politician and former King's Counsel. I must say I had little use for Reading. He was inclined to be a little too Oriental for my taste. I discovered in India that the old diehard British officials detested him cordially. They made a great point of British aristocracy and indeed all the previous Viceroys could point back to a long line of aristocrats, but Reading . . . began his tenure by declaring in a speech that when he had first visited India thirty-five years before it was as a seaman on a British freighter. Such a declaration would have had a marvelous effect in New Zealand or Australia, which both have strong radical traditions, but it shocked British society in India and apparently gave some offence to the Indians. 'Do we want a seaman as Viceroy?' was the question.

I think I can say that on this trip I began to mature mentally. I was no longer terrified by the endless round of ceremony. I took more interest in politics.

. . . There had been some doubt as to how I would be received in Bombay . . . Indian Nationalist leaders were seizing every opportunity to humiliate British rule and to protest against what they called British tyranny. However, they never attacked me personally. For this I was grateful. I visited dozens of Indian cities . . . and I remember India chiefly for its masses of people, an endless ocean of humanity. I saw it all from a distance through a screen of police and military . . .

The formality almost never varied. I would travel at night in a special carriage set aside for royal visitors like myself. Upon my arrival in a city the next day I would at once put on a full-dress uniform and drive through the streets to the Residency, where I would meet the Governor and his staff, all in uniform. Because the heat of the day soon grew intolerable, I would at once remove the uniform and join the Governor and his staff for breakfast. The first day as a rule would be fairly simple. The Governor would inform me of the plans that he had arranged for my visit and if I had any objections I would make them . . .

. . . The garden parties were always formal, almost unbearably so. Always there would be a brass band from the local garrison playing martial music under the banyan trees. I would stand beside the Governor and receive with him a long procession of the local elite, officials, wives, the richest and most aristocratic Indians. There was no color bar then, as the phrase is understood in America, but at the same time there were very few Indians invited . . .

There would always be a large official banquet on the second night, followed by a ball . . . and I would see again the same people with whom I had chatted in the afternoon. I must say it all struck me as quite unimportant, yet they all set great store by these stiff changeless ceremonies . . .

During the day I would be taken on a tour of the local countryside to inspect agricultural developments, visit the regiments and maybe have a drink in the officers' mess. I rather liked these meals with the officers for they gave me a chance to relax.

. . . I could sense the jealousy that permeated the whole British hierarchy of the order in which people would be presented to me or would sit at the great table. I used to feel sorry for the ADC [aide-de-camp] who had to keep the meticulous arrangements of Englishmen one to the other in hand . . .

. . . At the time of my visit Gandhi was in jail . . . but Nehru was out . . . Nehru had great power over the masses. Earlier when I arrived at Allahabad I had been met by the Governor of the province with the warning that I must be prepared for some discourtesy. The streets were empty and the officials were nervous. As usual I was in full dress uniform and an ornate carriage was waiting to take me through the city. A flustered official entered my carriage to explain that a 'hartal' or strike of resistance had been planned by Nehru's followers to express disapproval of my visit. I should add that we were never sure what the atmosphere in a town would be. It became a kind of game for public support. The Nationalist leaders on their side were anxious to make some show of dissent to show that their power over the crowds was greater than that of the British officials. And the British on their side were determined to prove that Gandhi lacked the power to interrupt anything that they had planned on.

Having complied with Nehru's orders to boycott his procession, a crowd subsequently flocked to see Edward play polo later that afternoon. 'Nehru has already demonstrated his power to handle the mob,' an officer accompanying Edward told him. 'Now he will let them go . . .'

Now this incident enable[d] me to have a little fun with Nehru.

During my stay at the Residency . . . I decided to see Nehru. He appeared in the Lodge, a most intelligent and charming fellow but obviously very much on his guard. He asked me politely, 'Sir, how are you enjoying your trip?'

'Very much indeed,' I answered. 'And indeed one of the high spots of my whole stay in India was the visit to your city Allahabad.'

He stared at me.

'It was a wonderful reception. I never enjoyed a polo game more.'

He bowed and a little smile played under his eyes. He wore the long coat and the tight pants and the box cap which even today remains his public costume. I was careful not to talk Indian politics. I had been advised that it was too tricky and dangerous and I knew too little to try a gamble.

. . . I suppose my views on India were very much with those of a British Tory. Winston Churchill in those days was always attacking the government for its mild policy in India. 'You can't let India go,' he stormed. But the Conservative Party was bent on reform and there was no turning back . . .

I must say that before the trip was over I got bored . . . I felt removed from all connection with India. The feeling of suffocation grew. I saw only British. The people of India, whoever they were, were at arm's length, beyond the police lines and the screen of civil servants . . .

From India, Edward sailed to Singapore, Hong Kong, and then Japan. There he met with Crown Prince Hirohito, who had recently been installed as Regent for his father Emperor Taisho, whose mental health had forced him into seclusion. Though his official biographer, Philip Ziegler, believed in Edward's 'indifference to the charms of Japan',[22] his recollections point to the contrary.

Palm Beach, 25 March 1948

. . . I was never taken to see the Emperor [Taisho] – it was said that he was not quite right in the head. The present Emperor [Hirohito] I had met at Portsmouth in 1921 on his arrival. He was a queer and amiable little fellow, very anxious to please. He had five or six set English sentences and several bad French ones which somebody had taught him. These he would use in circumstances which he considered appropriate. It surprised me at the time that the Japanese, so thorough in other aspects of their education and imitation, had neglected to teach the Crown Prince English . . .

My chief guide in Japan was the Consul at Yokohama, named Davidson [Sir Colin John Davidson], who in Japanese fashion we later called David-Sun. He was a charming, well-educated, friendly man with an immense knowledge of Japanese life. He took me to Geisha parties and taught me to drink sake, a sickening concoction. He taught me how to wear a kimono. I liked the Geisha parties with their tea, shrimp, lobsters and little dishes and the hot towel that would be brought halfway through the meal. We were always followed by Japanese police and in fact I was conscious of being watched . . . but I don't think this spying was done with the idea of picking up secrets but only to collect notes of how a British Prince conducted himself. I played golf with the Crown Prince and several Americans on a golf course which had just been built, with Hirohito dressed up in knickers [traditional golf trousers]. I must say that as a golf player he left something to be desired . . . I suppose he played merely to show how Europeanized he was . . .

I really had a good time in Japan. I visited lovely temples. One of the loveliest bridges I had ever seen was at Nikko – a bridge of red lacquer. The Japanese loaded us down with gifts – lacquer cabinets, swords, silks of all kinds. I was there a month altogether. The strongest impression I had was of regimentation and a childish hunger for Western ways. Japanese women in their kimonos have a unique charm but dressed up in European clothes they looked quite absurd. They wore huge floppy hats and dresses quite out of style . . .

With me the Japanese were always stiff and reserved. The only time I ever saw one relax was at a Geisha party . . .

The British Ambassador Elliot [Sir Charles Elliot] was a tall, heavy man whose hobby was collecting antiques. He had no interest in diplomacy and seemed wholly oblivious of Japanese politics. When he talked about the Japanese people they did not seem to exist; they were charming phantoms in a charming limbo.

From Japan, Edward made his way across the Indian Ocean, through the Red Sea, finally landing at Cairo for perhaps one of his most unusual royal audiences.

At Cairo protocol required a formal visit upon King Fuad. I stopped at the Residence with the High Commissioner, General Allenby [Edmund Allenby, 1st Viscount Allenby] . . . The little King was an extraordinary man. He was no Egyptian at all but an Armenian (the Khedives of Egypt were Turkish-Armenian). Fuad had been quite a politician in his time but he had the tactlessness to fall in love with the mistress of his brother. Surprised one night in the chambers of his lady love by the untimely arrival of his kinsman, he took refuge under the bed. But a sound gave him away and the angry kinsman shot him in the throat, inflicting a wound which thereafter left the Khedive with an impediment for which medicine was no cure. He spoke only with the greatest difficulty and if nervous or excited his language became a ridiculous series of barks.

Naturally this put an unusual burden upon visitors and Lord Allenby, something of a stuffed shirt himself, had warned me before taking me to the palace that the King had a little impediment and I must be on guard against it. 'Nothing very important,' he said promptly, 'just a slight defect.'

I was therefore not at all prepared for what must surely go down in history as one of the strangest sounds ever uttered by a monarch.

On our arrival at the palace we were taken up a flight of stairs to a big reception room. We passed through a screen of Egyptian courtiers, all bowing. Upstairs we passed through an enormous room with a parquet floor, then a second room at the far end of which the door was opened by a uniformed servant whose bow barely scraped the floor. There was a third room and yet another door. As this last door opened I found myself propelled into the largest room of all, at the far end of which sat a little man in the tarbush. (I was dressed in the uniform of a Welsh guard with pith helmet and miniature feathers of the Prince of Wales pattern.) Allenby clanked along at my side, a pompous figure, spurs clanging on the hard floor. Then from this figure came one of the most remarkable sounds I have heard on this earth – inhuman, animal-like, a bark but a pointless bark. It was all I could do to keep from bursting into laughter. Through the babble I could detect certain French phrases, which were barely intelligible. You can imagine the difficulty of developing a serious conversation. Any train of thought would be preceded by these weird barks. I tried to control myself but in spite of everything I noticed that my body was shaking and I could feel Allenby's immense disapproval; and finally in my nervousness I began to pluck the feathers from my pith helmet. Finally the ordeal ended and I escaped after the few pointless courtesies. All the way back through those vast rooms and endless corridors I tried to hold back my laughter. I think I succeeded but as soon as we got into the car and after the car drove off my controls vanished and I laughed and laughed and laughed. Allenby said nothing. He simply looked at me as if I were an urchin. 'Your behavior, Sir, was disgraceful, and if I might add, Sir, wholly beneath your dignity. His Majesty could not have failed to notice.' I am sure he did, for when I glanced at my helmet all the feathers were gone and I remembered a little pile on the floor beside my chair at the palace. It was a display of bad manners on my part because I was helpless . . .

'I was a traveler, rather than a sojourner,'[23] Edward recalled of the years between 1919 and 1925 when he traversed at least 150,000 miles and visited forty-five countries. His last great imperial tour from March to October 1925 covered the length of British colonial Africa and concluded in South America with stops in Uruguay, Argentina and Chile. Though constantly confronted by the barriers of officialdom the trips nevertheless afforded Edward the opportunity to see the world as no other Prince of Wales had ever done before. 'What had been mere abstractions,' he told Murphy, '. . . subjects of long leaders in *The Times*, official reports, now became invested with reality.'[24] He saw at first hand the slow but inevitable decline of the British colonial fabric: 'One could feel empire dying through inability to adjust itself to change,'[25] he told Murphy. Yet he had executed his brief and exceeded all expectations. His travels had recast him as an international celebrity, catapulting the British monarchy as embodied by its future sovereign onto a global stage. His popularity infused the institution with a dash of democratic modernity and Hollywood-esque glamour, qualities it had never had before. His success established a lasting model for the kind of soft power that would become the backbone of British royal influence in the twentieth century.

'Along with other things,' Edward wrote, 'I had come to be known as "BFA" [Britain's Finest Ambassador] [or] "BBS" [Britain's Best Salesman], two popular sobriquets which for all their obvious grandiloquence never the less gave me secret satisfaction.'[26] But his long trips had also separated him physically and psychologically from his family and traditional court life. His return to a settled routine in Great Britain did little to narrow the gulf, as he seemed unwilling or unable to return to the conventional royal formula. 'Life,' he told Murphy, was 'something more than driving down lined streets with uplifted hat and ready smile . . . [I] had got [the] impression I knew people, they knew me . . .'[27] His increasing obsession with America, where he had 'caught the infectious driving power of business competition and enterprise',[28] was the most outward manifestation of a desire to carve out a public and personal profile drastically different from any of his princely predecessors.

I gained something wonderful from them [the tours]. Men lived more freely. They were not afraid to speak to me or tell me what I thought because I was a prince. While they were civil and respectful they had no favor to seek . . .

To return from that to Great Britain was like returning to a trap. Back to the atmosphere of the tight little island, the rounds of Whitehall and Buckingham Palace; world of Ascot, and the grouse moors; where old ways [were] important because old.

Yet for all the outward manifestations of success, the tours had been gruelling and, as they came to a finish, many on Edward's staff felt increasingly disillusioned. His effervescent public performances were often matched by moody and depressive behaviour in private. His tendency to go off-script might have delighted crowds but it incited the irritation of those responsible for a meticulously planned schedule. He frequently failed to acknowledge their efforts or exhaustion. Yet with the hindsight of more than two decades Edward, in an undated draft, acknowledged the great debt he owed to the men who had accompanied him on these voyages.

If these tours were tough on me they certainly were tough on my staff as well but in a different way. I was on the stage all the time, but to keep me performing they each had their defined job but worked as a team taking care of all the details that would otherwise have hampered or interfered with or interrupted the imperial part I was trying to play.

I was, however, also indebted to the 'Retinue' composed of Clerks, Detectives, Valets & Orderlies, whose inconspicuous but invaluable contributions to the smooth running of these imperial odysseys never figured in the official diary – their efficient cooperation in their different departments at sea or ashore in trains or camps was such that not a piece of luggage was ever lost during the thousands of miles we traveled, never was a speech not ready typed . . .

But there were [two] men who must have special mention . . . my valets. Assembling a wardrobe for these lengthy expeditions was a task of considerable complexity. Not only did my public appearances range from full dress tamashas to polo clothes and rough hunting gear but the climates varied in extremes. On each trip from the Panama Canal or Hawaii to Invercargill or the slopes of Mount Cook, from Singapore to the Khyber Pass, from the Gold Coast to the summit of the railroad across the snow-covered Andes, the valets were responsible that I always had the right costume on hand for each part the schedule demanded of me and they never let me down . . .

After his return in October 1925 Edward began a more settled existence in Britain. In 1926 he 'caught the golf bug' and over the next few years he gradually gave up both foxhunting and the steeplechase. His love of the game endured for the rest of his life. 'The fact,' he wrote in an undated draft, 'that after all these years I still have a handicap of eighteen, and get a great kick out of breaking ninety, shows I picked the wrong game on which to devote so much of my leisure, but like all keen golfers, [I] was obsessed with the urge and the hope of improvement.'[29]

From 1926 to 1929 he rented a series of homes near his favourite courses in Kent and at Sunningdale until, he wrote, 'a chance windfall came my way': the discovery of Fort Belvedere. 'I loved it; my own home,' [30] Edward told Murphy, in an undated conversation. 'It was there that life began to mean something to me,' he continued. 'When I left I thought how wonderful if I could only pick [it] up, stuff it in a bag and take it with me.'[31] He described his affection for Windsor and for the place he later rechristened 'The Fort' in a lengthy undated draft written in pencil on his habitual yellow legal notepaper.

One of the 'Grace and Favour' houses in Windsor Great Park, a strange, castellated folly called Belvedere Fort, became vacant . . . Admiral Halsey, my comptroller, asked me to approach my father with the request that he occupy Belvedere

Fort . . . My father agreed, but in the end Halsey . . . found it too large and impracticable.

However, while the fate of Belvedere Fort still hung in the balance, Murray [Sir Malcolm Murray, Equerry and Comptroller to Edward's great-uncle, Prince Arthur, The Duke of Connaught] called me one day at Sunningdale and said, 'You like this section; why not come over to Belvedere this afternoon and look it over? I believe it is just the kind . . . of house you want.' So I accepted his invitation, and one look at the house and grounds was all that I needed to convince myself of the great possibilities of this hundred-acre Crown property. Next day I went to my father, explaining that I did not believe Halsey was very sold on the place, and that whether he was or not, I wanted Belvedere Fort myself, and would he please let me live there. He immediately agreed.

Built around 1746 . . . at the same time as Virginia Water was made into a lake – by William, Duke of Cumberland, second son of George II . . . it consisted originally of an octagonal tower one story high, protected on north and east by battlements, with cannon of the same period in the embrasures. Some seventy years later, George IV directed his architect Wyatville . . . to enlarge [it], in order to make it habitable, so the legend runs for one of the King's girlfriends. Wyatville's structure remains intact today . . . Such was the house that I saw that Sunday in July 1929, which was to become my cherished home for six years.

As soon as the Murrays moved out that fall, I started in to paint and decorate this unique, fantastic joke of a house . . . I dropped the redundant name 'Belvedere' and called it The Fort. But its basic charm was undeniable, and the setting, overlooking the birch and pine covered slopes with here and there a glimpse of Virginia Water Lake and tall trees beyond as a background, was enchanting. I made few structural alterations, beyond tearing down a few interior walls to enlarge some of the bedrooms, and putting in extra bathrooms.

The house eventually became snug and cozy, and from spending weekends there to begin with, I gradually came to live there far more than York House, and in the end virtually commuted to London most of the year.

But as the house itself gradually became my most prized personal creation and achievement from the comfort and decorating viewpoint, I started in to develop the gardens . . . I cut down all the gloomy yew trees that almost poked their dreary branches into the windows and made the house dark and gave one a feeling of claustrophobia. And even a magnificent beech tree in front of the entrance was sacrificed for light and air . . .

I transformed a neglected lily-pond below the battlements into a modern swimming pool, and built a spacious garage and rooms for my staff, which were concealed by vine-covered walls. The grounds were a paradise for the amateur landscape gardener, for Nature had provided all the drop scenes . . . It was all very beautiful and intimate, and the peaceful stillness, which was one of the great charms of The Fort, was only distantly broken over the weekends by the undisturbing murmur of traffic on the highway a quarter of a mile away.

It was a haven of rest, a private anchorage safe and secure from the turmoil which surrounded my public and social life. There I was as incommunicado as was conceivably possible, and I spent a lot of time there alone with my homework, my hobbies, and working in the garden . . . Gardening became an obsession for six years . . . In the summer I mowed the hay around the house with a scythe – backbreaking exercise until you scythe out the aches and stiffness. In the spring the cuckoos would remind one that summer was at hand, and pigeons and swallows disported themselves from the tall trees.

Most weekends I would have friends to stop. I had room for ten . . . But that was crowding the house too much, and I regarded four, five or six guests as enough for comfort . . . Nobody had to do anything, or go places they did not want to . . .

From the day I moved into The Fort, I began to take an increasing interest in Windsor Castle . . . I had always loved the atmosphere of Windsor where we had all had such a good time as kids. If the old castle seemed somewhat austere and forbidding, the spacious rooms and corridors and the acres of roof had provided a wonderful playground for children.

By now, [I was] nearing forty, [and] the chance proximity of my home to Windsor provided an outlet for my latent historical sense, inherited from my mother, and my taste for pictures, furniture and objets d'art. I was brought up on the history of the Castle and its contents, and delighted to take my friends on Sunday afternoons for a self-conducted tour. And the Great Park, too, gave many ideas for landscaping, and I began to be consulted by the Park Advisory Committee . . . In this way I kept in constant and permanent touch with the ancestral home of the British monarchy . . . [32]

On 11 April 1948 the Windsors boarded the Amtrak Silver Meteor at West Palm Beach station for the eleven-hundred-mile rail journey to New York City. In consideration of Wallis's lifelong fear of flying, trains were the Windsors' preferred mode of transport when travelling long distances in Europe and the United States. Met by their chauffeur and 'The Duchess' at Penn Station, they drove immediately to Severn, at 11 Horse Valley Road, Locust Valley, their rented eight-bedroom brick Normandy-style mansion on Long Island. Edward did not stay put for long. The next day, 13 April, he was back in New York City to meet Longwell and Murphy at the Time Inc. office. 'We all enjoyed seeing you today,' Longwell wrote to Edward, 'and, as always, you left behind . . . in LIFE a feeling of pleasure and warmth.'[33] Three days later the Windsors were on the move again, this time to West Virginia where they were to attend the gala reopening of the legendary Greenbrier Hotel in White Sulphur Springs. It was a fitting coincidence given the

current reminiscing. On leaving Washington D.C. in November 1919, Edward had spent a weekend at Greenbrier golfing and hiking in the surrounding pine forests before heading to New York City. Now guests of the hotel's owner, railroad magnate Robert Young – he and his wife Anita were two of the Windsors' closest American friends – they joined fellow guests who included the Marchioness of Hartington [née Kathleen Kennedy], Bing Crosby and William Randolph Hearst.

Returning to Severn on 22 April, Edward and Wallis found Murphy conveniently ensconced at a nearby cottage. With travelling at a stand-still, Edward's authorial pace quickened, and his dictation flowed. Gradually he began addressing more personal topics. On 3 May he reminisced about his parents, specifically their resistance to the modern world. He told Murphy that his mother had never spoken on the telephone except for one occasion, while his father 'never learned to drive a car.'[34] Cocktails were contraband.

Severn, 3 May 1948

I remember his [*my father*] coming to York House Cottage when we were having our little 7 o'clock drink, and he said what a terrible thing it was to drink before dinner . . . [he] never accepted new people . . . He was very conservative in that way . . . He was rather suspicious of trying anything new . . . No one had any influence over my father except my mother, especially as he became older. One had to go through my mother to prepare the way of broaching the subject . . . He was very much a man of habit. I think we all get that way a bit, though – one does as one gets older.

In his conversations with Murphy, Edward only alluded to the tensions that existed between himself and his father after he reached adulthood. His comments on George V throughout were sympathetic and on the whole admiring; they made no acknowledgement of the bitterness he had felt as a young man over his father's incessant criticisms of everything from his social circle to his style of dress. Returning to England in 1919, after nearly four years away from his parents, Edward felt overwhelmed by their censure. 'I know he [George V] doesn't approve of me,'[35] he wrote to his then mistress Freda Dudley Ward. 'How any human beings can ever have got into this pompous secluded and monotonous groove I just can't imagine,'[36] he added, in a subsequent letter, having spent just three days under the familial roof at York Cottage, Sandringham, over Christmas 1919. 'I feel quite a stranger here [York Cottage] somehow,' he wrote a year later, 'and I am not appreciated at all . . . I've absolutely nothing in common with the rest of my family and have drifted away from them altogether.'[37]

In a later undated essay entitled 'Family Life', which was never intended for publication, Edward addressed these tensions and the restrictive atmosphere under George V's paternal rule. His reflections offer remarkable insight into the causes of father and son's eventual estrangement as well as Edward's obsessive desire to carve out a life that was physically and emotionally independent from his parents.

The reader may wonder why my family life, so much a part of my early years, should seem to have become more remote and mean less to me as I grew older. It was no lack of affection on either side. I was always devoted to my parents and I believe they admired if silently my work for the Monarchy . . . Whenever I went to visit with them at Sandringham for Xmas [or] at Windsor for Easter and Ascot race week, at Balmoral for a week or ten days at the end of summer they did their best to make my stay pleasant in their own fashion . . . But it was the formality of their home life that I had grown away from and which discouraged relaxing in their homes.

The truth is that they and I would have been much closer if they hadn't been King or Queen; home life would have been far pleasanter and more enjoyable had it not been fenced in with court etiquette. For however biographers may have written up the legend of the simplicity of my parents' home life it was only simple in that decorum prevailed at all times . . .

Did Mary and my brothers feel the same stifling atmosphere at home as I did? The answer is NO. Certainly not in the case of Mary, for hers was an existence after the pattern of my family. She married an older man and assumed her duties as mistress of a large country house or estate with becoming ease. Her two sons were raised in the orthodox aristocratic manner and her friends [were] ever my parents' friends . . .

Bertie lived with his wife and two children in London. They spent their vacations with my parents who doted on the two little girls . . . Bertie got bored with the court etiquette after a while but he enjoyed the shooting and spent much longer under the family roof because his wife [later Queen Elizabeth The Queen Mother] being a commoner loved to bask in the glow of [being] a regal favourite . . . At least he had his family to keep him company for these long sojourns at home – away from his 'princing'.

The two younger boys were away most of the time, Harry in the Army, George in the Navy . . . When they got leave they lived at home and had rooms at Buckingham Palace . . . If the family were away or they had special dates they would stop with me at York House to avoid being questioned. I would say that they had both grown away from home life . . . George in particular, and preferred the atmosphere of live and let live which I would provide. Harry's tastes were sporting so Sandringham and Balmoral had more to offer him than George, who was more bohemian in his tastes and favored music or decorating to outdoor pursuits . . .

My brothers and I often discussed our family life and wondered why our parents wanted us to stop with them at home – they sometimes complained that we didn't stay often enough. They didn't make the house parties more congenial by inviting a few of our friends of our own generation. True some of our friends had committed the deadly crime of having had reason to divorce to escape from an unhappy marriage and had found another mate. But there were plenty of young married couples who from choice or conventionality had preserved their marriage ties who could have introduced a lighter touch to enliven the drabness of Balmoral and Sandringham. A few of the younger generation were invited to Windsor for the ultra-formal Ascot race week but the Castle was so large that the guests seemed to get lost within its spaciousness.

But there was an obvious and definite ban on our personal friends and this arose from the fact that my father, out of touch with the world outside his own, was fed gossip from unfortunate sources, usually malicious, critical, often inaccurate, and always playing for kingly favor. My father listened to the gossip and especially if it concerned us. If the stories became too consistent he would face us with them. That never made for a pleasant interview even if the whole thing was phony.

Boys are never pleased over parental lectures. If a father's diagnosis is correct and he is justified in his handling of a son's unfortunate escapade, the son will eventually appreciate the advice if he knows in his heart his father is right although he won't admit it at the time.

What boys resent are disparaging remarks or insinuations that arise unfounded. The resentment may develop into a row and the son will retire into his shell and hide his doings from the family.

What sons resent as they get older is family interference. Boys will be boys . . . but when men become men, they feel they have the right to work out their own lives for better or for worse. Some through temperament [or] character need more guidance than others or if they are good eggs will appreciate a father's action in intervening in an unfortunate friendship even if they don't admit it at the time.

But I guess that my father took the view that as King his princely sons must not be allowed to sow their royal oats or if they must do so they must keep their private lives behind the curtain of secrecy of Victorian times [and] out of the gossip of social drawing rooms. But, of course, by the 1920s this had long ceased to be possible.

I was once told . . . the King complained one day to him [Lord Derby] that in spite of all his assurances to his sons that he was their best friend they never seemed close to him or ever went to him with their troubles. He concluded by saying, 'You and I are the same age and your sons and mine are contemporaries yet you and your sons are the best of friends and they talk to you. How have you achieved such a happy relationship with all the young men of the generation? . . .' Lord Derby's answer was simple advice: 'Give your sons more rope, Sir. They aren't bad boys, only young and gay as you and I used to be. I never ask my sons to report their every movement or give them the impression that I disapprove of their lives. Your sons are not badly behaved any more than mine are. Give them their heads and they will come to you with their troubles like mine do.'

Though his great imperial tours had finished, Edward continued to make periodic official trips abroad. In January 1931, accompanied by his younger brother Prince George, he visited South America in an effort to boost British trade with the continent. During the three-month tour he visited Peru, Chile, Argentina, Uruguay and Brazil. The trip's highlight was his speech in Spanish at the opening of the British Empire Trade Exhibition in Buenos Aires, which he wrote shortly after his arrival. 'I feel one has to wait until in the atmosphere of the country one visits,' Edward told Murphy, on 5 May 1948. Typically self-effacing, he also added, 'My pronunciation wasn't good.'[38] *The New York Times* disagreed, and the speech made front-page news the following day with the headline, 'The Radio Carries His Voice Afar'. The paper praised his 'crisp and clear' enunciation, which made it 'easier to hear and understand than any other Spanish that went out over the radio'.[39]

Edward had been quick to adapt to the new medium and, by the late 1920s, many of his most important public speeches were written specifically for broadcast. Yet the art of public speaking had not come easily, as he noted in an undated essay entitled 'Speech-Making', most likely written in the late spring of 1948.

It has already been stated that I was not ever trained to public speaking, and this necessary part of a public life has always been a headache to me. By good fortune I was born with, or had unconsciously developed, a clear, carrying diction, 'a good radio voice', which seemed to make up for my shortcomings in the art of composition, technique and use of words and phraseology.

The first spring and summer of 1919 were of course the worst. Ponsonby had given me those few stilted samples of opening and closing paragraphs; Winston Churchill taught me the art of 'pile driving' . . . learning how to build and provide stands for one's notes by piling glasses one on top of another without upsetting them. When I would be so obviously nervous that my hand trembled, I was comforted by Ambassador Joseph E. Davies, and Lord Marshall, the Lord Mayor of London, to whom I often sat next at those first public dinners . . .

At any rate, these two older men always told me not to worry about my speech; that whatever I said would go with the company or the audience. It was lucky I did not take them too seriously, for my fellow diners might not have been edified had I succumbed to the temptation of telling them how profoundly bored I found myself in their company . . .

My overseas tours provided far better training [in] public speaking than I got in Great Britain. In Canada, Australia and South Africa I was always called on for impromptu 'ad lib' speeches, which helped me to overcome to some extent my extreme nervousness. It did not matter very much what I said to those up-country audiences, where speeches would not be reported, and when any attempt at formality would have been ridiculous. But the long, set orations at important functions in large cities, when I usually did not know my subject too well, and had to pad my remarks with fulsome platitudes, were an agony. Those speeches did matter and represented many anxious hours of preparation far into the night.

The 'public dinner' is a barbarous institution, and essentially Anglo-Saxon in character . . . The 'decorated circus' was what I called the pool of distinguished men in various walks of life from which the perpetrators or the organizers of these reunions would select the speakers to be invited. The victim had to show up in white tie and tails, festooned with decorations and medals, if he possessed any, at the appointed hotel or banqueting rooms . . . There he sat at the chairman's or president's table, toying with lousy food, waiting his turn. Even if the food was tolerably good, you could not enjoy it with this speech hanging over your head . . .

Much depended on who one sat next to. If the chairman was not a stuffed shirt, I would be able to pep up the prepared speech I had brought along with some interesting story or a topical joke about the organization or one of its members. I learned the technique of springing a joke early in a speech, for I soon began to realize that, particularly at public dinners, if one could not get the audience to laugh in the first two or three minutes, one's speech was doomed . . .

On 11 June 1935 Edward delivered a controversial speech to the British Legion. In it he endorsed the prospect of a forthcoming visit by members of the Legion to Germany, asserting that he could think of no one better 'to stretch forth the hand of friendship to the Germans than we ex-servicemen who fought them in the Great War and have now forgotten all about that'.[40] Influenced by the horrors of his wartime experiences, Edward was firmly committed to the prevention of any future military conflict. At the same time, he made little effort to conceal his recognition of Germany's renewed economic vitality under National Socialism.

Like Roosevelt's New Deal, which he also admired, Edward felt Germany provided a model for how government action could reverse economic decline. An inconsequential intervention, his words were nevertheless interpreted as evidence of his political inclinations. The incident delighted the German propaganda machine and complicated the Anglo-German naval discussions, which were taking place in Paris.[41]

Severn, 7 May 1948

The British Legion used to hold annual conventions on Whitsuntide and would invite me either at the inaugural session or at the end. I said it was best to go at the end: then I would know what resolutions were decided upon.

In 1935 . . . I addressed this meeting, and asked the secretary if anything [had] happened that I should add to my notes.

At one interesting session it was unanimously adopted that a delegation of top officers should go to Berlin to some German veteran organization. I said that was very good, and I would refer to it in my speech. So I heartily endorsed the resolution to send a delegation to Berlin, saying it was a good time to shake the hands of the German veterans and we could be ambassadors of goodwill.

This was published in the newspapers, and the next day my father sent for me, saying, 'I heard what you said yesterday. The Foreign Office is very disturbed by your remarks and you must realize you cannot make a speech giving your views in complete conflict with the views of the British Government. It so happens their views are completely contrary to what you expressed yesterday.'

I said, 'But I thought we were doing our best to avoid friction with the Germans at this time.' [He replied] 'Well, the Foreign Office didn't want you to do it nor to do it again.'

Edward had believed his words were in line with government guidance but the fallout was immediate. On 12 June 1935, the same day coverage of Edward's speech appeared in many British newspapers, Clive Wigram, George V's Private Secretary, wrote to the monarch relating in full the genesis of events: 'I . . . spoke to Sir Godfrey Thomas [Edward's Private Secretary], who said that he had understood that Sir Frederick Maurice [President of the British Legion] had spoken to the FO on the matter, and that Sir Frederick had informed HRH that the FO saw no objection to the proposed statement. I told Sir Godfrey that this was contrary to what V [Robert Vansittart, at the time head of the Foreign Office] had just informed me; and at the same time remarked that it seemed to me unfortunate that he himself had not ascertained what were the views of the FO.'[42] George V's reply to Wigram's letter was simple: 'Godfrey [Thomas] and no one else ought to have spoken to FO. We know Maurice.'[43] Thus it appears that although Edward may have agreed with the sentiments he expressed in June 1935, it was an administrative error rather than wilful disregard for advice that led to their public airing.

'I was not a politician,' Edward wrote in another undated essay entitled 'Lack of Political Comment'. 'In fact the opposite was the case, for my father had drilled into me that constitutionally the Royal Family had no politics and must at all times avoid them like the plague.'[44] Despite this training, as Edward aged and international politics became progressively more heated, he found a policy of enforced silence increasingly irksome. '[I] loved the clash and crisis of politics . . . the swift turn of [the] tide: the struggle,'[45] he told Murphy. But he noted, 'I was deprived by my status of power or even of the compulsion to act. I used to watch men like Winston Churchill with envy. They were free to act . . .'[46] Instead, he continued, 'I was a watcher of things. Never had a sense of accomplishment . . .'[47] [I] tried conscientiously to find my way through [the] maze of modern politics. Not sure [I] understood what was involved.'[48]

Forty pages of typed drafts exist from the period between 11 and 14 May 1948 while Edward and Murphy remained at Severn. Most focus on the social life of the 1920s and early 1930s. His nostalgia for a bygone era is clear. Edward fondly remembered nights at the Embassy Club and the many hours he spent either steeplechasing or foxhunting. 'Foxhunting,' he wrote, 'was one of the most democratic [sports] one could have, because once the hounds were off, all were equal – the farmer and the Prince of Wales . . . I enjoyed the speed, companionship and fun of riding more than what the hounds were doing.'[49] His cheeky irreverence for royal precedent was also evident. Of the system for bestowing 'Royal Warrants' upon establishments patronised by the Royal Family, he noted, 'I thought it a rather stupid association . . . Suppose,' he continued, 'I were crazy, or tight with money, or had curious or bad taste, it certainly would not mean the places having signs . . . were the best to patronize.' Remarking casually at a Royal Warrant Association dinner, he observed to a fellow guest that it was 'fortunate for many people that some people considered I had good taste, and that I didn't start a fashion not to wear pants'.[50] He even had a momentary digression on the subject of 'Courtiers'.

Severn, 11 May 1948

. . . Of course there were little feuds, jealousies, animosities, at Court . . . If my father ever called someone down, they might try to get back in his favor by blaming someone else . . . When I was young, there was always a bit of trying to get the eldest son in [the] wrong, and nearly always done to get back into favor. If they thought the King was especially annoyed with me, or there was a little period of coolness between us, they would perhaps dig into that and think it might please the King if they could tell about something I did that irritated him. Then he would say something to me, and I would say, 'But how did you know?' and he would not tell me. It was generally courtiers who would tell him little stories out of school, which never amounted to anything but just made unnecessary incidents full of intrigue; and not very edifying, I must say.

As their time at Severn came to a close and the Windsors prepared to return to France, Murphy made his first 'Windsor Diary' entry. His observations, witty and acerbic, capture Edward and Wallis at their most intimate.

Charles Murphy's Diary
Severn, 15 May 1948[51]

Up with the larks at nine o'clock.

His clothes beautiful. Pink with blue plaid, beautifully pressed. The shoes with a Guardsman's polish. The blue socks and the red socks. Beautiful shirt.

He filled a pipe with special cartridges made by Dunhill in London. Each cartridge was a cylinder of tobacco beautifully packed, wrapped in paper in such a manner that it could be stuffed into the pipe and the paper removed with a deft gesture . . .

The day the Duchess had a little cold, whole household stopped. Butlers tiptoeing around the Duke disturbed, harassed with a wild and worried look in his eyes . . .

. . . The Duchess said, 'Sometimes it seems almost too much. Why should we waste our energy trying to keep up this show and protect all these lovely things? Sometimes I think the happiest thing we could do would be to get a little apartment in New York and forget it all' – and, with a smile [she said], 'That mood doesn't last for long.'

3

Operation Belvedere

On 24 June 1948 Edward and Wallis returned to France, stopping briefly in Paris before heading south to La Croë. Murphy joined them on 25 July. It was the start of three consecutive months' work on 'Operation Belvedere', the code name Murphy gave to Edward's memoir.

Concurrently, Edward began informing a few select friends of his plans. One of those he chose to tell was the press baron and owner of the *Daily Express*. Lord Beaverbrook had been a vocal supporter of Edward in the weeks preceding the abdication and, not surprisingly, greeted the news of his writing with enthusiasm. 'It is clearly of high importance that such a work should be prepared without delay,' he told Edward on 24 July. 'If there is any postponement the facts will inevitably become blurred and distorted . . . It should shape the work of all historians of that era for all time. It is imperative that you should write the record yourself.'[1] Though appreciative of Beaverbrook's support, Edward's reply was noncommittal and brief: 'As you so rightly observe, the telling of the events of 1936 will be difficult and will require all the tact and skill at my command should I eventually decide to embark upon my version of so controversial an episode of British History.'[2]

Edward's cautious response was likely influenced by the disapproval of Sir George Allen and Sir Walter Monckton, who were both staunchly opposed to the prospect of a full-length memoir. Having objected to Edward publishing his boyhood reminiscences, they were even more concerned at the prospect of him writing about the abdication. 'Allen,' Murphy asserted to Longwell on 30 July, 'provided the main opposition' while Monckton 'merely concedes the danger to our friend – and the Monarchy'. Murphy believed their objections were unfair. 'Our friend,' he told Longwell, 'wants to go ahead and should be allowed to go ahead if he so wishes, and history requires him to do so.'[3] Yet the formidable opposition rattled Edward's confidence and left him 'quite upset'.[4] He insisted that Murphy fly immediately to London to consult with his advisers. A skilled diplomat, Murphy succeeded in securing the duo's momentary acceptance, if not their approval. 'I shall not be frivolous or capricious,' he promised Allen, after arriving back in Cap d'Antibes. 'The book will be difficult at best. I shall give it all the professional skill I possess. Rest assured that I grasp the meaning of your misgivings . . . I can only assure you on my side that there will be no conscious sensationalism; no improper pressures or enticement. Our famous friend seems able to take good care of himself in these matters.'[5]

These complex dynamics were a surprise to Longwell and Murphy, who, as Americans, approached the abdication without the cultural baggage of their British counterparts. The subject, they were warned, had the potential to rouse deep emotional divisions should Edward's family even allow its publication. Only by circumventing these potential difficulties could they realise commercial success. Murphy explained this and much more in a long letter to Longwell.

Charles Murphy to Daniel Longwell
La Croë, 3 August 1948[6]

. . . Our famous friend received the account of my conversation with his legal advisors with more satisfaction than disappointment . . .

The key to the project, as was plain from the beginning, is the abdication scene – the journalistic Homestake lode . . . [Allen] is sure it cannot be touched without (1) rousing the sleeping dogs of Britain, (2) offending the present occupant of the Throne, (3) and bringing a fresh heaping wrath upon the head of the author's wife. People in Britain of the upper middle classes – the County people – whom I tentatively sounded out, or who tried to sound me out, have no love for our author. That goes without

saying. They want to hear no more from him. He
shook their world. They want the skeleton to remain
in the closet. Mr Allen represents this class – just as
the readers of the *Express* represent the class with
whose unrest and dissatisfaction they are half inclined
to associate, not as a cause but as a symptom of our
friend's historic decision. Bill Aitken, Beaverbrook's
nephew who marketed the first series [of Edward's
Life articles] throughout the Empire, is willing to lay a
bet . . . The Royal Family, he thinks, would ban publication of the book, were it ever completed.

Is this possible?

The honest answer is – Yes. The other day, the
Duchess asked, 'And what will you do, Mr Murphy, if
one day the Duke receives a little note from his
brother, ordering him not to go on with his writing?'

'We shall cross that bridge,' I answered . . . 'only
when we come to it.'

'Habit is strong,' she said. 'A royal command is not
lightly put aside.'

'It was put aside once before,' I said. 'Let us first
wait for the command.'

So we start tentatively, outranged and outgunned
. . . Do I think we can pull this off?

I do . . . Our friend is torn; he wants no more
trouble; he is sensitive to criticism; he still loves his
family and his country if not the other England represented by Baldwin, Sir Samuel Hoare [the Archbishop
of] Canterbury, etc. If left alone, he would never write
the story – of that I am sure. But the pull upon him is
strong. He feels that his position was wrongly
presented. He wants to put his side of the affair down,
and at the same time complete, in the habit of Kings,
the account of a life otherwise not without significance. The deeper he is drawn into writing, the more

he begins to relive the old scenes, the harder it will be, I imagine, for him to throw the work away . . . This is what I am banking on. On my side, I must treat his story with the utmost circumspection. The slightest sensationalism would almost certainly cost us our investment. And if it were ever to seem that my interest in our friend was wholly entrepreneurial, his friends would be quick to spring between us. We must seek a mood; we must be light and deft and never obviously cynical or bitter . . . to be sensational without ever uttering a sensational word . . .

Longwell endorsed Murphy's approach, and on 12 August he wrote to Edward with words designed to calm his rattled nerves. Urging him onwards, Longwell assured the skittish author that *Life*'s motivations stemmed entirely from a 'sense of history' and belief that 'if you don't put down the record in some permanent form, someone will surely invent it . . . Most of all,' he concluded, 'I want you to know that neither Charlie, Luce, nor I want to do anything that would prove embarrassing to your country, embarrassing to your friends and family . . . If all this eventually goes into a vault we will all know that at least what we've done is right.'[7]

Longwell's 'well phrased'[8] letter had the desired effect. Work resumed, Murphy noted, 'not with a Churchillian swoop and hazza, but with Hanoverian indecision'.[9] Yet Edward was growing in confidence and determination. He was finally ready to tackle more difficult material. 'I Meet the Duchess' was drafted on 17 August.

La Croë, 17 August 1948

On a dank, cold and very foggy night in early January [1931], I first met the Duchess at a mutual friend's [Thelma Furness, Edward's then mistress] house in Melton Mowbray . . . I remember she said she never hated a weekend as much as that one for she was feeling very ill with a terrible cold. She arrived before dinner and was wearing tweeds . . . the hunting season was on, although the Duchess never rode or hunted at any time. She was very fond of being in her own home, and she was not too happy to be removed for a time to this 'hunting place'.

I was immediately impressed with the vivaciousness, wit and smart repartee of the Duchess – she certainly put most of the other people in the shade. One of the things I particularly admired about her was her complete frankness. If she did not agree with anyone, she said so, and I found this rarely due to the circumstances of my position, especially among my British friends.

Then I met the Duchess at mutual friends' several times . . . I was glad to have a few friends with whom I could really relax. I was a bachelor, alone, tired . . .

The Duchess and her husband had an apartment [5 Bryanston Court, Marylebone] . . . and served as good food as anywhere in London. She knew a lot about cooking, for had done quite a bit of it during her first marriage, besides which she came from Baltimore, Maryland, where food is marvelous and a main topic. I was always sure of the most delicious dinner in her home.

She had a host of friends and knew a lot of people from the embassies. The conversations were gay, witty and intelligent. I met Bill Bullitt at her apartment for the first time. He was Ambassador to Moscow then, and once on arriving from Paris, he telephoned her to ask if he might drop in at cocktail time. I was expected that afternoon, and I learned afterward that the Duchess telephoned my secretary to find out if it was all right for me to meet the American Ambassador to Moscow, for she did not want to do the wrong thing by having us meet. Of course it was all right . . .

Wallis, in conversation with Murphy on 22 September 1949, remembered their first meeting at Melton Mowbray chiefly for having the 'worst cold she had ever known' and that Edward 'hardly spoke to me'. When they met two months later at a reception, again hosted by Thelma Furness, she recalled overhearing Edward say to Thelma, 'Didn't I meet that woman somewhere?'

'You never looked at me,' she said to Edward, who was listening to the discussion.

'Can't believe that, darling,'[10] he replied.

Ernest Simpson's friend and the Editor-in-Chief of Reuters News, Bernard Rickatson-Hatt, who was also close to Wallis, thought her 'attractive and smart' and an 'extremely capable hostess', whose great achievement in London society was to 'transplant the life of Park Avenue to London'. Her home at Bryanston Court, comprising an entry hall, dining room, drawing room, two bedrooms and two bathrooms, was, according to Wallis's Aunt Bessie, 'pleasant but not ostentatious'.[11] Being a frequent guest, Rickatson-Hatt saw first-hand the evolution of Wallis's relationship with Edward. From 1934, he told Murphy in a conversation that took place in London in July 1949, 'The apartment . . . was full of flowers from [Fort] Belvedere and Wallis showed him expensive jewels which the Prince had given her.' Rickatson-Hatt noted that Ernest Simpson 'grasped what was going on but as a loyal Englishman was reluctant to make an issue of the situation. After the Prince became part of the menage,' Rickatson-Hatt continued, 'she [Wallis] invited only those friends whom she thought would interest him [Edward].'

'His days are filled with stuffed shirts,' Wallis explained to Rickatson-Hatt in late 1935. 'He comes here to be amused.' Murphy went on to record, 'R-H remembers how he [Edward] stayed up until four o'clock in the morning, pumping a Chicago architect who was involved in some huge mass housing scheme. The Prince was fascinated and hoped to learn from this American something that might be applied to Britain.'[12]

Though Edward's account of Wallis was circumspect, it opened the door to exciting territory that Murphy felt gradually able to probe. In a series of later conversations, Edward engaged with Murphy more freely about his feelings and how his relationship with Wallis had started. He eventually told Murphy he 'fell in love with the Duchess two years before abdication'. It 'happened in restaurant, no frivolous business, age on my side. I had sowed my wild oats. Made lots of mistakes, in [a] superficial way . . . I knew I was falling in love with another man's wife . . . but remarkable business about love is that one never knows (when found myself falling in love should have withdrawn) . . . love happens before [one] knows it.'[13] 'She satisfied something creative,' Edward continued. 'She brought into my life something not there before: curiosity, independence, impudence, questioning, warmth.' She was 'needed for my world . . . I saw things in a new light.'[14]

With bullet-point precision, titled by Murphy as 'HRH's Description of Duchess',[15] Edward listed in pencil on two pieces of Waldorf Astoria memo paper what he believed were Wallis's defining characteristics.

– Very proud
– Independent
– Demanding of highest standards of conduct
– Inflexible code of behavior
– Strict
– Exacting
– Elusive
– Chic
– Must have the best
– Very sensitive
– Easily hurt
– Great sense of dignity
– Perfectionist to the extent of wearing herself out.

At the end of August 1948 Monckton and his wife Bridget ('Biddy') joined the Windsors for ten days at La Croë. Monckton, 'the principal off-the-stage actor during the crisis', as Murphy described him, was there for one purpose: to engage with Edward on a subject he had thus far avoided: the abdication. 'The knightly barrister . . . and his famous friend are working together every day,' Murphy informed Longwell, on 22 August, 'refreshing each other's memory, dictating the story stage by stage . . .'[16] Murphy was thrilled by Monckton's presence and believed his arrival had induced 'a most optimistic turn'[17]. Until this point Edward had resisted discussing the abdication. He required the presence of an intimate not only to stimulate his recollections but also to create an atmosphere that was conducive to reliving this tumultuous drama. For Monckton, who arrived in the guise of a willing contributor, this was a chance to find out what was really happening with a project of which he still strongly disapproved.

Over two days in August, gathered in 'Fort Belvedere' on the top floor of La Croë – Monckton listening and Murphy furiously writing – Edward spoke about the crisis of 1936. Revealing freely and with uninhibited conjecture the major events of that momentous period, he talked at length, for probably the first time, about this defining episode of his life. The occasion offered evidence that he had begun to find a language in which, however fleetingly and rapidly, he could speak about the abdication. More stream-of-consciousness than full-length narrative, Edward went through events at breakneck speed, offering little in the way of context or elaboration for Murphy, who was astonished by the ex-King's directness. 'It is absolutely fascinating . . .' he declared to Longwell. 'Nothing is being held back . . .'[18]

As Murphy advised Longwell in the same letter of 22 August, these conversations were only the 'legal and historical framework . . . It will be some time,' he warned his boss, 'before we can crowd the canvas.'[19] By now Murphy understood Edward's limitations. Not trained to be reflective, these conversations were meant to build Edward's willingness to relive his past and establish his confidence to write it all down. Aware that everything Edward said would need to be revisited – to gain greater insight, to add further nuance and to be fact-checked – Murphy was content, at least for the time being, to listen unquestioningly to the tantalising but fleeting stories that were pouring out.

A year later Edward returned to these issues but here, in the summer of 1948, he spoke openly about the tumultuous events of the abdication: his decision to renounce the throne, his distrust of Baldwin, his feelings about his mother and siblings, his sense of isolation and his controversial decision to broadcast to the nation before departing into exile. At the end of the lengthy discourse, Edward added a note to Murphy: 'Check and make no accusations or incriminate anyone. I do not wish to alter the dignity [in] which I left.'[20]

La Croë, 25 August 1948

My mother knew the same evening – the 16th [November], after I saw Baldwin . . . Her feeling was one of regret; she was sorry but not understanding at all.

The decision to abdicate came to my mind after my talk with Baldwin, because he said it would never be possible for me to go on after the decree nisi [Edward meant 'decree absolute', which Wallis received on 3 May 1937]. There was a time when we thought it would be best if I were to go abroad, still as King. But the change in tempo came the Sunday before I went, and I felt if I could not remain under my conditions, I would not stay . . .

La Croë, 26 August 1948

Towards the end, I was getting all kinds of telephone messages from different kinds of people, but so strong was the discipline in the [Conservative] Party that never did many of my contemporaries come to see me . . . At the time they were all scared of spoiling their political efforts by running contrary to Baldwin's edict – afraid to 'buck the tide' – and thought it better to lie low . . . The people who tried to offer assistance to the King were not leaders in the Government . . . [the others were] afraid politically to show openly what they might have felt if in sympathy with me.*

---

* Those Edward referenced as having contacted him were Walter 8th Duke of Buccleuch, Josiah Wedgwood and Lionel Smith-Gordon.

The 'King's Party' was this surge of popularity in my favor Dec. 4, 5, 6, which began sporadically and had no Leader – it was just an imbroglio or atmosphere . . . no mass meeting or organization. But their [his supporters] feeling was they had given me their oath of allegiance and that now I was their King they must not change . . .

I was the figure in the Palace at that time . . . I had not yet gotten my feet and was handling much cautiously. Stanley Baldwin began to feel his strength when he realized I would not fight, and when they gave me credit for going with dignity credit was not given for going at all.

If I had done what Duff Cooper [then Secretary for War] said – 'While waiting for the decree absolute, you can be crowned, and get more popular with the people' – it might have paid. And that my answer to others should be, 'You can't ask me whether I intend to marry Mrs Simpson because she is not free. I know my constitutional duty, and the question does not arise.'

But I would not wait and felt the people should know. I had always been frank and my whole theme was to take people into my confidence . . .

What I should like to know is just what changed over the weekend. A quite friendly House of Commons up to Friday December 4th to one in which the entire tempo was different by Monday [December 7th]. On December 4, 5, 6 there was a real surge in popular feeling for me.

One of my aides happened to say quite naively, 'I can only tell you that I know there were Conservative agents going around the public houses saying, 'You are being fooled over this, and the sooner the King goes, the better.'

If there had been a directive, Stanley Baldwin would have had Margesson [David Margesson, his Chief Whip] get busy over the weekend and get the people to support Stanley Baldwin and not the King or it would hurt the Party.

But this is all a surmise; some forces must have been at

work, though, to be able to change all the feeling I had in my favor before December 6th.

. . . At my invitation, Winston [Churchill] dined with me on December 4th. I remember him coming in and sitting on my bed when he arrived.

During dinner, I told him all about things, and he said one must give time for 'battalions to mass' but he promised nothing . . . In my final broadcast, Winston Churchill made one or two additions or changes; they were slight, but one can spot them . . . Many people thought and said later that he wrote the speech, but he certainly did not. It was written by myself . . . I never wanted to withhold anything. At the end, 'Now that I am no longer King, I do not have to follow the advice of my ministers.' . . .

One day when I saw her [Queen Mary] at Royal Lodge [9 December], and she asked me what I was going to do, she also asked when I was leaving and would she see me again. I said, 'Yes, I am not going until (such-and-such a time) as I am going to broadcast at ten o'clock that night.' She said, 'Surely you are not going to do that?' I said, 'Of course I am.' When I saw her again the next day, she said once more, 'Surely you can spare yourself this extra emotion and strain of making the broadcast.'

Although not malicious, I can't help but feel she thought it would be easier for my brother to slip in as King if I did not make the speech. And yet I felt she really thought I had been through enough.

Drafting the speech went on for a day . . . Things that were running in my mind through all this time and that I put in the speech were such as: always determined to tell you (the people) this; I made my decision; can't go on without the help and support of the Duchess; a word about my brother . . . But my paramount idea was to go with dignity and make it easy for everyone. But how wrong that was – to give so much consideration: those I left behind could not have behaved worse . . .

I think my mother wanted me to stay, but she never made any particular effort that I do so. She was seemingly unmoved by it all. I think matters were a great shock to her; there was a certain amount of distress, but a lack of understanding because of the rigid adherence to duty and denying oneself things one wants to do, though she did not take the line of what my father would have done. Actually she did not make things difficult for me, but there was this complete lack of comprehension. She certainly was not demonstrative.

Gloucester [Prince Henry, Duke of Gloucester] was at the dinner party at Royal Lodge [on 11 December: the night Edward departed into exile) – all my brothers were. When we returned from the broadcast at Windsor Castle to Royal Lodge, and after the Queen and my sister had left, I had a drink with my brothers in a big room at the back of the Lodge. It was very informal, and we had whiskey and soda just as we would at any time . . . They all walked to the door with me, and everything was very normal, just as though we were going to Balmoral or a visit elsewhere . . .

But I think my sister [Mary, The Princess Royal] was more upset than anyone the last night; she was close to me. Kent [Prince George, Duke of Kent] and I were close, for we had been together a lot and on several trips together; and he felt I had a better grasp of things, and could get along better with me than our other brothers, as King.

Mary, did not advise me, of course, during this time. Throughout as a matter of fact, I felt it better to keep my family out of things . . . None of my family felt able to have a crack at trying to dissuade me . . .

My mother was of a generation where duty was above everything and one did not show emotions; so it was difficult for her to be sympathetic. Thus there was less warmth between us. While she did not try to dissuade me by her active argument, she did register her disapproval.

My sister was of another generation in thought and feeling,

and much under the influence of its rigour. She was a lot with older people, and her ideas are still of that time. She led a sheltered life, married a man older [Earl of Harewood] than herself by fifteen years and older in his ways than that.

Of my family, the Duke of Kent was the nearest to me and asked what was going on. He knew a good deal about it, I am sure, but not the other two brothers . . . And he worried about where I would go on leaving England; I don't recall any other member of my family doing so.

Gloucester was completely disinterested, except the one day when he had to be there.

. . . I remember sitting with him [George VI] in my room at the Fort . . . and I said to him, 'This is not a difficult job; there may be some difficulty with the speeches and broadcasting, but not much else. And you can ask me anything at any time.' I know Bertie hated my going . . .

Revisiting 1936 had unexpectedly left Edward 'full of excitement', as Murphy told Longwell. 'I would say,' he continued, 'that I have never seen him more enthusiastic, more eager, more confident, a condition for which our knightly barrister is chiefly responsible.'[21]

Fresh from these exhilarating discussions, and with the Moncktons en route back to London, Edward wrote to Longwell on 28 August informing him of his intention to complete the memoir and publish a further three articles for *Life*. 'I have decided to work along these lines,' he began. 'I will omit nothing, however secret and personal. Then I shall use my own judgement and sense of propriety in selecting from this unexpurgated work the portions to be published in book form. It will be from the material thus selected for publication, and no other, that "Life" Magazine will have the right to extract . . .'[22] The only provisions, Edward stipulated, were his refusal to be bound by either a deadline or a formal contract. Overjoyed, Longwell cabled back immediately and agreed in full. He was, he told Edward in a lengthy letter that followed on 10 September, 'delighted' with his news and encouraged him and 'Charlie' to press on at full steam while 'enthusiasm was running high', assuring his royal author that 'there is no time limit on finishing . . .'[23] Separately, Longwell urged Murphy, 'Keep after this thing as fast as we can . . . while he [Edward] has the leisure and inclination to do it.'[24]

Murphy credited Monckton for inspiring in Edward this newfound confidence. Now determined to proceed with his memoir, the 'knightly barrister' had inadvertently accomplished what he was most hoping to prevent. Deeply troubled by all that he had witnessed, he lost no time in writing to George Allen.

Walter Monckton to George Allen
London, 1 September 1948[25]

I returned late last night from ten days with the Duke. I spent two or three days discovering what the state of the prospect already was. I found that H.R.H. had prepared a considerable batch of material dealing with his life from 1914 . . . up to the Abdication . . . The secretary . . . has been busily taking down rather scratch and uncoordinated conversation by him. Murphy and he had had many talks . . . Moreover, the Duke obviously felt himself under considerable moral though not legal obligation to 'Life' to go on with the project. They have incurred considerable expense and he has led them to think that he wants and intends to write. I pointed out to him he need be in no hurry to sign any contract . . . To get a book by him dealing with the Abdication would be a scoop for any publisher and he could, to a large extent, make his own terms. I told him that he ought not to think of making a contract till he had your comments on the draft which he had just received through you.

I certainly persuaded him on two points: 1) He will not commit himself to saying when he expects to finish . . . 2) He will formally and effectively retain in his own hands the right to decide what is to be

published. His plan is to write an unexpurgated book
. . . This . . . will be his contribution to eventual historians . . . He is fully determined not to bring his family
into the picture and to stop the story when he left the
country on 11 December 1936. You will see the
advantages of this in that it avoids the family bicker-
ings, the question of the title and finance.

I found that his recollection, although vivid, was
untidy and I helped him so far as I could over facts
and dates . . . My part was only to stimulate his recollection.

I should very much like to have a talk to you about
all this at your convenience . . .

Edward had failed to detect Monckton's aversion to his endeavours.
To the ex-King, he appeared at La Croë in August 1948 in his usual
guise as Edward's constant, loyal and supportive adviser. 'I did so enjoy
your and Biddy's visit,' Edward wrote to him, on 11 September 1948,
'and the opportunity of undisturbed reminiscing . . . It was fascinating
to recall the stirring events of 1936 and to test our memories . . . with
those momentous days. I only hope you weren't too bored, and I am
most grateful for the use of your notes in the collection of material.'[26]
Monckton's role in Edward's life had solidified in the anxious days of
December 1936, when he, with George Allen, had shepherded the
King through his negotiations with the government. At least in Edward's
eyes, they were an outnumbered but loyal 'band of brothers', whose
efforts on his behalf had continued in the years that followed.

With Allen taking the lead on Edward's legal matters, it was left to
Monckton to serve as his proxy in the various family wranglings that
took place with his brother, King George VI, in the years after 1936,
including the denial to Wallis of the style Her Royal Highness. Despite
Monckton's lack of success in winning any of these battles, Edward
retained an unwavering confidence in his adviser's abilities. Monckton
was the lone establishment figure who had not abandoned him, and
Edward chose to overlook his more complex loyalties, the first of

which was always to the Crown. In serving Edward, Monckton was in fact serving the monarchy. 'One can influence him most,' Monckton wrote to George VI, on 11 August 1937, 'when one is most patient and avoids frontal attacks.'[27] Keeping an ever-watchful eye over him and seemingly always ready to drop anything in order to assist, Monckton retained Edward's trust while deftly succeeding in preventing the ex-King's embittered feelings towards his family from spilling over into the public domain, an eventuality that would have inevitably highlighted the Royal Family's often petty vendettas against the exiled couple. The beneficiary of Monckton's strategy was not the Duke of Windsor but his brother, the King.

Still emboldened by the August exchange with Monckton, Edward began to look about for others with whom he could reminisce. He quickly settled on Winston Churchill. But 'the great man', as Edward called him, who was 'vacationing and painting[28] in nearby Aix-en-Provence, proved a reluctant contributor to the slowly growing '1936 file'.[29] 'I was able to get Winston to talk a little about 1936,' he wrote to Monckton, on 2 October, but 'found him more reticent and cagier than I expected.'[30] Protective of his legacy and his political future, Churchill was disinclined to remind either the public or the Royal Family of his controversial support of the ex-monarch. In contrast Beaverbrook, Edward told Monckton, 'has been more than cooperative'.[31] On 24 September he and Edward sat down with Murphy at Beaverbrook's home on Cap d'Ail. Murphy's notes were brief on this occasion, but many lengthier conversations were to follow. Their primary topic was the King's Party – the apocryphal political group that for three days in 1936 had threatened to divide the country in support of a monarch against his government. The 'leader', Beaverbrook stated, 'was Winston Churchill'.[32]

On 10 October, Edward and Wallis returned to Paris with Murphy. From there author and ghost made their way to London. It was an important trip, an opportunity, as Murphy explained to Longwell, to clear 'the way forward with several of his [Edward's] intimates and confidants',[33] including Allen, who was now reconciled to the inevitability of the memoir and, at Edward's request, agreed to be interviewed. Allen was, Murphy later wrote, 'a cold fish, wholly impatient and unforgiving in his Anglican heart for what Windsor did in 1936, yet personally devoted to him, to the Duchess . . .'[34] Murphy recorded Allen's statements along with his own observations.

Charles Murphy: Interview with George Allen London, November 1948[35]

ALLEN: There was no question of Windsor's determination to marry Wallis. That idea was firmly fixed in his head eighteen months before the abdication . . . He was bent upon marrying her and making her Queen . . . and being crowned together.

　　He hated Buckingham Palace and Balmoral. He hated much of the royal existence. But at the same time he yearned to be King. At the outset there was no question of abdication. He took the job on with the hope of marrying her . . . He wanted the divorce secure and everything in preparation so they could be married before the Coronation.

MURPHY: Allen obviously disapproved of the whole business. A cold light burned in his eyes; his face grew longer and more severe. But his lawyer's taste for the fascinations of the human tragedy caused him at times to smile at some of the more ingenious turns.

ALLEN: The Duke had always been fascinated by sweet, pretty, domineering women . . . And because American women were more independent than most, more domineering, he was easily influenced by them.

　　[Final week of his reign] King in a frightful mood.

Almost hysterical. How do you explain it all? There's only one. It was a true love story, unique in history. Otherwise how would you explain the sinister details?

MURPHY: He spoke admiringly of the famous last supper. Baldwin turned up with Dugdale [Thomas Dugdale, Baldwin's Parliamentary Private Secretary], Walter Monckton, Ulick Alexander [Edward's Keeper of the Privy Purse] there. Kent and York . . . A 'tour de force'. Present King said, 'How well he conducts himself.' And Monckton whispered, 'Look at him. How can we bear to let him go?'

During the last week King sleepless. Light burned most of the night . . . Allen doubts that Beaverbrook exerted much influence. His chief interest was in news side of question.

ALLEN: He [Beaverbrook] kept asking, 'Will our cock fight? If we back him, will he let us down?' Churchill urged him not to press. 'Be crowned, hold your positions, work for marriage afterwards.' But King would not listen. He trusted few men . . .

ALLEN: [On Wallis]: The great tactical mistake was in permitting her to leave the country. Once she left he had but one thought: to rejoin her . . . Had she remained she could have stopped it . . . He was nervous, distraught, fearful she might be mobbed.

MURPHY: Day she left George drew up a simple will for her. They went into King's bedroom at Belvedere, wrote it sitting on bed.

ALLEN: Then she vanished and he became obsessed with the idea she might be killed – an idea not without justification . . . Baldwin failed to save King because he was piously high-handed. Had he gone to King and said, 'I want you to be together,' he and she would have crumpled. Doubt Baldwin wanted to get rid of King. He was a clever man. He put sentiment and reason aside to save Tory party . . .

Having decided to move forward with the articles, Edward also 'cleared the way'[36] for Murphy to interview former members of his staff. Tempering Longwell's expectations as to the ultimate rewards of these meetings, Murphy advised, 'It is not in their character or background to be easily anecdotal . . . or for a Dickensian sense of detail.'[37] One of the first people Murphy contacted was Godfrey Thomas, whom Edward had described in 1919 to his then mistress Freda Dudley Ward as 'my greatest friend'.[38] 'A thin, rather nervous man with sleek black hair, addicted to dark clothes and wearing horn-rimmed glasses,' he was, Edward explained to Murphy, 'very much the Foreign Office type . . . extremely intelligent.'[39]

Thomas responded to Murphy's request with reluctance. Of all Edward's former aides, he had been the most distraught at the abdication. 'For seventeen years I have worked to help this man prepare for kingship. All those years have been thrown away. I have failed,'[40] he exclaimed tearfully to Monckton, moments after seeing Edward depart into exile. He refused to be interviewed by Murphy and instead insisted on responding by letter to his questions. His responses were, as Murphy wrote to Edward, 'painstakingly composed – and the result was inevitably in the fine vintage flavour of the Ponsonby era!!'[41] Nevertheless, they were thoughtful ruminations on Edward's successful world tours, noting both the exhaustive demands of the schedule ('Naturally we all felt "stale" at times.') and Edward's undeniable charisma ('I should say few people were more skilled in breaking through the official screen than the Prince of Wales.').[42] Whatever bitterness Thomas and others felt at the outcome of Edward's reign, they retained an admiration for what he had accomplished.*

In late November Murphy, along with his *Life* secretary Monica Wyatt, returned to Cap d'Antibes, following on the heels of the

---

* Thomas was finally prevailed upon to be interviewed by Murphy during a visit to La Croë in June 1949.

Windsors, who had installed themselves at La Croë for the upcoming winter months. Though Edward's work ethic continued to fall well below Murphy's expectations ('It is hardly the schedule of a working man. The point is that it is the only schedule he knows . . .'[43]), the duo completed two chapters about 1936. Edward turned to the subject of his looming romance and his father's death.

La Croë, Autumn 1948

The choice confronting me was a bitter one . . . My father was almost 70; the time could not be far off when I would be called to succeed him. And while there was no desire in my heart to shirk my inheritance, the desire to marry and make a full life with the woman of my choice was equally strong. I thought out my problem in simple terms – too simple perhaps. I was in love; to live without love would have been intolerable. And more than that without it my service to the state would have seemed an empty thing.

La Croë, 9 December 1948

By now my father was failing . . .
   Invitations had gone out for the annual November [1935] shoot at Sandringham, [but] by the time the guests had arrived my father found himself unwontedly feeble and unable to go out shooting. Grumbling over man's ridiculous infirmities, he was irritated and depressed that the powerful engine that had supported him for seventy years should have chosen that particular junction to collapse. He presided over his dinner table in the evening, but in a manner unusual for this indestructible spirit he turned gloomy and introspective. Stressing his disappointment of the lost days in the field, a shiver of apprehension ran through the woman sitting next to him one evening when he complained that if his shooting days were really over – he rather expected they were without any damn

doctor having to tell him – there was not much point in going on living.

. . . When he went to Sandringham for Christmas . . . it was into virtual retirement for he never left the place alive . . . I realized [then] in the presence of my father's increasing infirmities how much time had changed us all – all but my mother, who remained serene, irreproachable . . .

Maybe because I was the eldest and next in succession, and had been away from home so much, I was more sensitive than the others to the extent of my father's decline. He would doze off in his chair, at table and in church, and when recalled to consciousness by some unknown compulsion he seemed unaware of his momentary exclusion . . . his memory, razor-sharp in the past, had lost its edge. It was painful to observe these melancholy signs and intimations . . .

On 16 January 1936, Queen Mary sent a note summoning Edward to Sandringham. 'I think you ought to know that Papa is not very well,'[44] it began. In January 1949 at La Croë Murphy and Wallis reread the letter. 'She underlined each phrase,' Murphy noted, and then said, 'Perfect English understatement . . . Imagine saying that . . . King [was] dead in a week.'[45]

. . . [W]hen I reached the house [17 January], my mother, who had evidently been watching from a window for my arrival, was at the door. For once her mask of self-control was pierced by an emotion that would not be put down, and she warned me to prepare myself . . .

I had expected to find the King in bed. Instead, with a final display of the will power that had been the despair of two generations of medicine, he was seated in his favorite chair in front of a cheery wood fire, dressed in an old Tibetan wrapper. The fireplace threw a cheery radiance over the unpretentious cretonne-covered furniture, and in a corner was the simple brass bed in which his father had slept before. Covering the walls or mounted in plain wooden screens were framed photographs of family groups, of his naval cronies and of warships in which he had served . . .

My sister Mary was in the room when I entered. He was lying back drowsily in the chair, and the small sounds attending my entrance in the room appeared to rouse him because he looked up and appeared to recognize me . . . But as I tried to make my presence known to him, Mary's signal to me with a finger to her lips from behind my father's chair, warned me not to overtax him by talking too much. Then a mist blurred his eyes; he no longer heard what I had to say, and after a few halting sentences, I tiptoed out of the room. And that was the last conversation I had with my father . . .

On 19 January Edward travelled to London to inform Stanley Baldwin that his father could survive no more than a few days. The audience was brief.

Baldwin was a strange, deceptive personality. He had the reputation of being ponderous, dull and insensitive, but as an astute political leader he had no rival. Although his public speeches usually struck a solemn note, he was capable in private conversation of quick and charming turns of thought. We said something about the advantage of having got to know each other over the years, which would help our formal relations as between King and Prime Minister, and I went away from No.10 Downing Street deciding that I liked him, a sentiment which I regret to say proved to be of only a few months' duration.

Edward returned to Sandringham the following day. George V died just before midnight on 20 January 1936. Edward's grief was, according to observers, intense. Yet he made no mention of it in this draft, stating merely that his father's death had been a 'harrowing experience'. The mechanics of kingship took hold and on 21 January he appeared before the Accession Council at St James's Palace and later in front of the committee overseeing his father's funeral. Edward wasted little time in upsetting royal tradition. He insisted that no more than a week pass until his father's funeral. Queen Mary, he wrote, 'had a horror of postponing a funeral too long, remembering the agony of the time between the death of my grandfather [Edward VII] and the day of his funeral. She said to me, "There is one thing we must not have and that is a repetition of what happened in your grandfather's time. This whole thing should not take more than a week."'[46] Even more controversially, he decided to watch as Garter King of Arms formally proclaimed him King Edward VIII – with Wallis at his side. Their appearance raised eyebrows. Duff Cooper observed, 'This is just the kind of thing that I hope so much he won't do. It causes so much criticism and does so much harm.'[47]

But Edward's genius for the innovative public gesture was still evident. 'All the time my father lay at Westminster,' Edward wrote, in an undated draft, 'officers stood vigil at each corner of the coffin. I had been to see it and was profoundly stirred. It gave me an inspiration. Here was a way in which my brothers and I could pay our respect to our father in a simple manner. We would do a tour of duty ourselves.'[48] The 'Vigil of the Princes' was a solemn yet modern touch that established precedents and was followed at the lying-in-state of Queen Elizabeth The Queen Mother in 2002 and Queen Elizabeth II in 2022.

La Croë, 12 December 1948

. . . There is something terrifyingly inhuman about official funerals. As they progressed from one stage to the next, the central characters seemed to become more and more the prisoners of the machine of State, and my brothers and I had come to feel more puppets in a vast and majestic show. But the dead King, after all, had been our father, so later that night as the last guest had left the Palace, we carried out a secret plan of our own which enabled us to show our respect in a simple and fitting manner.

. . . Just before midnight, having changed into our different

full dress uniforms, we motored to Westminster Hall and at
12.20 we descended the stairway opposite which the coffin
was resting, and took up our appointed positions at the head,
the foot and on each side of it between the four officers of
. . . Grenadier Guards, the battalion that happened to be on
the roster for the vigil that night.

That twenty-minute period while we stood motionless
resting on our swords reversed seemed the first time I had
been alone with my thoughts since my father's passing at
Sandringham and all that it had brought tumbling down upon
me. Standing there in that vast, dim, eerie, vaulted hall, lighted
by the tall candles surrounding the coffin, the deathly silence
broken by the booming of Big Ben striking the quarter hours,
one was conscious only of the muffled, shuffling steps of the
continuous divided stream of people passing at snail's pace
by the earthly remains of a much-loved sovereign. And it
seemed to me too bad that life could not return to my father
long enough for him to be conscious of the sincere tributes
of the affection that these hundreds of thousands of his
subjects were paying him that night.

As writing moved forward, Edward continued to report regularly to
Monckton. Neither his enthusiasm for the project nor his admiration
for Murphy, of whom he was growing increasingly fond, had diminished.
'He is a good egg and quite a brilliant journalist,' Edward told Monckton
on 8 December. 'The combination of his writing experience and my
intimate knowledge will, I hope, produce a very saleable product.'[49]
Naively, Edward remained unaware of Monckton's strong and at times
vocal opposition to his enterprise. On 17 December, Monckton wrote
to Gray Phillips, Edward's former equerry, expressing his continuing
reservations. 'I heard from the Duke last week,' Monckton began, 'and
fear that he is really getting down to writing the long threatened book.
I always hoped (a) that it would be postponed to the Greek kalends
and (b) that I should be able to operate an effective blue pencil. I am
still hoping to wield the latter; one cannot help seeing how much more

interesting it is for him to occupy himself in recapturing those exciting days than in any other pursuit now open to him . . .'[50]

Though Longwell had offered Murphy and Monica Wyatt a passage home for Christmas, Murphy chose to remain at Cap d'Antibes, hoping the period on the quiet deserted coast might turn out to be the most productive of the whole relationship. He spent Christmas with the Windsors at La Croë. As the festivities closed, he wrote to Longwell, 'Last night, for the first time, I began to get the distaff [Wallis's] side of the story – fascinating . . . She insists that he never asked her to marry him until after she had left the island – think of that!'[51] Adding to the intrigue was a telegram on Christmas Day from Max Aitken, Beaverbrook's son and editor of the *Daily Express*, informing Edward of the rumoured forthcoming publication in *The Times* of Archbishop of Canterbury Cosmo Gordon Lang's abdication papers as part of the serialisation of J.G. Lockhart's biography of the Archbishop. Edward and Murphy greeted the news with excitement.

Lang and Edward had never been close. Though they had no direct dealings during the abdication crisis, Edward had come to view the Archbishop, a close friend of Baldwin, as one of the Prime Minister's co-conspirators. This impression was fuelled by a BBC broadcast Lang delivered on 13 December 1936, just twenty-four hours after Edward had left England. In a speech that barely concealed his personal disgust for the former monarch, Lang decried Edward's irreligious and self-indulgent behaviour while congratulating the institutional bulwark that had prevented his moral failures from taking root in the monarchy, and by extension the British character. Lang denounced Edward's actions, and derided his decision to seek 'happiness in a manner inconsistent with Christian principles of marriage and within a social circle whose standards and ways of life are alien to all the best instincts of people . . .'[52]

Edward's fury over the broadcast was both immediate and long-lasting. News that Lang was yet again to offer commentary on a crisis

Edward believed he had helped to precipitate appeared to him and Murphy as an opening salvo in their own war of attrition. 'If true,' Edward wrote to Aitken's father, on 29 December, 'it should make easier the eventual presentation of my story. Besides, I could then never be criticized for being the first to rake up old coals.'[53] Murphy was even more jubilant: 'I would regard it as a wonderful stroke of luck for our side,' he told Aitken, on 26 December. 'That will give him two cracks at our man who so far has said nothing, and after that the accepted rules of fair play should entitle our man, wholly apart from other considerations, to have his day in court.'[54]

Setting aside momentarily the issue of Lang, Murphy and Edward returned to their desks, producing the final draft of 1948: the funeral of George V.

La Croë, 28 December 1948

. . . But most of all I remember the crowd. I have probably had as much experience with crowds as any man living, but I have never come face to face with a concourse quite like the one that had massed itself along the line of the route. The Metropolitan Police, assuming that my father's funeral would attract the same sized crowd as on the last occasion twenty-five years before, had made what they considered would be adequate dispositions of police and barricades. What they had forgotten was the increase in automobiles and the improvement in transportation that had taken place in a quarter of a century and that, apart from the people of London, hundreds of thousands could descend upon the metropolis from all parts of Great Britain. The police were prepared to cope with a flood. They were met by a tidal wave.

By the time we had reached St James's Street, under the sheer weight of the mass of humanity determined to see what it had come to see, the troops lining the streets were slowly pushed forward. The space left for the cortege shrank until there was barely room for the sailors marching . . . The shoulders of the blue-jackets on the extreme flanks actually pushed against the troops leaning back against the crowd, using their rifles as barriers to hold it in.

I shall never forget the faces of people – wrath contending with indignation. They had come to see their King buried and, if I rightly sensed their mood, they were furious with the authorities for putting them in so dangerous and uncomfortable a predicament. Though the day was cold, the atmosphere of the street seemed to grow almost overpoweringly warm with the suppressed passion of the crowd. For a moment I was afraid that one convulsive heave would engulf and break up the procession. But the British habit of self-control prevailed. Those in front held, those in back relaxed, and the procession marched on.

Even I, at forty-one and in good physical condition, was exhausted by the time the procession reached Paddington Station, for the . . . march in slow time had taken an hour and many of the top ranking mourners were in their sixties . . . Some of them indeed had become quite lame in their tight, uniform shoes and I suddenly realized for how long they must have been yearning for the horses, which I had unconsciously denied them in my determination that at a sailor King's funeral the Navy should predominate.

Only once during that seemingly endless funeral progress did my eyes stray from the caisson or the slowly marching figures immediately surrounding me. A swift scan of the windows of the second floor of a certain building rewarded me with a fleeting glance of recognition, of comfort and understanding of the mental and physical strain it was mine to bear that sad day.

A short railroad journey brought us to Windsor . . . It all ended in St George's Chapel . . .

As the coffin sank on slow and noiseless pulleys into the vault below, I scattered upon it the symbolic earth from a silver dish handed to me by the Lieutenant Colonel of the

Grenadier Guards: 'Man that is born of a woman has but a short time to live and is full of misery. He cometh up and is cut down, like a flower; He fleeth as it were a shadow, and never continueth in one stay . . .' So reads the burial service. I don't believe it was entirely so with my father who, if he had ever known any misery, doubt or fear, successfully concealed it from us.

1948 closed on a high. Edward's output had quickened, and his enthusiasm had never been greater. 'He [Edward] seems to enjoy the work so much, and especially Mr Murphy,' Monica Wyatt told Longwell when she met with him in late December. 'He [Edward] paid him a great compliment the other day by saying, "Charlie, we know each other so well now that I hardly feel like changing a word you write." The Duke is so pleased with the chapters that when we go there for dinner, he can hardly wait for the meal to be over so that he can read aloud the latest pages. I am not so sure the Duchess is quite so keen to live with the "work" twenty-four hours a day. But the Duke is thriving on it. He told me that he didn't have time to read a story in *Harpers* because, he said, "A man as busy as I am just doesn't have time for something like that."'[55]

4

Kingship

Edward, Wallis and Murphy welcomed the new year, 1949, at La Croë. Enthusiasm was high and Murphy wrote confidently to George Allen on 3 January, 'We are very close now to finishing . . .'[1] Edward and Murphy continued to work along the lines of the original proposition: drafting an unexpurgated book from which the three *Life* articles, now expected to be published in June, would be extracted. A publisher for the book had yet to be formally announced, but privately Edward had agreed to work with Ken Rawson at G. P. Putnam's, a close friend and professional ally of Murphy.

As writing progressed, the early habits of recorded conversations were largely abandoned, and Edward began the process of drafting the memoir himself. Having gained in confidence as a writer and as an authoritative narrator of his past, Edward turned to the difficult story of 1936. Sometimes he would write two paragraphs and sometimes twenty, before passing them to Murphy for corrections. Though Murphy smoothed the occasionally contorted syntax, he rarely made any substantive changes to Edward's text. Past his initial reluctance, the former King was plunging headlong into the chronicle of his brief reign.

Edward's accession on 20 January 1936 was a transformational moment in his public and private life. Created Prince of Wales on his sixteenth birthday, just seven weeks after his father succeeded as King, he had spent much of the following twenty-six years creating a 'modern version'[2] of an ancient office. But, as he freely admitted to Murphy, his part had not always been easy to play. 'My way was solitary,' Edward reflected. 'I was a watcher of things. Never took part in anything. [I was] permanently excluded from the excitement of creation.'[3] Yet he was clearly proud of his travels, and that, as he put it, his 'preparation for the throne' had been 'completed upon the trade routes of the world'. He had learned, among many things, about business, which, he noted with irony, royalty usually only encountered from 'persons who had ceased to discuss it – [like] J. P. Morgan . . .'[4] His 'Prince of Wales,' he said, was not the 'reproduction of my grandfather's top-hatted geniality', and 'without conscious intent' he became a 'spokesman of the rising generation – a restless, pushing iconoclastic generation'.[5] Edward faced the job of kingship with a similarly nonconformist outlook. He felt, as he told Murphy, a 'temptation to mould, change, influence affairs and men', to become 'a modern King'.[6] Not content to rest on the precedents of his forebears, his future was to be entirely forward-facing. 'I suppose it is the fate of modern monarchs,' he noted, 'to be unconscious of their historicity . . . Strange how little interested I was in kings.' They were, he said, 'strangers to me'.[7]

For Edward, kingship was a career. From the outset of his reign, he expressed a determination to separate his public role from his private world – a division he had successfully maintained as Prince of Wales. 'I refuse to become a prisoner of the past,' he declared to Monckton, shortly after his father's death. 'I must have a private life of my own.' Monckton believed Edward was 'haunted by the fear that his life had changed for ever, and he talked constantly about his right to an independent existence'.[8] His father's Private Secretary, Sir Clive Wigram, quickly disabused Edward of this notion. 'Sir, you are quite mistaken . . . the King has no private life whatever.'[9] Edward ignored Wigram's warning. 'I was suspicious of courtiers' advice,' he told Murphy. 'I had moved in the world of action,' but, he noted wistfully, 'this made for trouble.'[10]

These early reflections on kingship were uppermost in Edward's mind as he began writing in January 1949. The subject of his first lengthy draft was the mechanics of monarchy, which he described as 'a mixture of old and new, a mélange of up-to-date business accountancy, Victorian plumbing, Plantagenet ritual and Tudor costuming,' but ultimately 'a symbol of the continuity of British life, the long swing of British habit'.[11]

La Croë, 3 January 1949

Even among those whose conception of a King has gone beyond the medieval storybook picture of a little gentleman with a crown on his head who travels about in a gold coach, there is a disposition to regard the monarch as having, on the whole, an easy time of it – plenty of people to wait upon his simplest needs, no money troubles, fine clothes, travel, and, save for the odd chance of perhaps being potted by a lunatic, being quite without a care.

. . . Yet there is another side of the monarchy which few people comprehend, and that is that, wholly aside from the obvious ceremonial and political functions, the 'King business' is also a good-sized management operation in itself. The King must also be, in the modern corporate sense, an executive responsible for the administration of numerous large and complicated properties . . .

. . . I began to cast about for means to bring the running expenses in line with my income. And at that point my education in the power of the vested interests of the Court really began. For I was to discover that the monarchy is hedged in with all kinds of superstitions; the King cannot move without arousing some dormant prejudice or infuriating an obscure faction, or violating a tribal taboo.

La Croë, 4 January 1949

. . . My father loved Sandringham with a love that defied time, logic and reality. He had converted [it] into a Victorian fortress and there, in far off Norfolk, his private war against the eroding forces of the twentieth century had ended in the complete repulse of the latter. Had anybody suggested so

'The Four Generations'. Albert Edward, Prince of Wales (later Edward VII),
Prince Edward (later Edward VIII), Queen Victoria and George, Duke of York
(later George V) photographed after Edward's christening at
White Lodge, Richmond on 16 July 1894.

Edward at the wheel
of his Daimler outside
Magdalen College, Oxford.
12 December 1913.

Edward with members of
the Oxford Battalion of the
Officer's Training Corps,
June 1914.

Edward in the uniform of a
Royal Navy Captain signing
a visitor's book in Halifax,
Nova Scotia, August 1919.

Edward with his Private Secretary
Godfrey Thomas, *c.* 1933.

Edward dressed in a
ceremonial kimono during his
tour of Japan, April 1922.

Edward with the Begum of Bhopal
during his visit to India, February 1922.

'The Royal Family', photographed together after the wedding of
the Duke of York to Lady Elizabeth Bowes-Lyon, 26 April 1923.

Fort Belvedere, Windsor
Great Park, *c.* 1929.

Edward with one of his cairn
terriers by the swimming pool
at Fort Belvedere, 1936.

Edward with a group of miners at a colliery, *c.* 1920.

Edward with a miner and his family during a visit to Durham, January 1929.

Elizabeth (later Queen Elizabeth, the Queen Mother) with George V and her husband the Duke of York (later George VI), Balmoral 1935.

Edward and Wallis pictured during the *Nahlin* cruise, August 1936.

Edward, flanked by his brothers the Dukes of York and Gloucester, walking behind George V's coffin as it leaves Sandringham, 23 January 1936.

Edward, Lord Louis Mountbatten, Esmond Harmsworth, Katherine Rogers, Wallis, Gladys Buist and Lady Louis Mountbatten in the grounds of Balmoral Castle, September 1936.

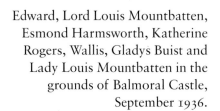

Edward with King Boris of Bulgaria on his way back to England from the *Nahlin* cruise, 7 September 1936.

Edward inspecting the crew of the Royal Navy ship *Royal Oak* during his visit to the Home Fleet, 12–13 November 1936.

Edward speaking to a group of unemployed men at the
Glebe Sports Ground at Abertillery, South Wales on 19 November 1936.

'The King's Party'. Demonstrators show their support for Edward outside Buckingham Palace, December 1936.

Wallis Simpson at
5 Bryanston Court,
1936.

much as altering one of the beloved structure[s], his answer would have been a salvo of Jovian thunderbolts of disapproval that would have left a stranger aghast.

Sandringham was the haven of my childhood; a place of perpetual happiness and activity. But long before becoming King I had ceased to care for the place and indeed come to regard it, sentiment aside, as a hideous place. Moreover it had become something of a white elephant. My father's valiant but notably unsuccessful forays into gentleman farming – model dairies – yielded a hair-raising annual deficit; and the outlay for the breeding of pheasants had led to a headshaking among his more observant friends.

Now my brother Bertie and I had often discussed Sandringham between ourselves. It was our idea that many economies were desirable and possible without affecting the quality of shooting or outraging my father's memories. So one day I said to my brother, who knew Sandringham much better than I did, 'You know what I'm up against. Why don't you go out to Sandringham, open the house, live there for a couple of weeks, and look around? See what can be done to cut down expense. Don't let anybody get the idea that I intend to close the place up. Explain things to the Land Agent. Tell him that we think a lot of money is going down the drain, and we'd like to stop it, if we can.'

To help Bertie, I sent along one of my personal financial advisors, Lord Radnor, an astute businessman. They spent a fortnight poking around the estate, and on their return presented me with an admirable report proposing a series of reforms. At their suggestion, I rented out farmland instead of continuing to farm it at a loss; I also reduced the scale of the pheasant breeding, and introduced other economies, some of which led, naturally, to a reduction of the staff, although nobody was taken off the payroll who had not already obtained another job.

I was congratulating myself at having accomplished all this

in business-like fashion, when one of my equerries (Aird), with an amused glint in his eyes, spread a London newspaper [the *Daily Telegraph*] on my desk. There, under ominous black headlines, was a sensational account of the new King's cruel eviction of the dead King's old and trusted servants at Sandringham.

Now that kind of publicity, which would never have turned a hair on the head of one of my Georgian ancestors, was the worst possible misfortune that could befall a modern King . . . The affair distressed and infuriated me, but the harm was past undoing. It furnished one more detail to the tongue-wagging: the King along with his other faults was a heartless landlord.

In a later undated draft Edward continued, 'Like many other things that strange year the tempest around the Sandringham pheasantry was unimportant and irrelevant yet it demonstrated how difficult it was to overcome the resistance to change which pervaded the British outlook upon the monarchy and why my every act however innocent was on that account being scrutinized.'[12]

Edward's vision, as he outlined it in 1949, was for a slimmed-down and more cost-effective royal establishment. Not confining his scrutiny to Sandringham alone, he quickly began delving into the framework of the entire royal property portfolio.

La Croë, 4 January 1949

. . . I was by this time too far along with my ideas to turn back, even were I disposed to do so. Simultaneously with the overhaul of the royal family's private establishment, I had also caused to be started a sober investigation of the state part of the royal machinery – the administration of the Palaces, the kitchen help, and so on. This had last been done at the outset of my father's reign, and I felt the occasion called for a brisk sweep of the broom. Since Buckingham Palace was close by, I decided before doing anything drastic to make a preliminary reconnaissance myself.

The actual management of the Palaces . . . was the province of the Master of the Household [Sir Derek Keppel]. An aging courtier of considerable charm and erudition, this functionary had been in my father's service . . . One morning I summoned him to St James's Palace and informed him that, with a view to increasing the efficiency and economy of the Household, I wished to make a personal inspection of the premises, and would he kindly make the necessary preparations.

Had I asked him for the keys to the silver vault, he could not have been more startled. His eyebrows shot up and his face flushed.

'Of course, Sir,' he replied. 'But what particular part did you wish to see? The kitchen, perhaps, or the Royal Mews?'

'Thank you,' I said, 'they all should prove interesting. But the fact is, I want to see all of it.'

'Yes, yes, but it is most unusual. Your father . . .'

'Tomorrow. We shall begin with the kitchen.'

In one corner stood a vast bin [in the kitchen]. 'What's in that?' I asked. Had the body of the Lord Chamberlain, hacked into small bits, been secreted inside, the Master of the Household could not have looked more stricken.

I am no gourmet, but the usual instruction in the culinary arts, which I had received as a young Prince under the benign Escoffier, taught me that this was hardly an inspired way to prepare potato chips. The results, when so flagrantly displayed at the King's table, could only add to the bad name already borne by English cooking.

In the months that remained of my reign, that interminable potato bin, as big as a locomotive coal box, loomed up in my mind as a symbol of the musty desuetude that prevailed throughout the royal establishments, on the other side of the state rooms . . .

All this was extremely instructive to me, opening up new

vistas of reform and improvement. But from the increasing coldness of the Master of the Household's demeanor, it was plain that he regarded my investigations as a flagrant breach of royal etiquette. His expression grew more disapproving, his glance arctic in its chill. And I presently discovered that my tours were being conducted along Baedeker principles. He took me to see only what he wished me to see; the rest he was determined to leave undisturbed in its millennial dust . . .

The deeper I penetrated the Palace fastnesses, the more my wonder grew. It was as if I had entered a Time Machine and been transported to medieval times. In the few months that remained to me as King, I was not able to press my explorations as far as I might have wished. Nevertheless, I saw quite enough to appreciate the tenacity of a community which, in the midst of London's metropolitan bustle, could persist for generations unchanged and unmoved in its ancient ways; an island of rigid habits in a rushing river of change.

What a strange and tough society it was; I say was because I assume that my brother must have brushed away some of the cobwebs. I did not really begin to appreciate how impervious and tightly woven it really was until my investigations carried me, all unsuspecting, into the weird and almost terrifying relationships governing the division of tasks among the multitudinous crafts and skills that serve the Royal Family.

These experiences convinced Edward that the monarchy needed modernisation. This required, as he wrote in an undated essay, 'to bring to the tasks of Kingship a fresh and original mind . . . The court,' he suggested, 'needed an airing – to allow the musty Victorian atmosphere to escape . . . What was really at stake,' Edward continued, 'was my right as King to a private life, to an independent existence, which in the real world is sometimes called "a life outside the office".' Having formed an implacable resistance to the idea that the monarch should negate all personal feeling in the pursuit of royal duty, Edward proposed 'to continue the regimen which I had developed among my contemporaries centered around the spontaneous informal amenities of The Fort in company of vigorous unprejudiced people'. He refused, he wrote, 'to convert to the rigid or withdrawn ordered ways that had come to be associated with Sandringham, Balmoral and Windsor Castle . . . What my critics forgot,' he concluded in this passage, 'was that the way I lived represented an outlook that had been formed by varied and constantly renewed experiences out of the journeys in settings and under conditions where the old order had to a large extent disappeared.'[13]

Implicit in this drive to modernise the monarchy was establishing the King's freedom to marry whomever he wished. Since early 1934 Wallis had occupied a dominant role in Edward's life. By the time of his accession, her marriage to Ernest Simpson was over in all but name, and rumours swirled in London society about her relationship with the King. One woman who did not address the speculation was Queen Mary. 'Mother never mentioned W's name,' Edward told Murphy, in an undated conversation. 'Thus curious for she knew about all my other flirtations, often chided, sometimes teased . . . about them. Perhaps she believed my bachelorhood permanent; or that my becoming King would sober me. But surprising. An observant woman. She must have noticed [a] change in my outlook as attachment deepened. My outlook [was] more serious, life stabler. Instead, she was silent. Her silence, coupled with inflexible opposition to divorce, meant she disapproved.'[14]

Though the question of his marriage had been discussed with his parents they had never exerted any 'ultimatum or pressure'.[15] 'I know . . . the fact that I did not marry bothered my father and mother . . . On my thirtieth birthday [1924] my mother raised the question tentatively . . . but I dodged, saying I had not met anyone I loved and I absolutely refused to enter into a marriage of convenience. In this my parents always backed me up and I shall be forever grateful.'[16] In an undated essay entitled 'Family', he expanded on these sentiments:

. . . His [George V] own happy married life must have given him a sublime faith in the magic propensities of the words of the marriage ceremony towards changing a man's make-up. Whatever may have been a son's transgressions, escapades and tendencies before, wedding bells to my father were the cure of all evils, if but only if he approved of the choice of wife . . .

I now realize that I must have been a disappointment to my father with respect to getting married in the orthodox princely way . . .

As I never even got so far as contemplating marriage before I met W the actual question as to whether I should marry a Scandinavian Princess for there were no other royal Protestant girls available except Germans or a suitable British titled lady of Aristocratic birth – Duke's or other exalted peer's daughter – never arose. W told me that George [the Duke of Kent] once discussed whom I should marry with her and was very definite in his view I should marry a royal princess like he had and not a British commoner for [he] asserted that Mary's and the other two brothers' marriages were not popular in Great Britain. He may have been voicing the opinion of my parents with regard to myself. As for the unpopularity of the other two brothers' marriages, I suspected a hint of jealousy over the fact that the two older brothers took precedence over his wife of royal birth . . .

I had developed an abhorrence of the idea of arranged marriages – 'mariages de convenance' – for they were no guarantee of real private happiness, which to me was the essential and basic element of existence in this world . . . I had seen too many unhappy marriages amongst my own contemporaries and had admired those who had found greater happiness with a divorce more than those who had chosen the path of conventional pretense to a life [of] matrimonial misery. But royalty lived in the fierce glare of publicity and presence of the State. There was no loophole for unhappy royal marriages or divorce as a merciful release. Once you took the step it was a life sentence and that I could not contemplate.

Now these conclusions may well be regarded as unfair and even insulting concerning 'mariages de convenances' and an overstatement of the case against them. Of course there have been many happy marriages of the kind, my brother's as a fine example. But it all depends on one's make-up and mine just wasn't that sort. My abhorrence of the system and my fear of getting trapped and losing my freedom until I had found the 'right' person – the 'right' person for me without regard to any other consideration – became so strongly engrained in me that I instinctively built up a formidable resistance to the very thoughts and idea of such a marriage. This accounts for my violent attitude and my determination to wait until I really fell in love, which didn't happen until I was forty.

In August 1936, six months into his reign, Edward chartered the luxury yacht *Nahlin* for a four-week cruise in the eastern Mediterranean. The party included, among others, Wallis, her friends Herman and Katherine Rogers, Duff and Lady Diana Cooper, and the Earl of Sefton. While Edward and Wallis's previous European holidays, in 1934 and 1935, had been relatively private, this trip took place under the full gaze of curious locals and a gathered international press. 'The cruise itself was unimportant,' Edward asserted to Murphy. 'It was a pleasant vacation but the clouds were rolling up – not only the clouds of war but the clouds of private trouble for me; for now the American press was intrigued with the relationship and pursued us everywhere.'[17] Crowds formed wherever *Nahlin* anchored, and, though the British press refrained from coverage, news-hungry American and European journalists relentlessly pursued the party. The informal way in which Edward chose to appear in public alongside Wallis (who was then still married to Ernest Simpson), sometimes shirtless, caused consternation for his staff and contributed to what Philip Ziegler believed was the general impression, albeit a false one, of the trip as 'the King, his mistress and a group of disreputable hangers-on carousing around the eastern Mediterranean, invariably under-dressed, usually drunk, shocking the local inhabitants and causing any Englishman who met them to hang his head in shame'.[18] Even as the media presence became more apparent, Edward refused to alter course. He seemed intent on proclaiming to the world his romance and this new style of royal informality. The publicity about the cruise marked a significant step on the road to abdication, but the informality was also combined with more formal moments, including meetings with prominent players in Balkan politics.

La Croë, 17 January 1949

But I had got into the habit of spending my summer holidays outside England. And the August migration to Balmoral, which in my father's routine had been as certain as the solar time-table, held little attraction for me. I wanted and needed a change; moreover, the gossip in the world press concerning my relations with W had reached a point where some action would have to be taken before long . . . One way or the other, I would have to declare myself. And I wanted to weigh my duty and my words . . .

. . . I chartered her [Nahlin] and, so as to avoid the long-wearing and sick-making voyage across the Bay of Biscay and through the Straits of Gibraltar, I sent her ahead, intending to join her with my party at Venice. This short-cut had the advantage of calming certain misgivings shared by the Admiralty. The Spanish batteries on both sides of the Straits of Gibraltar were taking occasional pot-shots at passing vessels and a royal yacht with a King aboard might offer an irresistible target to a trigger-happy Republic gunner.

But international politics dogged me even there. A few days

before I was to leave London Mr Eden [Anthony Eden, then Foreign Secretary] called at Buckingham Palace and I was treated to another demonstration of the incomprehensible contradictions in British foreign policy of the day.

In his polite and charming way, the Foreign Minister wished me a pleasant holiday – the Dalmatian coast had much to commend it. But a question had arisen in the Cabinet – nothing serious, at worse a minor inconvenience. Specifically, the Cabinet was of the opinion that it would [be] impolitic on His Majesty's part to board the *Nahlin* at Venice.

'What's wrong with Venice? It's the most convenient place.'

There was nothing wrong with Venice. The difficulty was that the political situation in Italy was obscure – as if it had ever been otherwise.

'Well, I don't mind a little obscurity. In fact, that little obscurity is what I am looking for.'

The Foreign Minister was in no mood for frivolity. There had been all that trouble over sanctions. Italian pride had been wounded. It was quite possible that the British King might be given a cold shoulder by the Venetians. Even worse, he might be openly insulted.

'Ah, Eden, but I'm travelling incognito. The question of my being given a reception does not arise.'

'Yes, of course. But there is always the *chef de gare*, and the municipal functionaries. There's bound to be some kind of affair.'

'Well, I'm not worried. I know the Italians. They're not going to pelt me with vegetables.'

Did I detect a faint smile pass across the Foreign Minister's features? 'Possibly Your Majesty is right. All the same, a too enthusiastic reception in Venice would produce equally difficult circumstances for His Majesty's Government in another direction. The League supporters would be upset if Your Majesty were to lend himself, even involuntarily, to an Italian celebration.'

In 1935 the League of Nations had condemned Italy's invasion of Abyssinia, imposing economic sanctions, which were largely ineffective due to the League's lack of international authority. The impasse was heightened in the summer of 1936 when Haile Selassie, the Emperor of Abyssinia, addressed the League's assembly, appealing for its aid in protecting his country from the European aggressor. Neither Edward nor, he claimed, his father believed the League an effective international arbiter. 'My father was troubled by the state of the world in his last months,' Edward wrote, on 18 August 1948. 'He had no faith in the League of Nations – thought it was bunk – especially as America did not get into it.'[19]

The League again. Now I said: 'We have truly arrived at a curious stage in British international relations. It is an incontrovertible fact that for the cruise I have in mind the most practicable place for me to board the *Nahlin* is at Venice. But the King is advised by his Foreign Minister that it is not possible for him to avail himself of this convenience; first, because he may get booed, and next – and what is even worse – because he may be cheered. This reminds me of *Alice in Wonderland*.'

Eden sat rigid. I went on, 'This absurd detour will put me to considerable added expense. Will the Treasury see that the King is reimbursed?'

Anthony Eden's aplomb was worthy of weightier issues. 'I assume,' he said, 'that the Government will follow the usual practice in such situations.'

As a good constitutional monarch must, I yielded to the advice of my Ministers, and gave Italy a wide berth . . . After crossing Europe by train, I took my party around the head of the Adriatic at Trieste, and we crossed the Yugoslavia frontier at Jesenice. There early one evening we were met by the Regent, Prince Paul . . . [he] had his own royal train pulled up on a siding and on his generous invitation our car was hitched on. Our destination was Sibenek, an obscure port on the Adriatic . . . My lingering impression of the interminable clanking night rail journey into Paul's realm is that the Yugoslav railway system is composed of a succession of freight yards, all employing rails of unequal height, and that Yugoslav engineers have reduced railroad techniques to two extreme gestures! When they are not flinging the throttle wide in an ecstasy of excitement for a lunatic swoop down a mountain side, they are yanking for dear life on the brakes in paralysis of fear . . .

Duff and his wife, Lady Diana, joined the party . . . Duff arrived with his countenance darkened by a frown, which boded ill for a yachting holiday. When I chided him, he laughed, apologized and asked if he might not see me privately. Over a drink in my quarters, he thrust at once to the point. He had just come from Venice, where he had been surprised and alarmed by the bitter comment of the Italians upon my action in passing up Venice and choosing an out-of-the-way place like Sibenek.

Duff-Cooper said, 'The Italians loathe and hate the Yugoslavs. They suspect that you purposely avoided Italy in order to pay a compliment to their enemies. It has been most unfortunate; the Italians feel that you have insulted them; serious harm has been done, and I am greatly worried.'

'So am I,' I said. 'Have you told Eden this?'

'No,' he answered. 'I've not been in London . . . Why do you ask?'

So I told the Secretary of War [Duff Cooper] what the Foreign Minister had told me in London. 'If this,' I finished, 'is a sample of how the British Cabinet works, God save the King – and England too.'

Duff Cooper was horrified and distressed. It is my impression that he sent off a cable or letter urging the Government to reconsider its first decision and, with a view to mollifying Italian sensibilities, to arrange for me to touch at Italy when I disembarked. If he did, nothing came of the idea. I bring the episode up . . . as an example of the confused counsel [from even] the supposedly best informed men of that volatile era.

Of all the drawbacks to a royal existence none is more exhausting than the absence of privacy. In the party, in addition of course to myself, were Jack Aird, Godfrey Thomas, Alan Lascelles – all of my household staff . . . We were a well-matched and agreeable company. Had I had my way, *Nahlin* would have steered into a healing void, not to reappear in the news until, tanned and refreshed, the holiday was over.

But a King, as my father once remarked, is always in session. Parliaments recess, Foreign Secretaries retire, generals and admirals take leave. But a monarch is a machine that is never allowed to run down. Although the trip was technically arranged in the guise of incognito, the relentless etiquette demanded a tiresome exchange of courtesies at every port. My guests were free to arrange impromptu shore excursions and wander happily and unmolested through bazaars. I was the one who made polite conversation with the bemedaled port officers and the excessively polite young men from the Foreign Office. There is no escape from formality; the fun always ends in an acre of state silver, a ten-course banquet, an eruption of speeches, and moist, outstretched palms extended in international fraternity.

Yet even these set pieces of protocol would have been tolerable had it not been for the staring curiosity provoked by most tentative sorties into [the] public gaze. The simple Baedeker pleasures of the sightseer are denied a celebrity; sooner or later he finds to his horror that he has become the spectacle.

The difficulties that attended my efforts to enjoy a few days of shirt-sleeved comfort are illustrated by the mob scene generated by *Nahlin*'s arrival at the port of Rab.

From the sea it promised to be an attractive, secluded spot. its antiquity proclaimed by a decaying fort surmounted by four towering campaniles . . . We put into the harbor, anchored, and went ashore in one of the barges.

One look into the crooked streets and our dreams of a leisurely afternoon evaporated. The sidewalks were swarming with tourists organized in two vast Serbian and German excursions. The news that King Edward of Britain had landed traversed these masses with electronic speed. In a moment we were engulfed; a thousand Leicas [cameras] were pressed into my face. For a few moments there was real danger that I might be crushed and trampled to death. The local Mayor, who was as surprised as anybody else by our unscheduled descent, saw the milling masses and excitedly called out the local garrison of soldiery to restore order and extricate his guest. Pushing into the mob, the soldiers tried to form a protecting wall around me; but they were powerless.

Abandoning the idea of ever seeing the cathedral, I shouted hoarsely to my companions that I was turning back. The crowd reversed itself and pursued us to the quay. While waiting for the barge to return to pick us up, the pressure of the mob upon our thin line grew heavier and heavier.

'By God, Sir,' cried Jack Aird, 'we're going to be pushed into the sea.' The barge arrived none too soon. One more surge of the crowd, and we'd have been swept over the edge into the water.

And always there was the press – persistent, tireless, ubiquitous. The American press, with that diabolical skill and enterprise in which it has no peer, had meanwhile whipped up the story of my interest in W until it had become a world topic of conversation. And while the British press at this time had still published not a line, the gossip had begun to seep through Britain, and Fleet Street was scrutinising *Nahlin*'s movements with even more morbid curiosity. The Adriatic became a vast ambush. Every height and headland crawled with photographers armed with telephoto lenses. They skulked behind the customs and dangled in grotesque attitudes from the rigging of fishing smacks that maneuvered around *Nahlin* whenever she put into port.

That relentless pursuit got on my nerves, and seeking privacy, we steamed up the Lanskinski Canal to the mouth of the Novigrad Inland Sea. Once inside these quiet waters, I breathed easily. They would never find us here. A picnic lunch was prepared, the hampers were stowed aboard a launch, and in high spirits we all set out to explore . . . Then from the mountains to the south came a familiar sound. From a low pass issued a bright yellow monoplane, which circled and dipped over the yacht, skimmed along the water in pursuit of the launch.

La Croë, 18 January 1949

. . . In my childhood and indeed all through my youth the British Royal Family had remained outside the ravenous appetites of the daily press. And on those occasions when its participation in state or private affairs called for public notice, a model of restraint and propriety with which its actions should be described was furnished by *The Times*. For us *The Times* exemplified everything that was proper and in good taste in journalism. All else was known as the penny or sensational or yellow press. It was, we were led to believe, owned and managed by wicked and treacherous men. Only depraved minds – scullery maids, coachmen and the lower orders – read these dreadful sheets. *The Times* was the journal of the gentry . . .

I have come to believe that one of the most unfortunate aspects of the crisis which before long burst around me was the long censorship which the British press in this connection imposed upon itself. As a result, when the facts were finally presented to the British people they came in a lightning burst. In the first shock of revelation much that was human and honorable was seamed by scandal and twisted by politics.

The people were staggered. Whether the eventual outcome would have been different had they known earlier what was involved, I cannot say; nor am I inclined to speculate, for what was done is done, and I am no longer King. But this I do believe: that had the facts seeped out during the summer of 1936, the frightful blow-up in the winter, a Hiroshima of constitutional politics, might never have come to pass; or had a crisis been inevitable, the cleavages might have been resolved without so heavy a legacy of bitterness.

But I was myself to blame in no small measure for this misjudgment; and the ordeal which was to break around me in December, shattering my world, lay hidden and wholly unseen beyond the golden evening mists of the Adriatic.

La Croë, 21 January 1949

To laze about in shorts after the rigid formality of the Court was an indescribable relief. But as all good things must, this unbuttoned dispensation all too soon came to an end . . . and eventually [we] arrived, after a brief visit to the battle-fields of Gallipoli,* at Istanbul.

Behind this informal and ostensibly unofficial visit to Turkey lay a highly official purpose. British foreign policy, elsewhere conspicuously unsuccessful in winning friends and influencing people, had succeeded in reversing the anti-British bias of the Turks, which had put the Ottoman Empire into Germany's camp in the 1914–1918 war. Far from siding once more with Hitler's resurgent Germany in the rising struggle for power, the Westernized Turkey of Mustafa Kemal [Atatürk, the founding father of the Turkish Republic] had begun to move tentatively into the British orbit . . .

---

* In conversation with Jack Aird, Edward recalled, in February 1949, 'It was a stirring day for me. I had never been there before, and so many of my friends had been killed at the Gallipoli time.'

My visit therefore was timed to take advantage of the current mutual good feeling and had, in fact, been enthusiastically promoted by the British Ambassador at Istanbul. *Nahlin* . . . lay four days in the Golden Horn. There was a whirl of sightseeing and entertainment, but the visit was memorable for me chiefly for what it taught me about Atatürk, one of the great revolutionaries of my generation.

Atatürk was . . . a wrecker of superstitions, an uprooter of traditions. The first Great [World] War had sundered the bonds of the Ottoman Empire. When I caught up with him he was past the crest of his power. His mind was no longer preoccupied with what he proposed to do. Instead, it dwelt lovingly upon what had already been done. His mind's eye looked backward over the road which he had travelled.

For a dictator Atatürk proved a surprisingly thoughtful, considerate host. *Nahlin* anchored off Dohne Baghe Palace, under the minarets of Istanbul, on the morning of September 4th. A vast crowd was massed on the waterfront. When I went ashore, Atatürk was waiting in a huge open car. In this machine, he escorted me to the British Embassy, a flattering gesture, I learned, for he never travelled the streets except in a bullet-proof car.

Altogether I saw Atatürk on three occasions during the visit – once aboard his yacht, and again at his summer villa, at Florya. The fact that he spoke neither English, French nor German hampered the exchange of ideas . . . I wanted to get down to brass tacks with him regarding Eastern European politics, especially as they related to Soviet Russia, whose subsequent expansionism he clearly foresaw. But he was wary of being drawn into a discussion of current politics, preferring to educate me upon the other side, the Turkish side, of the Gallipoli campaign – that glorious British failure which made Atatürk's reputation among the Turks while breaking Churchill's among the British.

Aboard [Atatürk's yacht] his face streaming with sweat,

for the day was boiling hot, Atatürk related with gusto the famous story of the chance practice maneuver on the Ismuth that enabled him, a Major General, to confront the surprise British landing at Suvla Bay . . . 'You British record Gallipoli as a fiasco,' he went on, with a twisted smile. 'You have never appreciated how close you were to complete victory.'

During this reminiscent excursion into the past, I studied Atatürk's face. In the unforgiving glare of the sun, reflected from the sea, the features were ravaged and dissipated. But Atatürk did not spring from a Puritan tradition. He was an Oriental with an open love for the fleshpots and made no bones of his lust for life. He was a hard drinker, with a thirst for fiery Turkish liquor called 'raki' . . . His Ministers and aides were in terror of him . . . But even more than Atatürk's savage temper, his Ministers dreaded his appetite for the night. If the mood for pleasure were upon him, Atatürk would summon them all, the carousers and the temperate alike, to the palace. He would keep them up, drinking, gambling and talking until dawn. He could always retire to his bed to sleep off the carouse. 'But,' as one of his Cabinet Ministers confided, 'the government meanwhile had to function next day. It was we who had to summon the resolution to stagger to the desk and wrestle with the stubborn problems of the day.' The regime of Mustafa Kemal was clearly one of the superb achievements. But it was also one of epic hangovers, bad breath, and bloodshot eyes – a Benzedrine dictatorship.

Yet power coursed through it – sheer, primal, absolute power to a degree never matched among the other governments which I had observed in various parts of the world. And the source of this power was the will of Mustafa Kemal. He was the main generator, the central plant that drove all the other dynamos. If I were asked to name the most commanding personality I ever met, it would not be Hitler or Mussolini . . . It would be Atatürk. Head, eyes, mouth, the set of the powerful shoulders, combined to produce an example of what a Hollywood movie director would call perfect casting for the role of dictator. His face in repose was fixed in a heavy, forbidding yet majestic scowl, but it could also be extraordinarily mobile. Cunning, wisdom, cruelty and love played across it with a theatrical versatility . . .

. . . On the night of September 6th we started home, and the journey . . . was pleasant and not without novelty for, among other things, it provided a quick but intimate view of the lives and interests of the Balkan monarchs who had long fascinated me.

Owing to the defects of my itinerary, I failed to meet such colorful monarchs as King Zog of Albania and King Carol of Romania. But the southern trip had afforded me the opportunity to visit both Paul of Yugoslavia and, on the homeward leg, King Boris of Bulgaria stepped forward in a most hospitable manner to conduct us through his wild, mountainous kingdom. Moreover, beyond Bulgaria Paul reappeared to bid us hail and farewell and to show us the costly new residence which he was building for himself . . . in Belgrade. So I did manage to improve my acquaintance with three of the more powerful rulers, just before the Iron Curtain clanged down upon Graustark. Now George [George II of Greece] and Boris [Boris III of Bulgaria] are dead, and Paul is in exile; except in Greece, the Commissars are everywhere in charge. Thus, without appreciating the drama at the time, I witnessed the golden twilight of the Balkan Kings and for this reason I have been impelled to describe what I saw. What follows are the casual jottings of a busman's holiday. The thought was in my mind, as I emerged from the Balkans, that the profession I shared with them could stand plenty of improvement.

Paul was . . . a self-made monarch. The progress of his family to the Yugoslav throne had reputedly been accelerated by one or two slight cases of homicide, which had the effect of eliminating the incumbent dynasty. George, on the other hand, was a genuine hereditary monarch . . .

George, in fact, was almost a stranger in his own realm
. . . I had come to know him during his long exile in London.
He had lived from 1924 to 1935, at Brown's Hotel on
Albemarle Street, then a fashionable and ultra-conservative
hostelry. My parents had sometimes had him in for family
parties but my brothers and I, being younger (George was
four years older than I), were inclined to regard him as stuffy
and lugubrious; he was, in fact, the most lugubrious monarch
I ever knew, a veritable sad sack.*

George had been recalled to Greece after a plebiscite and
restored to his throne only a year before I saw him in
Athens . . . He was vacationing in a handsome villa [Mon
Repos] . . . In the party was an English lady whom he
admired, Mrs Joyce Brittain Jones [the King's mistress].

But even these agreeable circumstances had not appreciably
lightened George's mood. The government of Greece was
firmly in the hands of the dictator [Ioannis Metaxas] and his
cohorts; the monarchy was only a showpiece.

'You cannot imagine how difficult my position is,' George
complained. 'There is nobody in Athens to talk to.'

During the first year of his kingship his weight had dropped
five stone – seventy pounds. Being King of the Greeks, I
reflected, must be an extremely trying job . . . If there was
ever a man who disliked being King, it was George.

Paul of Yugoslavia was, and is, a different sort. He was
easily the cleverest and most intelligent of the lot. I had known
him, though not well, at Oxford where, together with Prince
Chichibu [of Japan], he had been proudly exhibited by
President Warren [of Magdalen College] among the more
desirable samples from the *Almanach de Gotha*. And in a

---

* In the published version of *A King's Story*, Edward describes George of Greece
as follows: 'He had been recalled to his throne only the year before after an eleven-
year exile in Great Britain, where he had lived quietly and inconspicuously at Brown's
Hotel. There he had impressed me as a contented man, but on meeting him again
in his own land he seemed disillusioned.' (p. 309)

circuitous manner, we had subsequently been connected in a family way through my brother's marriage to his [Prince Paul's] sister-in-law, the Princess Marina.

But Paul was of a royal breed a world removed from the ponderous, conservative Saxe-Coburg strain. He was in the style of the Florentine princes – elegant, highly mannered, effete, with a dilettante flair for the arts. The . . . palace in Belgrade, built at the full flowering of the baroque era in royal residences, was a masterpiece of bad taste. Paul, who fancied himself an advanced thinker, had embodied certain architectural ideas of his own in a vast new structure . . . W was decidedly impressed by Paul's taste in and knowledge of paintings and furniture. 'He is the only ruler in Europe,' she insisted, 'who could be trusted to decorate a palace.'

Personally, I considered Paul's tastes, though undeniably elegant and refined, a trifle Byzantine. But I am no connoisseur. No doubt the cool, gray beauty of Windsor has spoiled me forever from enjoying other people's castles.

I come now to Boris, perhaps the only monarch of my generation who really enjoyed his job. And the air of contentment that pervaded his outlook could no doubt be attributed to the fact that he had developed a genial philosophy. Winston Churchill, the most prodigious worker of his age, has often remarked that it is not great responsibilities that wear down a man; it is the lack of a distracting hobby to rest and replenish the spirit. 'Change,' he says, 'is the master key.' Winston has managed to ring in the indispensable changes in his own life by becoming an amateur painter and bricklayer. Boris achieved the same tuning up of the psyche by driving locomotives.

By means no longer clear in my mind, Boris learned to drive or pilot locomotives while a young prince; and after becoming King, instead of letting this novel skill lapse, he utilized it both as a means of escaping from the cares of his office and as a means for travelling about his realm. Long before I ever went to Bulgaria, various friends of mine in the diplomatic service had described the remarkable experience, while traveling about Bulgaria in the royal private train, of having the King excuse himself from the drawing room, to reappear fully equipped with coal-smeared overalls, engineer's goggles and a bright kerchief looped around the neck. The train would stop, Boris would mount the cab, and the train would proceed with Boris at the throttle, proclaiming his progress through his realm with prolonged joyous toots on the steam whistle.

Since the current trend of proletarian politics is not likely to bring forth any more locomotive-driving kings, I am happy to be able to record among the souvenirs of that trip the experience of having traveled through Bulgaria in a train driven by King Boris.

While we were still some distance outside Sofia, capital of Bulgaria, the train jolted to a stop. First a bevy of peasant girls in bright costumes trooped into the drawing room to present me with flowers; then behind them came Boris and his brother Cyril . . . Altogether, it was a charming interruption, and I thanked Boris for traveling so far to meet us.

'Not at all,' he answered. 'No trouble at all. As a matter of fact,' he added, with a theatrical wink at brother Cyril, 'I welcomed the excuse for getting away from the desk. Now I shall have the honor of personally driving your train into my capital.'

The meaning of the mock wink became clear when Cyril at once uttered a mild protest. Cyril disapproved of the idea, though I was not sure whether it was because he thought Atatürk might take a poor view of an amateur's running his train [Atatürk had lent Edward his train for the journey], or merely because he was apprehensive of the international complications that might result if Boris bungled things while the King of England was aboard. But Boris would not be put off. When his brother's attention was distracted, he slipped away, and before long I became sensible of a livelier motion to the train, a gayer tootle in the whistle. And Bulgaria clicked away under the wheels, memorable chiefly as a mountainous landscape permanently half smothered in black smoke. When Boris returned to the car to say goodbye, he was elegantly clad in morning coat and striped trousers; but I observed with admiration that his eye sockets were still black from coal dust. He wore a more jubilant expression than is customarily seen on the countenance of a modern monarch, and on being asked how I enjoyed the ride, I was obliged to respond, in all sincerity, that it had been, so far as I could tell, a moderately well-driven train.

This flair for mechanics has unquestionably helped to sustain Balkan monarchs through the swift changes in fortune. Only the other day, on the French Riviera, a conversation with my friend the Princess Margrethe de Bourbon-Parma [born Princess Margaret of Denmark] set me to ruminating upon the wisdom of teaching future kings a useful trade along with the customary principles of constitutional law.

The Princess Margrethe de Bourbon-Parma and her husband [Prince René of Bourbon-Parma, known as Pierre] are the best of all possible friends. It was their daughter, Princess Anne, who married Michael of Romania after his forced abdication in 1947 under Kremlin pressure. All the family – the ex-King and his young wife, Princess Margrethe and Pierre – live as a family in Villefranche, not far from the villa La Croë . . . where W and I have passed many happy summers . . . I never really appreciated how much of a treasure she regarded him until one night, over the Napoleon brandy brought out in her honor, she exclaimed, 'Pierre and I have acquired not merely a King as a son-in-law, but the finest mechanic in Europe.'

Indicative of the adaptive processes at work on the youngest generation of monarchs, Michael has a passion for engines and is rather widely read in electronics, nuclear physics and petroleum chemistry. In the afternoon, after he has dealt with the not inconsiderable business that accumulates around even an exiled monarch, he will leave the house, slip his great bulk behind the wheel of a souped-up American car, and head for the lower Corniche. Then, for an hour, happily removed from the frustrations of exile, he will drive at fantastic speeds over the swooping levels of Provence, listening to the motor's hum with a professional's ear. If there is the slightest skip in the rhythm, the faintest suggestion of a passing flaw in the carburation, Michael will head home and make the necessary adjustments himself, with an easy competence that delights his mother-in-law. 'The view of the former King of Romania with which I am most familiar,' she announced, with pride, 'is of a large rear end protruding from the open bonnet of a Buick. It may be something less than royal, but it keeps down the garage bills.'[20]

Following the cruise, Wallis, and her friends, Herman and Katherine Rogers, joined Edward at Balmoral. Although they were among a group that included the Duke and Duchess of Kent, Lord and Lady Louis Mountbatten and the Duke and Duchess of Marlborough, Wallis's presence was controversial and overshadowed the aristocratic tenor of the gathering. Even the usually sympathetic Churchill deplored 'Mrs Simpson going to such a highly official place upon which the eyes of Scotland were concentrated'.[21] Adding to the contention was Edward's insistence that she be named in the Court Circular as one of his guests. A published record of the comings and goings of the British court, the Circular was, Edward wrote, 'before the persistent insistent newspaper publicity, the only source of information on the daily activities'[22] of the Royal Family. The inclusion of Wallis Simpson in the King's official business transformed the typically dull report into what the socialite Diana Mosley described as 'a source of endless gossip and conjecture in London society'.[23] In an essay entitled 'Notes on the Hypocritical British Attitude Toward Divorce', Edward defended his decision, asserting, 'I could have camouflaged her presence and catered to gossiping tongue-wagging by merely stating . . . "The King is entertaining a few friends at the Castle." It was my honesty, my chivalry and my good manners that offended in certain quarters, whereas duplicity and camouflage would have satisfied my hypocritical critics.'[24]

In the chronology of Edward's brief reign, the cruise on *Nahlin* and his unconventional stay at Balmoral were critical milestones. Each tested public and official appetite for his relationship with Wallis, and in both instances failed to garner either sympathy or support. Yet the woman at the centre of these events remained, as Edward told the story in 1949, firmly on the periphery. While Edward glossed over the personal and intimate details, Wallis tackled them head on with Murphy. 'He lost his head over me,' she explained, in an undated conversation. 'I was pleased. I was flattered. I was happy. But all the time something inside me kept saying, "One day something will stop it" . . . I was in love with him and he with me . . . I liked what was happening – being taken to fine houses, people sucking up to you. Reminded me of Navy days [Wallis's first husband Win Spencer was a naval pilot]. When you're the commandant's wife the world is your oyster; wives play up to you. Fine car, chauffeur. All the perks. Then your husband ordered to sea. Car taken away. Servants. House boys. Thought same thing could happen to me . . . Go back to where one lives . . . I'd be Mrs Simpson again – the discarded woman.'[25] Yet the excitement of her new life was intoxicating as she explained to Murphy: 'Everybody succumbs to glamor; defy anybody to say otherwise.'[26]

Murphy correctly understood that Wallis held the key to their joint lives. He trained his eye assiduously on her throughout.

Charles Murphy's Diary
Cap d'Antibes, January 1949[27]

Duchess touched [on] her childhood. Always stresses southern background – poor, but aristocratic.

It developed: [the] mother married not once but three

times. Apparently she was something of a problem to her mother who knew exactly how to handle her. W would show off, talk a lot. One day when a stranger interrupted to contradict something her mother said, 'Oh, no, you mustn't bother. Wallis is right. Wallis knows everything, don't you, Wallis?'

Her hatred of British. Their cruelty. Cruelest people in world. Also cleverest. They know all about world. Know all about money. All about trade. All about shipping. And all about vices.

An isolationist – but an emotional one. A means of vengeance.

The narrative of 1936 was momentarily interrupted by Edward's former equerry, Sir John Aird, who arrived at La Croë on 22 January 1949. Aird was, according to Murphy, 'wispish and shrewd'. The 'perfect caricature of an Englishman,'[28] observed Leopold, ex-King of the Belgians, who with his wife Princess Lilian dined with the Windsors during Aird's stay.

Aird, alongside Godfrey Thomas, had been one of Edward's longest-serving aides. He had accompanied Edward to South America in 1931 and was present for the private holidays he and Wallis took in the summers of 1934 and 1935. Aird resigned in 1936 shortly after returning from *Nahlin*. The cruise, he told Murphy in 1973, was 'my last crusade. I had come to realize earlier what was afoot.' Yet he and Edward parted on good terms. Aird, like many who had worked for Edward, found his sometimes-errant ways frustrating but retained a fondness for him personally. 'There was a wild streak in him – something he could not control.' Though not 'notably intelligent,' Aird reflected, 'neither was he a fool. He was attracted by the thought that problems, a problem, might have more than one solution, and that the one pressed upon him was not necessarily the right one.' Aird refuted the allegation that from the beginning of his reign Edward had wished to abandon his duties as King: 'He loved the job, really.'[29]

Aird stayed at La Croë for over three weeks, reminiscing with Edward over their many shared experiences. Murphy labelled the over forty pages of typed material created 'Notes on Conversations Between His Royal Highness and Sir John Aird'. Among the many topics they covered was Edward's trip to France to consecrate the memorial at Vimy Ridge to the Canadian soldiers who fought in the First World War and a highly unofficial memory of George V's Silver Jubilee in 1935.

La Croë, 3 February 1949

With a galaxy of former Governor Generals and (top-ranking) Canadians for a background, we stood together on top of the famous ridge, which twenty years before had belched flame and fiery steel and now seemed a gentle slope dominating the plain of Lens devoid of any . . . historical significance. The land was bright and green; new trees had grown to replace the dead trunks blackened by shellfire. The trenches had been filled in and grass and Flanders poppies hid the scars of war. How much time, I thought, had already passed over my generation. The survivors of the charge up Vimy Ridge in the smoking sleet were middle-aged. Battalion commanders had become grandfathers. But the grimness and reality of this epic feat of arms needed no confirmation for those who had come to remember.

La Croë, 7 February 1949

. . . After the Jubilee service [6 May 1935] was over, my father and mother returned from the procession and went out on the usual little balcony at Buckingham Palace to accept the cheers of the crowd and wave to them.

My sisters and family subscribed to a rather nice cup to present to the King and Queen. My brother brought it to the Palace and I was asked to present it to the King. But I said I thought the King was tired and that we had better give it the next day. But my brother [George VI] thought that was too late: it should be given on the day of the Jubilee Celebration. So I told him to do as he wished but I advised him not to give it that day.

Meanwhile the cup was in the little room leading in from the balcony. My father was very tired and left the balcony with the Queen and we followed; and he passed right by the cup in his anxiety to get to his room as soon as possible and get out of his uniform to rest. My brother tried to draw his attention to the cup but was unsuccessful. So we all trailed along, taking the cup, and went right with my father into his room. When he saw us all there, he asked, 'What do you all want here?' My brother tried to present the cup, and my father said, 'Get that damn thing out; I don't want another cup.' My brother felt very downcast. Had he waited another hour, it might have been all right . . .

Aird's presence prompted Edward again to revisit the controversial speech he had given to the British Legion in 1935, and to remark, 'Sir John Aird says that my great weakness as a member of the Royal Family was that I would act myself instead of expressing my views through someone else who might report, "The Prince of Wales was annoyed at this or that . . . " but a King or Prince must work indirectly, not directly, it seems, and I never learned that. My father worked indirectly; he was a master at it. But the days when the censure of the sovereign was feared by Prime Ministers, as in the time of Victoria, had gone.'[30] Towards the end of his visit, Aird remarked wistfully one night at dinner, 'There never was Edward VIII. That was fantasy. In my lifetime only two Kings – George V and George VI. Some say there was another King in between, but no trace of him survives today.'[31]

The Windsors and Murphy remained at La Croë until late March. Writing, Murphy admitted to Hank Walter, had 'fallen behind but I trust we shall make it up'.[32] As the Windsor household prepared to decamp to Paris, Murphy once again cast his penetrating eye on Edward and Wallis's world.

Charles Murphy's Diary
La Croë, March 1949[33]

. . . House bustling with activity day before. Duke supervising packing of his own things.

Then in the morning the caravan drawn up in front – first the maroon, canvas-topped Cadillac, next the Buick (for the secretaries . . .), then the Citroën for the footman, then the red Jeep station wagon piled high with luggage.

Marchand [the butler] had packed Cadillac with a confectioner's care; the two rugs, with red Coronets, folded; the Duke's worn leather case (from grandfather), marked E., stuffed with maps; sandwiches. Coroneted pillows. Mink coats neatly folded

Duke supervising everything . . .

Swish off – servants waving goodbye. In the wake a Citroën containing two secret service men of the Quai d'Orsay who are assigned to HRH whenever he travels.

5

The Crisis Unfolds

Murphy arrived in Paris on 27 March 1949 and immediately made his way to the Windsors' new home, 85 rue de la Faisanderie, a grand mansion in the 16th arrondissement, rented from their friend the French industrialist Paul-Louis Weiller. Though the house was filled with treasures and possessed an enormous drawing room, the Windsors were not enthusiastic about the property. It had only a small garden and a rather gloomy dining room that curtailed the style and size of their dinner parties. But the move at least offered Edward and Wallis their first permanent residence in the city since 1946, when they had vacated 24 boulevard Suchet, their home since 1938. Edward could have purchased the elegant four-storey townhouse, also located in the 16th, when the owners decided to sell, but he dallied, and it was sold to another buyer.

Edward was still resisting putting down any permanent roots. Sensitive to the political instabilities in post-war Europe, he also held on to the hope that he would be allowed eventually to return to Fort Belvedere. Between 1946 and 1949 the Windsors' Paris residence was a suite at the Ritz Hotel. The MP and diarist Harold Nicolson, who saw them in Paris around the time they left boulevard Suchet, commented wistfully on this nomadic existence: 'She says that they do not know where to live. They would like to live in England, but that is difficult. He retains his old love for Fort Belvedere . . . He likes gardening, but it is no fun, gardening in other people's gardens . . . They are sick of France. He likes America but that can never be a home. He wants a job to do. "You see," she [Wallis] says, "he was born to be a salesman. He would be an admirable representative of Rolls-Royce. But an ex-King cannot start selling motor-cars . . ."'[1]

Having decided not to renew their lease on La Croë when it was set to expire in August, the Windsors were forced into this temporary residence. As they busied themselves with settling into their new house, Murphy observed with quiet amusement the confusion that reigned.

Charles Murphy's Diary
Paris, Spring 1949[2]

. . . Marble house. Enter through series of chambers, like Egyptian tomb. Narrow. Flight of stairs – at top . . . a marble horse, presumably finest example of Greek sculpture. This hidden behind luminous curtain – figure dimly seen.

Tremendous organ; this concealed by a false painted bookcase, in which central feature was opened book across which written 'Not yet finished.'

Table with green velvet cloth upon which disposed old silver regimental badges & dirks. All this surmounted by a two-foot silver figure of British Guardsman of Napoleonic wars, with knapsack, bayoneted rifle. If touched, Duchess angry; left mark on velvet.

Duke pleased as punch, shirt open, coat off, opening boxes, humming to himself, examining finds – his blond head darting among French workmen.

One day gardener making racket in court. Duke shouted in French at him. Confused exchange. Duke returned, shaking head: 'That confounded fellow said, "Pardon, I do not understand English."' . . .

Windsor: Loves to do everything himself . . .

Two French *ouvriers* standing idle while Duke and Duchess move small boxes, bibelots about. Old equerry [Godfrey Thomas] murmured, 'Exactly like his father. Masters of unessential details.'

The stay in Paris was brief. On 5 April Edward and Murphy left for London to spend two weeks researching and visiting 'the scenes of his princely youth'.[3] The trip was quickly extended for a further ten days so that Edward and Wallis could spend Easter with the Earl and Countess of Dudley, two of their oldest friends, at the Dudleys' home, Ednam Lodge, near Sunningdale. News of the diversion reached Longwell, who was beginning to feel uneasy about Edward's productivity. Murphy had, after all, been with Edward for more than a year and Longwell was eager to see a return on *Life*'s already substantial investment. He urged Murphy to sprint to the finish and aim for a June publication.

Until the trip Murphy had remained confident that they could meet Longwell's deadline. But work had slowed, and on 14 April he telegraphed Longwell confirming the first of many delays. Longwell and Luce were both upset. Murphy was summoned back to New York for a full explanation. Confronted with the inevitable, the bosses at *Life* were left with little choice but to accept the situation as it was. Chastened, Murphy returned to Paris to resume his task. 'The main thing,' he wrote to Longwell, 'is to keep the work going . . . There are many people in England, and even around the Duke, who would like to see this work killed.'[4]

As efforts recommenced a familiar pattern resumed. Edward wrote – in pencil – while Murphy followed close behind, refining and choreographing his text into coherent chapters. Edward's output was erratic. Some days he filled barely a page while on others he wrote upwards of twenty. This unpredictability was agonising for Murphy, who was trained to the discipline of hard and fast deadlines. 'Privately,' Longwell wrote to him, 'my editorial concern with the Duke is that he writes too little.' Longwell, who was also overseeing the completion of Churchill's articles, which were to appear in January 1950, continued, 'With Mr Churchill it tends to be the other way around. My life would be more serene if these eminent gentlemen could trade their great and strongly developed traits for a few months.'[5]

Between April and August 1949, in Paris and later at La Croë, Edward, albeit at his own pace, set to work and wrote his history of the abdication. Following an established pattern, episodes were tackled in chunks irrespective of their chronology.* Much of what was written during this period found its way into his eventual publications and demonstrates that the words Edward eventually published were very much his own. But the more intimate details of what was for him and Wallis a personal calamity were missing.

The dramatic events of the abdication lasted less than two weeks. Yet trouble had been brewing since Edward's return from Balmoral in September 1936. The controversy surrounding Wallis's stay at the castle alongside American publicity of the *Nahlin* cruise had stirred gossip in Britain and precipitated the final break-up of the Simpsons' marriage. 'In the end,' Wallis told Murphy, 'Ernest saw what was happening. I'm sure he was in love with me. The situation hurt him. He drifted away.'[6] Wallis's aunt, Bessie Merryman, echoed this sentiment. 'Wallis was truly happy with Ernest,' she told Murphy, in February 1950. 'Had the Prince not appeared she would have gone on with him and they would have had a happy life together. But the Duke was stubborn and persistent. What woman could resist him? He demanded her time.'[7]

Wallis's upcoming divorce suit on the grounds of Ernest Simpson's adultery threatened a full-scale exposure of her relationship with Edward. The case was scheduled to be heard in Ipswich, Suffolk, on 27 October 1936. Conscious that 'a good many people in Britain, especially in government circles, and amongst the upper classes, were only too well aware of what was being printed in America',[8] Edward took drastic action. To control the British press, he turned to an unexpected ally. Lord Beaverbrook, known to his friends as Max, founder of the Conservative-leaning *Daily Express*, had briefly been Minister of Information in the last months of the First World War under David Lloyd George, an office that had taught him the full

---

* The treatment of the abdication in chapters 5, 6, 7 and 8 has been organised according to the events of 1936, rather than the chronology of Edward's drafts.

potential of media to shape mass public opinion. He and Edward had not been historically close, though they had met intermittently in the 1920s. Beaverbrook, Murphy believed, 'seems to have liked' Edward 'very much'. 'He was a serious young prince,' Beaverbrook remembered. 'I am convinced that he wanted to be the poor man's king.' And 'contrary to the rumours that he hated the idea of being king,' he was, Beaverbrook believed, 'a serious candidate for kingship'.[9]

Edward in turn admired Beaverbrook's independence and believed he 'could be expected to see W's predicament in a human and modern light, detached from cant and prejudice'.[10] He was pleased to find in him a willing ally, and the press baron succeeded in securing a 'gentleman's agreement among the principal newspaper proprietors of the British Isles to report the divorce action . . . with restraint.'[11] As Edward's writing in 1949 progressed, Beaverbrook became an integral source in the retelling of the abdication story. As Murphy wrote to Longwell on 29 August, 'Having been both a King's man and also privy to the Government's secrets, Beaverbrook probably knows more about the abdication than anyone else – more than even the Duke and more than Baldwin or the other agents.'[12]

Shortly before Wallis's divorce hearing, Edward was summoned back to Fort Belvedere from a shooting party at Sandringham to meet the Prime Minister, Stanley Baldwin, who implored him to intervene and stop the proceedings. Edward refused and, on 27 October, Wallis appeared at the Ipswich courthouse accompanied by her lawyer Theodore Goddard.

La Croë, 18 July 1949

But of course readers of the Court Circular could never have guessed that while I strove to carry out these duties with my usual punctiliousness, part of my mind was that morning understandably occupied with what was taking place at the Ipswich courthouse. It did not require much imagination to appreciate that there can be few more trying experiences to a woman, especially a sensitive woman, than her appearance as the petitioner in a divorce action. My sympathy would have gone out to W in any case, but after my talk to Mr Baldwin and his ominous question, 'Must this case really go on?' I could not help but view her situation with some concern. Since the Prime Minister had clearly assumed that the divorce, if granted, would be a prelude to my marriage – a marriage which he obviously deemed contrary to the interests of the monarchy and of the established Church of England – and historical responsibility might well devolve upon the shoulders of the judge who removed the legal obstacle. I yield to no one in my regard for the incorruptibility of the British judiciary. But a word here, a hint there – anything was possible . . .

Thus, while my personal affairs moved one step nearer to the torment of decision, the mechanics of kingship went forward undisturbed. The art of being a proper constitutional monarch consists in no small measure of appearing to be not only above politics but above life. To be above politics entails no strain; despite my occasional yielding to temptation, discretion had by now become instinctive. But for a person of my philosophy and temperament – not to mention what was going on within me at the time – the mere idea of preparing to be above life, to appear austere, remote and oblivious of the human comedy, was something I could not accept. And so as I conscientiously pursued my round of duties, the ceremonial side, designed to impress the people with the symbolism of kingship in all its panoply, began to take on an air of unreality.

Edward carried out his last ceremonial duty as King on 11 November 1936, Remembrance Day. Considering his experiences in the First World War it proved a poignant final appearance on the public stage of British royal life. At 11 a.m., having stood before the Cenotaph to observe the customary two minutes' silence, he laid the first wreath. The occasion moved him deeply. His father, he wrote on 20 July 1949, was 'very much in my mind that day and,' he continued, 'after dark I was moved to drive over to Westminster Abbey. Outside is a railed-off patch of grass. For some years it had become with many a custom to plant tiny wooden crosses in memory of someone close who had fallen in the war. In the rain at first unnoticed I joined a throng of some hundreds of people who had paused there on their way home from work. I bought one of the crosses, which I planted in honor of my father.'[13]

After paying this private tribute, Edward boarded a night train to Portsmouth. Accompanied by Samuel Hoare, First Lord of the Admiralty [later 1st Viscount Templewood], and Ernle Chatfield, Admiral of the Fleet [later 1st Baron Chatfield], he was to spend the following two days visiting the Home Fleet at Portland.

La Croë, 20 July 1949

The train pulled up in the navy yard early next morning and I was awakened by the sound of a furious wind lashing around the sleeping car . . . As if to provide a prelude for the constitutional storm about to break around me, a heavy westerly gale, one of the worst in local history, howled down over the harbor . . .

The royal yacht *Victoria and Albert* . . . steamed over from Portsmouth. She was my headquarters for the visit . . . Flying my standard from the main I entertained all the flag officers and captains of the Fleet at dinner . . . It was good to be back with the Fleet. Going from battleship to cruiser, from cruiser to destroyer, and from destroyer to submarine, I met many old friends who had been with me at Naval College or shipmates on my long Imperial voyages. The lower deck gave a concert in honor of my visit. In the hangar of the aircraft carrier *Courageous* I joined the blue-jackets and Marines in the latest vaudeville choruses to the music of a mouth-organ band. Before returning to the royal yacht, I made a little speech in which I told the Fleet how much it

meant to me to be with them again. I spoke from the heart.
I understood these sailors and they understood me. In their
company I had been able to put aside for a little while the
burning issue unknown to them which demanded my decision.

Edward returned to Fort Belvedere late on the evening of 13 November.
Waiting for him was an unexpected letter from his Private Secretary,
Major Alexander 'Alec' Hardinge, marked 'Urgent and Confidential'.
The letter was a crucial turning point in the drama. Beaverbrook
interpreted it as a 'direct challenge to the King', which obliged him to
finally 'face up to Baldwin'[14] about his relationship with Wallis.

Edward wished that his memoir would reproduce the letter in full. He
was dissuaded by the horrified warnings of Monckton and Allen, who
feared both the breach of royal propriety and of Hardinge's copyright.

Alexander Hardinge to Edward VIII
London, 13 November 1936[15]

Sir,
    With my humble duty
    As Your Majesty's Private Secretary I feel it is my duty
to bring to your notice the following facts which have
come to my knowledge, and which I know to be accurate.
    1) The silence of the British press on the subject of
Your Majesty's friendship with Mrs Simpson is not going
to be maintained. It is probably only a matter of days
before the outburst begins. Judging by the letters from
British subjects living in foreign countries, where the
press has been outspoken, the effect will be calamitous.
    2) The Prime Minister and Senior members of the
Government are meeting today to discuss what action
should be taken to meet the serious situation which is
developing. As Your Majesty no doubt knows, the
resignation of the Government, an eventuality which
by no means can be excluded, would result in Your

Majesty having to find somebody else capable of forming a Government which would receive the support of the present House of Commons. I have reason to know that, in view of the feeling prevalent among members of the House of Commons of all parties, this is hardly within the bounds of possibility. The only alternative remaining is a dissolution and a general election in which Your Majesty's personal affairs would be the chief issue, and I cannot help feeling that even those who would sympathize with Your Majesty as an individual would deeply resent the damage which would inevitably be done to the Crown, the cornerstone upon which the whole empire rests.

If Your Majesty will permit me to say so, there is only one step which holds out any prospect of avoiding this dangerous situation, and that is for Mrs Simpson to go abroad <u>without further delay</u>, and I would beg Your Majesty to give this proposal your earnest consideration before the position has become inevitable. Owing to the changing attitude of the Press the matter has become one of great urgency.

The way Hardinge chose to deliver his message shocked Edward almost as much as its content. Yet he should not have been overly surprised. Despite the importance of Hardinge's position in Edward's official life, the two men, as Edward had already explained to Murphy, were not close. Describing him as 'an irrelevant figure. Wooden. Stiff; embittered,' he had been, Edward told Murphy, 'all right' in the 1920s but had by 1936 'turned sour'.[16] A veteran courtier, Hardinge had served as George V's assistant private secretary for sixteen years, but he was temperamentally unsuited to work with Edward. Walter Monckton believed he 'took too pessimistic and critical a view' of Edward and the relationship with Wallis, while at the same time expressing these opinions 'too emphatically and widely to have any hope of retaining the King's confidence when the crisis came'.[17]

La Croë, 21 July 1949

Time heals many wounds. Words and actions which in the heat of controversy assume abnormal and decisive significance when surveyed in retrospect are often found to be merely incidental. Alec Hardinge's letter should, I think, be read in this light. A stranger studying this document today, against the accomplished fact of my abdication, might well decide that under the given circumstances it was [an] entirely proper and reasonable letter for the King's Private Secretary to write his sovereign. Be that as it may, when I read the letter . . . I was stunned and angry.

If, unknown to me, matters had come to such a pass, why had not Alec Hardinge come and told me these things? There could have been no question of his lacking an entrée, for I saw him every day I was in London. He brought me my official correspondence each morning, so there had been many opportunities for him to have raised the question. And even if the perfunctory nature of our relationship would not have predisposed me to welcome this intrusion into so personal a matter, a warning from Alec Hardinge would have caused me at once to have summoned Mr Baldwin and have thrashed it out with him. That would have been the traditional procedure by means of which a monarch and his Private Secretary would have dealt with such confidential business. No doubt I was in part responsible for this unfortunate breakdown in our official association. I had never taken Alec Hardinge into my confidence; we scarcely ever saw each other outside working hours. And the fact that I had not included him in my intimate circle may have made him in his turn cool and distant towards me. So I reaped the whirlwind in the form of this cold-blooded, unempathetic letter; and not merely a letter but what was in effect a demarche with its brutal suggestion that W leave the country without delay.

. . . After some dinner I read the letter again in a calmer frame of mind . . . It was the motivation of Alec Hardinge's action that puzzled me. However one looks at it, it was a strangely bold one on his part. He was a courtier – and I know courtiers. I cannot imagine any courtier, even one who privately endorsed the various contingencies and propositions raised in this remarkable letter, plunging headlong on his own initiative into so dangerous a position. To begin with there was that astounding categorical statement that not only were the Prime Minister and his Cabinet contemplating resignation unless I gave W up, but also that sounding of other parties in the House of Commons showed that I stood little chance of inducing anyone else to form a government. Now Alec Hardinge was far from being either impulsive or irresponsible. It was impossible to imagine him making such sensational statements except on the highest authority. Had he not used the phrase 'I have reason to know . . .'? Who could have told him this but Mr Baldwin? But what was S.B.'s game, I wondered. That was more difficult to fathom. Were he and the senior members of the government trying to scare me with an ultimatum, for how else could I regard the letter? Yet if their game was to intimidate me into capitulation without a public clash by pointing their big pistol of resignation at my head, they had made a gross tactical error in suggesting that the simplest way out was for 'Mrs Simpson to go abroad without further delay.' I was obviously in love; they were striking at the very roots of my pride and only the most faint-hearted man would have remained unaroused by such a challenge.

. . . Until now, after making due allowances for the constraints and restrictions imposed by my high-born position, my life, I reflected, had gone on much as I wished. No one had ever seriously interfered with it. I had succeeded in establishing a delicate and harmonious balance between duty and desire, which had made my princely existence tolerable. But now my life was challenged . . . This was no simple affair of the heart; it had become a tremendous constitutional issue shaking the foundations of the world's greatest empire. And feeling the need for not only advice but support, I decided to send for Walter Monckton . . .

Over the phone I had already warned him of the purport of the meeting. Without further words I handed him Alec Hardinge's letter; he read it slowly and deliberately; his expression turned grave. 'What do you make of it?' I asked.

'Sir, it looks as if S.B. is trying to smoke you out.'

'Well, if that is his intention, he has.'

I then went on to tell Walter Monckton that if Alec Hardinge had truly reflected Mr Baldwin's attitude, then time could not wait. I must send for him at once and declare myself . . .

Although Walter Monckton demurred at the mere thought of my going, he agreed that I had no alternative but to send for the Prime Minister. 'I certainly don't look forward to this unpleasant interview,' I told him, 'but I must put it behind me. I can't leave Alec Hardinge's letter hanging in the air. I shall see S.B. tomorrow.' . . . We then turned to the other dilemma created by Alec Hardinge's letter, namely, the impossibility of my continuing to work with or through him in the difficult negotiations which his own action had made inescapable and in which he had already displayed so strong a bias. And the net effect of his action was to block the channel of communication between Buckingham Palace and Number 10 Downing Street – a channel which by custom is confined to the King's Private Secretary . . . Unless the confidence placed in the Private Secretary is matched by sympathy and loyalty to the master, the link with government snaps. The absence of teamwork between Alec Hardinge and myself, therefore, was doubly unfortunate, for was there ever an occasion, in a century not devoid of disagreements between sovereign and ministers, when this teamwork was more essential to a clarification of the personal and constitutional issues at stake? I therefore decided to bypass him in my dealings with Mr Baldwin.

. . . The simplest solution was to dismiss Alec Hardinge. Walter Monckton, however, dissuaded me from the step, pointing out that with Whitehall already full of rumors, the mass interpretation that would undoubtedly be placed on Alec Hardinge's dismissal would only add to the confusion. So I left him where he was but decided to bypass him in my dealings with Baldwin.

La Croë, 23 July 1949

But where would I find a man to restore the broken link? . . . The obvious man for the job was sitting right there in the room with me, but it was with some diffidence that I approached him. Walter Monckton was one of the leading barristers of London . . . To give it up, however temporarily, and enlist in the King's cause – a cause perhaps already lost – might mean a considerable sacrifice to him, and not merely of money. Yet Walter Monckton never hesitated . . .

So it came to pass as events shaped themselves that whatever contribution Alec Hardinge may otherwise have made to British history, he must be credited at this juncture with having been instrumental in making up his sovereign's mind. However that may be, his letter turned out to be a blessing in disguise. Things were bound to come to a head anyway, and if the letter hastened it, what matter? It gave me a reason to bring Walter Monckton into my personal service, and the part which he played thereafter satisfied Mr Baldwin as much as it helped me. Despite the passions that were soon to envelop us, neither the Prime Minister nor myself ever once had cause to complain of any misrepresentation by my chosen instrument. For all the hullabaloo in the press, the constitutional negotiations were in fact handled by Monckton calmly, expertly and always with dignity. And while there were no doubt times when Walter Monckton might have wished that I could have been persuaded to take another line, he never allowed his personal feelings to impair the impartiality required of him as intermediary.

Edward met Baldwin at Buckingham Palace on 16 November. His future, he declared, was 'marriage and a home with the woman I loved'.[18] The woman was, of course, Wallis. Stating emphatically that he wished to marry and remain King, he nevertheless acknowledged that should the government oppose the union he was prepared to stand aside for his brother and successor, the Duke of York. Baldwin, according to Edward, took little time to reflect before pronouncing the view that neither Cabinet nor country would accept Wallis as Queen. 'He might have been Gallup Poll incarnate,'[19] Edward wrote. But despite Baldwin's surety, 'I was not,' he continued, 'going to accept without a challenge, his bold statement . . . A number of the ministers were my personal friends; some were my contemporaries, and therefore I had reason to believe that many of the old objections to divorce had lost some of their relevance in modern society. I therefore asked the Prime Minister to consult them.'[20]

That same evening Edward dined with Queen Mary, his sister Princess Mary and sister-in-law Alice, Duchess of Gloucester, at Marlborough House. After dinner and the Duchess of Gloucester's departure, Edward 'told them the whole story'.[21]

The declaration, as he told Murphy in August 1948, was not a surprise to either. 'Things like that go along in whispering campaigns,'[22] Edward recalled, and he suspected Hardinge of having informed Queen Mary's Comptroller, Lord Claud Hamilton, to whom he was close. Queen Mary received the news with stoic, albeit silent, disapproval. 'Whenever personal desires or private predilections cut across the accepted traditional forms of royal conduct,' Edward reflected, on 25 July 1949, 'they must be suppressed. By her standards one followed a lofty and rigid principle of self-denial, thrusting aside the importunities of the outer world, however heartrending the choice.'[23] She refused her son's request to receive Wallis and they parted that night with a silent recognition of the gulf that had opened between them. It was, as Queen Mary's biographer James Pope-Hennessey defined it, 'a conflict of realities'.[24]

In the midst of this emotional turmoil Edward left London on the evening of 17 November for a two-day visit to inspect the coal fields of South Wales. Planned in the early summer, his trip was designed to highlight the region's poverty and draw attention to the 'terrible evidence', he wrote, in an undated draft, 'of Britain's decline, and the failure of old-fashioned politics to cope with the unemployment'.[25] It was also a continuation of the type of work he had championed as Prince of Wales. 'I went among crowds,' he told Murphy, in an undated discussion. 'I went into the slums. I tramped the factories. My father had done none of those things. Many of the old courtiers thought I was letting down the dignity of the office. But I realized it had to be done.'[26] Yet as the economic depression of the 1930s worsened, there was very little that Edward could do, except to call attention to the plight of the unemployed in what became known as the 'distressed areas' of Britain. 'I wanted to focus public opinion on conditions there . . .' but 'I was powerless to promise them anything concrete. I spoke to them as individuals . . . I went into their homes . . . They would thank me for coming up. I said it was all new to me and I did not have remedies but would report conditions when I returned.'[27]

Some of Edward's most poignant experiences were his visits, as Prince of Wales, to the working men's clubs established by the social campaigner Bill Adams, whom he first met in 1929. Entering the spartan halls filled with idle men, Edward saw at first hand the human impact of economic paralysis. 'Clearly the usual Prince of Wales speech would have sounded mocking in such a setting. What could I say?' he reflected. 'That it would all be fixed up? That it was their fault? That living on the dole wasn't half bad? Or keep a tight upper lip?' There was nothing to do, he told Murphy, except to acknowledge their 'difficulties' and assure them that he was not 'oblivious to their hardships . . .'[28] These appearances offered little scope for a prince who was, as he put it, 'in search of importance'.[29] Yet despite the limitations, Edward believed it was work worth continuing as King.

Paris, 28 April 1949

. . . Yet in the atmosphere of suspicion attaching to all my movements, even this sad journey among the poverty-stricken families gave rise to a fresh set of rumors that tended to widen the breach between me and the Government . . .

The Rhondda's black hillsides, with its dingy towns and slag heaps, were a familiar sight and I had been visiting the mining valleys ever since 1918. In the light of all that has since happened to Britain and the revolutionary changes that have come over its way of life, South Wales is now seen to have been a curiously prophetic place in which to make my last public appearance . . . That unhappy country whose once rich mines and industrious people had made the Britain of my youth seem invincible had already become one huge monument of the transitoriness of human institutions. As new needs arise, the old forms fall. Even a king, who would be among the last to feel the pinch of a depression, could see that people left in so dismal a plight must sooner or later take power into their own hands.

In fact, by their ill-concealed agitation the two Ministers [for Health and Labour, Kingsley Wood and Ernest Brown respectively] in attendance obviously shared my views. Sensing the temper of the crowds, with which we mingled freely at each stopping place, they showed an almost fearful reluctance to become separated from my well-guarded person. The spectacle of these two portly and perspiring politicians, panting at the King's heels all the while darting nervous glances at the sullen miners, drew scornful jibes from onlookers.

While I obviously sympathized with the plight of the people

of South Wales, I also recognized that the miners' leaders themselves were not always wise in the methods they used to publicize it. For example, the hunger marches on London had particularly unfortunate repercussions in the capital; they had alienated some of the sympathy felt for Welsh labor and given it a bad name. So strongly did I feel this that I undertook to point this out to the local Members of Parliament as each one rode with me through his constituency. How could they expect industry, I asked, to risk capital by establishing new plants in South Wales so long as local labor persisted in such hostile and unreliable behavior?

As Beaverbrook told Murphy, Edward's 'idealism was high and sincere'. He was genuinely 'alarmed over unemployment' and, Beaverbrook emphasised, 'over the apparent inability of British society to resolve the human crisis'. Believing in a 'man's right to work and in a nation's responsibility to supply him with work', Edward chafed at the inaction that dominated the political landscape in Britain. But 'the Beaver' also noted that 'the remedies that he proposed were not always appropriate', and that without the ability to act politically, he fell back 'upon wishful thinking, upon the supposition that a good king could improve the misfortunes of the world'.[30]

Paris, 29 April 1949

Wherever the fault might lie, the tragedy of the depression was everywhere visible. In the Rhondda there is a place called Dowlais, and when I first went there many years before, a large steel mill with collateral industries gave employment to 9,000 men. But gradually the mill had become obsolescent and by 1936 it had been completely abandoned, leaving the community stranded like castaways around a wreck. The spectacle of that rusting plant and the forlorn crowds clustered on the surrounding hillside struck me with the force of an accusation; and I was moved to remark that as this great mill had brought people to Dowlais something must be done to provide work now that it had failed.

<u>Something must be done</u>* – that wholly innocent phrase, the minimal humanitarian response seized upon by the reporters at my elbow echoed throughout the United Kingdom. The more liberal newspapers took approving note, but Government circles were not pleased. Unemployment having become a political issue, it was argued that the King should have concentrated on the positive side of the Government's attempt at rehabilitation and kept his mouth shut insofar as its failures were concerned. For in saying 'something must be done' he had in effect accused his ministers of not having already done all they might, a criticism that could well encourage the unemployed to increase their demands. The King, in other words, by this definition while remaining outside politics must play the role of 'front man' for his government of the day.

In an already charged atmosphere, Edward's pronouncement was construed by some as a populist rallying cry from a king who seemed on a collision course with the Prime Minister. The most vocal rebuke came in the *Times*, which implied that Edward's words had been a naive intervention that ignored government action, which had already done 'a great deal' to alleviate the hardships of the area through social welfare, and that efforts must be concentrated on relocating the unemployed to areas where 'the distribution of government orders has improved the economic circumstances of those . . . areas which had the greater inherent power of recovery'.[31] It was a remarkable reprimand from the cultural mouthpiece of the class to which Edward belonged. The denunciation demonstrated how far he had become alienated from that milieu because of his views and actions.

---

* Edward's complete statement, according to Philip Ziegler, was 'These steelworks [at Dowlais] brought the men hope. Something must be done to see that they stay here – working.'

Paris, 30 April 1949

Just as in the most cultivated Oriental gatherings, an almost invisible gesture conveys depths of meaning hidden from the untrained eye, so a *Times* editorial by subtle alterations of the ceremonial prose will convey to its habitual British readers meanings of the most subtle character. The foregoing example must be studied with this peculiarity in mind. Besides, Geoffrey Dawson, the editor of *The Times*, was not only close to Baldwin but was also a friend of Cosmo Lang [the Archbishop of Canterbury] . . . From numerous signs, all three were at one concerning me.

Was Mr Dawson afraid that in preparation for the approaching showdown on the marriage question the anti-Baldwin press was attempting to rally to my side the unemployed and the discontented of Britain? In rebuking those who had sought to use the King as a stick with which to beat the Prime Minister, Mr Dawson was really reprimanding me. It was *The Times*'s way of saying that the King was meddling in politics and that he would be well advised to confine his 'well known sympathy' to less restless and contentious subjects.

The trip to South Wales had given Edward a momentary reprieve from his personal drama, but it also served to remind those around him, both his supporters and his detractors, of the personal and potentially polarising charisma he still wielded. During the visit, as his biographer Philip Ziegler noted, he was 'indefatigable, endlessly interested, sympathetic without being mawkish, bringing . . . a ray of hope and the conviction that one person in high places at least cared about their plight'.[32] The situation showed him at his most relaxed and most confident. As he reprised the winning formula he had mastered as Prince of Wales, Britain glimpsed the sovereign they might have had, the 'modern King',[33] 'the self-made monarch',[34] who 'loved to circulate . . . to escape the confinement of the court; to pick up information, hear new viewpoints, see what was going on . . .'[35] It is easy to imagine how successfully Edward's style could have been tailored to meet the needs of a wartime Britain, had he remained on his throne.

But, by his return to London on the evening of 19 November, that future was quickly fading. Though moved by what he had seen, his attention shifted back quickly and permanently to his impending crisis.

Paris, 2 May 1949

Directly upon my return from South Wales, I set about mustering all the support I could in preparation for the coming struggle. Surveying the possible employment of forces from Buckingham Palace, I derived comfort and confidence from the knowledge that, in answer to innumerable radios and shore-to-ship telephone calls, Max Beaverbrook, who had only that morning disembarked in New York from the *Bremen*, sent word from the Waldorf Hotel that he was sailing back to Southampton at midnight in the same ship.

Before his visit to South Wales, Edward had met on 17 November with two Cabinet ministers who, he hoped, might prove sympathetic to his cause.* The first, suggested by Beaverbrook, was Samuel Hoare, who had accompanied him on the recent tour of the Home Fleet, and the second was his and Wallis's friend Duff Cooper, Secretary of State for War.

Hoare was an unlikely choice but, as Beaverbrook explained to Murphy in an interview at Cap d'Ail on 16 July 1949, the First Lord of the Admiralty was 'ambitious to succeed Baldwin . . . You must remember,' Beaverbrook went on, 'that the King has the power for at least one moment to name anybody whom he pleases as Prime Minister . . . Were Baldwin to resign in a clash over policy, Hoare's turn might have come . . . but the risk scared him [Hoare] . . . and the King made the risk all the greater for a potential supporter by his refusal to fight.'[36]

---

* In both Edward's published and unpublished versions he misrememberd the chronology of these meetings, writing that they took place immediately after his return from South Wales.

Beaverbrook's tactics were those of an astute political operative but fell flat with a monarch who was already uneasy about how far to push the boundaries of his office. When Edward met with Hoare he asked only that Hoare might 'speak up in the defense of a King's right to marry'.[37] And though he 'replied in warm, sensitive phrases', Hoare refused to offer any support. 'I then and there,' Edward wrote on 2 May 1949, 'regretfully struck his name off my list.'[38]

Duff Cooper was next. His advice, Edward wrote on 2 May, was 'subtle and practical'. He urged Edward 'to steer away from all risk of an immediate collision with Baldwin. After all, he said, the question of my marrying W could not arise until her divorce became absolute in May, and meanwhile Baldwin could not press me on the constitutional issue. Duff in substance said, "You must be patient. You are to be crowned in May. Say nothing now; let the people get used to you as King. You should then be able to marry on your own terms."'[39] Duff, Edward told Murphy later, 'didn't understand [the] curious position of King in [the] Coronation ceremony; a sanctified person; Head of Church; taking a sacrament.' Edward had, he declared, 'no intention of going through this, then springing on an unsuspecting public a plan to marry a divorced woman.'[40]

Had I followed it [the advice of Duff Cooper], the subsequent course of events might well have been radically altered and I might even still be King and W my Consort. However, although profoundly impressed by Duff's reasoning, I could not bring myself to adopt the course of action that he recommended. For one thing I did not possess the subtlety and patience to play so tricky a game, and not only with Baldwin but with the British people. But what was even more important, the scheme was hopelessly flawed for me for the obvious reason that it would have required my resorting to a subterfuge on a matter affecting the highest and most delicate sentiments of the British people. But this opportunistic approach . . . overlooked the anomaly of my dual function as King: not only was I Head of State, but I was Head of the Established Church of England as well. As Head of State I was technically free to marry whoever I pleased. The British constitution imposed no bar upon the King's choice of Consort other than that she must be a Protestant, and actually Mr Baldwin could have ransacked the legal libraries of Britain in vain for power to stop me. But as Head of the Church I was under restraints which were nonetheless powerful for being unwritten . . .

Few have credited Edward's belief in the sacred nature of the Coronation as the real reason for his unwillingness to pursue Cooper's suggested subterfuge. Instead, it has been interpreted as a suitable excuse for a man now committed to escaping his high office. Yet Edward returned to the point repeatedly with Murphy. Though quick to admit he was not a religious man, he could, as he wrote on 2 May 1949, 'never have brought myself to submit to the Coronation Service with the secret intention of later on marrying under circumstances at variance with the doctrines I would have sworn to uphold'.[41] Raised as he was in the dual religions of royal custom and the Anglican Church, it is hardly surprising that he was unable to rebel against one of its most fundamental rituals. 'I was,' he told Murphy, 'greatly troubled over my position at the Coronation.'[42] But the concealment of his intentions was only part of Edward's conflict. The ceremony would also have entailed him taking, very publicly, the sacrament of Communion – which Wallis, as a divorcee, was not allowed. This hypocrisy, he declared, did not suit. I 'would not wish to take that which my wife [was] denied,' he told Murphy. Believing the Church held 'a rather narrow view of the world', Edward noted with amused but mournful irony that the 'very thing that he [Henry VIII] created in order to divorce wives operated years later to defeat me . . . a travesty of morals'.[43]

Having given up on finding any support among the Cabinet and now also having dismissed Cooper's ideas, Edward turned his attention to an alternative plan: a morganatic marriage with Wallis. Defined by Edward as a union 'between a male member of a royal or a princely house and a woman of not equal birth', it meant that Wallis would not adopt

Edward's rank and her children would not have any rights of succession.[44] Proposed by their friend and the Chairman of the Associated Newspapers, Esmond Harmsworth, it was, Harmsworth argued, 'a way to outflank Baldwin and to allow the King to marry without bringing on a clash with the Government'.[45] Wallis, he thought, could become 'Duchess of Lancaster' – a nod to the dukedom of Lancaster, which had become one of the British monarch's subsidiary titles in 1413.

When Harmsworth raised the idea with Wallis over lunch at Claridge's she was, she told Murphy, 'taken aback. Truth is,' she continued, 'that the King had not then asked me to marry and never did until after the abdication. I was deep in my own private struggle. My husband had let me down. He had done what men do – and I knew he knew I knew it. The only thing I was interested in was getting a divorce, and I did not want it caught up in the silly business of a constitutional crisis . . . The divorce was what I wanted – that took precedence over everything else.'[46] That extraordinary confession indicates the degree to which Edward acted entirely on his own behalf, without consulting the person who would be most affected by his decision.

Paris, 3 May 1949

It is the content of things, not the form, that matters. My first reaction to Harmsworth's plan was one of instant aversion . . . Furthermore, in not standing upon the right of my wife to a Queen's status I would leave an obvious opening for a thrust that if she were ineligible to be Queen, she was manifestly unfit to be the King's wife – and this opportunity I must confess was afterward exploited to the full, by no one more fiercely than the hostile *The Times*. Yet, after considerable thought, I accepted the idea for it must be remembered that at this stage I was in a mood to welcome any reasonable suggestion that offered any hope of resolving my personal dilemma – allow me to marry on the throne. If the constitutional barriers standing in the way could be leveled by my forgoing for W the claims to queenly prerogatives which normally accrued, then a morganatic marriage might indeed prove a practical solution . . . So, when Harmsworth asked if he might submit the morganatic proposal to Baldwin, I gave him my blessing.

'The gambit,' Edward wrote, was 'risky'. For the proposal to succeed it would require the Cabinet's approval and parliamentary legislation. Despite these challenges, Edward instructed Harmsworth to present the plan to Baldwin. Four days later, having heard nothing from the Prime Minister, Edward summoned him to Buckingham Palace. Having given the idea 'careful thought', Baldwin believed it unlikely to succeed either with his ministers or in Parliament. 'It seems to me,' Edward responded to this pronouncement, 'that you are taking a great deal for granted.'[47] He insisted that Baldwin formally present the idea to the Cabinet and the Dominions.

With that, the Prime Minister hurried off, and he was hardly out of the room before I realized that I had sealed my own fate.

It is now clear that this audience was the turning point in the whole affair, for in asking Mr Baldwin to present the case to the Cabinet and the Dominions before my side had been heard, I had played into his hands. Under the Statute of Westminster, the Prime Minister had no authority to approach the Dominions directly in political matters. That prerogative remained the King's. But I had all unwittingly put the imperial pass-key into Baldwin's hands, and once inside the door, he would close it against me. Not I, but he would compose the telegrams to the Dominion Prime Ministers. Would they be compassionate pleas on behalf of the King's right to marry a lady who had been twice divorced and whom he had found was essential not alone to his private peace but to the discharge of the public duties of the Empire he had served in his youth? Not if Mr Baldwin wrote them!

'The misgivings induced by the realization that I might have blundered, at least tactically,' Edward wrote on 4 May 1949, 'were heightened by Max Beaverbrook's dramatic return from America.'[48] Beaverbrook had already proven himself a useful ally in silencing the press, and Edward had implored him to return forthwith to England. He was determined to secure help from someone he believed could be a formidable adviser in any future negotiations with Baldwin.

'You must get one fact straight,' Beaverbrook freely admitted to Murphy. 'I was not drawn into this struggle by a desire to serve the King or to keep the King on his throne. I am not a Royalist. I have never been impressed by kings. I am an avowed republican. I don't believe in the hereditary principles. I was after Baldwin. I seized upon this issue because it promised to be a way to drive Baldwin from office.'[49] Edward was under no illusions about Beaverbrook's intentions. 'Max,' he told Murphy, was 'panting for a battle'. For Beaverbrook, Edward exclaimed, 'To overthrow Baldwin and keep the King – what a victory.'[50]

Over their lunch at the Fort on 26 November 1936, Edward realised 'The Beaver' was horrified that he had given his permission for Baldwin to formally consider the morganatic proposal. 'Max,' Edward wrote, 'perceived at once my constitutional error in seeking the advice of my Dominion Ministers,' which once given, 'I was bound by constitutional usage to accept . . .'[51] Beaverbrook later told Murphy that he had seen the unfair wording of Baldwin's cables. 'Tapping a copy of the memorandum which he had prepared,' Murphy recorded, 'he said: "Here are the exact words." He read, "Do you recommend the King's marriage to Mrs Simpson on one basis or the other, or if the King must marry do you recommend abdication?"'[52] Beaverbrook pressed Edward to take swift and decisive steps.

Paris, 4 May 1949

. . . Max urged upon me four courses of action:

One: Withdraw the plan of the morganatic marriage – the British public and the people of the Dominions would never stand for anything so radical.

Two: Stave off an immediate Cabinet decision until I had been able to determine how the individual Ministers would line up on the question, and until I had had time to sound the sentiments of the Country.

Three: Try to persuade a friendly Minister to present my case to the Cabinet.

Four: Lay my case for the marriage before the British public in a systematic way.

Max was a publicist, and he instantly measured the situation as an exercise in the art of forming and directing public opinion. If what he called the 'King's Case' were to prevail there must be time for an influential spokesman to emerge, for supporters to rally, for sympathy to spread. Meanwhile, he was all for Fabian maneuver and retreat, leaving Mr Baldwin to grapple with a phantom. His parting words were: 'We need time, sympathy, patience – and, above everything, patience.'

All that Max said made excellent sense, but having already taken the one leap into the dark, I hesitated to leave again until a safe lodgment was in sight. And when I did turn to act, it was too late.

On 27 November the Cabinet met to discuss the morganatic proposal. As Baldwin had warned Edward, it was dead on arrival. Only the lone voice of Duff Cooper dissented. Not exactly endorsing the idea, he at least cautioned against any hasty action. Edward did not receive the full minutes of the meeting, but he quickly learned of its outcome. Beaverbrook was probably the source of his information. When Murphy asked Beaverbrook on 16 July 1949 why Edward had not received these minutes, 'the Beaver,' he wrote, 'smiled and said, "You must remember that the Cabinet keeps secrets even from the rest of the government."'[53] Baldwin and certain members of the Cabinet, Beaverbrook told Murphy, were 'determined to get rid of the King. The Duke,' he insisted, 'must stress the point in his book. It is the key to Baldwin's actions and the abdication crisis. Baldwin was against palliation, conciliation or temporizing in any form. He was determined to dethrone the King.' Baldwin's 'enmity', Beaverbrook believed, stemmed from his dislike of 'the King as a person' and the feeling, shared by the Cabinet, that 'the King was lowering the tone of the monarch' and was 'an unworthy occupant of the throne'.[54]

Paris, 6 May 1949

. . . The Prime Minister had evidently finessed with his well-known adroitness the question of the morganatic marriage as a compromise solution. Instead he thrust straight away to the alternatives: the Government must either accept the lady in question as Queen, or if the King persisted in his determination to marry, he should abdicate. And Baldwin even prepared his colleagues for the dire eventuality of His Majesty's going ahead with this plan and refusing to abdicate; if that should happen, his Government would resign. Therefore so far as the British Cabinet was concerned it was to be, for me, a take-it-or-leave-it proposition.

But how was the matter broached to the Dominion Governments? That particular detail even today still remains something of a mystery . . . The coded telegrams went out secretly to the individual Prime Ministers from Mr Baldwin's offices. He never showed them to me, and strange as it now seems in retrospect, I never asked him to do so. After all, the issue would be decided in the 'Old Country'. But from the accumulated information of the intervening years, it seems reasonably certain that Mr Baldwin's messages to the Dominion Governments were couched in much the same terms in which he had presented the case to his Cabinet . . .

That Mr Baldwin should win over his Cabinet came as no surprise. I came to suspect that some of the senior members had been irked by my inclination to take an independent line in certain matters. Were they seizing upon my desire to marry as a long-awaited excuse to come to grips with me? Whatever the reasons that moved them I could not look to them for something in a matter of this kind. What did come as a disappointment was that none of the members spoke up for me. Without exception they fell in line silently behind their leader.* The irony of it all is that the members of the Cabinet are styled 'His Majesty's Ministers' but how tenuous was that claim alongside the call of the party machine.

And behind my Government now ranged against my project was . . . the Archbishop of Canterbury [Cosmo Lang]. Concerning his role in what the Archbishop's biographer described as the 'King's matter', his biographer says, '. . . Lang saw and talked with many of those principally concerned. There was no argument for there was no disagreement . . .' I never saw him yet all the while I had a vague disquieting sense that he was invisibly and noiselessly about.

Curiously enough we were both fighting for a principle: I for the right to marry someone who for me possessed all the womanly qualities essential to my happiness, and he to prevent the marriage because the lady had been involved in divorce. The issue dividing us was intensified by the circumstance that my desire cut across the drive the Church of England under his leadership was making on the rising trend of divorce in British life. Cosmo Lang was acutely conscious that the power of the Established Church was ebbing and, in an effort to restore its prestige, was preparing to use my Coronation as a spectacular background for an intensive campaign of Christian revival.

I was by no means oblivious of the quandary in which I was placing the Archbishop for, were he to acquiesce, the attack on divorce, which was to be the central theme of his program would lose its point. What a strange situation it all really was, and reflecting upon the breach that was opening between us, I often pondered the complete reversal in historical positions of monarch and primate on the question of

---

* Edward later acknowledged that Duff Cooper had expressed some reservation during the meeting.

marriage. The Catholic sway of the Pope over Britain was broken, the Church of England established, and a Protestant Archbishop installed in place of the great Cardinal Wolsey in order that my Tudor ancestor, Henry VIII, might divorce his Spanish Queen. For centuries later this same religious device . . . invented to satisfy Henry VIII's personal whim now wheeled around to block my marriage on the moral argument that the lady of my choice had been divorced.

'Many find any assertion of a religious side to the problem impossible to contemplate,' Monckton wrote, in a private memorandum entitled 'October–December 1936', 'but it was there. The King had the strongest standards which he set himself for right and wrong . . . It was the cant which he saw on all sides which made him out of touch and out of sympathy with the leaders of the churches and other conventional moral advisors.'[55]

Against this backdrop, Edward's attention moved to Wallis. On 27 November a brick was hurled through the window of her rented home at 16 Cumberland Terrace, where she had moved after her separation from Ernest. Already on edge from anonymous death threats, Wallis was shaken and afraid. Edward insisted she and her aunt Bessie Merryman, who was visiting from America, should move permanently to Fort Belvedere, where they could take full advantage of 'the protection at all times thrown around the King's person'.[56] 'Her physical timidity played a more important part than was generally realized,' Beaverbrook told Murphy. 'The misguided wretch [who threw the brick] . . . was probably an even more influential factor than Baldwin in the King's decision to abdicate without a fight. For that act, alien to British character, filled her with fear. It convinced her that the British people were plotting to kill her. And in so doing he found himself taking her side against his own people.'[57]

For Edward, it was a defining moment in the crisis, eliciting a recognition that his world had begun irrevocably to alter.

Paris, 4 May 1949

Today [1949] I circulate on the other side of the royal transonic wall; on my abdication I passed from the sure and sheltered life of a King into the stormy realm of the private citizen. Somewhere along the route of decision I must have reached a point at which I had to make up my mind whether to try to have it both ways – to chance a fight for the right to marry on the Throne or to abandon it all and go forward with W into what, for me, would be 'terra incognita'.

Airmen, I understand, have a term for such a situation, what they call 'the point of no return' – a point in time on arriving at which the pilot, if apprehensive of the conditions ahead, may safely turn back while still possessing enough fuel to return to his starting point, yet which once passed leaves him committed beyond recall to fly on into the uncertain hazards surrounding his original destination. Such a moment, I think, happened to me on the afternoon that I persuaded W to leave Cumberland Terrace . . . For in deciding that it had become too unpleasant for her to remain in London, I had unconsciously made up my mind that the struggle to save my throne was hopeless, and that in the end I would follow her wherever she might go.

6

The Story Breaks

In the late spring of 1949, from his desk at 85 rue de la Faisanderie, Edward paused his writing to muse aloud to Murphy, who was, as ever, listening and recording. 'HRH wonders why no historian has ever attempted to write [a] serious study of details of [the] abdication . . . His mind,' he wrote, 'has [a] habit of going over [the] past. Speculates on what would have been the effect if he had informed Baldwin that since he was free under the law of England to marry whomever he wished, he would abdicate as head of the Church . . .'[1] With Murphy as his almost constant companion, reflections such as these, alongside the history he continued to write, became more frequent and increasingly more intimate.

'That the crisis was upon me was all too evident,' Edward wrote, in a draft dated 9 May 1949. It 'had become the only issue'.[2] On 29 November 1936, two days after Wallis's hasty retreat to Fort Belvedere, Baldwin dispatched Samuel Hoare to see Beaverbrook. It was only a matter of hours, Hoare warned, before the story of Edward's romance broke in British newspapers. When it did, he insisted, it was imperative that both the government and the press unite in opposition to Wallis becoming Queen. 'The argument,' Beaverbrook told Murphy, 'was presented with skill. It was to the effect that such a marriage was manifestly impossible . . . It would . . . destroy the monarchy . . . The King's desire . . . was itself an example of a poor judgement too frequently displayed in the past. If he persisted, abdication was the only solution. And abdication might spare the nation the ordeal of other crises in the future.' Beaverbrook's reply to this 'invitation that he should join them [Baldwin and Hoare] in dethroning the King' was simple. 'Once I had taken the King's shilling,' he asserted, 'I could not be diverted from my course.'[3]

Hoare's visit left Edward in little doubt that 'even if Baldwin had been all indecision and for delay before, he was now all purpose and action'[4] and, as Hoare predicted, the media avalanche began just four days later. On 1 December, the obscure Yorkshire prelate Bishop Blunt 'made the speech that touched off the publicity gunpowder barrel',[5] as Beaverbrook later described it. 'Inspired' was how the press baron characterized Blunt's message to the gathered diocesan conference. 'What did Blunt say?' Beaverbrook exclaimed. 'All he said was that the King almost never went to church. But who did? Of course there was Baldwin. Baldwin not only went to church, he often read the lesson. But who wanted to be Baldwin?'[6]

Paris, 10 May 1949

But for some unaccountable reason this prelate, whom I had never met, was moved to criticize the King by expressing his regret that His Majesty had not shown more positive evidence of his awareness of the need for divine guidance in the discharge of his high office. There was a veiled suggestion of a want of sustained habit in my church-going. To the extent that I did not follow my father's unfailing custom of attending divine service every Sunday morning, Bishop Blunt's criticism was no doubt true. But if he really wanted to impute to the monarch a want of faith, then he overlooked the spiritual enrichment and the private enjoyment that I derived from the choral evensong services at St George's Chapel. There I would quietly occupy my stall as Sovereign of the Order of the Garter whenever the spirit moved me – and it often did. In the light of its consequences, the Bishop's censure of me seems mild indeed; but it was nevertheless *lèse majesté* . . .

For twelve years, it was my unshaken belief that Bishop Blunt's statement had been 'inspired' from Lambeth Palace. The Archbishop's biographer, J. G. Lockhart, on the other hand,

refutes as 'totally untrue' the story that Cosmo Lang had been
privy to the outburst. That being the case, the incident must
be put down, in the British manner, as an extraordinary coincidence – a coincidence in which the converging interest of
the Archbishop and the Prime Minister were simultaneously
served, and Hoare's warning to Max was swiftly fulfilled . . .

Edward had at first refused to believe that Blunt's speech would have
a national effect. 'The London newspapers won't touch this,'[7] he told
his friend Bernard Rickatson-Hatt, the Editor-in-Chief of Reuters, who
went to Buckingham Palace on the evening of 1 December to show
him advance copies of editorials that were set to appear the next day
in the *Bradford Observer* and the *Yorkshire Post*. Rickatson-Hatt, who
had by 1936 become a trusted member of Edward and Wallis's circle,
was a useful source of press insider information. 'What the provincial
press says tonight,' he warned Edward, 'the London press will say
tomorrow.'[8]

Finally convinced that the story would break nationally, Edward
summoned Baldwin 'with the idea,' he wrote, 'of forcing a showdown
. . . The instant the Prime Minister entered my room . . . I realized
from his demeanor that I would not get one.'[9] Baldwin confirmed that
neither his Cabinet nor the Dominions would be willing to support
Wallis as Queen. Three options remained: to give up the marriage, to
marry against the advice of his ministers or to abdicate. Baldwin told
Edward he 'prayed'[10] for the first of these three outcomes. 'The idea,'
Edward wrote, 'of abandoning W was so preposterous that I would
not even dignify his prayer with a rejection.' Baldwin had declared it
would be 'manifestly impossible'[11] to pursue the second option. There
remained, according to the Prime Minister, only one choice: abdication.

Paris, 12 May 1949

. . . In saying [that], I thought to myself, Mr Baldwin was
certainly taking a great deal for granted. If I did insist upon
marrying as King, the only constitutional way I could be

forced off the throne was for him and his cabinet to resign, for me to fail to find someone else to form a new Government and for a general election to return him to power with the mandate from the country. All I did was to shrug my shoulders. Never taking his eyes off me, he went on ponderously to say that if then I would not abandon the project upon which my heart was set there really was nothing left for me but to abdicate.

. . . A few hours later, from The Fort, I had a long telephone conversation with Max. The last vestige of his control of Fleet Street had gone with a whoop. The facts of the virtual ultimatum backed by a unanimous Cabinet, which Mr Baldwin delivered to me, was by now common knowledge, and all the London newspapers were going to press that night with sensational stories. Max still refused to panic. He never stopped counseling patience. And he urged me again and again to allow his two great dailies [the *Daily Express* and the *Evening Standard*] and Esmond Harmsworth's [the *Daily Mail*] and other friendly groups to strike out vigorously on my behalf.

. . . At The Fort, nothing seemed changed. W and I walked out along the flagstone path around the house after dinner. The fog was rolling up from across Virginia Water, and the night was utterly still. Peering out of the battlements in the direction of London, I seemed to feel the atmosphere vibrating as from ultra-frequency soundwaves to the distant den of the Fleet Street presses. In those last hours, before the pent-up fury of the press burst upon us, I saw one thing very clearly. W must leave Great Britain without delay. With a strong sense of responsibility for all that was happening, I was anxious to move her off the path of the main blow. After all, the great decision was mine, and mine alone; this was something which would have to be thrashed out with my own people. And whatever the outcome of this struggle, I did not intend that her right to a divorce should be jeopardized by the fierce struggle over the Throne. I therefore urged her, not to flight, but to a change of residence so as to detach her affairs from mine. However painful the prospect of parting, especially at such a time, she saw the cruel wisdom of my suggestion, though it was obvious to both of us that the move from the protection of The Fort would expose her to many inconveniences.

Paris, 18 May 1949

While we were discussing what was best for her, she had a proposition as to what I should do. It was that I should not abdicate, as I had told Mr Baldwin I was prepared to do, but rather that I remove myself temporarily from the constitutional struggle in Great Britain, with a simple announcement to the British people that I would go abroad and wait quietly for their verdict. This idea also appealed to me; it had the virtue of simplicity. Moreover, my father's Christmas Messages to the British Empire, not to mention Mr Franklin Delano Roosevelt's Fireside Chats to the American people, were spectacular examples of how to reach immense audiences. Although nothing was decided then, I went to sleep that night with the substance of a broadcast slowly taking form in my mind . . .

If the public was to know where I stood, then I must speak out. The idea of the broadcast crystallized almost instantly, and I resolved to make it if the Government would agree. Flinging the offending newspapers on the floor, I started in to write. When the draft had progressed far enough I telephoned to Mr Monckton and Mr Allen to come to The Fort at all speed to help me. Just at that moment W walked in with a newspaper. 'This is the end,' she exclaimed, handing me the paper. I had already seen it: the whole front page surmounted by a sensational headline was given over to a picture of her. She was furious. 'You were quite right when you said last night that I must leave Great Britain; I cannot remain here with all that is going on. I never thought it would be so bad.' I tried to comfort her, but without success. She thought for a few seconds before replying, 'It is not only my divorce that is becoming imperiled or that you are being attacked personally. They are attacking the King.' It was all extremely painful. W said something that she had said many times before: that it was not too late; I could always draw back. 'I always thought you would manage it,' she said. 'Nobody has ever bothered to tell me about these constitutional questions.'

The upshot of this conversation was a decision on her part to follow the harsh counsel I had so reluctantly given, to leave for the Continent before nightfall. But where to go? A hotel was obviously out of the question, for she could expect no peace from the press. 'How about asking the Rogers?' W suggested. They were old and close friends and that charming villa [Lou Viei] above Cannes would be a haven until the whole question was settled. It was no easy decision to make. We knew that the world press would hound her right to the Rogers' doorstep and that a burden would be imposed upon the household. But knowing they would not fail her, a discreet telephone call was put through to Cannes. It was dangerous to say much for I had good reason to believe that The Fort telephone had been tapped . . . The Rogers grasped the nature of our request, and their invitation to W was clear and unreserved.

Rickatson-Hatt, who had provided astute advice on the Blunt publicity just two days before, was called back to Fort Belvedere on 3 December to advise Edward and Wallis further on the media fall-out. 'I am sending to you the most precious thing in the world,'[12] he overheard Edward tell Herman Rogers when he telephoned on the morning of 3 December.

'Please don't worry,' I told W. 'I will take care of all the arrangements for your motor journey to Cannes.' Since she could not travel alone, my first care was to provide a trustworthy and congenial companion for the trip. This delicate responsibility I entrusted to our mutual friend and one of my Lords-in-Waiting, Lord Brownlow . . . They would use W's Buick, driven by my trusted chauffeur, Ladbrook, who had been with me seventeen years . . .

Thus this day of decision hurried on amidst a fever of preparation to the climax of parting . . . Owing to the danger of being recognized and pursued by the press, it would have been unwise to stop for dinner on the way to Newhaven so I had high tea prepared in the dining-room. The warm glow from the fireplace, the shining tea silver, made a perfect setting for the British afternoon rite. But little of the fine food was ever eaten.

Lord Brownlow (Peregrine 'Perry' Cust, 6th Baron Brownlow) was, as Monckton described him to Murphy on 23 October 1949, 'a close friend' of Edward and Wallis, whose 'pleasant' personality and 'adaptable nature' made him an ideal travel companion for the nerve-racking journey ahead. 'The King,' Monckton recalled, 'telephoned . . . and asked him to come out [to Fort Belvedere] ready to leave at once.'[13] Brownlow, without knowing the exact nature of his mission, agreed immediately. When he arrived at Fort Belvedere shortly before 6 p.m. he found the atmosphere, as he told Murphy, 'depressing and desperate in the extreme'. Edward and Wallis were, he remembered, 'on the point of tears throughout'.[14] 'I did my best to reassure her,' Edward wrote on 20 May 1949, 'that she and I would be together before long and that nothing in the world would prevent our being together . . . But,' he continued, 'having felt the forces converging upon the throne, she left hoping that she would see me again, but never expecting that she would . . .'

In preparations that seemed to Brownlow 'almost melodramatic',[15] three cars were deployed for the journey so as to evade the press now encamped outside the gates of Fort Belvedere. The first car, Wallis's own Buick, was dispatched with luggage to the ferry at Newhaven, a second was sent in the direction of London as a decoy, and the third, driven by Edward's chauffeur, Ladbrook, was for Brownlow and Wallis. As they drove the eighty miles to the East Sussex port, Brownlow, who feared the consequences for Edward of Wallis leaving England, urged her to reconsider. 'Let me take you to Belton [his country home in Lincolnshire]. I have my own staff there. They are trustworthy. You could lie low and think and be within easy reach if any important decision has to be taken. If you go to France the King will long for you,' he concluded. 'You will be out of touch . . .'[16] But Wallis refused. Fearful for her safety and horrified by the media explosion, she was adamant that she should get as far away as possible.

'That was a terrible day,' Wallis confided to Murphy, in an undated conversation. 'I was close to the breaking point. I drew back into my shell. That is my way . . . I knew the meaning of trouble. I had learned to discipline myself, never to reveal my true feelings. I had never discussed with Ernest Simpson my troubles with Win Spencer [her first husband]. I never told David [as Edward was known to his family and friends] my troubles with Simpson. And that terrible day I never told David how deeply wounded I was – how desperately anxious I was to escape; to be away from the uproar.'[17] In a later conversation, she declared, 'It was bad enough to be attacked by the British press. I could understand that. But the failure of anyone in my own country to speak up for me hurt deeply. I felt like a woman without a country. It was this that made me decide to leave for Cannes.'[18]

According to Wallis's aunt, Edward was 'a pathetic figure that night – distraught, oblivious of everything but his desire to be with her'.

'She [Aunt Bessie] had the feeling that he [Edward] looked to her for comfort,' Murphy recorded in their February 1950 interview. 'Mrs Merryman said, "But, Sir, you have your mother." "The Queen," [Edward] said almost fiercely. "My mother is the Queen."'[19]

On 3 December 1936, with Wallis en route to Cannes, Edward's attention eventually returned to writing his proposed broadcast.

Paris, 20 May 1949

... As it took shape, with the help of Monckton or Allen's suggestions, the underlying conception became more and more important. My conflict with the Government having become public property, the immediate danger was that if the deadlock persisted, with neither they nor I yielding, the country might become fatally split on the issue of my personal happiness. Short of abdication, which I was desperately anxious to avoid and to which I was not yet committed, there remained but one alternative that promised to save my throne: that I should go before the British people, explain to them the sincerity of my desire, and then announce that I was preparing to leave the country temporarily so that they could make up their minds calmly without the distraction of my presence. Such an act of effacement, it seemed to me, would calm the uproar.

I had it all figured out. I would go to Belgium, just across the Channel, and wait out the judgment there. And with regard to the discharge of my constitutional duties during my absence, it would have been a simple matter to reconstitute the Council of State, composed of my mother and my brothers, which had functioned in the last few hours of my father's life. But of course I fully realized that before I could even make a broadcast, let alone present such a novel idea, the agreement of the Prime Minister and the Cabinet would be necessary. I had, in fact, arranged for an audience with Mr Baldwin at Buckingham Palace for nine o'clock that evening. The probability that they would ever give my project their blessing, on the grounds that I would be appealing to the public over the heads of my Ministers, did not discourage me. I wrote on and finished the speech.

'As a modern man,' Monckton told Murphy, in an undated conversation, 'he [Edward] wanted to broadcast and lay his case before the people.'[20] Despite the constitutional conflict such a speech could precipitate, Edward was determined to speak directly about his feelings to the only group left that he felt might support him: ordinary Britons. With the adulatory headlines of his tour of South Wales still fresh in his mind – the Daily Mail had declared, 'Never has the magic of personal leadership been better shown than by the King's visit'[21] – Edward was resolved to take back control of the narrative through the only means he felt available to him: the radio. Broadcasting his position to the people afforded him the opportunity to communicate in unequivocal terms, uninterrupted by the voices of either government or press. It was a radical concept, one in which the private life of the King would, as the poet and critic Stephen Spender later wrote, be 'a matter of public debate – a debate in which he [Edward] wished to take part himself'.[22]

The Draft Broadcast of King Edward VIII[23]

By ancient custom the King addresses his public utterances to his people. Tonight, as King, I am going to talk to you as my friends, Britishers, wherever they may reside within or outside the Empire.

When I talked to you on St David's Day I told you that I was that same man whom you had known so much better as Prince of Wales. I am still that same man whose motto was 'Ich dien', 'I serve.' That motto has guided all my actions for the Country and the Empire through my life and tonight I have specially in my thoughts the great Dominions beyond the seas where I have always received an open-hearted welcome.

I want to say to all of you that I realize that the newspapers of other countries have given you full cause to speculate about what I am going to do, and here may I express my gratitude to the newspapers of this country for their courtesy and consideration. I have never wanted to hide my intentions from you. Hitherto it has not been possible for me to tell you of them, but now I must.

I could not go on bearing the heavy burdens that constantly rest on me unless I could be strengthened in the task by a happy married life and so I am firmly resolved to marry the woman I love when she is free to marry me.

You know me well enough to understand that I never could have contemplated a marriage of convenience. It has taken me a long time to find the woman I want to make my wife. Without her I have been a very lonely man. With her I should have a home and all the companionship and mutual sympathy and understanding which married life can bring. I know that many of you have had the good fortune to be blessed with such a life and I am sure that in your hearts you would wish the same for me.

Mrs Simpson has had no wish to become Queen and she would assume such status as would be fitting.

Now that I have taken you fully into my confidence, as I have long wanted to, I feel it is best for me to go away for awhile so that you may have time to reflect calmly and quietly but without undue delay on what I have said.

Nothing is nearer to my heart than that I should return but whatever may befall I shall always have a deep affection for my country and for all of you.

Paris, 20 May 1949

With the draft of the broadcast in my briefcase, I took myself to London. Monckton was waiting at the Palace, and I showed him the copy of the finished product of the day's labor. Like myself, he was dubious of the chances of my ever being able to make the broadcast, but he was all for my trying . . .

As soon as Mr Baldwin left, I summoned my two waiting friends [Allen and Monckton]. From Mr Baldwin's attitude it was pretty clear that my Ministers would oppose the project unless pressure was put upon them from outside. Here was work for Max, and he was in the mood to do it. Not wishing to go off half-cocked, I decided also to ask the advice of someone else, my old friend Winston Churchill, whose reverence for the monarchy and knowledge of British constitutional conduct was unequalled. He had been in and out of my life so long that I was confident he would not desert me in my hour of trial. Since they [Beaverbrook and Churchill] were then brothers in politics, united in a common purpose to unhorse Baldwin, it was possible to deal with him and Max simultaneously. So I dispatched Monckton and Allen to Stornoway House [Beaverbrook's London home] with a copy of the broadcast . . .

Churchill and Edward's association was long-standing. 'Winston,' Edward wrote on 18 August 1948, 'flitted in and out of my life,'[24] and was, he declared to Murphy in an undated conversation, 'drawn to me by old affection'.[25] In 1911 Churchill had presided over Edward's debut on the public stage when at Caernarfon Castle he had read out the Letters Patent that invested the seventeen-year-old prince with the title Prince of Wales. Their relationship strengthened in the 1920s with Churchill, assuming the role of a quasi-mentor to Edward, corresponding with him on public affairs and providing guidance on public speaking. Believing as he did in Edward's personal appeal, he viewed his accession optimistically. Just weeks into the new reign he sent Edward a 'gracious and grandiloquent letter',[26] offering his 'faithful service' and hope that Edward's 'name will shine in history as the bravest and best beloved of the sovereigns who have worn the island crown'.[27] The letter was received appreciatively, and Churchill was one of the first politicians invited to dine with him as King. When they met at Blenheim shortly before Edward's speech at the unveiling of the Vimy Ridge Memorial on 26 July 1936, the new King asked Churchill to 'look over the draft of the speech', which, he recalled, 'was the beginning of the new association'.[28] Thus, as tensions heightened later that year, Churchill was a natural ally to whom the beleaguered monarch could turn.

According to Beaverbrook, Baldwin had opposed the idea of 'an alliance' between Edward and Churchill, whom the Prime Minister considered a Tory 'troublemaker'. Even more unnerving for Baldwin was the coupling of Churchill with Beaverbrook – two of his fiercest critics. 'We shared one common ambition,' Beaverbrook declared, of his and Churchill's mutual political interests. 'To cause Mr Baldwin the utmost inconvenience and difficulty . . .'[29] Anything that Baldwin wanted must be wrong.'[30]

Edward was also attuned to Churchill's other, less altruistic, motives. He 'hated Baldwin', Edward declared. Beaverbrook was even more forthright. 'You realize,' he told Murphy, '. . . that Winston now sees everything he says or does, every word and action, in terms of history. You would never get him to admit that in this affair he had an ulterior motive. But he did. We were together in a game to overthrow Baldwin.'[31]

'Churchill and Max,' Edward told Murphy, in an undated conversation, '[were] hammer and anvil . . . Winston the aristocrat . . . Max suspicious, speculative, irreligious. Great love between them. Each strengthens the other. Winston furnishes the high line, Max the cunning, the tactics . . . Winston,' Edward continued, 'sees monarchy as [a] luminous institution. Max, the Canadian view, [as a] useful instrument.'[32]

Paris, 26 May 1949

Mr Churchill and Lord Beaverbrook were attracted to my side by a variety of reasons . . . As aggressive Empire Builders, they were determined to defend another who had tramped the outer marches. But, in addition, they were both political animals, possessing a highly developed instinct for controversial issues. In my personal struggle with Mr Baldwin they saw opening up a brilliant opportunity for the play of their combined strategic genius. To save a hard-pressed friend, rescue a popular king and bring down Mr Baldwin – here was an adventure that not only appealed to their robust natures but promised at the same time to yield a handsome political dividend in the shape of Mr Baldwin's downfall.

Edward did not tell his mother about any of these political manoeuvres when he saw her over dinner that evening, 3 December 1936, at Marlborough House. Having read the morning's headlines about her son's relationship with Wallis, Queen Mary insisted Edward offer, in person, a full and immediate explanation of what had transpired between him and the government. The two had not met since 16 November, and, though they had exchanged a few brief letters, Edward had consciously kept his mother and the rest of his family in the dark over what was happening. Queen Mary was anxious to break the silence. Yet it proved, for both, a disappointing experience.

. . . It was not, of course, that I was avoiding her, but knowing how grieved she was by a situation the human aspects of which she could not comprehend, I had been at pains to spare her the crude details of my negotiations with the Prime Minister.

What seemed to trouble her most that evening was that I had stopped going to see her. 'Why have you not proposed yourself?' she asked. That question was hard to answer at the end of a harrowing day. As simply as I could, I explained to her the reasons for this apparent aloofness. 'I didn't want to bring you into all this. This is something I must handle alone.' As we talked on, I became sensible of the slow descent between us of the Iron Curtain with which my mother almost mechanically shut herself off from the outside world [when] things didn't always go according to plan. I left her, regretting that I could not give her the answer that she expected.

Returning to Buckingham Palace, Edward found Monckton and Allen already waiting for him. Their news was not hopeful. Neither Churchill nor Beaverbrook believed the government would allow the broadcast. Nor were they particularly encouraging of the idea overall. Churchill, Monckton told Edward, believed that it was 'a tactical blunder of the first magnitude', which would leave Baldwin 'in physical possession of the field of battle'. 'This was all,' Edward wrote, 'very discouraging but

I was too exhausted to cope with any more that night . . .'[33] Despite it being after midnight, he was determined to return alone to Fort Belvedere. 'I shall be all right,' he told Monckton.

'The King,' Murphy recorded, after a conversation with Monckton on 23 October 1949, 'was apparently accustomed to returning late. The staff did not wait up for him. Usually a light was left burning over the front door. As the Duke says, "I had a key of my own and let myself in."'[34]

But Monckton was adamant that Edward should not be left on his own. He had arrived at Buckingham Palace that evening with a bag already packed and insisted on accompanying him. As they passed through the gates, a small crowd gathered outside let out a cheer. It was a heartening gesture, Edward wrote, after a day of 'successive shocks, rebuffs and failures'.[35]

'I wanted no demonstration,' Edward told Murphy, in a conversation from 1949. 'Walter said to me, "They're with you," but it was no longer important . . . To have changed the outcome,' he continued, 'would have required different tactics. It was too late for that . . . I suppose [with] Max and Winston to guide me I might have made quite a fight of it. Suppose I had let the news get about that the King would address from B.P. . . . fine balcony there . . . easy to fix a spotlight . . . the lonely figure. And my speech, "I am grateful for this show of sympathy, and mindful of my duty. I shall fight this old ogre." This was the age of the balcony . . . But I did not want to divide [the] country, or to make things hard for my family . . .'[36]

Events were moving swiftly, which Edward himself recognised. 'Yet when looking back the thing that sticks out in my mind is the fantastic acceleration of events and the unbelievable compression of emotions. The whole drama in its public aspects ran its course from haphazard beginning to sudden end in exactly ten days.'[37] His final seven days in Britain were spent in seclusion at Fort Belvedere. 'It was,' Monckton told Murphy, 'a fabulous setting for such a drama.'[38]

7

The King's Party

Paris, 27 May 1949

In withdrawing to The Fort, I detached myself from the normal routine of the Court. I left behind me at the Palace the private secretaries, the equerries, and other officials . . . I had a special reason for excluding all but one of them from this last stage of my struggle. It was not that they lacked competence . . . to deal with any sort of constitutional emergency. But my problem was more than constitutional. And knowing from long association their ingrained prejudice, their courtier's outlook, I doubted that they could give me the reasoned and above all the impartial service that my particular problem demanded.

Indeed, only the day before, a small incident revealed how far they had all become removed in thought from me. In the midst of all my preoccupations, two of the oldest members of my household* who had both served me as Prince of Wales, appeared at The Fort during the forenoon. They had come out of a sincere desire to help me, but I soon realized that what brought them was a mistaken belief that I had not understood all the implications of what I was doing. They were against my going no matter what the cost to me personally, and they had considered it their duty as old friends to tell me what they had evidently decided amongst themselves no one else had presumed to bring up. They pointed out that if I persisted in my present course, it would mean the life of an exile abroad.

---

* In an interview with Murphy on 23 October 1949, Monckton revealed them to have been Tommy Lascelles and Godfrey Thomas.

'And how,' asked one of them, 'will you find happiness and contentment in that?'

'There is one thing I do know,' I said. 'There will be neither happiness nor contentment if I stay here.'

They went away depressed over their failure to move me, yet their manner suggested that they jointly derived satisfaction from having done their best to deflect me from what was to them a tragic choice. Yet on my side, their failure to comprehend what the alternative meant for me was truly disappointing, for with so wide a gulf between us I could not give them my confidence in this one.

What my negotiations with the Government called for were unbiased and highly professional minds. Monckton, who had given up his practice temporarily and was already installed at The Fort, had become my key man, the recognized go-between for Mr Baldwin and myself. But he could not carry the burden single-handed, and at his suggestion I summoned his close friend and my solicitor, A. G. Allen, long familiar with all the aspects of the matter at issue. My senior by several years, a gallant and much decorated officer of the First World War, he had a fine reputation in the City of London as a corporation lawyer. He is a man of few words, has a poker face, and his character is well summed up by a stern remark he once made on an occasion of considerable tension: 'I refuse to be stampeded.' Putting aside his practice, as Monckton had done, he also moved on this day [4 December] into a room at The Fort.

Although, insofar as my private affair was concerned, I had cut myself adrift from the Court, the enmeshed wheels of Palace and Government kept turning remorselessly, heedless of the momentous issue that was monopolizing the waking thoughts of millions. In continuous, undiminished volume, the daily batches of state papers continued to arrive in the red boxes from London. Almost to the last hour there were the usual submissions to be approved, commissions in the armed forces to be signed, dispatches to be read and noted.

To help me in coping with this river of paper, in maintaining close contact with the Palace secretariat and in administrating my estates, and in general to ensure that the daily routine of the King-business did not bog down, I called to The Fort my keeper of the Privy Purse, Major Ulick Alexander. Although of the Court, he was not a courtier in the familiar derogatory sense of that much-abused term. For one thing I had only appointed him to his position in July; he was still outside the pervasive, entangling alliances of Court life; he still had the detached outlook of the businessman. Sir Ulick moved into The Fort . . . to complete the team . . .

'I had made up my mind to go,' Edward told Murphy, in an undated conversation, 'and spiritually I had left. I had made up my mind to do that when I brought W to Belvedere.'[1] Yet despite this assertion, the following two days, 4 and 5 December, were an inflection point in the crisis. Pivoting between a resolve to abdicate and mustering the forces of Beaverbrook and Churchill, Edward watched as the government's resolve tightened against him. On the morning of 4 December, the Cabinet met and formally rejected the idea of Edward's broadcast. Later that afternoon Baldwin appeared in the Commons and addressed the country for the first time about the crisis.

Paris, 15 August 1949

. . . Mr Baldwin struck hard. Until then he had made no public acknowledgement of the conflict between us. No doubt the furor of the idea of the morganatic marriage, the spectacular emergence of Max and Esmond [Harmsworth] as my champions, forced his hand. In any event, he resolved to blast out the 'middle-way' with a single well-aimed blow. With regard to the Government's possible sanction of a morganatic marriage, the Prime Minister now put the House of Commons

– and the nation and Empire – on notice as he had a few days before done with me . . .

There was to be no . . . middle-way . . . If the King married, the Government would resign, the Empire would be riven. Mr Baldwin had declared himself . . .

After addressing Parliament, Baldwin drove to Fort Belvedere formally to deliver the news that Edward would not be allowed to address his people. He brought with him a memorandum prepared by the Home Secretary, Sir John Simon, outlining the reasons for this rejection. Simon was, Edward told Murphy in an undated discussion, a 'dour' statesman – 'Even on a warm day his appearance chilled; made one want to put on a coat.'[2]

'The Sovereign,' Simon wrote, 'can make no public statement on any matter of public interest except on the advice of his Ministers. Whether the medium is the B.B.C. or any other form of address . . . The reason for the above rule is that "The King can do no wrong." Consequently, the King's Ministers must take responsibility for every public act of the King. This is the basis of constitutional monarchy. If the King disregarded it, constitutional monarchy would cease to exist.'[3]

'With as much grace as I could muster,' Edward wrote, on 22 May 1949, 'I once again accepted the inescapable.'[4]

Before departing, Baldwin urged Edward for an immediate decision, 'if possible . . . before he started back to London'.[5] 'The Beaver', Murphy recorded, after their meeting on 16 August 1949, 'insists that the Duke from the beginning was subjected to pressure – the most abominable kind . . .'[6] Edward echoed this sentiment. 'The Times,' he wrote on 15 August 1949, 'rejected with outraged sanctimoniousness the "abominable and malignant insinuations that pressure had been brought to bear upon the King by his Ministers". And to the extent that no active pressure was ever applied the statement is technically true. But pressure of a sort was certainly there – the passive yet implacable grip of a vize [sic], which, having fastened upon its victim, never relaxes.'[7] Even Monckton conceded this point, writing in his unpublished memorandum of the abdication, 'The Cabinet's anxiety was for a speedy decision . . . as early as this [4 December] [the Cabinet] felt that his immediate abdication upon generous terms was desirable.'[8]

'Mentally,' Edward concluded 'there now remained but a last short step down from the throne.'[9]

The arrival of Winston Churchill at Fort Belvedere just minutes after Baldwin's departure at least momentarily halted Edward's eroding confidence. Though 'almost an outcast'[10] in Tory politics in 1936, he was still a powerful symbolic rival to Baldwin's authority. Churchill was also, Edward affirmed to Murphy, 'an ardent monarchist'. Having witnessed the demise of many of the great European dynasties at the end of the First World War, now replaced by dictatorships, Churchill had become a staunch advocate of monarchy as the only effective protection against authoritarian rule, and he was moved by his wish to 'rescue a popular King'.[11] According to observers, Churchill was visibly upset by the plight of a man who in certain respects he considered his protégé. Brownlow, who drove Churchill to the House of Commons after lunching with him and Beaverbrook at Stornoway House on 3 December, told Murphy on 8 December 1949 that 'Churchill was almost in tears' throughout. 'He referred to his many associations with the King. His tremendous promise and opportunity. As he talked, tears welled in his eyes. Hot ashes fell from his cigar in his mouth into the expensive astrakhan collar on his coat. The smoke curled upwards . . . I hated to see the vast collar burned. But Churchill's discourse was so moving that I hadn't the heart to say, "Pardon me, Sir – I think you are on fire!"'[12]

Moments after leaving Brownlow, Churchill stood up in the House of Commons to demand Baldwin's assurance 'that no irrevocable step will be taken before a formal statement has been made to Parliament'.[13] 'Winston hated the idea of any break in the succession,' Beaverbrook told Murphy, on 25 July 1949. 'It looked too much like random picking among the royal litter.'[14]

Paris, 25 May 1949

Now I waited for Mr Winston Churchill with mixed feelings. I was confident that whatever else might result from his audacity, his strength, his unquenchable confidence would rid my mind of the gloom left by the discouraging encounter with Mr Baldwin that afternoon. But I was unable to see how anything positive could result there from. Mr Churchill was announced as I finished dressing. I hurried out to welcome him for I had not seen him since all this had started. His manner was grave and belligerent – grave because of what had come to pass, belligerent because there was no thought in his mind of my giving up.

We were five for dinner [Allen, Monckton and Ulick Alexander were also present]. He told us how he had spoken the night before at a huge rally of veterans at the Albert Hall, and described with pride and pleasure the great roar that had gone up at his mention of the King's name. Mr Churchill must have sensed what was running through my mind, and as the meal progressed he began to argue against the idea of abdication. He had evidently given considerable thought to the constitutional aspects of my difference with Mr Baldwin, for he ranged easily and learnedly over the field of the relations between King and Parliament.

Paris, 15 June 1949

. . . It always takes Winston a little time to warm up. In that respect the workings of his personality follow the principles of an internal combustion engine . . . And as the words rolled out, revealing the foundations of his faith, I saw Winston in a new light, in the full magnitude of his greatness.

When Mr Baldwin had talked to me about the monarchy it had shrunk and diminished, like something viewed through the wrong end of a telescope. Mr Baldwin's monarchy was sheltered, arid, remote. It had to be protected from the vulgar forces of life. But when Winston spoke the institution became infused with living spirit. Max had said: 'Winston understands what moves the hearts of men and women when they look upon Princes and Kings.' Winston is a monarchist in politics and, for that matter, spiritually. Indeed, I have never myself met anyone of royal blood who in his approach to life exemplified in such high degree the ideal of the 'good king'.

Paris, 26 May 1949

In Mr Churchill the flair for the sublime is married to a true sense of the ridiculous. His game was to make Mr Baldwin look foolish, which, given the existing situation, should not have been too difficult. What Mr Churchill apparently had in mind was a regal adaptation of the sit-down strike then disturbingly in vogue in America and France. Suppose I had taken Mr Churchill's advice and left The Fort, only to reappear dramatically at Windsor Castle with the announcement that here in the ancient abode of British monarchs I intended to stay. There seems little doubt that Mr Baldwin would have at once been confronted with a decidedly awkward eviction problem if for no other reason than that I would have been innocent of breaking the law of the realm or of any actual transgression of the British constitution. I would have been guilty only of the human lapse of having, by the Prime Minister's standards, loved unwisely.

Mr Churchill had but little use for Mr Baldwin. In his eyes, the other man represented all the evils of the politician of accommodation hidden behind a mask of hokum and high-mindedness. It was Mr Churchill's thesis that, contrary to the assertion of certain journals, no constitutional issue had as yet arisen between me and my people. This being so, Mr Churchill insisted wrathfully, Mr Baldwin and his Cabinet had no authority to force me to abdicate, the more so as the particular point at issue, my marriage, could not possibly be consummated under British law for another five months. They were hurrying the pace, taking advantage of the agitated state of my mind to maneuver and push me forthwith into abdication before public sentiment had a chance to crystallize behind me as Winston was convinced it would, given time. If any stepping down was to be done, Mr Churchill maintained, let it be done by the Government.

Mr Churchill's bold plan alarmed my closest advisors. They visualized the King becoming a pawn in the fierce play of politics – invested in his castle, Mr Churchill directing the defense from the Tory back benches, and Lord Beaverbrook thundering forth from Fleet Street. Viewed across the span of thirteen years, much that went on around me must now seem strangely quixotic; far removed from the harsh materialism of contemporary politics; from the spectacle of Mr Churchill, now in Mr Baldwin's place as leader of the Tory party, absorbed in the task of writing the history he so largely made. Yet it was all real enough. And months after it was all over, I still felt the strain.

Paris, 16 August 1949

I studied the faces of my advisers [Allen, Monckton and Alexander]. Their countenances individually expressed fascination and alarm. I knew their minds . . . It was not a program they would recommend for their King.

Earlier that day I had informed Max through Walter that I could not see him any more. If I were to begin negotiating with Baldwin on the conditions of abdication I could not in justice continue to deal with his opponents. There could be no riding of two horses. Though the right words stubbornly refused to come, I undertook to tell Winston as much.

'But it's too late, Winston,' I said. 'I am going.'

Winston would not listen. When he set off into the night

it was in the mood of a Field Marshal about to set a great offensive in motion. First, a private letter to the Prime Minister to be read in the Cabinet, warning the Ministers of the grave responsibility which they are assuming in pushing the King into so precipitate a decision. Then simultaneously an appeal to the public, urging the wisdom of delay for further reflection.

'Must give time for the battalions to mass,'[15] Churchill told Edward, as he said goodbye to him that night. Though vague about the form those 'battalions' might take, there was the feeling, as the MP and diarist Chips Channon noted on 3 December, that 'London is dividing into Roundheads and Cavaliers'.[16] 'The King's faction grows,' Channon recorded the following day. 'People process the streets singing "God Save the King", they assemble outside Buckingham Palace, they paraded all night. After the first shock the country is now reacting . . .'[17] The 'King's Party' was the name given to what Edward described to Murphy as a 'tremendous surge of feeling'[18] that sprang up between 4 and 5 December. A term first used in Scottish politics to refer to the group of Scottish aristocrats who in 1567 deposed Mary, Queen of Scots, in favour of her son, the future James I of England, the King's Party in 1936 was symbolised by the sporadic crowds that gathered in London to support Edward.

'It began spontaneously,' Edward told Murphy, in an undated conversation. 'It was an organic thing. It had no organization and no formal leader.' For those in his immediate circle, Edward believed it was 'a sentimental thing . . . They had sworn allegiance to [the] King and now when hard-pressed [they were] determined to live up to it.' Among the ordinary people, Edward believed it was more straightforward, the 'sense of injustice coupled with a sense of suspicion of Baldwin'. They believed that the King 'was being railroaded'.[19] 'The Beaver,' Murphy recorded, after their interview on 16 July 1949, 'is still convinced that had the King been prepared to fight, he might still be King of England.'[20]

Having refused to rally behind Baldwin, Churchill was considered, along with Beaverbrook, a leading member of this phantom-like movement. Many grew suspicious that Churchill might even try to form an alternative government should the Prime Minister be forced to resign in opposition to the marriage.[21] And though Churchill never openly encouraged these suspicions or attempted to rally the crowds amassing in London, he certainly tried to fortify Edward's stamina in a fight for time and sent a stirring battle cry from his London home, 11 Morpeth Mansions. 'News from all fronts,' he began. 'No pistol to be held at the King's head.' Churchill urged Edward to remain calm – heed the advice of Beaverbrook – and take heart from the support of Lord Craigavon, Prime Minister of Northern Ireland, who remained 'deeply moved by loyalty to the King'.[22]

Unexpressed to Edward was Churchill's conviction that, given time, his fascination with Wallis would fade and the crisis, by virtue of delay, would come to a natural and anti-climactic conclusion. Had he contemplated the possibility of Mrs Simpson as Queen of England? Churchill's Principal Private Secretary Jock Colville asked him in 1953. 'He said,' Colville recorded, 'that he certainly had not. He was, however, loyal to the King whom he wrongly believed to be suffering from a temporary passion.'[23] Yet his public championship of Edward and his proximity to the King's Party cast an uncomfortable shadow over his later political career. Basking in the glow of his wartime triumphs, Churchill distanced himself from the combative approach he had assumed on Edward's behalf in 1936 as he crafted his 1948 memoir, *The Gathering Storm*. His brief summation of the crisis was a far cry from his passionate exhortations at the time. Baldwin, he wrote, 'perceived and expressed the profound will of the nation. His deft and skilled handling of the Abdication issue raised him in a fortnight from the depths to the pinnacle.'[24]

'He didn't think that about Baldwin then,' Edward exclaimed to Murphy as he read Churchill's comments 'with a grimace'.[25]

As he tackled the history of the King's Party in 1949, Edward offered a stirring commentary on the divide between Churchill's past and present loyalties.

Paris, 30 May 1949

Because of their prominence and avowed championship of my cause, the two men most closely bracketed in the public mind with this so-called 'King's Party' were Winston Churchill and Max Beaverbrook. Today even they have difficulty in remembering much about it. In the summer of 1948 Mr Churchill was Lord Beaverbrook's guest at the latter's villa on the Cap d'Ail . . . not far from the Duchess of Windsor's and my place on the Cap d'Antibes. One day we were invited over to lunch. Lord Beaverbrook met us at the door and led the way out to the garden where Mr Churchill was painting. Seated before an easel and commanding a fine view of Monte Carlo across the bay, the artist presented an impressive study in purposefulness, the oft photographed ten-gallon hat throwing into shadow a heavy scowl of concentration. All three of us, a few feet away, waited for the assault on the canvas to commence. Now, I thought, at this quiet hour by the edge of the Mediterranean with my two friends in a relaxed mood, was a good time to reminisce. They both knew I was working on my memoirs, and I wanted to compare notes with them, particular with regard to this 'King's Party.'

'Tell me Max,' I began. 'Was there really such a movement?'

Lord Beaverbrook: 'There certainly was.'

Mr Churchill (studying the scene): 'There never was a "King's Party."'

Lord Beaverbrook (with an impish grin): 'Sir, Mr Churchill is guilty of an historical lapse. There was a "King's Party."'

The Duke: 'Was it an important movement? Was it taken seriously?'

Mr Churchill (making furious passes at the canvas): 'The "King's Party" was only a name.'

Paris, 12 August 1949

The Duke: 'Who was its leader?'

Mr Churchill (paint going on at a terrific rate): 'There was no leader.'

Lord Beaverbrook: 'It had a leader, Sir.'

The Duke: 'Who was it?'

Lord Beaverbrook: 'He is right here; this artist fellow with the big hat! Isn't that so Winston?'

Mr Churchill: (silence)

During the last half century Winston and Max have hurled any number of thunderbolts into the British political firmament. They could hardly be expected to keep track of them all. Yet there was no question but that Max in his teasing had flicked a sensitive nerve. The King's Party was a climactic episode in Winston's Tory rebelliousness, a gallant but reckless gesture that brought him into crashing opposition with the party diehards at a time when, almost simultaneously, he was striving to lead the nation to higher ground on the issue of war against totalitarianism. Yet in thus repudiating the movement that vainly sought to attach itself to his sturdy and invincible frame Winston is supported by historical evidence. In the usual sense of the term the King's Party had no existence. It was not an organization, but only an idea in men's heads. Yet ideas are also real, as Winston understood better than most men. And for an incredible hour or two this idea threatened to shake an empire to its foundations.

. . . Viewed across the span of thirteen years, much of what went on around me then now seems improbable and even quixotic. Fort Belvedere, which I loved so much, now stands deserted and decaying among its lovely woods, which, untended, have once again begun to thrust a devouring undergrowth among the mossy battlements. With undiminished vigor, Max still hurls thunderbolts into the sky, exhorting his countrymen to defend the Empire which in spite of all that

Max can do steadily shrinks away. And in Baldwin's place as head of the Tory Party now stands Winston, the soul of orthodoxy, yet still the eloquent champion of the right of men, including Kings, to compose their lives according to law and reason.

One of the most striking phenomena of the whole affair in the absence of any action . . . was the violent ebb and flow and ebb again of public opinion in my favor.

This was a subject in which Max's genius and Winston's found sure exercise. And when in the second stage of the crisis Max, in concert with Harmsworth, struck out in support of me, they were not firing wildly in the dark. It had taken a little while for all the facts at issue to sink into the public ken. Then sentiment formed and flashed through the country as Mr Churchill thought it might. Letters poured into the editors . . . A far higher proportion than was expected bespoke understanding and sympathy for their King. And reporters sent into public places to listen to what people were saying returned with the information that wherever the question was discussed . . . the King never lacked champions.

. . . However something else appears to have been at work – a side of British character which Mr Baldwin may have temporarily overlooked, that saving capacity for second thought combined with a deep-seated sense of fair play that can be counted upon to restrain the British people from the partisan excesses that tear more volatile people to pieces.

Paris, 27 May 1949

Whatever the origin of this broad upsurge, there it was. It lit up the sombre background of the constitutional crisis like a display of fireworks . . . It hung only for a moment in the sky before it went out. Yet in that moment, its flashing transit impressed and startled not a few – among them Mr Baldwin. This was 'The King's Party.'

The 'King's Party,' even today, is something of a mystery. Presumably it was composed of those who opposed a change in the succession; who, though they may have viewed the prospect of my marriage with varying emotions, nevertheless stood firm upon the right of the British monarch to compose his private life in accordance with the more modern standards enjoyed by his subjects . . .

So for one fleeting interval, at least, times were breast-high for me. By the Saturday [5 December], many elements essential to the formation of a considerable popular movement . . . had evolved, though still in inchoate form. Winston and Max were stimulated by its latent power. They longed for the shock of battle.

Paris, 12 August 1949

Yet the truth is that the King's Party was a party in a vacuum. Even as it strained for an impossible climax the only possible justification for its existence – the abstract question of the King's right to marry . . . had ceased to exist. On Saturday I began to negotiate with Mr Baldwin the terms of abdication.

My decision to do this was reached alone at The Fort on Friday [4 December] night, during the hours between Winston's departure and the dawn. The considerations that moved me were complex and perhaps not all of a piece. It may be that at bottom I really had little relish for a fight. No doubt there are circumstances upon which a constitutional monarch in modern society might go down among his people as the protagonist of a broad controversial issue, but I could not bring myself to believe that a matter affecting only my personal happiness was properly one. From the outset my conduct had been governed by a single thought. If the verdict of my Government went against me, I would close my reign with dignity, clear the succession for my brother with the least possible disaccommodation, and avoid all forms of faction.

The Cabinet remaining firm in its opposition to the marriage, I now prepared with heavy heart to inform the Prime Minister that I would step down from the throne . . .

'It is no use. I must go,'[26] Edward muttered repeatedly, as he and Monckton sat up into the early hours of Saturday [5 December] morning at Fort Belvedere. According to his adviser, as 'the sentiment in the country turned more and more hostile his determination to go through with the abdication became absolute. He decided to marry at any cost. At the same time, he had an innate sense of loyalty to the people. In so doing he threw down the advice and counsel, not only of Churchill, but also Beaverbrook.'[27] Beaverbrook, in contrast, remained convinced, as he told Murphy on 14 July 1949, that 'had the King been courageous and resolute and willing to take risks, his marriage . . . could have been carried off . . .'[28] 'With boldness and courage,' Beaverbrook continued, 'everything favored the King. He had fighting for him the two most powerful newspapers [the *Daily Express* and the *Daily Mail*]. But he had no fighting spirit. He was afraid . . . The campaign collapsed because . . . the King's men soon discovered that the King would not allow them to go into battle . . . When the hope of a crusade loses faith, will weakens, plans turn foolish and frivolous . . .'[29]

Edward's refusal to rally the supporters that Beaverbrook might have gathered was not, as is often assumed, out of his lack of desire to remain king. Rather, it was the only possible decision that he, as a constitutional monarch, could make. To have acted against the advice of the Prime Minister would have plunged the country into chaos as King and government clashed openly on a constitutional issue. That, he knew, would have created a true crisis. 'I did not want to hurt the monarchy,' he said to Murphy, on an undated occasion. 'I might,' he continued, 'have made a fight of it . . . but that would have wrecked [the] monarchy.'[30] He told his companion in a separate discussion, 'To have changed the outcome would have required different tactics, a whole new program, something called a campaign . . . But I did not want to divide the country, or to make things hard for my family.'[31] In the act of abdicating, Edward believed he had demonstrated to both country and Cabinet that he was unwilling to jeopardise the foundations of British constitutional monarchy in the pursuit of personal desire. Framed in these terms, his sacrifice was a last heroic act of royal duty. But in holding on to the idea of the King's Party in exile, Edward retained a belief in his popularity with ordinary Britons.

As he grappled with these dilemmas Edward's mental state became increasingly frayed. 'In the last weeks,' Monckton told Murphy, 'he came to the end of his natural resources. He was like a rat in a trap. His nervous system was strained to the breaking point.'[32]

On Saturday, 5 December, after a two-day drive through France, Wallis finally arrived in Cannes. She had had only sporadic hard-to-hear telephone conversations with Edward during the intervening two days. Settled at Lou Viei, their communication did not improve either technically or emotionally. 'Over and over,' Wallis told Murphy, in an undated conversation, 'I said to the King, "You must not abdicate. You must never abdicate. You must see somebody. You must get advice."'[33]

'It was a very bad line,'[34] Monckton recalled. 'There was much shouting and confusion but the outcome was that the Duke utterly refused either to give up the project or to acquiesce in her doing so . . .'

On 7 December Wallis issued a statement of her own, offering to 'withdraw forthwith'. This only got Edward's assent,' Monckton asserted, 'in order to protect her from criticism and not because he had the slightest intention of letting her go.'[35] Churchill was also left unaware that his counsel had fallen on deaf ears. In the hope of buying time and rallying public opinion, he released a lengthy statement to the nations' newspapers pleading for 'time and patience' in resolving the stand-off, concluding that if 'an abdication were to be hastily extorted, the outrage committed would cast its shadow forward across many chapters of the history of the British Empire'.[36] Regardless of either's opinions to the contrary, the 'mechanics of abdication'[37] began to take shape.

On the morning of Saturday, 5 December, Monckton informed Baldwin, whom he met at 10 Downing Street, of Edward's determination to go. Later that afternoon, with Edward's approval, he advanced to Baldwin the idea that Parliament should introduce two bills: the first to formalise Edward's abdication and the second to make Wallis's divorce absolute with immediate effect, staving off any potential action by the King's Proctor. That 'most elusive and awkward ghost',[38] as Murphy described him, was in fact an office held by the prominent solicitor Sir Thomas Barnes. Invested by Parliament in 1860 with the power to apply greater scrutiny to English divorce practice, the King's Proctor had the authority to nullify a divorce proceeding on the grounds of either collusion or any other illegality that was discovered before the granting of a decree absolute. A British monarch could not be the subject of civil or criminal proceedings but, once Edward ceased to be King, he would be vulnerable to court action like any other subject. While Ernest Simpson had obliged Wallis with evidence of his own extramarital affair, the exposure of her relationship with Edward had the potential to raise questions about the validity of her original petition as the wronged party. 'The truth is,' Edward wrote, on 15 August 1949, 'in the torment of decision I had given no thought to the future beyond the fact that I should one day marry W. All that lay between was unknown and vague and forbidding. I embraced Walter's idea gratefully – it was a lifeline thrown across dangerous seas.'[39]

Monckton, Murphy recorded after their meeting on 23 October 1949, 'became obsessed by the thought that the King in the end would lose everything – "No Throne, no wife."' He, Murphy continued, 'says there were two grounds under which a Decree Nisi might fail to become a Decree Absolute. First, if collusion were proved and second, if the petitioner was himself or herself proved guilty of misconduct. There was,' in Wallis's case, 'a strong possibility of a challenge on both grounds.' Moreover, 'Once the King ceased to be the King he was no longer master of the King's Proctor.'[40]

Monckton arranged for Baldwin to call at Fort Belvedere that afternoon.

'He [Baldwin] and the King,' according to the description Monckton gave to Murphy, 'entered the drawing room. The door closed. A moment later Monckton knocked on the door, and he entered, saying, "May I have leave to speak, Sir?" And then he presented the matter which both knew so well.'[41] Baldwin agreed to sponsor the Bill for Wallis's divorce in a Cabinet meeting the following day.

Paris, 27 May 1949

He [Baldwin] had evidently weighed the pros and cons of the proposal quite carefully, and after predicting that some of the more formal religious element might oppose yoking a special divorce Bill to the Instrument of Abdication, never-theless he was confident that the Cabinet would agree. And in an unexpected outburst of generosity, he made so bold as to state that he would stake his political career upon securing for W and myself this one concession, and in the unlikely event his colleagues should take the narrow view and turn down that which in simple humanity belonged to us both, he would resign as Prime Minister of Great Britain.

I never knew what caused the cautious Mr Baldwin to make this rash promise. Perhaps he was carried away by the intoxicating realization of the magnitude of the tremendous historic coup which he had brought to pass. After all, had he not unseated a new King, and would not that brilliant act lift his career from mediocrity to splendor? A man who had won so much on a single throw could afford some such sacrificing gesture . . .

However as matters turned out, Baldwin proved to be also a prisoner of his own case against the King. Not only did he fail to win over his colleagues at a Sunday [6 December] Cabinet meeting; he also found compelling reasons for not resigning. And Walter Monckton [who had travelled to London and waited at 10 Downing Street while the Cabinet met] was an uncomfortable witness of his defeat – a defeat which Baldwin had accepted with a show of philosophical forbearance exceeding any of which had hitherto been displayed . . .

Meditating upon the one-sided results of my struggle with Mr Baldwin, I came to realize as never before how lonely and powerless is a monarch alongside a shrewd Prime Minister armed with all the apparatus of a modern state. And the irony that pervaded our relationship was all the sharper for the reason that the terms of mastery continued to be conveyed in the elegant idiom of an outmoded fealty: '. . . with my Humble Duty . . . In accordance with Your Majesty's command . . .'

A cheer went up for the King's car as Walter drove away from No.10 . . . Several ministers who followed were booed. These appear to have provided the last audible demonstration of the 'King's Party' . . . An autopsy might have revealed certain contusions and bruises not entirely consistent with a wholly natural death. Over this last weekend of my reign the party machine went to work. The Government whips and, I suspect, the whips of the opposition parties as well, instructed the Members . . . to repair each to his own constituency, ostensibly to poll their electors and assess public opinion. But in many places the poll was something less than neutral. Party agents were active in the public houses of every city and village of the kingdom, primed to argue down any voice raised in my defense and to maintain that Mr Baldwin must be supported.

Paris, 30 May 1949

Only Mr Churchill refused to give up. Having from the outset pitched his argument on the thesis that the Government had no authority to force the King to abdicate without consulting Parliament, he went forward with his plan to attack it on the floor of the House of Commons on the following Monday

[7 December]. Lord Beaverbrook, however, had seen the hand-writing on the wall, for during this weekend at a meeting in Mr Churchill's house, he had broken sorrowfully with his old friend after a clash of views on the question of challenging Mr Baldwin. Lord Beaverbrook explained it to me afterwards: 'Churchill was prepared to stand up against the executive. In a quarrel with the Government, he was bound to be beaten. And even if he won, the victory would be useless. So I left Churchill's house without coming into conflict with him, but making it plain that we were taking different paths . . .'

All this notwithstanding, Mr Churchill strode into the House of Commons . . . to launch his assault on the Government. But hardly had he arisen to put a supplementary question than the hostility smote him like a great wave and stunned him momentarily. The memorable scene of Mr Churchill being howled down by his own party has often been described, but out of sight it had a sequel quite as poignant, which he once described to me. Shaken and dismayed, he made his way out of the House and took the elevator to his office in the Parliament Building. The attendant, whom he had known for many years, closed the gate and pressed the button. As they began to ascend, the old man, oblivious of what on the floor had just happened, contemplating Mr Churchill's bowed head, was momentarily moved to commiserate.

'Oh, sir. I do feel so sorry for poor Mr Baldwin.'

That hapless remark roused Mr Churchill from his despondency and, as he put it, 'I was almost at the man's throat.'

And so that was a bad day for Mr Churchill; possibly one of the worst of his life. I have always regretted it . . .

'Walter said that the last days at The Fort were indescribable. They verged on madness,' Murphy recorded, after a conversation with Monckton that took place in early July 1949. 'People were rushing in and out. Motorcycle couriers would drive up with dispatch boxes from London. The telephone off the octagonal room never stopped ringing.

Pick it up and you would find yourself talking perhaps to Downing Street or Beaverbrook or Churchill or Alec Hardinge at Buckingham Palace.'[42]

'While all was still seething around me, a calm now descended upon my spirit,' Edward wrote on 31 May 1949. 'I had made my decision. There was nothing more to be said between Mr Baldwin and myself. There remained only the mechanical formalities of abdication . . . and – as the French so charmingly put it – *faire mes adieux*.'[43] Despite failing to secure passage of the Bill that 'would have given security to my intended wife',[44] Edward was determined to abdicate before further political division could arise. He believed the Crown was 'a symbol of British life', as he told Murphy, in a later undated conversation. His was, Edward reflected, a 'conflict between two ways of life; and while I was sure mine was not dangerous to [the] other, [I was] prepared to give way'.[45]

As Edward readied for his departure, attention shifted towards Wallis, who remained cloistered inside Lou Viei and under siege from the encamped press. On Monday, 7 December, Baldwin summoned her divorce lawyer Theodore Goddard to 10 Downing Street. Goddard found Baldwin 'irresolute and uncertain', he told Murphy on 8 December 1949. 'He [Baldwin] looked exhausted, complained of fatigue . . .'[46] but insisted that Goddard depart immediately for Cannes to try to persuade Wallis to abandon her petition. Monckton, as he told Murphy on 23 October 1949, believed Goddard was 'a friend of the King's', and he agreed to Baldwin's suggestion because he 'wished the King to remain on the throne. And, having perceived there was no possibility of persuading the King to give up Mrs Simpson, he had therefore undertaken to persuade Mrs Simpson to give up the King . . .'[47] Edward feared that he would find fertile ground for Baldwin's suggestion. Brownlow, Edward also believed, had from the 'moment he took his seat beside W in the motor' been 'subtly and persistently' working to convince her to abandon him.[48] Brownlow denied there had been a conspiracy between him and Beaverbrook to prevent the marriage, something Edward later came to believe, but did admit to having done everything possible, as he told Murphy on 8 December 1949, to stress to Wallis 'the historical consequences of her action. "If you marry the King," he told her, "you will be the most hated woman in British history. You are laying up a dreadful future for yourself." She,' Brownlow remembered, '. . . was herself close to hysteria.'[49]

'The common end,' Edward wrote on 31 May 1949, 'was to keep me on the throne by persuading W that the protection of the monarchy as the binder of the British Commonwealth . . . demanded from her a great act of renunciation which would make the marriage impossible.'[50] Discussing the 'plot' with Murphy, on 13 May 1949, 'The Duke,' Murphy recorded, 'said, shaking his head emphatically, "They must have been mad!"'[51]

Paris, 31 May 1949

In his first conversation with Mr Monckton and Mr Allen, when he was pressing to be allowed to plead the King's case, Lord Beaverbrook kept on asking, 'But will our man fight?' What he really, and not unnaturally demanded before committing himself to a knock-down drag-out fight with Mr Baldwin, was an assurance that I would not desert him. But for reasons which must by now be clear, such an assurance was impossible to give. Max on his side realized why this was so – why I shied away from all his stratagems. He struck out on his own in a manner which, however well meant, all but supplied for me the last straw on the camel's back. For his game, as he afterwards explained, was to slip past me with the secret object of inducing W to settle the issue for all concerned by declining to go on with the prospect of the marriage.

. . . I provided him with an accomplice . . . when I delegated to Lord Brownlow the delicate mission of escorting W to Cannes. He and Lord Beaverbrook had long been intimate friends, and it transpired that he arrived at The Fort to fetch W primed with the instructions which Lord Beaverbrook had drummed into him the night before at Stornoway House.

While Brownlow and Beaverbrook had thus far been unsuccessful in persuading Wallis to take any irrevocable steps to halt the crisis, she was still, according to Brownlow, 'willing to do anything to prevent the King from abdicating'.[52] Goddard's sudden arrival in Cannes in the early hours of 9 December forced Edward to confront Wallis directly and the power she still held over their future together.

Paris, 9 June 1949

W's answer was that in any case she would have to see him [Goddard], but she would do nothing without telling me. The conversation was inconclusive and disquieting, and left me wondering what was really on her mind. Now, when I reflect upon her position, I realize that in some ways she bore the heavier load. Once away from me and the shelter of my position as King, she turned unsure and even terrified by the violent passions which we had all unknowingly aroused and to which she had become more vulnerable. What really alarmed her was the growing conviction that it would be wrong for me to abdicate in order to marry her; for in so doing I would bear a heavy responsibility in history. Because of this, she had come to fear for me and the abstract thing that I was. How, then, could we any longer expect happiness from marriage? Far away in Cannes, in a manner of which the tense watching world remained oblivious, W was thinking hard, and next day when lawyer Goddard arrived on the scene to add the power of his arguments to those of Lord Brownlow, she was in a mood not only to listen to them but to cooperate with them in compounding a drastic remedy.

'Don't be influenced by anything he says,' Edward demanded of Wallis. 'There is no turning back for either of us now.'[53]

8

Abdication

Edward's anxiety about Wallis was momentarily overshadowed by the unexpected arrival of his brother, the Duke of Kent, at Fort Belvedere on the afternoon of 8 December 1936. Throughout the ordeal, Edward had maintained a 'self-imposed isolation'[1] from his siblings and refused their requests to either see or speak to him. Only after his decision to abdicate was made did he agree to meet his successor, the Duke of York, on the evening of 7 December. The future George VI had returned to Fort Belvedere the following afternoon [8 December] for a 'preliminary talk' about Edward's financial future when the Duke of Kent suddenly appeared. The eleventh-hour arrival of his favourite brother provided Edward with little comfort. 'The end came under sad and melancholy circumstance,' Monckton told Murphy. 'His brothers gave him no strength, least of all George who had particular reason* to be grateful to him. George thought he was mad.'[2]

Sir Edward Peacock, Edward's long-time financial adviser, was also at Fort Belvedere on 8 December, having assumed the role of chief negotiator in the discussions now taking place. As his father's sole heir, Edward had inherited the private estates of Sandringham and Balmoral. Their future, along with that of the vast hoard of royal treasures that were also his, was still to be determined.

Baldwin's unexpected arrival on the same evening halted these negotiations. 'I have nothing more to say to Mr Baldwin,' Edward told Allen, when informed that the Prime Minister 'wanted to pay me a last visit . . .'[3] For the final time, Edward's attention shifted back to the politics of the abdication.

---

* Edward had helped Prince George recover from a tempestuous affair with the American socialite Kiki Preston, who had, according to rumour, introduced the prince to drugs.

Paris, 10 June 1949

Mr Baldwin reached The Fort at five thirty, accompanied again by [Baldwin's Parliamentary Private Secretary] Captain Dugdale. As I went forward to greet them in the hall, I noted the latter in the act of depositing near the door what was unmistakably a suitcase.

'Good God!' I swore softly to myself. 'Surely that old "turnip" doesn't intend to stop the night?'

As fast as I could, I ushered him into the living room. Then on some excuse I left him with my brother George and closed the door. Peacock was outside.

'Like hell, he will sleep here,'[4] Edward exclaimed, when Peacock informed him that Baldwin had come prepared to stay the night. Peacock was tasked to prevent such an outcome – a duty he quickly discharged.

Paris, 14 June 1949

I rejoined the Prime Minister in the living room, and he had as usual made himself comfortable in the same armchair to which habit now propelled him. Puffing away at his old pipe, he never looked more convincingly the part of the apple-raising Squire of Bewdley in Worcestershire. He heaved himself to his feet as I entered and, bidding him again be seated, I asked him point-blank: what was his motive in sending the lawyer Goddard to Cannes? He answered easily, 'Sir, it was the same motive that has brought me here tonight – a desire shared by all your people to keep you with us as our King.'

Telling him that while the motive was high, the means were deplorable, insofar as they involved the British Government in an effort to destroy the one thing I wanted more than anything else in the world – my marriage. He sat unmoved as I went on to say that he was wasting his time if he thought such stratagems could deflect me from my purpose now.

'I take it, Sir, that you are telling me that you are now prepared to abdicate?'

'That is so, Mr Prime Minister,' I answered.

'I shall convey this your formal intimation to the Cabinet when it meets tomorrow morning. But until you make a formal declaration in writing, the door will still be open.'

'You will have that tomorrow,' I assured him.

Then I took up another question. Since Mr Baldwin had opposed my presenting my case to my people as King, I now claimed the right, following my abdication, to say farewell to them over the radio upon leaving the country.

'As a private citizen, Sir?'

'As the subject of my brother,' I answered.

'I shall so advise the Cabinet.'

Paris, 15 June 1949

As dinner time drew near, Mr Monckton tried to dissuade me from joining the party. 'You have had the devil of a day,' he said. 'Why don't you have your dinner sent to your room? Your brothers and the rest of us will take care of S.B.'

But with the Prime Minister as a guest, the rules of hospitality demanded the presence of the King at his own table. So, after changing, I led the company into the dining room . . . Exactly what we talked about, I have no memory whatever. No doubt we ranged over the usual masculine fields – politics, sport and the great topic of the day, President Roosevelt's New Deal. But one thing I do remember is that the one subject we never even approached was the one that in its myriad workings had brought us all together that evening . . .

Though the crisis had another three days to run, the dinner was its denouement. Emerging briefly from the exhaustion and emotional strain of the last weeks, Edward delivered a captivating performance before his assembled guests. It was, Allen remembered, a 'tour de force'.[5] 'The whole conversation was led by the King – politics, personalities, trips,' he told Murphy. 'There was no mention of the abdication.'

'Isn't he wonderful?' the soon-to-be George VI whispered to Peacock. 'I could never do that . . . I can never do this job of King.'[6]

As Edward and Baldwin parted for the final time that evening, the Prime Minister was heard to say, 'There are no two people in the country who have shared your anxiety of the last few weeks to a greater extent, nor wish for your future happiness more than the missus and myself.' Though he made no mention of it in his writings, the statement appears to have moved Edward, who remarked the next day, 'The Prime Minister is the only man who has said any kind word to me about the future and wished me good luck.'[7] 'I have never seen, Sir,' Allen boldly asserted to Edward, in a conversation on 13 May 1949, 'any justification that Baldwin wanted you to abdicate. He wanted you to stay.'[8] Monckton supported Allen and told Murphy, on 23 October 1949, 'He [Baldwin] was sure that in the end when aroused to the consequences of his action the King would give the woman up.' The Duke (who was listening in), 'nodded his head sagely', noted Murphy. 'Have no doubt,' Monckton continued, 'having been married so long to Lucy [Baldwin] he no doubt could not imagine any other course.'[9]

Despite the dissent, Edward remained resolutely unconvinced that Baldwin had done anything but help manoeuvre him off his throne. In an undated note in his own hand, Edward wrote of Baldwin's role in the crisis as having been not 'so much that of a Prime Minister trying to help his Sovereign thru a personal situation of almost indescribable complexity but that of a political Procrustes determined to fit his royal victim into the iron bed of rigid convention'.[10] It is perhaps an indication of how blurred Edward's emotional landscape became that his former Prime Minister was eventually transformed into the drama's arch-villain.

Having finally dispensed with Baldwin, Edward's attention shifted back to Cannes and to the 'scheme' that he dubbed 'almost Machiavellian

. . . manipulated out of my sight', which tested, he wrote, 'the last remnants of my patience . . .'[11]

Paris, 11 June 1949

The first crashing revelation of the progress of the plot was supplied by W. She informed me that Mr Goddard had telephoned at 2 a.m., when she had arranged that he should call upon her at Lou Viei immediately after breakfast. In fact, he [Goddard] was even then in the room as she was speaking. She went on to say that Mr Goddard was urging her in the strongest terms to withdraw her divorce petition. Allen was at my elbow, and when I told him the line Mr Goddard was taking, his legal mind reacted at once.

'Tell Mrs Simpson,' he said, 'that to do that would be tantamount to an admission of guilt.' This advice I impressed upon her, but I had a sinking feeling that my words were unheeded.

Thus began a hellish day [9 December]. As it wore on, the telephone conversations between The Fort and the Villa became more and more intense and alarming. For eventually Mr Goddard persuaded W that, come what may and whatever the means, the abdication of the King had to be prevented. If the King would not renounce the marriage, then she herself must perform the act of renunciation by withdrawing the divorce action and confronting the King with an impassable barrier. With Mr Goddard goading her on and Lord Brownlow prompting from the wings, W did everything in her power to make me give her up. And yielding to their pressure she finally telephoned me at mid-day that she had instructed her lawyer to destroy the material evidence upon which the divorce petition had been based. If by reason of this act she was forever barred from marrying again, what would it profit me to give [up] my throne? And thus, even as all the exits of my kingly life were closing one by one, I found myself confronted by a void – a void made almost unbridgeable by the bad telephone connections which were our only means of trying to make each other understand.

. . . I was frantic. Speaking very slowly, enunciating every word, I told W that I had already informed the Prime Minister of my intention to abdicate and that the machinery for changing the succession was already in motion. She could stop the divorce if that was what she needs must do, and she could leave France and go wherever she wanted . . . but wherever she went I would follow her. That was in essence what I said. Lest there should have been any misunderstanding, I repeated this to Mr Goddard. It was enough to convince him that nothing would move me. Conceding defeat, Mr Goddard retired at once from the stage upon which he had played so fleeting if portentous a role.

'Only afterwards,' Edward told Murphy, in an undated conversation, 'did I realise what a difficult position she was in. Nobody ever explained . . . to her, constitutional questions.' He also acknowledged that in many ways he had been to blame for her ignorance. 'Beaverbrook makes the point,' he continued, 'that he could never reach Mrs Simpson. Curious how important that fact looms now. Fact was that I had given orders – I shall deal with Mrs Simpson. And because I was King my orders were obeyed. Nobody,' he noted, 'went near her . . . Queen Mother, Cabinet, family. I saw to that. Knew my own people . . . They would have made her see the impossibility of her position . . . It would have ceased to be a matter between a man and a woman.'[12] Even Monckton believed that had Queen Mary spoken to Wallis 'the entire crisis might have been avoided, for she of all women had the power and love to make this other woman understand what was involved . . .'[13] Cocooned from reality, the outcome, when it finally came, was a profound and unexpected blow to Wallis. Edward, she confided to Murphy, in an undated conversation, 'did not disclose to me his plans. He never told me that he intended to abdicate. The word abdication was never mentioned.'[14]

'But I don't know what you're talking about. You've never asked me to marry you,'[15] Herman Rogers overheard her tell Edward, during one of their endless telephone conversations. Wallis's agonised pleas against abdication fell on deaf ears and she, like everyone else, had only one choice: to accept the inevitable.

At 11 a.m. on 9 December the Cabinet met and was formally told of Edward's decision to renounce the throne. Later that day he went to see Queen Mary at Royal Lodge, the Duke of York's home in Windsor, to inform her of all that had passed since they had last seen each other on 3 December. 'If she had come to Windsor with the idea of adding her voice to the many which that day had assailed me, then she must have decided, after hearing me . . . that particular aspect of her errand was hopeless.'[16]

There remained only the signing of the Instrument of Abdication, which was printed in the early hours of the next day. Eight copies were delivered to Fort Belvedere at 9.30 a.m. on the morning of 10 December. In the presence of his brothers, Edward signed all of them: one for Parliament, one for the Royal Archives, one for each of the five Dominions and one for India. The informal ceremony was brief, and at 10.30 a.m. Monckton departed Fort Belvedere for Buckingham Palace so he could deliver the signed documents to the King's Private Secretary, Alec Hardinge, who remained Edward's official liaison to the government. Having been expunged from the drama in mid-November, Hardinge emerged again at the very end of a crisis that he had helped spark. Politically, all that remained was for Baldwin to deliver his final report to Parliament.

All that remained for Edward was to finish writing his broadcast to the country and closing the financial negotiations with his family. Edward was purposefully vague about the details of the agreement. He wrote only that after the signing ceremony, he, Peacock and his successor met 'for various arrangements . . . to be made . . . with regard to the disposition of family estates and property'.[17] The eventual agreement signed at Fort Belvedere on 10 December 1936 granted Edward an annual income of £25,000 in exchange for his relinquishing any claim to either the property or estates he had inherited upon his accession.

In the event that this allowance would not be covered by the government in the new Civil List, George VI agreed to fund it personally. Amid the haste of these financial talks, Edward crucially failed to include any provision for either Wallis's title or specifics around his eventual return to Fort Belvedere.

The amicable resolution was short-lived. In early 1937, George VI discovered that Edward had taken into exile a large private fortune. During negotiations, Edward had not revealed the extent of his wealth, saying only that he would be 'badly off'[18] in his new circumstances. George VI cited the omission as reason to nullify the existing terms. It took another thirteen months of wrangling before he finally agreed to pay his brother £21,000 per annum for the property he had relinquished. But with the new agreement came an added clause. Should Edward ever return to England without the government's (or his brother's) permission, the allowance would cease forthwith.

Paris, 24 June 1949

On the last morning [11 December] I was up early, striving to finish the broadcast . . . In some ways this was the hardest thing I have ever done. It was a good deal like composing a message to be consigned to a bottle. It was largely patterned upon the speech prepared the week before . . . Certain indispensable things had to be said, yet because this broadcast was my farewell, I had to be brief, for under the intense emotional stress there was the temptation of saying too much. Indeed, my mother urged me to abandon the idea of the broadcast altogether.

Undeterred by his mother's plea, Edward finished a draft of the broadcast shortly before Churchill arrived for lunch. 'I wanted to say goodbye to my old friend,' Edward wrote, on 24 June 1949, 'and I took advantage of his visit to ask him to read my modest effort, the substance of which he was already familiar with. He made a few brilliant suggestions . . .'[19]

'The King,' Monckton recorded in his private memorandum, 'was in excellent form . . .'[20] As they ate, at 1.52 p.m. precisely, the Speaker of the House of Commons announced the passage of the Abdication Bill and Edward formally ceased to be King. The moment, Edward wrote, 'passed by unnoticed and without comment', though everyone was 'acutely conscious of the imminent change in my status from monarch to citizen'.[21]

The immensity of that change was emphasised when at 7.05 p.m. the new King, George VI, arrived at Fort Belvedere for what Edward described to Murphy in an undated conversation as a final 'handover talk'.[22] 'It was hardly necessary for me to say,' Edward wrote on 24 June 1949, 'that I was distressed that circumstances had obliged me to give up the throne; he knew as few others did how seriously I had taken my position and how anxious I was to succeed in it. I in turn appreciated the tremendous change my action was beginning to make in his set and well-ordered family life . . .'[23] Sitting on his bed, amid the chaos of a room Edward described as 'littered with papers, clothes and other belongings',[24] the brothers discussed what the now ex-King would be called. In another sign of the chaos that pervaded Edward's final hours in Britain, this question had been entirely overlooked in any of their preceding conversations.

Paris, 24 June 1949

'Only this afternoon,' Bertie went on, 'I was wondering about this, and remembering that you were going to broadcast this evening, I made inquiries at the British Broadcasting Company as to how the director intended to announce you. I was astounded when they told me that Sir John Reith was proposing to call you "Mr Edward Windsor"!!'

'But isn't that rather forward of the director?' I asked.

Bertie was furious. 'I soon stopped that,' he told me. 'You will be announced as "His Royal Highness Prince Edward".'

'Why, of course,' I said. 'That is the proper way to address the son of a sovereign until such time as he is created a royal duke.'

Instead of bestowing upon Edward an existing royal title, George VI opted to create a new dukedom for his brother. He would be transformed, in the first act of his reign the following morning, into His Royal Highness The Duke of Windsor. The name their father had used to rechristen his family and his dynasty in 1917, 'Windsor' evoked simultaneously the British monarchy's ancient foundations and its modern rebranding. It was unconventional, but also uniquely appropriate for a man whose royal career had embodied both.

A few minutes after 8 p.m., Edward said goodbye to his staff and climbed into the waiting car, which was to take him to Royal Lodge for dinner with his mother, brothers and sister. His maternal uncle, the Earl of Athlone, and his wife, Princess Alice (daughter of Queen Victoria's son, Prince Leopold), were also present. As he drove away from Fort Belvedere he caught a final glimpse of his beloved home 'ablaze with light', and he was moved to reflect on the enormity of his impending loss. 'In that moment,' he wrote, on 24 June 1949, 'I realized how heavy were the penalties of kingship; the price I had paid for rejecting my official inheritance was the severance of all personal ties in my country as well. I was now irretrievably on my own, and it was in this mood, touched perhaps with defiance, that I joined my family . . .'[25] Edward made no mention of what Monckton described to Murphy in July 1949 as the 'state of anarchy' that existed at Fort Belvedere on this last day. 'The staff,' he declared, 'had turned insulting. Allen, who was also present, grumbled, "You cannot imagine how rude they all were. I felt like knocking down the butler."'[26]

Paris, 15 June 1949

In spite of the blood bonds that united us, a faint but distinct tension prevailed. It was not merely that they could not reconcile themselves to my leaving; their apprehension as to

what I might say made them one in their silent opposition
to the idea of my farewell broadcast . . . My whole being
was drawn taut in anticipation of the broadcast by which
posterity would judge me. All over the world, wherever the
English language is understood, people would be listening. I
was determined not to fail.

The broadcast was set for ten o'clock. A half hour before,
while we were still at dinner, the butler announced the motor
was at the door to take me to Windsor Castle. Saying I would
be back in an hour or so, I excused myself. Mr Monckton
was waiting beside the motor. 'You have the broadcast,
haven't you?' His question startled me, and convulsively my
hand sought my pocket. It was there. I stepped into the
motor . . . On the way down the Long Walk, I asked Mr
Monckton whether he had had further word from Cannes.
'Yes,' he answered. 'Mrs Simpson has telephoned to say that
your Austrian friends are glad to offer you hospitality at
their castle [Schloss Enzesfeld]' . . . In my relief at knowing
that at the end of my journey I would be assured the protection and privacy of a baronial estate, I inwardly thanked W
for her thoughtfulness of me . . .

Edward, accompanied by Walter Monckton, arrived at Windsor Castle
at 9.45 p.m.

. . . The senior functionaries of the permanent staff received
me; at their heads stood Lord Wigram, my father's old Private
Secretary who had emerged from the shadows of his retire-
ment 'to be in attendance' in the dual capacity of Lieutenant
Governor of the Castle and Deputy Constable of the Round
Tower, to which I had appointed him. 'Is everything all set?'
I asked. 'Yes, Sir,' he answered, as he accompanied me up the
Gothic staircase, leading towards the room in the private
apartments where I had arranged to have the microphone
installed. This room, which I had selected, before all the others

in the Castle was the sitting room of the suite in the Augusta Tower, which I had occupied as Prince of Wales . . .

Sir John Reith [Director General of the BBC] was already in the room, supervising the technicians he had brought with him from the British Broadcasting Company. The microphone was on a table . . . During the few minutes that remained while I read the speech over once again, I was conscious of the presence of the director – a tall, cadaverous Scot whose cheek bore the scar of a severe war-wound – hovering behind my chair, watch in hand, measuring the seconds. This was no place for strangers, I decided, and, turning to him, I said, 'Sir John, will you please leave the room as soon as you have announced me; it is my wish that only Mr Monckton be with me while I am speaking.'

'The King,' Monckton remembered, 'ran through the draft broadcast rapidly in the last five minutes . . . He also tried his voice on the microphone.' At exactly ten o'clock, Reith returned to the room and 'stood over the King, who sat before the microphone'.[27]

. . . In a deep voice, Sir John Reith boomed into the microphone, 'This is Windsor Castle. His Royal Highness Prince Edward.' . . . When I began to speak, all the tension went out of me . . .

'At long last,' Edward began, 'I am able to say a few words of my own. I have never wanted to withhold anything, but until now it has not been constitutionally possible for me to speak.' Declaring his allegiance to his brother, now George VI, 'Prince Edward' shifted to the heart of the matter.

You all know the reasons which have impelled me to renounce the throne. But I want you to understand that in making up my mind I did not forget the country or the Empire, which, as Prince of Wales, and lately as King, I have for twenty-five years tried to serve. But you must believe me when I tell you that I have found it impossible to carry the heavy burden of responsibility and to discharge my duties as King as I would wish to do without the help and support of the woman I love.

Edward's stilted tone at the outset of his address betrayed his nervousness. But his delivery grew in confidence, particularly as he spoke of the subject he cared most about: Wallis. 'This was a thing I had to judge entirely for myself,' he said emphatically to his listeners. 'The other person most nearly concerned has tried up to the last to persuade me to take a different course . . . The decision,' he continued, 'has been made less difficult to me by the sure knowledge that my brother, with his long training in the public affairs of this country and with his fine qualities, will be able to take my place forthwith without interruption or injury to the life and progress of the Empire.' A drastic overstatement: his brother was by any standards less handsome and less charismatic, but he still possessed, as Edward emphasised, 'one matchless blessing, enjoyed by so many of you, and not bestowed on me – a happy home with his wife and children'. And having paid the obligatory homage to his mother and his former Prime Minister, the now ex-King solemnly concluded, 'I now quit altogether public affairs, and I lay down my burden. It may be some time before I return to my native land, but I shall always follow the fortunes of the British race and Empire with profound interest, and if at any time in the future I can be found of service to His Majesty in a private station, I shall not fail.'

Though a sombre message, Edward was carried through its passages by the euphoria of having been at last liberated from a terrible burden. The American radio correspondent Lowell Thomas noted of the speech, 'Take all the great speeches of history, of the stage, of impassioned orators, of great statesmen – there is nothing approaching in poignancy that of the man who today spoke to the Empire for the last time.'[28] Listened to across Britain, the Empire and the world, it became one of the twentieth century's most iconic broadcast moments.

Unlike the words Edward had hoped to deliver earlier in the month, this message was not designed to alter the course of events. Breaking the silence his constitutional position had imposed, Edward delivered a highly personal message whose sentiments were authentically his own. 'He felt,' Walter Monckton wrote, in his unpublished memorandum, 'that he and Mrs Simpson were made for one another and that there was no other honest way of meeting the situation than marrying her. When he said in his final broadcast that he could not carry on his task without her by his side, he said what he really meant from his heart. They were not merely his own words but words which he insisted upon inserting and retaining against the suggestion of others.'[29]

'Well,' the author Virginia Woolf noted, after listening to the message, 'one came in touch with the human flesh.'[30] Nothing like this had ever been attempted by a king with his people. Its reception among Edward's peers or the Establishment, a term he defined in an interview with Kenneth Harris in 1969 as 'authority',[31] was muted at best, disdainful at worst. References to the 'woman I love' and the contrast created between himself and his brother's 'happy home' were intimate phrases that people such as Alec Hardinge's wife thought made the speech 'very vulgar'.[32] The historian Elizabeth Longford, herself a member of British aristocratic circles, labelled the syntax as 'women's magazine language', noting that it 'simply wasn't the way a King spoke'.[33] Yet for the average Briton, and for an American audience captivated by the aura of romance, these passages lifted the speech outside the norms of traditional royal oratory and into the realm of popular imagination. The effect was to humanise both Edward and the crisis from which he had at last emerged.

Shortly after 10.30 p.m. Edward arrived back at Royal Lodge, where his family remained gathered. 'I had the feeling – a good feeling,' he wrote, on 24 June 1949, 'that what I had said to some extent levelled the barrier which earlier had stood between us.'[34] But the emotional gulf between Edward and his family had already widened. One exception,

Edward later noted, was his great-uncle, the Duke of Connaught, the last surviving son of Queen Victoria. His 'understanding', Edward wrote, 'prompted him to write . . . one of the most human letters of the many I received after the abdication, when from his character and background one would have judged him to be one of the last to understand my action'.[35]

Charles Murphy's Diary[36]
Paris, Spring 1949

> At his last meeting with his mother, 'just before the iron curtain clanged down', the Queen Mother [Queen Mary] asked HRH [Edward] if he would leave with her the Garter star. 'I realised of course that she wanted it to wear at the coronation of my brother and the thought that crossed my mind was how inhuman it was in the midst of this tragedy and sorrow and my departure that she should have asked for this bauble. But I realise now that she was not being thoughtless at all. It was merely a question of the show going on, the royal show. The King is dead. Long live the King.'

Having said his final goodbyes, Edward and Monckton departed for Portsmouth at 12.15 a.m. on 12 December. 'Because,' he wrote, 'the destroyer [HMS *Fury*] that was to take me across the Channel was even then standing by, we drove fast.'[37]

Thus at two o'clock in the morning the *Fury* slid silently unescorted out of Portsmouth Harbor, its destination no longer of significance to a people confused and exhausted by the great constitutional conflict that had forced their King to abdicate. It had been hard enough to give it up. Watching the British shore recede I was swept by many emotions. But of one thing I was certain, it was my fierce conviction – it was that a deep true love had triumphed over the exigencies of Church and state. A sweet and sublime perfect close, firm solid, strong.

Though not part of this original draft, Edward left a haunting addendum titled simply 'Abdication'.[38]

The position of a King is perhaps the only vocation that a man can never leave. He can cease being a lawyer, a banker or an industrialist. He can give up his board chairmanships and retire to an honorary position of the Boy Scouts, or as a trustee of a county hospital, become a farmer. But there is no question of a King ever ceasing to be a King and living with any measure of comfort.

9

The Finish Line

It took Edward five months to write the story of 1936. Between April and August 1949, fifty-five thousand words had been produced about his reign. He and Murphy had worked continuously – reviewing dates, events and people – so that Edward, whose memory at times was hazy, could tell his story. 'When did I actually decide to abdicate?' he wrote to Monckton, on 13 August 1949. 'Was it during the night of December 4th–5th after Winston had dined with us at The Fort? Further, when did I inform Mr Baldwin of my decision or did I send you to No. 10 Downing Street the morning of Saturday December 5th to tell him first, and that I wanted to see him at The Fort that afternoon?'[1] In writing these drafts, Edward had relied on the voluminous research and interviews that Murphy had compiled over more than the year he had spent working on the memoir. Typed out and assiduously labelled by theme, these served as prompts for Edward, who at times struggled to put his experiences into words. Murphy had recognised this problem early on in their collaboration. His system was designed to compensate for Edward's deficiencies and supplement his sometimes vague recollections with what Murphy said were 'a succession of revealing personal anecdotes . . . and a sense that the reader is constantly sharing the thoughts, emotions and beliefs of the writer'.[2]

Murphy's strategy and his reassuring companionship had transformed the once reluctant author into an enthusiastic storyteller. Though the research stage of the project had largely ceased, Edward was still eager to continue reminiscing and even succeeded in luring the hesitant Godfrey Thomas to Paris in late June. 'He has been pressing me for some time past to discuss with him "various aspects" of his tours and help him fill some gaps,' Thomas reported to Monckton, on 19 June 1949.

'He [Edward] rang me up this morning,' Thomas continued, 'and sounded full of life and good spirits – likely, I should say, to see us both out!'[3]

By early July Edward was sufficiently confident to dispatch Murphy and his completed drafts to London so that his two chief advisers, Monckton and Allen, could weigh in. As well as offering legal advice on issues such as copyright and libel, both men had been principal participants in the abdication drama, and they were ideally placed to comment on the veracity of Edward's account. Having advised him from the outset of the project, their feedback was an important next step in the pre-publication process.

Though Allen's views at this stage are unrecorded, Monckton was immediately alarmed by what he read. Over dinner with Murphy on 6 July, he gave him his 'hurried notes of candid criticisms', and spelled out a list of the manuscript's further 'dangers', which included 'errors of fact', 'breaking the rules of constitutional propriety' and 'libel'.[4] Anxious that Murphy had not taken his concerns seriously, Monckton sent him an aide-memoire of the conversation two days later itemising for the 'record'[5] these three concerns.

Monckton's notes do not survive and neither does any record of what Murphy subsequently relayed to Edward, but the drafts clearly sparked a new level of anxiety regarding Edward's memoir and a concern that his influence was now being filtered through the voice of an American journalist. Though he found Murphy 'pleasant and under-standing' he was, Monckton believed, 'mainly interested in the sales of the book' and thus eager 'to publish just those things I want to stop'.[6] Monckton, who had never really supported the project, was even more fearful after reading Edward's chapters. He became increasingly uneasy that their publication could have a harmful impact upon the monarchy. Seeking what he termed 'wise and helpful advice',[7] Monckton turned, as he had done previously in containing Edward's unwieldy inclinations, to Buckingham Palace and specifically to Alan 'Tommy' Lascelles, George VI's Private Secretary. He was on friendly terms with Lascelles, who had, coincidentally, met with Murphy just a few days before.

Lascelles was, the editor of his diaries Duff Hart-Davis noted, 'every inch the Private Secretary. Six foot one . . . elegantly thin, with dark hair,' he possessed a 'moustache . . . that gave him a quizzical, almost challenging look.'[8] From 1920 to 1929 Lascelles had served as Edward's Private Secretary, but he resigned his role, frustrated with Edward and too depressed to continue. He rejoined the Royal Household under George V in 1935. Retained by Edward VIII after his father's death, Lascelles was pleased to observe with the benefit of proximity a 'marked improvement'[9] in the new sovereign's behaviour and temperament. However, Edward excluded Lascelles from the abdication drama, believing he possessed the unhelpful 'ingrained prejudice' of a 'courtier's outlook'.[10] He remained in office under George VI and took over the role of Private Secretary after Hardinge's retirement in 1943. He subsequently established himself as one of Edward's most vocal critics and was instrumental in shaping the lasting perception of the ex-King as a royal delinquent, even after his retirement in 1953. As late as 1965, while corresponding with Nigel Nicolson on the treatment of the abdication in his father Harold Nicolson's diaries, Lascelles could not resist the temptation to express his contempt for the now seventy-one-year-old Duke. 'Words like "decency", "honesty", "duty", "dignity",' he advised Nicolson, 'meant absolutely nothing to him.' His 'moral development,' Lascelles continued, 'had for some reason been arrested in adolescence . . . An outward symptom,' he assured Nicolson, 'was the absence of hair on the face . . . E.P. [Edward] only had to shave about once a week.'[11]

Murphy was aware of Lascelles's attitude and his pre-eminence as an institutional gatekeeper. When the summons to meet him at Buckingham Palace came via Godfrey Thomas in January 1949, Murphy had purposefully avoided it. But, as he wrote to Longwell on 11 July, he was eventually 'maneuvered into a position' where he was 'obliged to face up to the King's private secretary and confidant . . . Our friend,' he hastened to add, 'was against my doing this but I had no choice . . . Clearly the royal family and the courtiers are worried about how far our friend intends to go and whether he intends to pay off old scores. In my answers I was both discreet and wary . . .'[12]

Murphy's encounter with Lascelles provided Monckton with the perfect pretext to involve the formidable courtier in scrutinising Edward's memoir. 'I think it might be helpful if we had a private talk,'

Monckton suggested, in a letter to Lascelles on 8 July – just two days after he had dined with Murphy '. . . for what I have written to the proposed author will undoubtedly cause offense. If I go too far I shall lose what chance I have of exercising the pruning fork, which becomes more and more necessary at every stage.'[13] Away from the officialdom of his office at Buckingham Palace, in which he had deliberately met Murphy, Lascelles spoke discreetly with Monckton over lunch at his home in St James's Palace. It was an undeniable breach of the trust Edward had placed in Monckton. Yet, as neither he nor Murphy suspected any disloyalty, Monckton remained an integral voice in the project and, on 15 July, Murphy wrote to assure him that 'our friend' has taken 'your candid comments in good grace', and he looked forward to receiving more 'specific criticism and aid when the manuscript entered a second and more precise stage'.[14]

If Edward felt disappointment at Monckton's reaction, it did not dampen his enthusiasm for writing. Monckton was, after all, only one of the voices that Edward wished to hear from as he prepared his manuscript. Next on his list was Beaverbrook, the project's most enthusiastic proponent.

'Our famous friend,' Murphy informed Beaverbrook's son Max Aitken on 1 August, 'called upon him [Beaverbrook] yesterday, alone, and read him certain chapters of the work – always a mistake.'[15] Beaverbrook was not impressed. 'The story,' he wrote to Murphy on 3 August, 'does not stand up . . . I give some examples . . . The narrative suggests,' he began, 'that Mr Churchill was actuated by dislike of Baldwin . . . He was the sincere and unswerving friend of his King. The Duchess,' he noted, 'is praised for her self-abnegation, for her willingness to stand aside from the marriage. And yet Lord Brownlow and others are criticised because they suggested to her such a decision.' He continued, 'The narrative is not clear to me on the Baldwin issue. Did Lord Baldwin wish to keep the King on the throne? Did he treat the King abominably? I am in doubt after reading the text.' Beaverbrook further noted, 'An account is given which justifies the dismissal of Hardinge. Yet the King drew back from taking such action . . . I gather,' he went on, 'that the "conspiracy" record [Brownlow's and Beaverbrook's attempts to persuade Wallis to give up Edward] is drawn from a free reading of my account of the crisis. I had no intention of entering into any "conspiracy". But you will see . . . that Monckton and Allen are involved as well as Lord Brownlow . . . It will be necessary to include the names of these gentlemen.' He proclaimed adamantly that the elusive 'King's Party' had in fact existed. 'We were indeed the King's Party,' Beaverbrook insisted. 'But unfortunately, the King was not a member of it.'[16] He opted to send a more diplomatic version of his letter to Edward, who, along with Murphy, accepted the criticism in good spirit. 'The whole work,' Murphy assured Beaverbrook on 11 August, 'is in the process of thoroughgoing revision.'[17]

By 20 August, the day that Edward dined at Cap d'Ail, Beaverbrook's home, the 1936 chapters were complete. Churchill's arrival as Beaverbrook's guest was imminent, and Edward had brought with him two completed chapters, both relating to Churchill's role in the crisis. He hoped that the former Prime Minister would read and offer him the kind of editorial counsel he had once eagerly volunteered for his public addresses as Prince of Wales and King.

But Edward faced disappointment as Churchill proved unwilling to assist and left it to Beaverbrook to relay the bad news. 'He [Churchill] told me quite emphatically,' Beaverbrook wrote to Edward, on 22 August 1949, 'that he did not wish to be consulted; he prefers to stand apart altogether from the preparation of the narrative.' Churchill was also against Edward publishing before the next general election, which was predicted for February 1950. 'This feeling,' Beaverbrook advised, 'is due entirely to his position as leader of the Conservative Party.'[18]

'Churchill,' Murphy concluded, in a letter to Ken Rawson (Edward's editor at Putnam's), 'has come to regret his role in the abdication crisis and from time to time feels it was one of his worst political mistakes.'[19] From the outset, he had shown a polite reluctance to be drawn into the writing of Edward's memoir. He had tactfully refused to be interviewed and distanced himself overall from a project whose narrative he understandably suspected would clash with his own published account of the abdication. Churchill, as his long-time aide Jock Colville noted, had an unshakeable belief in the verdict of history because 'he intends to be one of the historians'.[20] Confronted at first hand with Edward's account of his combative stance during the crisis, Churchill recoiled.

Unfortunately for Edward, Beaverbrook's letter was merely the beginning of further problems. 'We have been through a severe crisis,' Murphy again confided in Rawson, on 24 August:

> Winston Churchill has visited Beaverbrook here and is dead set against the publication of the articles and book. He has given our author a severe talking to. Evidently, he is not actuated only by his own belief that it is improper for a former King of England to reveal his heart's innermost secrets to the general public. The present King apparently approached him. And the Beaver seems also to have been playing a little game of his own. Remember the scandal around the throne involved the most orthodox elements in British life, which is to say the Tory Party – Baldwin and all the others. And it happens also to have been one of the most controversial episodes in Winston Churchill's life, an episode which marked the climax of his Tory rebelliousness. With an election impending in Britain this winter or spring, neither Churchill nor Beaverbrook would necessarily welcome a sensational retelling of the abdication incident . . . I have not elected to inform my own colleagues. It would inevitably have led to a panic . . . I was tempted at one point to ask Harry Luce [who was also overseeing the publication of Churchill's memoir] to bring an end to this unseemly cannibalism among his own authors . . .[21]

Edward, Murphy told Rawson, 'caught the full blast' of the drama. Though determined to move on with publication, the disappointment at these initial reactions to his memoir left him 'bored and weary. Very often,'

Murphy acknowledged, 'he has stopped working for days without my knowing it, or he will be present in the body but not in the mind.'[22] And rather than returning to Paris after leaving La Croë for the final time, Edward and Wallis headed for three weeks' rest in the Tuscan spa town of Montecatini. 'He considers himself fatigued,' Murphy wrote to Longwell on 23 August, 'and wishes for some relaxation and detachment . . .'[23]

On 14 September Murphy joined the Windsors at their rented Italian villa. With work on the memoir in abeyance, Murphy had the leisure to return to his diary. He had known Edward and Wallis for nearly two years, but he was still fascinated by their foibles and determined to learn what made these two enigmatic people tick.

Charles Murphy's Diary
Montecatini, 18 September 1949[24]

Sunny day. HRH returns from cure. Bang on door. 'Charlie.' 'Sir.' 'Have you heard the news?' I hadn't seen a newspaper. He enters room with Italian newspaper. Pound sterling has been devalued from 4.02 to 2.80. 'A terrible blow.' 'Those damn socialists.' It took me a little time to realize why it had hit him so badly: their Treasury allotments are still in sterling. Their trip to U.S. affected.

Duchess telephones. 'Good morning. I have been devalued.'

She was poring over the Italian newspapers, translating with a dictionary . . . the Italian word was 'mutilated.'

HRH dispirited. We went for a walk. Up to Montecatini Alti. 'This greatly affects our plans.' He had hoped to settle in the U.S., to buy a house and set up a pied à terre. 'I have come to like, yes, love your country. After England, it is the one place in the world where I am truly contented. I like the people. I like the spirit. Now all that is gone. I can no longer afford it.'

She was more practical. 'Well, this is a victory for me. I had not wanted to go to America. Let's be candid. I am one of those Americans who while enjoying the U.S. for short stays find it more pleasant to live in Europe . . .'

But HRH depressed all day; his shoulders sagged; his face heavy with sorrow, and eyes dulled . . .

The Duchess was in one of her anti-British, anti-monarchic moods tonight. How long are we Americans going to be fooled by all this? The British hate us – let's face it . . .

Her attitude toward the brother [George VI] is riddled with bitterness . . .

While Edward, Wallis and Murphy were in Italy, 'the Beaver' channelled his combustible opinions into full-scale rewrites of the chapters Edward had given him on 20 August. Though he had conveyed Churchill's reaction, Beaverbrook held off on communicating his own negative impressions of the material. He eventually shared his revisions with Henry Luce and Murphy – but never with Edward. Both were impressed by the skill and sagacity of his narrative but there was, Luce pointed out to him in a letter of 23 September, a fundamental flaw. 'The trouble with it is,' Luce began, 'that it is too good for a royal autobiography. Your version provides the King with a grasp and understanding of the larger political situation posed by the Abdication which he obviously did not have in 1936 – and probably does not have today.'[25] The redrafted chapters were dropped without Edward knowing anything about them.

Before leaving for Italy Edward had also dispatched the same completed abdication story he had left with Beaverbrook to Monckton and Allen. This was their second reading of his material, and this time both men were appalled. 'I must make my position clear,' Monckton wrote to Allen on 4 October 1949. 'I can take no responsibility for the book, for its presentation of the Duke's case, or for the accuracy of its statements of facts, except in the instances where I have a record . . . It is of vital importance that this should be made plain.' Monckton decried Edward's portrayal of Baldwin and believed that his free use of Cabinet information was inappropriate. In an addendum, which his secretary annotated with the note 'NOT included in the copy of this sent to A. G. Allen', Monckton added, 'I ought to let Tommy Lascelles know in the near future that while I think that the articles are now likely to be published soon, I have succeeded in securing the deletion of the attack on Hardinge and practically all criticism of the Archbishop [Cosmo Lang]. There is and could be nothing critical of the Royal Family or any member of it. Any minor observations in relation to any of them to which objection might be taken I have already been able to delete . . .'[26]

Allen's response, which he gave to Monckton in a letter on 13 October, was even more visceral. 'I feel that they [the chapters] are so bad that I am impelled to suggest to you that it may be our duty to advise him against publication, because if they appear in their present form they will be condemned and must do him untold injury.' Allen believed that the drafts constituted 'a charge against S.B. [Stanley Baldwin] of forcing the King's abdication . . . Legally, the criticism . . . might be said to go beyond fair comment and to constitute . . . an attack upon him personally . . . that if S.B. were now alive . . . would not be safe to publish . . . because of the laws of libel.' The material, Allen continued, was fuelled 'by political controversy and speculation', which impugned the propriety of Edward as 'a former King'. Allen also felt Brownlow might take 'strong exception' to his part in the story, while the representation of Goddard's intervention constituted an 'element of defamation'.[27] The strength of the criticism affected even Murphy, who met both men over dinner in London during the first week of October. 'I had a sense of having talked perhaps too emotionally,' Murphy wrote to Monckton, on 5 October, 'and yet, now that the champagne fumes have dissipated, I still would not change anything important I said.'[28]

On 13 October Murphy warned Longwell of the impending danger posed by both men's disapproval and, for the first time, expressed an awareness of the complex loyalties underlying their service to Edward. 'Lately some difficulty has arisen,' Murphy began, 'over the reluctance of his lawyers, the men closest to him during the abdication, to contribute additional material. You will recall from earlier advice,' he continued, 'that both of these men now have connections with the Royal Family. Their lives are in England. He has departed, they remain; and they are not without reason concerned about their future positions.' Murphy gave no hint about how much of this criticism had been conveyed to Edward, but enough must have been said to weaken some of his earlier resolve. '[O]ur principal,' Murphy concluded to Longwell, 'has fallen steadily behind . . . and each day his power to act seems a little less.'[29]

Seeking Monckton's reassurance, Edward tried ringing him repeatedly during the second week of October. But Monckton avoided the calls and instead wrote to Murphy on 14 October to tell him that the drafts were not 'something which can be advised upon over the telephone'.[30] Assured by Murphy that Edward 'would not wish to go ahead without the benefit of your criticism and counsel',[31] Monckton spent 22 and 23 October in conference with him and Murphy at 85 rue de la Faisanderie. Exercising his signature deft touch, he secured Edward's promise of substantial rewrites. 'I am now convinced,' Edward wrote, just a day after Monckton's departure, that 'it is imperative that Charles go to London soon to discuss with you the restringing of the abdication "pearl necklace". I will impress on him to be guided by your suggestions as to the cutting of the material . . .'[32] From Murphy's more practical standpoint it was an unenviable setback, as he helped Edward rework material that constituted only a third of the text they were meant to deliver to *Life* in less than two months.

'At times,' Murphy wrote to Allen on 28 October, 'I grow depressed.'[33] Having expended their enthusiasm and resources on the book-length chapters of 1936, Murphy and Edward faced the considerable task of not only cutting and revising that material, which was only one of three articles, but of drafting the first two instalments, which were to cover Edward's life prior to his accession. On 7 November, Murphy informed Longwell that there was no possibility of meeting the deadline for December publication. The best they could aim for was mid to late January. But Longwell and Luce were impatient. 'They argue,' Murphy explained to Allen, 'that each day sees a deterioration in the value of the series, but I have . . . not bothered to show the cables to my principal on the theory that it is better not to shake him now.'[34] In desperation Longwell finally appealed to Edward directly. 'I fully realize,' he wrote, on 2 December, 'the difficulties of the task but must dutifully report my disappointment that the work is not in hand.' With a busy publication calendar for 1950 that included *Life*'s syndication of the third volume of Churchill's memoir and the serialisation in *The Ladies' Home Journal* of royal governess Marion Crawford's memoir about Edward's nieces, Elizabeth and Margaret (*The Little Princesses*), the 'schedule', Longwell emphasised, was getting extremely crowded. 'I promised,' he concluded, 'never to pressure you but for the good of all concerned I think I am only being a good Editor in advising you that the final stint should be done now.'[35]

But Edward was unmoved. 'I appreciate your point of view as Editor,' he cabled back to Longwell in reply on 7 December, 'but I am sure you also comprehend [the] magnitude and unique responsibility of my task as author. We have worked unremittingly for many months . . . we shall however require a little time on it in New York before the articles can be ready . . .'[36]

Edward's reply and Murphy's assurances eased Longwell's anxiety, and he was optimistic that the articles could be published in January 1950. On 26 December Edward, Wallis and Murphy arrived in New York. Two days later Longwell and Edward lunched together at the Time Inc. office. 'I was so happy to hear,' Longwell wrote to him the next day, that 'you and Charlie really want to get this task finished. It has been a long and difficult one, and you show a very proper sense of history in wanting it to be exactly right, which makes it more difficult. If you get the bulk of it done in the next two weeks,' he concluded, 'we will see that you have plenty of time for last minute changes and correction . . .'[37]

Longwell's confidence was short-lived. Less than twenty-four hours after he had seen Edward, Murphy informed him that the articles were nowhere close to being in publishable form: only one, the third instalment – the story of 1936 – was complete. 'We have at last faced up to realities,' Murphy informed Allen on 30 December. 'Publication . . . has been postponed indefinitely.'[38]

Depressed but determined to see the two-year assignment to completion, Murphy established himself at the Hotel Marguery, just two blocks south of the Waldorf Towers – with the aim of making the four weeks before the Windsors departed for a holiday in Mexico as productive as possible. With the series now set to begin in late May and a submission deadline of 1 April, Edward accepted that a different strategy was required. He ceded control of the process and allowed Murphy to write the first drafts of the two opening instalments, which he would then review and revise. Both men agreed it was the only way to meet the deadline. But this strategy also proved challenging. Edward made slow but voluminous changes, often rewriting entire paragraphs but rarely with the intimate anecdotes that Murphy felt were essential. 'It is because of the absence of truly personal details and observations that the writing . . . has taken so long,'[39] Murphy told Edward in late 1949. But Edward proved recalcitrant. Murphy recorded him saying in January 1950: 'Charlie, as I have said often, I just can't describe a state dinner at Buckingham Palace. It's one of the things I can't do.'[40]

In spite of his disillusionment, Murphy continued to observe the Windsors closely – especially Wallis, who remained an enigma. She had had no active role in the reminiscing and writing of the preceding two years, and therefore Murphy's interactions with her remained limited. As in December 1936, Wallis was left merely to observe as Edward took sole responsibility for the story, even though she and their relationship were at its heart. But as publication neared, Wallis's voice began to be heard. Her sudden participation in January 1950 elicited one of Murphy's most revealing and intimate encounters with the couple. It also produced one of Edward's most reflective statements on what might have been had he remained King. He was notably honest about the opinions he had held in the 1930s and the clash with his government they might have provoked.

Charles Murphy's Diary
Waldorf Towers, New York, January 1950[41]

The Duchess told me how when she first went to
England she used to read four or five British newspapers a day – *The Times*, the *Telegraph*, the *Express*,
the *Evening Standard*. She always read the Court
Circular. The phrases delighted her. ('And no term
delighted me more than the one "Lord and Lady
So-and-so visited the King and Queen and remained
for dinner."') She remembers also seeing the present
Princesses [Elizabeth and Margaret] in the garden at
Buckingham Palace, the 'two little girls in four-button
red coats behind the railing.'

She is impressed by the thought of what has been
lost. Half angrily she said, 'People keep saying that if
the Duke kept his Crown and remained on the throne
there would have been no war. I don't know about
that. Wars are made by politics and politics are made
by men. And I suppose that by this people meant that
had the Duke remained King, because he knew men
and got along well with them, he might have kept the
politics (politicians?) from driving Britain into war. He
was stronger than the present King.'

As she talked the Duke sat by, nodding in approval.
Her contempt of the present King cut like a knife
through everything she said. On the table was a copy
of the current issue of the London *Picture Post*. It was
covered with a photograph of the present King and the
Duke taken during their childhood. 'Look at that,' cried
the Duchess. 'Whenever did you see the differences in
their character more tellingly expressed?' She pointed to
the attitude of the young Prince of Wales – erect, hands
just so alongside his sailor's pants, heels together, toes
out in the proper military attitude. Young Bertie looked

harassed and fidgety, his feet apart, his hands nervously plucking at his pants, his collar in some disarray (they were both in old-fashioned children's sailor suits with straw hats and short pants).

In further proof of his wife's point, the Duke told the story of a meeting with his brother in Buckingham Palace last year. The King showed him samples of the new ribbons that were being awarded to the British troops who had served in the last war. One was for the desert army that had fought under Montgomery. The King held it up for his brother to see. 'Isn't that a marvelous ribbon?' He pointed to a somewhat muddy yellow band. 'Know what that is supposed to represent?' he asked.

The Duke answered, 'I haven't the faintest idea.'

'The desert. And do you know where we got the color for it?'

The Duke again said he hadn't the faintest idea, adding, 'Then a light came into my brother's eyes. "From the mud on the back of Monty's car – it was my idea, too."'

There was a discussion between them [Edward and Wallis] over the power of the King. The Duchess insisted . . . that the King was indeed a powerful man, that he could bring things to pass in Britain that no one else could bring. The Duke shook his head. 'If I had been powerful there would have been no question of our marriage. I would have married you on the throne.' She contradicted him. 'The difficulty was that he had been too impatient; he would not listen.' The Duke only shook his head. 'I was an absolute puppet.'

She said that the decision to give up on the throne was his alone. 'Why did he do it? I can't answer that. I would have stopped him if I could. Nor was there any question of giving up his duty. Nor did he give up the

throne because he could not live without me. It was no
fiery passion. If so only ashes would remain where
today there burns an even flame. The British hoped
that we would fail. They would then have said, "Come
back, little boy. All is forgiven. You have learned your
lesson."' From the side the Duke said, 'No, no, darling.
You don't understand. They would never have had me
back. There is no room for two kings in Britain.'

Of kingship the Duke said, 'It was a fine job, a great
job. It could have been an exciting job if I had been
allowed to do all that I felt ought to have been done. Yet
if on the other hand I had done it automatically – if I
had pranced when I was told to prance – then it would
have been the dullest job in the world. I took it over full
of high hopes. I had my own ways of doing things. It
was a bigger and better job than I had ever had before,
but once I discovered that I could not do it the way I
wanted to do it, then it no longer held me.' He said
somberly, 'Perhaps it all worked out for the best. Had I
remained my reign might have produced quarrel after
quarrel with the Government. I would have clashed with
them, I am sure, over Germany. I would never have lent
my name to the measures of socialization. I would not
have allowed myself to be pushed around.'

There was a discussion between them also about
whether the other women in the life of the Prince
should be mentioned. The Duke insisted that there
were no others. The Duchess scolded him. 'I should
not like people to get the impression that I was your
first love affair. I want them to know that I married
an interesting man, a man who had known many
beautiful women.' She spoke admiringly of Freda
Dudley Ward. 'She was the Duke's true love. She was
a fine woman. She had a good influence on him. I
admire her.'

By mid-February Murphy had completed drafts of all three *Life* articles. Edward received a portion of the manuscript while in Mexico, but he made little progress working alone. 'As you doubtless know, the Duke returned on February 24th,' Murphy advised George Allen on 6 March. 'I would judge that his obligations to his hosts took precedence over everything else. However, last Monday we resumed our work.'[42]

There is no hint that Edward had lost interest in the project. His 'Season Kalendar' for early 1950 is filled with entries 'WORK' or 'HOMEWORK' written in his own hand, often covering both his morning and afternoon entries. But it was also evident that he was incapable of accomplishing much without his collaborator. Unmoved by the commercial pressures of *Life*'s schedule, Edward's slowness may also be attributable to a reluctance to finish something that had given him a vocation and the stimulating company of a round-the-clock male companion. The writing also afforded the camaraderie of being part of the Time Inc. world – and he rarely missed an opportunity, when in New York, to join Longwell at his weekly editor's lunch in the conference room at 9 Rockefeller Plaza. On 7 March, he sat around the table with a group that included, among others, *Life*'s Editorial Director, John Billings, whose 'infectious enthusiasm',[43] as Longwell described it, was on full display throughout the afternoon. While Edward revelled in these continuing encounters, Murphy was increasingly frustrated by what seemed to him a never-ending assignment. 'The famous work,' he wrote to Beaverbrook's friend and colleague at the *Daily Express* Michael Wardell, on 28 February, 'is now entering its last stage. If the present schedule can be maintained – and there is nothing in past performance to suggest that it will be – I shall have completed it in somewhat less time than the Napoleonic wars.'[44]

On 15 March he joined the Windsors in Palm Beach. In a last-minute editorial decision Edward insisted the article on 1936 be divided and the series be expanded from the original three to four instalments. 'Full justice to the story was not otherwise possible,'[45] Edward advised George Allen, on 19 March, and Longwell agreed. This sudden change was likely due to Wallis, who was now actively reading the near-completed drafts. 'She left the story until now,' Murphy advised Allen

Wallis, Edward and Fruity Metcalfe on the balcony of the Château de Candé after their wedding, 3 June 1937.

Lord Brownlow, Katherine Rogers, Wallis and Herman Rogers
outside Lou Viei, 10 December 1936.

Edward and Wallis
reunited at the Château
de Candé, 7 May 1937.

Wallis and Edward being escorted to their car by Adolf Hitler after their meeting at the Berghof on 22 October 1937.

Edward and Wallis hosting the annual inspection of the Bahamas branch of the Red Cross, of which Wallis was president, at Government House in Nassau, 1942.

Edward in his study at La Croë by *Life* photographer John Swope, summer 1948.

Wallis and Edward in the grounds of La Croë by John Swope, summer 1948.

Edward and Wallis pictured on holiday in Montecatini, Italy on 11 September 1949.

Stanley Baldwin at his desk in 10 Downing Street, May 1937.

Cosmo Lang leaving 10 Downing Street on 6 December 1936.

Walter Monckton, c. 1956.

Daniel Longwell photographed
by Philippe Halsman in his office
at 9 Rockefeller Plaza, 1949.

Clementine Churchill, Winston
Churchill and Edward walking in
Antibes on 11 September 1948.

Lord Beaverbrook, *c.* 1946.

George Allen, *c.* 1937.

Charles Murphy with Benquethra Dirque, the cairn terrier that Edward gave to his daughter Edythe, Cap d'Antibes, August 1949.

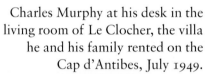

Charles Murphy at his desk in the living room of Le Clocher, the villa he and his family rented on the Cap d'Antibes, July 1949.

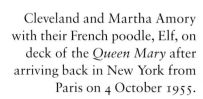

Edward with his dogs, inscribed to Charles Murphy's daughter: 'To Edie, Edward, Dizzie & Thomas, Belleair Florida March 1953'.

Cleveland and Martha Amory with their French poodle, Elf, on deck of the *Queen Mary* after arriving back in New York from Paris on 4 October 1955.

Edward at La Croë by John Swope, summer 1948. Swope later told Murphy, 'It's a funny thing but when you look at all the pix you get the unmistakable idea that when the Duchess is around the Duke freezes up and loses a lot of the young boyish charm which he evidences in pix of him alone.'

Edward waving from the train with Charles Murphy looking on from his right, Belleair, Florida, March 1953.

a few weeks later, 'and in consequence points that should have been disposed of long ago have only lately come under study.'[46]

Murphy was ambivalent about Wallis's sudden interest, in part because he blamed her for Edward's lack of progress. He cited the endless social whirl, which she orchestrated and which engulfed their lives. The routine, he told Allen, left Edward 'nervous and exhausted'.[47] But, Murphy concluded, 'he depends terribly as you know upon her'.[48] Despite these reservations, Wallis's engagement in the most sensitive areas of the memoir elicited another revealing exchange, which Murphy diligently recorded.

Charles Murphy's Diary
Palm Beach, March 1950[49]

Today for the first time the Duke and Duchess faced up to the issues involved in the abdication. It was a weird experience. The Duchess appeared in the white room overlooking the sea at 11 o'clock. She was dressed in a bathing suit and was on her way to the Wrightsmans' [Charles and Jayne Wrightsman]. The Duke was exhausted.

The conversation that followed only confirmed for the nth time my original surmise, that he and she had never discussed alone with searching inquiry the circumstances of his abdication. He seemed quite at a loss. Her point was that the manuscript in its present state failed to give proper credit to her for having wished to withdraw from the marriage on her depar-ture from Britain. The Duke was most apologetic. His hands fluttered. Whatever she said went with him . . . 'That,' she said, 'was foremost in my mind. I wanted him to stay. I felt he ought to stay' . . .

She said that when she left The Fort it was with the conviction the whole business was finished. She would never see the King again. It was in her mind either to go off to the United States or even to China – a place she also knew. 'That would have been a simple matter. I could go wherever I wanted. The King could not. He was chained to England. After a time he would find new interests and the British are very clever – they would have never allowed me back in England. In time it would have all been forgotten. That was in my mind.' She mentioned at one point in connection with her departure from England, 'I was fleeing for my life.'

The Duke injected a mild demur. 'Darling, it was not for your life. It was not like that.'

She looked at him severely. 'I was fleeing for my life.'

. . . She spoke of the change in her relationship with the Duke after he became King. He was hard-driven thereafter with many appointments. She went on to say that he was 'busy as a bird dog' in Buckingham Palace trying to change things around. 'He went too fast. That is why he got into trouble.'

. . . She said of the Duke, while he listened, 'He was pretty smart as Prince of Wales. He knew his way around. He knew how to get things done. He knew what he wanted. But after he became King the reins pulled tightly. He tried to save himself. He was always looking for ways through the restrictions – like holding part of his speech back. But in the end they beat him.'

Of their early relations she said, 'The first bond between us was his job. I was fascinated by his job. I was anxious to learn about it and to help him with it. And I was desperately interested in his job as King. I felt I could help him there.'

His idea, as she put it, was to make the King over into the image of the Prince of Wales he was – the man who got around.

It would seem that from the beginning the Duchess recognized that her real adversary was the old Queen

Mary, who remained on in Buckingham Palace. The Duchess said, 'I told the King again and again, "You must get her out of there. You must get her out of Buckingham Palace. The British people are not accustomed to their King being in York House."' And the Duchess repeated what she said before, namely that she was sure that the old Queen's idea was to remain on in the Palace and become her son's hostess and the matriarch of a great Empire. The Duke then chimed in to say that he had finally told his mother that she must leave. There, I think, is one of the keys to the tragedy. The Duchess underestimated the power of the Queen.

She spoke wisely and with insight about the importance of . . . Fort Belvedere in the Duke's life. Prior to that time he had been much on his own but now he needed companionship. 'He wanted a woman there and fate decided that we should meet at this time. It might have been anybody else.'

She spoke of the Duke's hold upon the imagination of the British public. When he became King he was a man thrice fortunate. He had been a popular Prince of Wales, he had shown himself to be good at all the sports except cricket, which they love, he was unconventional, 'which fascinated them', he was a bachelor and thereby demonstrated his independence. 'But when he refused to give up a woman for them it was a terrible thing. It hurt them deeply. They could never forgive him.'

On 6 April 1950 Edward and Wallis left Palm Beach and headed north, again by train, to Canada. They stopped in Chicago, where Edward inspected the Donnelly Printing Plant and saw the color engravings being made for his articles. Their trip rounded off with a visit to Calgary and

a three-day stay at the E.P. [Edward Prince] Ranch, the four-thousand-acre property Edward had purchased on his 1919 tour. Though he had visited it only twice since 1927, the ranch was, as he told reporters who greeted them in Calgary, 'the only land in the world I have ever owned'.[50] As usual, Murphy was not far behind. Thirty years before Edward had been surrounded by private secretaries and equerries as he crossed the Canadian–American border for the first time. Now it was only Murphy who rode back with him and Wallis to New York – 'Our last chance for more or less uninterrupted work,'[51] he informed Allen.

Despite his fatigue, Murphy could finally concede that Edward had met his deadline. 'Taken together,' Murphy wrote to Monckton on 6 April, after sending him and Allen the completed articles, 'these four instalments represent the King's story as he wishes to tell it.' But Murphy felt disillusioned by the result. 'There are many places in it where, had I had my way, the story would have taken a different form. And much is lacking that would have given breadth and depth to his life. But this, after all, is the Duke's story; there comes at every stage a point beyond which he cannot be taken, and there, always, the narrative stops . . . But on the other hand, the tale is told simply and with a minimum of platitudes; and if occasionally it suddenly splinters off into a startling naivety, that too is in character.'[52] Having made drastic revisions to the previous year's 1936 material, Murphy assumed Monckton's and Allen's comments would be few. The earlier sections, sent as a matter of courtesy, were as far as the content went, Murphy advised Monckton, 'outside your specific responsibility'.[53]

Monckton and Allen were still horrified by what they read, particularly in the second instalment, which told the story of Edward's meeting with Wallis. She was, the article read, 'a light . . . a gleam from an unseen headland'. 'It was my fate,' the passage continued, 'to fall in love with her and for that love to become ever increasingly the controlling force of my existence.' In addition, there was a forthright assessment of the hypocritical code that governed the British court's attitude towards divorce – a proceeding that, though 'proper under the law and increasingly accepted in British life . . . brought to me an agony of decision and cost me my throne . . .'[54]

'I am very anxious,' Allen cabled Longwell on 19 April, 'concerning the treatment of this friendship [Edward and Wallis]. As represented in this article it is a story of a love for a married woman and the alienation of her affections with ultimate divorce and marriage as the objective. I do not know what husband might do but legal action cannot be ruled out . . . I doubt wisdom,' he continued, 'of stating views on divorce and in my view the less said about this subject the better.'[55] The following day, Monckton added his own voice to the alarmed chorus. 'I suggest that readers ought not to be given smallest hint when author admitted to himself his love for the lady, still less his wish for marriage. Such information,' he continued, 'invites criticism that either he was ready to break a home or divorce was collusive. It would also draw criticism on lady.'[56] 'It is obscene to write gainfully about one's own love affairs,'[57] Lascelles commiserated to Monckton, after seeing the proposed new sections.

Further bruising comments came via Churchill. 'Difficult situation has arisen with Winston,'[58] Allen warned Edward, on the morning of 20 April. At Longwell's requests, passages of the fourth article had been sent to Churchill via Max Aitken. 'Churchill states the story of Windsor Castle incorrect,' Allen followed up, in a cable to Longwell later that day. If not removed, he 'will injunct *Life* and publish a personal statement'.[59] 'I strongly advise,' Allen continued, 'all references to Churchill should be carefully scrutinised and rewritten in such a way that no damage will be done to Churchill's political reputation.'[60] Faced with an onslaught of condemnation, Beaverbrook's was the lone congratulatory voice. He cabled Murphy on 14 April: 'I congratulate you on brilliant story which Duke has provided. I hope you will not alter even one word.'[61]

Edward received these criticisms gracefully but the effect on him, as Murphy wrote to Allen on 28 April, 'proved almost crushing . . . I feel for the Duke,' he continued:

He could hardly have accepted all the points without perpetrating a historical gloss which I think would have been more disastrous to his position than the existing manuscript. For the heart of the story concerns the growth of his relation with Wallis S., and for the life of me I cannot see how a great love story can be written without mention of love and indeed with almost no traces of the woman in question . . . I can only say that he took the cables in good heart and has struggled conscientiously and even heroically to meet the criticism and corrections.[62]

What followed in the final weeks before publication was a tug of war between Edward's words and worlds, old and new. Once he had accepted most of Allen's and Monckton's suggestions on the earlier drafts of the articles, the bosses at *Life* were left disappointed. Henry Luce, who had until now remained above the fray of what he called 'the intricate problem of this production', urged Edward to rethink the revisions, which had 'condensed' Wallis to an 'irreducible minimum' and left the reader 'unprepared' for the events of 1936. He urged Edward to 'make clear your position at the moment of accession' and retain the parts of the story that spoke to 'the honorable hope of a marriage based on deep affection and mutual respect'.[63] The 'letter was masterly,' Murphy told Luce, and it 'proved persuasive in a moment of wavering'.[64] Accordingly, Wallis was reinserted.

But Monckton and Allen refused to give up. They 'bombarded him [Edward] with more and more outspoken criticism', as Monckton reported to Lascelles on 5 May, forcing Murphy to make a last-minute visit to London. Backed by the bosses at *Life*, Murphy's message to the duo was firm: the offending passages about Wallis were to remain and he/Edward would concede only the most minor of further alterations. 'All we have succeeded in doing,' Monckton wrote wearily to Lascelles, '. . . has been to make what was horrible a little less so.'[65] But Buckingham Palace was still appreciative, as Lascelles confirmed on 10 May: '. . . Allen and you had done all that mortal men could do to make this wretched publication as decent as possible, and you may be very sure,' he continued, 'that all here are deeply grateful to you . . .'[66]

'Showed to AGA [Allen] 11 May 1950,' Monckton recorded on the letter before it was filed – confirmation that both of these trusted advisers had betrayed Edward by colluding with Lascelles.

The same day, 11 May, Edward's four articles finally went to press. The first instalment appeared on 22 May 1950, with a striking portrait of the couple on the magazine's cover taken in November 1947 by the photographer Philippe Halsman at Longwell's request. 'Believe me, Charlie,' Longwell wrote to Murphy on 14 June, two days after the final article appeared, 'it was a unique piece of work. I know it took you three years, but I am not at all certain it wasn't the most import-ant magazine piece published in our times. I know of nothing that created such a wide interest, and the odd part about it was that it wasn't the sensationalism of a former king writing his memoirs, but it was how it was done – the intimacy yet the good taste, the good humor, the artistry with which you wove it all together as an editor and writer are what make it unique. I have heard nothing but praise from all sides . . .'[67]

'The articles have been a tremendous success,' Murphy wrote to the Duke's American lawyer Hank Walter on 26 June 1950. *Life* estimated that five million copies of each of the four issues were sold, translating into the projection that between sixty and seventy million people read one or more of the articles.[68] Appearing in Britain via serialisation in Beaverbrook's *Daily Express*, they had, Murphy told Walter, produced a 'circulation increase in excess of 500,000 weekly . . . the longest and fastest jump in the history of British journalism'.[69]

One of Edward's less than enthusiastic readers was his mother, who swiftly communicated her disapproval to him after receiving the articles from her son. Owen Morshead, the Royal Librarian, who shared his copies with Edward's nemesis Alec Hardinge, received back from him what he described as an 'indiscreet but revealing letter'.[70] Though Edward had settled for including only the first three lines of Hardinge's November 1936 letter and a subsequent summary, the former Private Secretary was still enraged. 'What a deplorable performance,' Hardinge wrote to Morshead on 28 July 1950, 'a real apologia . . . Beastly things about poor old Baldwin . . . It is of course monstrous to publish a very confidential letter from his P.S. – and not even that in full. And he has no-one to protect him. No doubt they like the publicity – and they are not going to get it from me . . . What a man!'[71]

Edward doubtlessly anticipated the disapproval in court circles, but he could at least feel satisfied that he had pleased Longwell and the other bosses at *Life*. 'I have been away on holiday, but I returned to the office to find people still talking about the success of the memoirs . . .' Longwell wrote to Edward on 10 July. 'I believe that the three articles three years ago and the last four are about as notable a magazine contribution as I have seen in my time . . .'[72]

Though delighted with the articles' commercial success, Longwell must have breathed a sigh of relief that he was no longer responsible for Edward or for the completion of his full-length autobiography, to be titled *A King's Story*, which had been announced on 21 January 1950. Hoping to capitalise on the commercial success of the articles, Edward's editor at Putnam's, Ken Rawson, pressed him to publish no later than January 1951. It was part of the *Life* contract that Murphy would help Edward turn the articles into a book, and he, with a new secretary, Hildegarde Maynard, was dispatched to Paris in early June for the duration of three months.

Murphy quickly complained about the lack of progress. 'It's the old business,' he wrote to Hank Walter on 26 June, of 'too many late nights, and an inability to concentrate. He is supposed to be piling up for me material for the earlier chapters: the month has produced perhaps two new small anecdotes.'[73] Using material from the uncut *Life* articles and the completed 1936 chapters of 1948 and 1949, the core of the book was finished by late summer. But Edward still needed to write about his childhood and youth – which he did slowly and in his usual non-chronological fashion. 'The difficulty,' Murphy told Edward on 1 September, 'has been one that I have often explained: how to weld the scattered incidents into an autobiographical narrative; how to deal with your little brushes with Court Pooh-bahs, yet hold the impression that you were always a serious monarch.'[74] The book, Murphy continued, must demonstrate that while 'the later hours of your life made for controversy, the first part represented your years of success'. It was an 'asset' that 'must not be thrown away'.[75]

By mid-November all hope of finishing the book for a January publication was over. Murphy described himself as 'depressed and frustrated' but still determined, as he told Walter on 11 November, to see the project through to its completion. But finishing remained a challenge. Edward, Murphy told Walter, was 'prepared to spend every day with me,' but he is 'in a mood to work effectively only a fortnight out of every two months.'[76] Finally, increasing pressure from Putman's alongside Murphy's looming return to Life on 1 January 1951 forced Edward into realising he had to get the book finished.

On 16 November Wallis sailed alone for New York while Edward and Murphy remained in Paris. The decision provided the project's final burst of drama and what Murphy described twenty years later to his then agent Phyllis Westberg as Edward's 'first abdication in December 1950, as an author'.[77]

Charles Murphy to Phyllis Westberg
Washington D.C., 23 January 1973

. . . At 7:30 one morning in Paris, there was a call from the Duke. Astonishing! I'd never heard from him before 10:30 in the morning. He was so distraught that he could barely frame his message. What he said was that he had been up all night, packing, he was taking the boat train in the early afternoon for Cherbourg, to sail in the evening for New York. He was sorry; he was giving up the book. He had too many things on his mind. There was a danger of war (the Chinese had crossed the Yalu); he was worried about the Duchess.

What he did not know was that I knew the cause of his distress. The Duchess, before leaving for New York ahead of him in . . . November, had failed to cut off her standing order with a newspaper clippings service in New York. The Duke had opened the envelopes and come upon a large batch of clippings from the New York gossip column, and most disconcertingly the lurid offerings of Walter Winchell, describing the

Duchess's 'romance' with Jimmy Donahue and even
hinting at the break-up of the marriage. She was
refusing to take his panic-stricken telephone calls.

Before the morning was out, I telephoned the Duke's
lawyer in New York [Walters] . . . and informed him
the Duke was giving up the book. I also notified the
Duke's lawyers in London, the barrister Monckton and
the solicitor Allen. And the publishers . . .

I did one thing more that morning. I made up my
mind to return with him, rather than see him go off
alone, facing five days at sea, uncertain of what he
would find in New York. I truly feared that he might
commit suicide. So I joined him on the boat train.

By the time Edward arrived in New York, his mood had calmed, and
he had decided, after all, not to abandon the book. In a very public
demonstration of unity, Wallis greeted Edward affectionately at the
dock, but speculation about their marriage continued. With Edward
once again preoccupied with the memoir, which was eventually published
in April 1951, the Duchess continued to be seen in public with Donahue.
An heir to the Woolworth department store fortune, the Windsors
had met Donahue in 1947 and socialised with him frequently in both
Europe and the United States, often being entertained at his expense.
Handsome, rich and unapologetically gay, Donahue shared Wallis's endless
appetite for parties and nightclubs. It remains a topic for debate whether
he also shared her bed. Still, the pair were seen out together evening
after evening as Wallis seemed impervious to the gossip that swirled.

Murphy had returned to his desk at *Life* in the new year, as planned,
but he continued to assist Edward as the manuscript reached its completion. He also kept an observant eye on the Windsors' marital state and
witnessed at first hand the emotional pain Wallis's behaviour inflicted on
Edward. 'The Duke,' Murphy reported to Allen on 23 February,
'true to his nature, although apparently hurt and affected, has closed his
eyes to all the implication. He is inclined to blame the demand for the
book for everything that has happened. He is nervous and distraught, and

I worry for him . . . I tell you these things, not with the idea of conveying gossip, but only to keep you advised in matters related to a mutual friend.'[78]

Wallis's flirtation with Donahue was the only public crack that arose in the Windsors' thirty-five-year marriage, and it occurred, coincidentally, at exactly the point when she and Edward had collectively confronted the trauma of 1936. While it is doubtful that their marriage was ever in any serious danger, the episode betrayed an underlying vulnerability at the core of Edward and Wallis's relationship: the abdication. They had experienced this defining event separately and without a mutually agreed approach. Edward had decided Wallis's future for her, and, once the drama had subsided, she faced not only the ineviitability of their marriage but a life that would always be defined in relation to his. The outcome left Wallis consumed by desperation and nervous agitation. Besieged physically by the reporters who were camped out around Lou Viei at the end of 1936, she felt herself a prisoner in a world that despised her. Wallis poured out these frustrations in the letters she sent to Edward in the early days of his exile. But even as she complained bitterly about her circumstance, she never questioned her position as his future wife. Her quiet acceptance of the new role was the silent agreement in their relationship. But Edward's memoir challenged the nature of that accord and resurrected old wounds. Donahue provided a convenient escape from a painful past and its present retelling.

Added to this strain was Wallis's recognition that her presence in Edward's memoir was negligible. Readers were given only the barest of biographical details about her life. Rumours that swirled in society gossip columns about her childhood, her early marriages and her supposed sexual exploits while living in China were left unaddressed, and there was no mention of the outsider status she occupied as a fringe member of the British Royal Family. Had Monckton and Allen had their way, she would have been expunged entirely. But, as it was, Wallis remained a one-dimensional detail amid the panoply of Edward's more illustrious royal past – little different from the position she had first occupied when the scandal of their romance broke in 1936.

But the story was not over, and in the coming years Wallis began to find a voice. She would emerge in the mid-1950s, with Murphy at her side, as a pivotal narrator of the emotional consequences of the abdication.

IO

The Duchess Speaks

'I am delighted, and I congratulate you as an author,' Longwell wrote to Edward on 13 April 1951, a few days after the American publication of *A King's Story*. 'The book reads at a gallop, and that's how a good book should read. It's modest and charming, tremendously interesting, and makes its point firmly but unobtrusively.'[1] Most reviewers agreed with Longwell's assessment, including the poet and critic Stephen Spender, who believed the memoir a 'solid but vivid piece of social history' that affirmed 'The Duke of Windsor's true vocation . . . not so much to be King as to be a critic from the inside.' Edward, Spender believed, had given 'new life to the concept of what a constitutional king should be in a modern democracy'.[2]

'HRH is in terrific form,' observed his secretary Anna Seagrim on 19 April, four days after Spender's review appeared in the *New York Times*. Edward, she noted, was 'very happy about the book, which has had a wonderful reception . . . the reviews have been too marvellous — completely beyond our wildest expectations.'[3] But Edward remained modest about his efforts. 'I've had G. P. Putnam Sons forward you a copy,' he wrote to his long-time friend Eric, Earl of Dudley, on 3 May 1951, 'but you don't have to read it.'[4] He said the same to the exiled head of the House of Hapsburg, Archduke Otto of Austria, but added, 'If you do peruse the pages, I believe you will better understand the passages on the difficulties of kingship in a modern world than other readers.'[5]

After a brief stint in New York, Murphy was reassigned to *Life's* sister magazine *Fortune* and relocated to Washington D.C. But he and Edward remained in touch. In May, the Duke was invited to speak at a luncheon hosted by the American Booksellers Association in Cleveland, Ohio, and Murphy, in a role that Churchill had once occupied, provided the finishing touches to his keynote address. In September, to more muted acclaim, the British edition of the book was published, and Edward sent an inscribed copy of the new version to Murphy's thirteen-year-old daughter, Edythe. She was, Murphy assured him, 'delighted to come into possession of a signed copy', and 'in her patient and persevering way has almost finished the book'.[6] When Murphy arrived back in New York at Christmas, he joined Edward for a lunch hosted by Longwell at the fashionable Rockefeller Center restaurant, Louis XIV.

Murphy was still in New York on 6 February 1952 when Edward received news that his brother, George VI, had died at Sandringham. Summoned to the Waldorf Towers, he helped craft Edward's statement to the press, then accompanied him on board the *Queen Mary* to watch as he delivered the prepared remarks to the throng of gathered reporters. A year later, Murphy provided 'editorial and research assistance' on Edward's article about the upcoming coronation of his niece, which neither he nor Wallis were invited to attend. Simultaneously, Ken Rawson, now an editor at David McKay, also proposed Murphy as a collaborator for a children's book he thought Edward should write about his royal upbringing. Though Murphy got so far as to create a first draft of the manuscript, Edward showed little enthusiasm for what he irreverently labelled 'the Kids' Book',[7] and the project was eventually dropped.

Murphy and Edward's ongoing collaborations meant he was the leading candidate to help Wallis when she began to consider writing her own memoir. As far back as 1949 Longwell had tried to interest Wallis in authoring a 'series of little essays on the American girl or entertaining'.[8] This was to be in a similar light vein to her 1942 recipe book published in aid of the British War Relief Society, *Some Favorite Southern Recipes of The Duchess of Windsor*. She was unenthusiastic and discussions soon turned towards a full-length autobiography. From the outset, Longwell was sceptical. 'I am afraid,' he wrote to *Life* colleague Roy Larsen on 22 November 1950, 'that anything we did after the Duke's memoir would be an anti-climax.'[9] In the spring of 1952 Hank Walter offered *Life* first option on the project, but with an advance even higher than the one they had paid Edward. Longwell refused, and he also cautioned Murphy against any involvement in the enterprise. 'The thing is so nebulous,' he wrote to him on 31 July 1952, 'I think you would be wasting your time.'[10]

But, eager to supplement his income from Time Inc., Murphy dismissed Longwell's warnings and pursued the project. It took a further year but eventually three contracts were signed – one with McCall's for a series of articles, the second with the publishing firm David McKay, now headed by Ken Rawson, and the third with Murphy. On 8 January 1954, the day he formally signed on as Wallis's ghostwriter, Murphy joined the Windsors for dinner in their apartment at the Waldorf. 'They seemed delighted to see me,' he recorded in his diary. 'The Duchess once more expressed her misgivings over proceeding . . . But for the first time she announced her intention to go ahead with it.'[11]

Wallis's sudden determination surprised even Murphy. But over the course of the almost two-year negotiation, the Windsors' lives had changed dramatically, giving new purpose to an enterprise that might otherwise have been dismissed. By 1954 they had finally accepted that their exile was permanent. The death of George VI had severed an important emotional link with the abdication, but it did nothing to alter prevailing attitudes among Edward's family. Queen Mary still refused to receive Wallis. 'My mother's mind was set,' Edward later told Murphy. 'There would be no reconciliation. The fact that my marriage was manifestly a true and felicitous one did not move her.'[12] Influenced by her grandmother and her own mother's implacable disdain for the Windsors, the new Queen, Elizabeth II, made no attempt at a meaningful reconciliation with her uncle. And though Fort Belvedere remained vacant and uncared for, it was made clear to Edward that he would never be allowed to return.

In a gesture of quiet acceptance, the Windsors began to put down permanent roots in France, something they had resisted since 1937. In the summer of 1952 they purchased 'The Mill', an eighteenth-century converted water mill an hour's drive outside Paris. Consisting of four stone buildings and twenty-six acres, the River Mérantaise ran through the estate, making it the ideal setting for Edward to renew his passion for gardening. Murphy described it as 'a gem of its kind – a miniature French village', and it became the Windsors' weekend escape and Edward's preferred residence.

Alongside the acquisition of the Mill, the Windsors also changed their Paris homes. In 1953 they relocated from 85 rue de la Faisanderie to 4 route du Champ d'Entraînement, a sprawling mansion tucked inside a garden of more than two acres on the edge of the Bois de Boulogne. Built in 1929, and later occupied by Charles de Gaulle during the Second World War, the lease was owned by the city of Paris, which offered it to the Windsors for a nominal annual rent.

Murphy believed the costly renovations of both houses accounted for the Duchess's 'heightened interest in the autobiography'.[13] Wallis was no doubt influenced by financial incentives, but the deaths of her brother-in-law and of Queen Mary on 24 March 1953 may also have emboldened her to consider breaking the code of enforced silence that even fringe membership of the British Royal Family entailed. As Edward told Murphy in 1962, with his mother's death 'my last strong link with the past was severed. Queenship,' he added, 'the iron rules of convention, had formed her nature, and however sensitive her inner feelings, she could not bring herself to reveal them.'[14]

Having remained dutifully silent as others, including her husband, told her controversial story, Wallis seems to have decided that the time was right for her to speak. 'You have had an extraordinary life,' Murphy wrote to Wallis on 31 October 1953. 'It has been touched by history . . . It would be a mistake to leave the last judgement with those dreadful characters who have . . . addressed themselves to the subject of your life.'[15]

Work on the memoir began tentatively in late January 1954 in New York but did not begin in earnest until Murphy arrived in Paris on 15 October. Wallis had no pretensions as a writer, and Murphy's plan, as he informed her on 5 August, was 'to develop the basic material through conversations . . . using a tape recorder'.[16] To Murphy's frustration their first lengthy interview did not take place until 28 October, almost two weeks after his arrival. 'I thought grimly,' he recorded in his diary on 19 October after another cancelled meeting, 'the pattern was repeating itself.'[17] But once they got going, Murphy was impressed by the precision of Wallis's memory and her 'fairly sharp gift of description'.[18] As with Edward, Murphy went straight to 1936, tackling head-on the most controversial components of her story. The planned tape recorder was not yet in place, so Murphy transcribed Wallis's words as she spoke.

Wallis, Duchess of Windsor, on 'The Abdication' Paris, 28 October 1954[19]

It was a whirlwind affair – an explosion. It was upon me before I realized what was making up. I have often gone back over the event in my mind. It is possible that if I had stayed in England I might have persuaded the King not to abdicate. But I doubt that I ever could have changed his mind.

Perry Brownlow thought I was making a mistake in leaving The Fort . . . But I had already answered the question in my own mind. If I stayed in England, and if the King abdicated, then I would be blamed for the result. It would be said that I was afraid of losing him . . .

Yet while I think I did the right thing I realize now that the minute I put my foot inside France I had ceased to exist, so far as my being able to affect the situation . . . I couldn't make myself understood. As for the King, he was hard driven himself. The people around him were pulling him apart. A time came when he could not endure the pulling. His one desire was to get away.

David [Edward] can be influenced and persuaded. But it must be done in a certain way. His reason can be appealed to. But if you try to force him he will walk out of the room, close the door between and make up his mind alone. That was what happened after I left.

All the talk of his not wanting to be King makes me angry. He always wanted to be King. He often discussed with me what he proposed to do as King. He intended to be not so much a new kind of King as a King who rules in a more modern way. That did not mean that he intended to stand on his head in Piccadilly. He wanted to introduce to kingship some of the ideas he had learned as Prince of Wales.

The fact is that the King never told me until the storm broke, how serious was the issue between him and Stanley Baldwin. He told me of the details and I realized that he was worried but he always reassured me . . .

Where the British Government erred was in pushing him into a decision. If Baldwin had not pushed him, the idea of a marriage might have been put out of [his] mind. The King had a strong sense of duty. He was profoundly troubled. Above everything else he wished to do the right thing. But he was new in the position. He was trying to change from being the Prince of Wales with all of his accustomed independence and relative freedom, to being monarch. He was in love with me and it both saddened and angered him that others disapproved. He does not react well to criticism. He was unaccustomed to it. He felt he was being censured like a willful boy. This infuriated him.

There was a time when, if somebody wiser than I was in these matters had come to me, and told me what was at stake – the views of the Dominions, the attitude of the gentry, the politics of the Church of England – I might have persuaded the King to abandon any idea of marriage. But no one ever did. I was without weapons. All I could say was no to a man who was determined to marry me, and he would not listen.

. . .[T]he British . . . at least paid me the compliment of not trying to buy me off. That was the only insult that was not tried.

Yet in retrospect I see now that the people around the King were also confused. No such situation had ever occurred before. Nobody knew quite how to deal with it. The natural instinct was to stand aside and apart, leaving it to the King to make the decision. It was difficult to decide where and how to intervene . . .

One thing that angered me was the failure of the British Government to make any provision for the King. I could not believe that it had not acquired for him . . . a place where he might stay in dignity until our marriage. He himself did not complain. But he was so accustomed to having things done for him as to be almost helpless. The Rothschilds had asked us to spend Christmas with them. I asked them to take in the King. This they generously offered to do. They too were friends in need.

Could I have persuaded him not to abdicate? The question has haunted me ever since. I believe now that if someone in Britain who knew what was involved had taken me into his confidence I might have prevented this tragic thing. But by the time I realized what was going on it was too late. The King was just as glad that I made up my mind myself to leave the Fort. He said, 'I must fight out this thing alone.' He didn't want me directly involved. He kept his family out of it . . . He said to me afterwards, 'I was alone on the bridge. I even sent my navigators below.'

Wallis was hesitant to allow Murphy to record her speaking, but Edward encouraged the plan, and at his instigation the duo finally got the 'tape recorder into action' on 30 October. Their first attempt at a recorded conversation was not successful. 'The Duchess,' Murphy noted in his diary, 'was acutely conscious of the fact she was being recorded: her answers were mannered and almost painfully restrained. She was rather rude to me at dinner. I declined to be trodden upon and told her so, politely. That cleared the atmosphere. To bed at 1:15 a.m.'[20]

After several days of further experimentation, the situation improved. On 6 November, after having lunched alone with Wallis at the Mill, Murphy and she began again. 'The Duke,' Murphy recorded in his diary, 'had the tape recorder ready to go except for a click of the switch. In response to my questions she talked almost steadily for nearly three hours – our best performance to date.'[21] The transcript of the conversation, which Murphy's secretary diligently typed, stretched to fifty-six pages.

The interview began by discussing Edward and Wallis's decision to be married at the Château de Candé. A small but luxurious Renaissance castle in the Loire valley, the estate was owned by the French efficiency millionaire, Charles Bedaux, and his American wife Fern, friends of Herman Rogers's brother Edmund. Bedaux had unexpectedly written to Herman just five days after the abdication, offering his home as a sanctuary to Edward. He declined, but Wallis accepted in his place. Candé offered her privacy and a suitable backdrop for the wedding, which was planned for early June.

Wallis and the Rogers arrived at Candé on 7 March, and Edward joined them on 4 May, just a day after Wallis's divorce from Ernest became absolute. They were married at the château on 3 June 1937 in a small ceremony witnessed by only a handful of guests. 'Everybody was asked that had a reason to be asked,'[22] Wallis told Murphy. Among those present were Wallis's Aunt Bessie, Edward's long-time friend Edward 'Fruity' Metcalfe, his wife Lady Alexandra Metcalfe, who photographed the ceremony, Herman and Katherine Rogers, Walter Monckton, Charles and Fern Bedaux, Randolph Churchill (Winston's son) and Eugene and Catherine 'Kitty' Rothschild, Edward's hosts at Enzesfeld in Austria, where he had gone immediately after the abdication. None of Edward's family attended. Preparations for the ceremony, Wallis remembered, 'were not very gay'.[23]

Though Murphy was meant to be focusing on Wallis, their conversations inevitably turned towards Edward. Having said goodbye to him in *A King's Story* on the deck of HMS *Fury*, Murphy resumed the narrative by exploring, through Wallis, the emotional and practical fall-out from the abdication.

Interview with Wallis, Duchess of Windsor
The Mill, 6 November 1954[24]

MURPHY: What was the Duke's feeling about his family?

DUCHESS: The Duke's feeling towards his family was— There wasn't a week went by when they didn't do one or another disagreeable thing to him. So I think his feelings are pretty numb regarding his family by the time the six months had gone. I think by the time his brother wrote and said that I wasn't to have his name I think he had no feeling at all, as far as that goes . . .

MURPHY: Do you remember the Duke's appearance when he arrived [at Candé]?

DUCHESS: Yes, I thought he looked very thin and strained but I didn't expect him to look otherwise . . . I mean he looked like a man who had been through a great deal, which indeed he had . . . I don't think he regretted his decision to go, but I think he was absolutely struck down by his family's behavior after he'd gone. Because he left them in a very friendly way and he expected to be treated with friendliness, instead of that he was treated in a most horrible way by all of them, and I think that was a terrific shock to him . . . I think it hurt him a great deal, but he keeps things to himself. But I think it showed on his face. And I was of course beset with newspapers and these outrageous stories about me which were not true at all, about who I was . . . and I had no redress. I had to keep myself from getting an inferiority complex over all the things that were being said

and of which there were so many terrific lies – that's the
hardest thing. And that requires a great deal of patience,
and you have to make some sort of an arrangement with
yourself how to deal with that. And, of course, the Duke
who had never been anything but yessed all his life and
had been protected in every way, he was completely on his
own and with his family turned against him, though they
knew he was going, they had accepted that fact and all said
goodbye to him, and no sooner was his back turned they
began to attack him. That I think was unfair.

Edward had parted with his family on 11 December 1936 in a spirit of
goodwill, completely oblivious to the enormous institutional shock he had
inflicted upon them. He interpreted their affectionate farewells as a tacit
approval of his decision and left England believing it was only a matter of
time before he, with Wallis at his side, would be accepted back into the
royal fold. His first few weeks at Enzesfeld did little to dispel that impression. He remained in almost daily communication with the new King and
wrote frequent letters to his mother. Visits from both the Duke of Kent
and his sister Princess Mary in mid-February reinforced the view that there
had been no serious disruption in either his royal or familial role.

But as February wore on, the situation began to change, and relations between Edward and his family frayed. By the time he joined
Wallis at Candé they were irretrievably broken. The collapse of the
financial agreement signed at Fort Belvedere was key to the breakdown. But other less consequential factors were also at play. In late
February, Monckton was dispatched to Enzesfeld by George VI to
put an end to Edward's incessant phone calls to Buckingham Palace.
The new King was feeling harassed by his brother's demands over
his future status and overwhelmed by his unsolicited advice on kingship. Monckton was sent to tell Edward that this routine must stop.
As he later noted, this 'started a stream of division between the
brothers and, indeed, between the Duke and the rest of his family,
which widened into a gulf over the title to be given to his wife'.[25]

But additional forces added to Edward's mounting sense of grievance.

In March he was removed as Colonel of the Welsh Guards, a post he had held since 1919. Though ostensibly a regimental decision, Edward believed his dismissal had been at his family's behest. Shortly thereafter, he was also informed that he would no longer be a Privy Counsellor – a position he had held as Prince of Wales since 1920.

'Well, I suppose I have no standing of any kind now,' Edward supposedly told Fruity Metcalfe, who was staying with him at Enzesfeld. 'I used to be a Field Marshal and an Admiral of the Fleet – but now I'm nothing.'[26] Further disappointment followed on 11 April 1937, when George VI wrote and informed his brother that, in accordance with the advice of his government, no member of the family would attend his wedding at Candé. Edward's former aides, now serving under the new King, were also advised to stay away and none accepted Edward's invitation. Even Lord Brownlow, no longer serving at Court (he had been unceremoniously dismissed from his role as Lord-in-Waiting in late December 1937), was warned by the Bishop of Lincoln that he would be forced to resign as Lord Lieutenant of the county should he or his wife appear at the ceremony.

Edward also faced the implacable resistance of the Church of England, who refused to grant his request for a religious ceremony. Though a priest was eventually found who was willing to defy the ecclesiastical edict (Reverend Robert Jardine, who was subsequently relocated to the United States when he was forced out of the Church of England), it further fuelled Edward's resentment. On 26 May, now reunited with Wallis at Candé, he wrote coldly to his mother, with whom he had stopped corresponding regularly: 'After the way that Bertie has continued to take advice that the Government and the Church of England are giving him according to their policy to ostracize us – I am definitely disgusted . . . Thank you for your good wishes, but it saddens me that the present conditions do not make me feel that they ring very true.'[27]

These issues were at the fore of Murphy's mind as he continued questioning Wallis on 6 November 1954.

MURPHY: Did you have any plans for your life, any specific plans after the marriage?

DUCHESS: No, we had no plans, we never discussed any plans. In the first place we were exhausted, we were so glad to be married and so glad to be left alone that we didn't have any plans . . .

MURPHY: It was very clear in the Duke's mind and in yours that the Duke would not return to public service?

DUCHESS: Yes, well, we knew from the attitude . . . that his family would block anything, and I say I think that his family would block it more than the Government . . . One of the great reasons was because they did not want me to have any [position]. The more they could get me down, the more they thought they could destroy. I think they would really like to have seen the marriage become unhappy, so as to get him back, and so I think they thought that by destroying me in every possible way, I mean to make it difficult, to make it possible for the world to be rude to me, that I would succumb under it. Well, they miscalculated that.

MURPHY: It was a form of cold war?

DUCHESS: Yes, it was a form of cold war, and I think they thought that that would make me so unhappy that I would become cross and disagreeable . . . that I would not be able to take the snub which they were forcing upon me. But it had just the opposite effect, it made me more and more determined to make a success of it. I was determined that they should not get me down.

MURPHY: Did the Duke ever discuss with you the subject of his family's attitude?

DUCHESS: No. We had one discussion about it, and I felt that a man's family has the right to disapprove of a marriage and take whatever attitude they want about whomever their son marries, and even if they . . . do not want to give it a try, I think that is their privilege. His mother was a great character and I think she was devoted to him and I did everything in my power to make him keep in contact with his mother and he wouldn't, I know that, he wouldn't have done it if I hadn't forced him to go and see her. I used to force him to go to England when he first started to see her. I sent all telegrams, Christmas telegrams and different things to them, I wrote them all out for him, but he never would have, he was too hurt and he never would have had any contact with his family again if it hadn't been for me. So I have no feeling about it, at all.

MURPHY: Yet, in a sense, the subject was a closed one?

DUCHESS: Yes, and I never would have come, I was not going to come, between a mother and her son, that is too dangerous a thing to ever have on your conscience . . . I did not want him to think I had, because I did not want him to be unhappy about it. So I made him understand that I did not mind at all. We made our lives without even considering England or his family. We made the sort of life we would have made if they did not exist. We would have done exactly the same, what the Duke always wanted, I think – to have a house of his own which was not a palace and to be able to live that sort of life. Not that if he had been King he wouldn't have been an excellent King, but I think he enjoys his own home and he always has something to do. People always say to me, 'Well, what does the Duke do?' Well, I say if only he could only find he did not have something to do . . . I have never seen a busier person. And I think it is marvelous, when you have not got a job to be able to make so many jobs for yourself, which he has the gift of doing . . . I can't say that he doesn't miss knowing what is going on behind the scene that he always had known, he would like to be informed of what the policy is of his country, so that he would not express an opinion that they would not want said. But we had no idea of anything. If they had given him a job we would have done it to the best of our ability, as we did at the Bahamas . . .

MURPHY: How easily did he adjust himself to this life?

DUCHESS: Well, you see, it was not hard for him, because he'd always lived in the simplest way. I mean he always took the worst room in the house. I meant if he went anywhere, he always took the smallest room, and he bought that ranch, which could not have been more uncomfortable, and he always liked simple things. So the fact that he was not living in a palace, it was not that different to him. He had always mixed with people – in fact he mixed much more with people with less money than he had than with the people who had everything in England. He did not really go so very much to the big houses in England and so forth, he knew people who had smaller flats [such as Wallis and Ernest Simpson] and those were the people he liked better, which of course has been the criticism, because all the upper class, so to speak, turned against him. Because he never made very intimate friends with them.

Murphy was back at the Mill the next day and this time, as he noted in his diary, 'Both the Duke and the Duchess took turns recording. Again, a good day's work by prevailing standards.'[28] Interviews continued throughout November. The next surviving recording was with Edward, who began discussing George VI's decision to deny Wallis the style of 'Her Royal Highness'.

Interview with Edward, Duke of Windsor[29]
The Mill, 5 December 1954

MURPHY: But it never occurred to you, Sir, at that time when the final arrangements had been made that your wife's position would be in any way . . .

DUKE OF WINDSOR: Never. Never at all, never. And that only was conveyed to me two or three days before we were married.

MURPHY: How did you receive that news?

DUKE OF WINDSOR: It came in a letter from my brother. I was warned of it, actually, by Sir Ulick Alexander, Ulick Alexander who came to our wedding. And, erm, he told me. He said, 'I think that I shall be getting a letter that I am to deliver to you, and it doesn't contain very good news.' Well, I said, 'I'm pretty used to that but what is it?' I couldn't believe my ears when he told me what it was. And this letter, which was obviously written by Simon [John Simon, Home Secretary in 1936] and by the secretaries, and God knows who, I mean my brother just took a piece of paper and copied it, do you know. I mean, it was very— well, cleverly— more it was not the kind of letter that I think he'd have thought up himself because there was (laughs) no loopholes but there was no blame on him, at all. No blame.

MURPHY: Do you think he wished to do it himself, Sir? Or was there pressure on him?

DUKE OF WINDSOR: I really don't know. No, I like to give him the benefit of the doubt, I don't think he did. But I think that, er, well, it's as though there were other influences, some very close and others possibly ministerial, and no doubt that Archbishop of Canterbury. I'm sure that he probably dabbled more than anybody else.

Edward was not entirely honest with Murphy. The uncertainty over whether Wallis would be styled as 'Her Royal Highness' after they married had worried him from the outset of his exile. The question of Wallis's style also preoccupied George VI, who, backed by Queen Mary, believed that it was a status she should not receive. Yet the consensus among government officials, including the Home Secretary, Sir John Simon, was that legally it was unavoidable. But the Royal Family were persistent, and eventually Simon found a solution. He advised George VI that he should issue new Letters Patent conferring upon Edward, but not his future wife or heirs, the style of 'Royal Highness' on the pretext that having abdicated his place in the line of succession he had also given up the style that had been his since birth. The premise was shaky, particularly as it contradicted George VI's own insistence at the time of Edward's abdication broadcast that he be announced as 'His Royal Highness Prince Edward,' but that detail was ignored. On 27 May 1937, just a week before Edward and Wallis were to marry, the new Letters Patent were issued. The document ensured that the Windsors' marriage would be morganatic – which only five months earlier they had been told did not exist under English law.

Reprising his role as a go-between, Monckton was dispatched to Candé with a letter from George VI confirming the decision. 'This is a nice wedding present!'[30] Edward exclaimed, after reading the message. The ceremony went forward as though nothing had happened and Edward insisted (as he would for the remainder of his life) on everyone referring to his new wife as 'Her Royal Highness', and addressing her as such.

But while they were on honeymoon in Austria, Edward continued to fume. On 14 June, Allen advised Monckton that Edward intended to release a lengthy public statement denouncing the 'insult to his wife',[31] and declaring his intention to give up his own title. Monckton and Allen were predictably horrified and eventually dissuaded Edward from any action. Though Monckton noted in his later memorandum that he was always 'strongly in favour'[32] of Wallis having the title, he confided to Allen, on 9 June 1937, 'He was determined to be married at all costs – and the cost goes on mounting. This present trouble is one of the items in it . . . I do think it has to be paid.'[33]

At Edward's behest, Allen made extensive legal enquiries, which included enlisting the services of the prominent barrister Sir William Jowitt, who concurred with Simon's original opinion and said that legally Wallis was entitled to the style. But it was to no avail and in the end Edward's sole recourse against the edict was the defiant reply he sent to his brother on the eve of his wedding. 'I wish to place on record to you,' Edward wrote to George VI on 2 June, 'that I do not deem myself to be bound by the Letters Patent of 27th May 1937.'[34] But Buckingham Palace was adamant and, via instructions invariably sent by either Hardinge or Lascelles, made sure that wherever the Windsors went, British officials obeyed the mandate. The subject of Wallis's title remained a source of permanent frustration for Edward and poisoned all hope of a future reconciliation with his family. The 'curtain had gone clanging down', Edward told Murphy. 'I doubt that my brother ever really wanted to see me isolated so peremptorily. But the Monarch and through him the entire Royal Family are prisoners of the tight little world – the Establishment . . . that regulates Royal conduct, even its private affections . . . It meant . . . that I would go forward to my marriage and my new life with my own family standing aloof and disapproving.'[35]

Shortly after his conversation with Edward, Murphy raised the subject directly with Wallis. Though the style was hers, their discussion remained focused on the effect the decision had had upon Edward.

Wallis, Duchess of Windsor, on 'The Question of Title'
Paris, December 1954

The brother's order, denying me the title of HRH, was a deep wound to him. It meant nothing to me but it hurt him. It gave my enemies a stick to beat me with. For the exclusion was a permanent reminder to him that, in the eyes of the Royal Family, I was of lesser status than he. Women curtsied to him; they did not have to do so to me.

The matter was overlooked in the negotiations concerning the abdication. It never occurred to me that his wife would be denied that which was part of his birthright. He was shocked by his brother's action. To him it seemed a deliberate trick. He insisted upon having the title. The matter was brought up many times, through his lawyers. But the Royal Family refused to unbend. The Duke cannot understand this. In his eyes I am entitled to the styles and titles accruing to him . . .

I will say, too, that it has hurt me. There is no pleasure in being a second-class citizen, or a second-class Duchess for that matter.

I cannot understand the attitude of the Court . . . They have never given me a chance to show that I am different from what I have been painted . . . He [Edward] cannot understand why his blood kin should close the doors to his wife. Their attitude has hurt him desperately.

I am tired of being the problem child of the British Empire.

British friends are afraid to receive us for fear of not being invited to Court. Some of our former American friends are equally apprehensive. Our life, in consequence, has been circumscribed. I would gladly have worked for British charities. But where would I find the right British names to help me?

In other families even if a man or woman marries a person of whom the family may disapprove reconciliation usually takes place after several years. Sensible people, kindly people, make up. But that has not been so in my case. The Iron Curtain has never lifted. For my husband it has meant permanent exile.

Even as these candid conversations took place, Murphy was aware that Wallis remained hesitant about delving too deeply into the emotional landscape of her past. 'It is extremely difficult,' Murphy recorded in his diary, on 21 November 1954, 'almost impossible, to penetrate her caution. Her life, I suspect, frightens her.'[36] Yet Murphy remained drawn to the Windsors as actors on the historical stage, and his renewed intimacy with them, nine years on from his first meeting with Edward, enabled him to observe their lives as they settled into old age and permanent exile. Over lunch at the Mill on 28 November, Murphy met the artist James Gunn, who had been commissioned to paint a portrait of Edward in his Garter robes – a Christmas present from Wallis. 'I was impressed,' Murphy wrote, 'by the quick working sketch, which had caught the tragic look in the Duke's face – the pinched features, the sunken mouth; a look trying to be determined and resolute but succeeding only in being desperately sad. It is a look I have seen often.'[37]

As interviews carried on, Murphy began writing chapters. But as usual he needed more information to move his narrative beyond a merely superficial retelling. On 5 December, the date of their next surviving recorded conversation, he tackled Wallis's arrival at Candé. But Wallis quickly changed the subject, moving on to topics she felt much more passionate about – the abdication, the American press (which Edward and Wallis blamed for stirring up the sensationalist speculation about their romance), the hate mail she received and, as always, their treatment by Edward's family – playfully suggesting at one point that, left up to her, the book would be called *Turn the Left Cheek*. It was, he noted in his diary later that evening, 'one of the most fruitful afternoons'[38] they had spent together.

Interview with Wallis, Duchess of Windsor
The Mill, 5 December 1954[39]

MURPHY: Could you perhaps tell me a little bit about the difference between your life at Cannes and that which you led at Candé?

DUCHESS: Well, you see, Cannes – it was the beginning, the whole bubble burst. The interest in the whole thing was at fever heat when I arrived at Cannes. It was then that I was beginning to understand the world wasn't made up of good-will, but rather jealous people, a great many crazy people, and spiteful and all the things I'd never really had time to bother about because they weren't in my mind. I'd really never had any spite in my make-up or envy of other people. I'm afraid again comes my selfish side. I was always so interested in myself, whether it was the smallest thing that was going to happen to me – people were nice, attractive, and I never went down into what all human nature was made of until it was absolutely thrown at my head like a bombardment. I got the full crag of what life really is.

MURPHY: Which is as though the world had blown up on you?

DUCHESS: Well, yes, my world had certainly blown up, and I was thrust into being a public character in twenty-four hours. People who become public characters generally become so because they want to be one. I mean, a politician knows he's going to be a public character, in a way, a successful politician.

MURPHY: You used a very striking phrase a moment ago – your world blew up, on a breakfast tray?

DUCHESS: Tray of letters. But I had to train myself. I used to get terribly bitter at times, because I thought it was unfair to judge a person you'd never seen, you didn't know the circumstances surrounding it, you were to put pen to paper to damn someone that you didn't know. I mean the letters that were of sympathy to me were from the most human people, but they were in the minority. I used to get terribly depressed from them. I used to wait sometimes in the morning till I got a little stronger before I'd begin opening them . . .

Wallis told Murphy that she 'never read one newspaper about myself'.[40] In fact, she pored over press clippings, complaining bitterly to Edward about her treatment in British and American newspapers. 'The world is against me,' she exclaimed, in a letter on 14 December 1936. 'Not a paper has said a kind thing for me.'[41] Murphy may have suspected that she had not told him the truth and pressed her on her reaction to the coverage she received. He even managed to get her to address the notorious 'China Dossier', a report that was alleged to have been commissioned by the British government and passed to George V, which suggested she had received sexual training in Chinese brothels. Wallis had travelled to China in January 1924 hoping to resuscitate her marriage to her first husband, Win Spencer. She spent most of her almost two years in China living with Herman and Katherine Rogers at their home in Peking. Neither the dossier nor any evidence of an investigation exists. Eventually, as it always did, the conversation veered back to Edward.

MURPHY: I see. But then you did mention these outrageous things being said about you in the press?

DUCHESS: Well, Herman used to tell me these certain things, because we used to have debates whether we'd write [to complain]. But what could you do because I mean the press made up – I think the British put out a terrific propaganda. I always think they did. I don't know, I have no proof of it. But Lady Astor [Nancy Astor] goes around talking about some dossier of mine. We've never been able to trace some dossier. We got hold of George Allen and he could never trace anything at all. Well, if anyone put out a dossier it must have been the British. And then different friends of mine told me that fantastic stories about me came back from China. There was nothing fantastic about my life in China, the Rogers, I was living with them. I would see every possible story of invention simply made by venom, feminine venom . . .

MURPHY: You also mentioned to him that after reading these letters, hearing the criticisms, that 'I am a woman without a country. I have no place to go – only France.'

DUCHESS: Yes, because you see I had my own country against me, and the whole of England and the Dominions. I mean there wasn't anybody that said, well, 'Stop it, she can't be that bad. This thing can't be that bad.' No, everybody just got out their whips and lashed. Nobody tried to see any other angle to it except that I could have prevented the abdication. They didn't stop to think of the Duke's make-up – whether you can prevent a man of his character to do things or not. They never stopped and said, 'Well, maybe she tried.' Not one break was I given in the whole thing. I don't think anybody ever tried to put themselves in my position in any way to realize what I was thrown into – without any guidance. And there wasn't absolutely anybody of any power connected with me, who could have said to someone in power, 'Listen, let's tone this thing down, this is getting pretty bad.' And that is one of the things I had to rise above. I felt I couldn't go out and show my face. It's as though I committed some horrible murder. And that was very hard, and Herman was the one that helped me during that time, because I had to talk it over with him. Sometimes I used to say, 'Well, it's really more today than I can take.' Something, some bad news from England would come, or they'd done another thing to the Duke, you see. I mean, it's the things he'd tell me on the telephone, and I heard no word of complaint. He'd say, 'Oh, they removed me from the Welsh Guards', things that meant a great deal to him, you see, and I'd come back to Herman, I'd say, 'Well, just one more slash at the Duke now.' All those things upset me, just as much as they upset him. The whole six months we were separated, they thought up some devilish thing to hurt him about every six weeks. And then they crashed down with my title at the end. They saved the atom bomb for the end. The week before the wedding or something, they saved that one, but each thing was done with a reason, to flatten him out in England so that if there was any piece of popularity left they could destroy it. It was a sense of destruction, one of the most cleverly devised pieces of destruction of a public man in the eyes of the people that I've ever seen worked. Why? He'd gone in good grace, they knew his make-up, they didn't have to do that. He was never going to take advantage of his popularity in England or any sympathy that he might have had in his cause. He went and in a very fine way, and they should have taken his word for it. Instead of that, having built him up to the sky, they went out with these really fine propaganda ways of destroying him, one of which was to make me a terrible character. That he'd married an adventuress and Heaven knows what. That was one of the methods they used, so in destroying him they even destroyed me with the British. He was a desolate man who'd fallen in love with this adventuress. That was the basis of the propaganda. And they – they just really did everything they could to make him unpopular with the British people. Why not let him alone? Let the British people make up their own mind. I have great bitterness there.

MURPHY: You made the point that when the Duke came to Candé you were conscious of his strength.

DUCHESS: Oh, naturally once you see the person that's in the same [predicament]. I was alone, he was alone – naturally two people are stronger than one to combat things. But we both had to fight out the worst part alone. With a bad telephone communication and listened in to, to boot.

MURPHY: But he never, he refused to allow himself ever to . . .

DUCHESS: Wouldn't discuss it. I mean if I said, 'I think that's outrageous what they've done,' he wouldn't answer. The conversation ceased then. I suppose he didn't want me to know how badly he felt. Oh, no, it was a very, very difficult thing.

MURPHY: Did you write very much during that period?

DUCHESS: Oh, yes, we never sent a letter through the post because it would certainly have been opened and read. I mean, don't forget that England would have – having kicked him out and beaten him down, they'd have done everything in the world to prevent him marrying me.

MURPHY: In other words, that was the strategy then to prevent the marriage if possible.

DUCHESS: After all that, but when they couldn't do that then they decided on the title. Quite a nation!

No further recordings by Murphy exist after 5 December. On 9 December Edward and Wallis sailed for New York, with Murphy following shortly thereafter. But the partnership became uneasy. 'Her mood has changed,' Murphy recorded in his diary on 12 February 1955. 'She was irritable, snappy, and not intelligent.'[42] A few days later he added, 'She complains that I am not fully sensitive to her personality.'[43] Even as they continued to work, Wallis complained that Murphy's chapters had 'not caught her spirit, her youthfulness and gaiety'.[44] Murphy took the complaints in his stride but, on 9 April, just hours after saying goodbye to the Windsors as they set sail for Europe, he was fired over lunch by Hank Walter. Wallis chose the writer and society commentator Cleveland Amory to replace him. A few days later, Edward and Wallis explained their decision to Murphy directly.

Edward, Duke of Windsor, to Charles Murphy
Paris, 27 April 1955[45]

Dear Charlie,

I am sorry to have taken so long to thank you for your two letters . . .

In the first place, as to the manner chosen to acquaint you of the Duchess's decision to cancel your contracts. As Hank has dealt directly with you in all legal and financial matters . . . we decided that he should be the one to tell you that in the interests of the memoirs, the Duchess has decided to seek other editorial assistance.

We hope that in his conversation with you immediately after we sailed from New York, Hank followed our instructions by making it clear to you that the cancellation of your contract is no reflection whatsoever on you personally, nor on the quality or substance of the material you have prepared as a first draft. On the contrary much of what you have written is excellent, especially the chapters dealing with the Duchess's actions and reactions before and after the Abdication.

No, as you say, you and our friendship for you, do not enter the picture at all. For want of better words, I, as a watcher on the sidelines, attribute the difficulty to a clash of two very strong personalities, the one ultra feminine and the other complete masculine counterpart. While you and I could not have teamed up better over *A King's Story* and I could not have found an abler or more congenial collaborator in a long and tough writing project, with the Duchess it was quite different. As you well know, protracted and sometimes agonizing concentration on writing and drafting has never been down her alley, as it has had to be down mine all my public life. Her mind works like the proverbial lightning – a great gift in many ways – but she just cannot undertake the 'yellow blank' system the way I can . . .

Actually the Duchess had grave misgivings from the start as to whether you and she could ever work together and, in all fairness to you, blames herself entirely for not having said so frankly to you, Ken and Hank a year ago.

. . . We hope that you know that if there is anything we can ever do for you and Mrs Murphy you will let us know. Our long association with you is something we value greatly and your loyalty to us has been and always will be appreciated . . .

Wallis, Duchess of Windsor, to Charles Murphy
Paris, 27 April 1955[46]

Dear Charlie,

I am so terribly sorry that things have turned out this way. It isn't, please believe me, that I don't think what you have written is excellent, but I do not feel myself in the pages. That is no fault of yours; it is most likely the fashion in which I have tried to put myself over to you.

However, as the book will surely come under the hammer – (like I myself have) – more than the average, I feel I must have another try at it.

I do hope this turn of events will not in any way impair a friendship which the Duke and I have valued and enjoyed these past years . . .

But the partnership between Wallis and Amory did not go as planned. In late August, Murphy began to hear rumours of the 'kiddish quality' of Amory's work and suspected, 'A new crisis is in the making.'[47] By October, according to Otto Wiesse, the president of McCall's magazine, Amory was in 'an almost hysterical condition,' and the publishers, including Max Aitken, who was overseeing syndication in the *Daily Express*, 'had lost all confidence in the project and in Amory personally'.[48] By the end of September Amory was officially out. 'The Duchess terminated her contract with Amory,' Edward wrote to Murphy on 14 October, 'for the simple reasons that her publishers had rejected the work and it was therefore impossible to continue with him.'[49] Murphy was rehired, and in March 1956 the first of five weekly articles appeared in *McCall's* magazine. Wallis's full-length autobiography was published on 28 September. The title, *The Heart Has Its Reasons*, was lifted from the chapter in Edward's memoir that recounted their fateful first meeting.

As with Edward, Murphy's steadfast resolve saw Wallis's project through to completion. The five months with Amory was largely a waste and little, content-wise, was salvaged from the short-lived collaboration. 'If you are lucky,' Weisse had warned Murphy over cocktails in New York, on 20 September 1955, 'you'll be able to save [from Amory's work] a couple of commas and a period.' But unlike Murphy, who had always remained firmly in the background, Amory took centre-stage in the drama of his dismissal and in doing so took control of the book's public reception. 'You can't make the Duchess of Windsor into Rebecca of Sunnybrook Farm,' Amory famously asserted to reporters as he arrived in New York in the wake of his sacking on 4 October 1955. In referring to the classic American novel about an innocent orphan who, through strength overcomes adversity and makes a new life for herself, Amory aimed to undermine Wallis's credibility and sow the seeds of doubt that her memoir could ever be anything more than a hack job sprung from her own vanity. The analogy stuck, and in the coming years Amory would repeat it time and again as he rehashed his experience with the Windsors. It was a key punchline when he appeared on the American television network NBC's *Today* programme a few days after *The Heart Has Its Reasons* was published. When asked what he thought about the book, Amory replied simply, 'I would say never have so many worked so hard to keep so much out.'[50]

Amory was a skilled tactician in the game of public relations, and his embittered and catty remarks succeeded in diminishing the public's perception of the memoir to such an extent that it was largely ignored by the critics. The reviews that did appear were, as Murphy noted in his diary on 26 September, 'certainly not good'. 'In general', he reflected, 'the reviewers have taken the line laid down by Cleveland Amory. They are reviewing not the book but the woman and since they cannot bring themselves to endorse the woman, they refuse to endorse the book.'[51] The gossip that swirled prior to its publication remained, and Wallis had little success in humanising her controversial story. When Murphy questioned noted *New York Times* reviewer Charles Poore over drinks at the Century Club on 10 October 1956, Poore advised him that no review had appeared in the famed newspaper because 'neither he nor his colleagues considered it important enough'.[52]

But Murphy did not share Poore's assessment. He had crafted the work authentically and translated, into diplomatic language, the spirit of Wallis's candid conversations. Yet along the way, he realised any significance the book had was entirely in terms of Edward. In telling Wallis's story he had inadvertently added a sad but necessary postscript to *A King's Story*, a work that, as the years passed, he came to regard with increasing admiration. As he wrote to Max Aitken on 12 April 1956,

> The more I have struggled to deal with the lives of the Windsors, the more I found myself concentrating on and developing the theme of the former King's re-adjustment to life. I did this not for calculated purpose, at least in the beginning, but rather because everything else seemed so meaningless and purposeless. Then, suddenly, it dawned on me that this was the only way for her to tell the story; the little man emerges as the central character and for the first time we have the account of a former monarch trying to make a life for himself in a relatively inhospitable

world. The technique has an additional merit; it enables us to traverse the years of empty wandering without directly accounting for them, although all the implications are there.[53]

The German Question

Edward died at his home in Paris on 28 May 1972. In Britain and the United States, his death was front-page news. Three days later his body was flown to Britain, and on 5 June, after a service at St George's Chapel, Windsor Castle, he was laid to rest in the royal burial ground at Frogmore. For the first time, the Duchess was welcomed by the Royal Family. She was invited to stay at Buckingham Palace and appeared alongside Queen Elizabeth II and the Queen Mother at Edward's funeral. But she declined to attend the ceremony of Trooping the Colour on 3 June, the annual parade held to honour the sovereign's official birthday. From a window of Buckingham Palace, clad in black and wearing pearls left to Edward by Queen Mary, she watched the parade march back to the forecourt, the close of a ceremony that had honoured the memory of the former King with a minute's silence. By the time his two-day lying-in-state concluded, more than sixty thousand people had filed past his coffin.[1]

Murphy did not attend Edward's funeral, but he watched the television coverage with interest from his home in Washington D.C. He had last seen Edward in early 1971. Since the publication of Wallis's memoir, the pair had remained in regular touch, working together on intermittent projects and keeping up with each other socially in New York and Paris. In 1969 they began a book about Edward's youth, which seemed a more promising subject than the biography of George III that Beaverbrook had proposed in 1962. But in the face of Edward's declining health the writing never gained momentum, and, in January 1972, now undergoing painful treatment for the throat cancer that would eventually kill him, Edward wrote, telling Murphy it was time to 'forget the whole thing and classify it as project abandoned!'[2]

Disappointed but aware that all was not well, Murphy kept a vigilant eye on news about Edward during the spring of 1972. 'My affection goes out to you afresh,' Murphy wrote to him on 22 March, after learning that he had recently undergone surgery. When no information was forthcoming, he turned to Wallis, with whom he was not in the habit of corresponding. 'We three have passed a good deal of time in one another's company, time that did have a creative value,' he told her, in a letter on 17 April. 'I know that the Duke's means enable him to command whatever he may need. But . . . if I can do anything for you that you may judge useful and helpful, it will be gladly forthcoming . . . In the midst of work, even of some strain, we had good times together. The memory of it all remains strongly in my mind.'[3]

More than most, Murphy appreciated the poignancy of Edward's final return to Britain, set as it was amid the backdrop of the scenes of his princely youth. Murphy was moved by the final chapter of a life in which he had played a unique role.

'The things I learned about these places from the Duke, and the relationship of the two of you with that world, came hauntingly back to my mind . . .' he wrote to Wallis, on 9 June, just four days after Edward's funeral. 'In London, when I was about with HRH, I heard more than once older men call, "Good old Eddie" – the war greeting. All the while, as we both know, there was, barely heard but there all the time, that other powerful reservoir of emotion at the time of the Abdication – affection and pride in the Prince of Wales, a gallant and famous and attractive man. Then at the end, half a lifetime removed, it was expressed again.'[4]

Yet Murphy's sympathetic epitaph has not endured, nor have his insightful reflections on the struggles Edward faced in exile as he tried 'to make a life for himself in a relatively inhospitable world'.[5] Instead, in the fifty-one years since his death, another, far less nuanced and historically dubious, portrait of Edward has emerged to dominate the popular understanding of him.

'There is no possibility of my forgiving you. The question is how on earth can you forgive yourself?' exclaims Queen Elizabeth II to her ageing uncle, the Duke of Windsor, as she sends him back into exile after learning that he had conspired with the greatest enemy of the twentieth century, Adolf Hitler, to remove her father from his throne. Set in the mid-1950s, this is Elizabeth and Edward's final scene together in the highly successful but heavily fictionalised television series *The Crown*, and the moment is composed as a triumph of the young monarch's moral fortitude as she brushes aside their shared bonds and condemns Edward as a traitor to his family and his country.

Back in Paris, the episode closes with a dejected-looking Edward suffering the pointless monotony of an evening card game with Wallis amid the splendour of their gilded exile. What has led him to this abject existence, he wonders. Glancing away from the table, he stares into the mirror, back into his past, back to Germany, and viewers are presented with a seamless transition from the fictitious to the factual as five carefully selected historic stills from the Duke and Duchess of Windsor's 1937 trip to Germany close the episode. Edward, the real Edward, is pictured basking in the glow of Nazi admiration, surveying its militaristic might and standing proudly in the presence of Hitler. A final photograph, the most horrifying of them all, shows Wallis beaming as the Führer, in a chivalrous bow, grasps her outstretched hand. In an otherwise grainy image, the swastika on Hitler's armband is boldly captured and it leaps to the fore, framing, with Wallis, the ex-King, who looks on in admiration – as though entrapped by the two forces that have held him hostage: his wife and the Third Reich. In the director Peter Morgan's first use of still historic photography in the series, these undeniably striking pictures seem meant to offer irrefutable proof of Edward's guilt.

Morgan's treatment of Edward as the 'traitor king'[6] is now the overriding impression we have of him. Not created by *The Crown* alone, this portrayal has been built by a body of material that has flourished since Wallis's death in 1986 when, freed from the threat of libel action, their more 'venturesome biographers',[7] as Philip Ziegler called them, have cemented the assumption that Edward was a Nazi sympathiser. This judgement is based primarily on two periods in the ex-King's exile, which, though considered minor by Murphy and other of his contemporaries, have now overtaken all other biographical threads of Edward's story: his visit to Germany in October 1937 and the four weeks in July 1940 he spent in Lisbon, where he and Wallis had sought refuge after fleeing Nazi-occupied France. Both events took place amid complex personal and political circumstances for Edward. In the absence of diligent scholarship, the facts surrounding each have been merged with further hearsay about Edward's political allegiances, which have in turn been augmented by supposition and gossip. As a result, the man whom Prime Minister Edward Heath declared had 'made monarchy a living reality'[8] has been lost and contemporary perception rests on a sensationalist but highly skewed narrative about Edward's life, which has confused his political inclinations towards appeasing Hitler with accusations of full-blown treachery.

Edward had not shied away from discussing his brief engagement with Nazi Germany in 1937 when he and Murphy began compiling material for his memoirs in 1948. Though the meeting with Hitler fell outside the chronological scope of their work, a description of both the encounter and the man evolved seamlessly from Edward's other recollections of Joachim von Ribbentrop, who had been appointed German Ambassador to Britain in August 1936. Edward approached the subject without trepidation and treated both men in a style not unlike his other descriptions of the world leaders he met in the 1930s. His comments were intended as a record of fact, objective in detail and forthright in language. He showered neither with praise nor bestowed upon Germany the type of adulation he accorded to the United States.

La Croë, 18 August 1948

The first time I saw Ribbentrop was at Lady Cunard's when he was the German Ambassador to London . . . He never stopped talking about the German regime. I left England and did not know until later of his bitterness against the English. He was a buffoon and rather a ridiculous man, and his wife was never without a headache due to sinus. As things boiled up between Germany and Great Britain, people began to ostracize them, and he acquired a hatred for the British. This was unusual, for generally the Germans that were anti-Communist actually had a deep-lying respect for Britain and wanted her as an ally.

The second time I met Ribbentrop was when I was King, and he came to present his credentials as Ambassador* [30 October 1936]. This is a formality, and an entire Embassy staff accompanies its Ambassador on this occasion, then withdraws leaving him in a few minutes' conversation with the King. Later, and as is usual, the King summons him one day and sits down with him for an hour or so, and this was the third time I saw him.

The fourth time was in October 1937, when the Duchess and I were in Germany. When he heard that we were traveling in Germany under the auspices of Hitler, Ribbentrop rushed to Berlin, and it was written in our itinerary that he and Frau Ribbentrop would like to give a dinner for us. We attended, and that was the time when the Duchess sitting next to him was told, 'When your husband left Britain, Germany lost a friend.' He gave us a fine dinner, attended by officials, Nazis and some friendly Berlin society.

The end of the trip, we met Hitler. We never knew if we would see him or not, and each day it seemed to be a matter of great mystery as to whether the Führer would see us. On the way by train from Stuttgart and Munich, suddenly our whole train was changed, and we found [out in] the car we were going to Berchtesgaden . . . and at the little station were met by Hitler's aide . . . and were taken up the mountain to

---

* In *A King's Story* he described Ribbentrop in this encounter as 'polished but bombastic', words Edward himself wrote.

the house. We were shown into a large room, and the aide said he would like to take me to Hitler's room. I went up with an interpreter named Schmidt. I told Hitler that I could speak German and did not need the interpreter, but he said, 'I always have a record of my talks.' I think I only had to ask the interpreter about two words.

I was with Hitler about two and a half hours, then we went down to the room where the Duchess was waiting with the aides, and we sat around a large tea-table and had coffee, tea and cakes. Hitler talked about all the things he had done in Germany, extolled the excellence of his party and system, and as good as said he would have no quarrel with the British unless they were stupid enough to oppose him in any way. But he did not talk war, mostly about civilian life, and he asked me questions about Britain's housing and the welfare of the British people.

Hitler was taller than one imagines, very vigorous, very serious.

After about an hour, we were told it was time to go to the train; so we took leave of Hitler and went on, to Munich.

Edward's meeting with Hitler at his home in Berchtesgaden was an unexpected finish to the two weeks he and Wallis had spent touring Germany's industrial centres and holding meetings with senior Nazi officials for what he publicly stated was for 'the purposes of studying housing and working conditions'.[9] The brief encounter eventually eclipsed any other narrative surrounding the trip. Gushing descriptions in the American press of Hitler's 'affectionate farewell'[10] to Wallis on the steps of the Berghof made international news, and created an impression that Edward's political views were decidedly pro-Nazi.

Yet Edward saw things rather differently. Though he had, just ten months earlier, promised to 'quit altogether public affairs', much had happened in the first seven months of his exile to change his outlook. Now faced with what he believed was the implacable hostility of his family towards him and Wallis, he became convinced that he must carve out a new separate future under his own auspices. Without the traditional advice that had been available to him either as Prince of Wales or as King, Edward began to listen with enthusiasm to other, less conventional, voices, who were offering to guide his post-royal career and without whom he would most likely never have ended up in Germany in October 1937. First among these individuals was Wallis's host at Candé, Charles Bedaux.

'Not particularly attractive' but 'full of energy'[11] was how Wallis described Bedaux to Murphy – a man whom neither she nor Edward had ever met when she accepted the use of his home in December 1936. Bedaux's gesture was audacious but well-timed and appealed to a couple who felt increasingly rejected by a hostile world. They appreciated what Wallis recalled as his 'great sympathy with the way the Duke had been treated'.[12]

He was also just the sort of man that Edward tended to admire. A self-made millionaire and amateur explorer, Bedaux embodied all the dynamism in American life that Edward revered. He had arrived penniless in the United States in 1906, and over the following thirty years transformed himself into one of the country's leading industrial consultants. In 1917 Bedaux established his first efficiency consultancy and began selling the 'Bedaux System of Human Power Measurement', a standardised labour measurement unit called B that could be applied across a range of industries. His efforts were satirised in the Charlie Chaplin film *Modern Times*, and he was despised by many American labour leaders. As his biographer Michael Weatherburn notes, with the expansion of his business and by extension his wealth, he became over the course of the 1930s 'a well-known socialite, womanizer, big game hunter, and adventurer'.[13] He had purchased Candé in 1927 and spent the next two years transforming the fourteenth-century Renaissance castle into a paragon of modern luxury. His renovations epitomised the power of American wealth to transform decaying European heritage and were part of Bedaux's evolving plan to cultivate the society of the international elite.

A man who craved fame and historical permanence, Bedaux leapt at the chance, through his friendship with the Rogers family, to insert himself and his house into the ongoing drama of Edward and Wallis's romance, which the Baltimore journalist H. L. Mencken described ironically as 'the greatest story since the Crucifixion'.[14] But what began for Bedaux as a much-longed-for publicity coup swiftly evolved into an even greater opportunity, which was designed to place him at the fore of the Duke's future life.

In early April Bedaux arranged, via Wallis, who had formed a quick and close friendship with his wife Fern, for Edward to receive a letter from Oscar Solbert, an American military attaché who had briefly served on Edward's staff during his 1924 visit to the United States. Solbert, now an executive at Eastman Kodak (a Bedaux-company client), made an eloquent appeal for him to lead an international movement dedicated to European peace. Rooted in the strength of working-class support, the campaign would entail Edward making extensive investigative tours of housing and industrial conditions. 'I believe,' Solbert wrote, 'you are the ideal man to head such an establishment . . . You would confound every critic, would become a power to be reckoned with, and would stand ready for any eventuality.'[15]

By the time Edward and Bedaux met in May 1937, the now embittered ex-King was primed to listen with interest as his host began to elaborate on Solbert's proposition. Bedaux, a master salesman, argued that even without the support of the British monarchy Edward could still wield his personal charisma, as Solbert suggested, in service of the causes he had championed as Prince of Wales. It was an appealing argument for a man who, after a lifetime of steady employment, faced an uncertain future. And after the wedding at Candé in June, in concert with others, including Thomas Watson, the founder of IBM and confidant of Roosevelt, Bedaux persuaded Edward to begin making practical plans for a series of international tours that would kick-start a new chapter in his public life.

Watson was a particularly influential voice as Edward and Bedaux's collaboration developed. In August, Edward met Watson and his wife, Jeannette, over lunch at Schloss Wasserleonburg, the rented Austrian castle where the Windsors had spent part of their honeymoon. The meeting had been arranged at Bedaux's instigation and took place while he and Fern were staying at Wasserleonburg. It was a major turning point in the evolution of Edward's plans. Watson was himself fresh from his own tea-time visit to Hitler. Having travelled to Berlin to preside over a meeting of the International Chamber of Commerce, he had met the German leader on the afternoon of 28 June, just a few days before he became the first American to be given the Order of Merit of the German Eagle in recognition for services to the Third Reich, specifically 'the improvement of international economic relations . . . in the maintenance of peaceful relations'.[16] Watson encouraged Edward to believe there was a void on the international stage that he was primed to fill. A proud exponent of the slogan 'World peace through world trade', Watson believed free trade and better social conditions would lay the ground for a lasting international peace. The philosophy chimed perfectly with Edward's, and the encounter further encouraged his alliance with Bedaux, who presented himself as Edward's link to a new group of dynamic and powerful men. Bedaux eventually added a third voice to the chorus, that of the Swedish founder of Electrolux, Axel Wenner-Gren, whom Edward met in Paris in the autumn of 1937 and who pledged to finance any future tours he might undertake in Europe.

Surrounded by a new set of advisers and buoyed by their enthusiasm, Edward confidently agreed to Bedaux's proposal: a programme of two immediate tours that would focus on an inspection of housing and labour conditions in the world's leading industrial nations, Germany and the United States. The visits, Edward was encouraged to believe, would replicate the success he had enjoyed as Prince of Wales and most recently as King, offering him an international springboard from which to begin a new life of purposeful post-royal employment.

Bedaux's efficiency consultancy had only tentative roots in Germany but it had firm foundations in the United States, where companies such as Kodak, General Electric, DuPont and Goodrich made up his client list. He agreed to oversee and fund Edward's American tour, which was planned as a month-long inspection of companies throughout the United States. Edward also agreed to allow Bedaux to announce publicly that he was sponsoring the tour, ensuring he was at the fore of press reporting when details of the trip emerged towards the end of October.

Without the same network in Germany, Bedaux passed logistical and financial responsibility for Edward to the German government, who leapt at the opportunity to host the ex-King. Robert Ley, Chairman of the National Front (the national labour organisation), was put in charge of Edward's tour. While Edward would doubtless have been aware of Bedaux's high-profile business links in the United States, he was probably less familiar with the precarious state of his German company, a much smaller enterprise, which had been seized by the government shortly after Hitler came to power in 1933. After five years' careful wooing of Nazi elites, Bedaux's company was returned to him in exchange for fifty thousand dollars and an agreement to hand over a percentage of his profits to the National Front. As Janet Flanner noted in her profile of Bedaux, published in the *New Yorker* in 1945, 'Bedaux figured that, as a result of the Duke's visit . . . the Party in general, and Dr Ley in particular should feel they received a favor from Charles E. Bedaux, one he could hope they would return right away, or pretty soon anyway.'[17]

The dangers inherent in Edward's visit were immediately clear to the British Ambassador to France, Sir Eric Phipps, who arranged a meeting with Edward shortly before his departure and reminded him that the Germans were 'past masters in the art of propaganda'. Edward brushed off the warnings and assured Phipps that he was more than aware of the potential dangers and would be 'very careful and not make any speeches'.[18] Phipps was the lone Establishment voice who questioned Edward directly on the decision. Monckton seems to have absented himself from the role of Edward's adviser-in-chief, and no one in the British government intervened formally to dissuade him from his plans. As the British Ambassador to Portugal, Sir Walford Selby, later noted, 'What guidance of any kind did he or anybody else get from our paralysed Foreign Office? [Lord] Halifax [then Secretary of State for War] tells us he visited the Sports Exhibition and Hitler in November 1937 with full approval of Eden, in other words the approval of the Foreign Office.'[19] Instead, Buckingham Palace accepted the inevitability of Edward's decision and their chief concern revolved around matters of protocol – ensuring that embassy staff virtually ignored the Windsors' presence. Edward, as Monckton later reflected, had always had 'constant access to the best advice in every sphere'. Now, devoid of 'responsible advisers', he left for Germany in a spirit that was as enthusiastic as it was naive.

When they had worked on the *Life* articles and *A King's Story*, Edward had held back on providing Murphy with a detailed explanation of why he and Wallis were in Germany. It was an understandable omission as both took place almost a year after the events in his published auto-biography ended, and therefore were irrelevant to further discussion. But when it was time to assist Wallis, whose memoir was to cover her life up to the 1950s, Murphy's remit could include questioning the couple about the visit. Both Edward and Wallis freely recorded their memories of the prominent Nazis they had met. They framed their recollections of these encounters as social rather than political occasions, highlighting their impressions of individuals who were, by 1954, infamous. These anecdotes dominated and obscured more detailed descriptions of the strenuous programme of inspections of German infrastructure that Edward undertook. Following an itinerary created by Ley, in consultation with Bedaux, Edward approached the trip as he would have any other royal tour. He conformed to the schedule that had been made for him and greeted crowds and his hosts with the expected (royal) enthusiastic goodwill. Over the two weeks, he visited, among others, a model machine-making factory in the Marienfeld district of Berlin, the porcelain factory at Meissen and a newly created settlement of working-class homes near Stuttgart.

Interview with Edward, Duke of Windsor, and Wallis, Duchess of Windsor
Paris, 6 November 1954[20]

MURPHY: Were you primarily interested in housing?

DUKE: Yes, in housing

MURPHY: Rather than labour?

DUKE: Sure, far more than in labour. I could exert no influence on labour, but I had studied housing and I had formed committees, and in Great Britain when I was Prince of Wales I did a great deal towards housing improvement in Kennington [London], the Duchy of Cornwall property. I was very interested. I was identified with various housing schemes. I visited housing schemes in . . . Denmark, Sweden, Austria, France, and other countries besides Germany . . . We arrived at the Bahnhof in Berlin . . . Ley [Robert Ley, their escort for the tour] was there . . . a number of German officials, but there was nobody from the British Embassy . . . And I had not been at the hotel more than, oh, half an hour when I had a call from the British Chargé d'Affaires [George Ogilvie-Forbes] because Nevile Henderson, who I believe was the British Ambassador there at that time, was away on leave or whether he had absented himself because of my visit I couldn't tell, to show that the British Government were not identifying themselves in any way with our visit . . . Anyway, he asked if he [Ogilvie-Forbes] could come and see me. And he was quite a nice spoken man and I said, yes, I would receive him any time he would like to come. So he came about an hour after we had arrived. And he said, 'I must apologize, Sir, for not being at the station to meet you, but I had orders not to do so, but I have come to pay my respects to my former King and to tell him that I was sorry that I was not able . . . was not allowed to do it.' And then we talked a bit. He told me some quite interesting things about Göring and about the different officials, which was very useful, and it was a very amicable meeting, but he didn't . . . couldn't offer us lunch or dinner at the British Embassy because he was under orders not to do . . .

MURPHY: Could you tell something about the details of the trip?

DUKE: I could tell you a little more about Dr Ley. Dr Ley we
hated from the start. He did drink quite bit . . . He was
very lewd, a very coarse man . . . Fortunately the Duchess
could not understand but some of his jokes were very much
off colour . . . I was always glad when we were not in his
company. Otherwise, we had some quite nice people with
us . . .

MURPHY: What about your visit to Carinhall [Göring's home]?

DUCHESS: . . . We had tea in this very modern type of room,
an enormous tea-table, the biggest table I had ever seen,
round. And he was in his white uniform, and I spoke French
with him. And she spoke English . . . The house was very
interesting. He was very proud of his maids . . . all dressed
in a sort of peasant costume and he was very proud of the
rooms he made for them, and each room had the name of
the maid on the door. They were very nicely furnished with
bright-coloured cretonnes and then we went upstairs and
he showed us his bedroom.

MURPHY: What was that like?

DUCHESS: Well, that had sort of Italian paintings in it, a
strange bedroom, rather gloomy, darkish . . . And then we
saw the gymnasium and then we saw his library where he
had maps . . . And then we left, and then she [Frau Göring]
tells me she is going to have a baby . . . There was no
discussion of politics. No.

DUKE: Well, except the only one actually, if I can intervene
for a moment, when the Duchess mentioned the maps. One
of them was a big map of Europe, and Germany was
painted in a very outstanding colour. And I told Marshal
Göring that we'd just come from Austria where we had

spent our honeymoon, we had been there three or four months, and I looked at this map and he obviously saw that I was a little surprised because I saw that there was no Austro-German frontier, the whole of Austria was incorporated into Germany, so I thought, well I'm not going to say anything, and he picked it up and said, 'Oh, yes, I know what you are looking at, you see that Austria is coloured the same colour as Germany. It's a new map, and as it will be Germany very soon, it will save the trouble to have the man change it.'

DUCHESS: And he also said, 'Where are you going to live?' And we said, 'Oh, we have not quite decided.'

DUKE: And we liked Austria very much.

DUCHESS: And we like Austria very much, and we are going to America and we will decide . . . 'Oh,' he said. 'You ought to decide to come and live in Germany.'

MURPHY: What response did you make to that?

DUKE AND DUCHESS: Oh, we just skipped it, turned it off.

DUCHESS: No, there was no political conversation, it was a typically social tea. People making conversation.

DUKE: It was interesting to see the way he lived. And he actually was far the nicest of all of them. He was the only, well, gent, you could say. He was the only one who really knew how to behave . . . the only one. And he was the only one that at the end anyone could talk to. Even Nevile Henderson went to see him and various people . . . at the last moment, because they felt that he was the one who really did not want the war. But he could not prevail on Hitler. He was much the less aggressive Nazi. Himmler was a horrible man. Do you remember? He was a brute. Goebbels was a cripple with an enormous head, very thin.

DUCHESS: He was clever, and he had the prettiest wife . . .

DUKE: Hess had great charm, and spoke very good English . . .

MURPHY: What about your visit with Hitler?

DUCHESS: Well, we didn't expect to see Hitler. It was not in the books to see Hitler. We were in Munich and we got a message saying that the Führer would like to see us the next day. I mean it wasn't on the schedule at all.

DUKE: Well, it was in the air. It was never done until about the evening before when we were told that the train was ordered for us at a certain hour.

DUCHESS: . . . We were not met by Hitler. He saw us off. We went into the house and we sat on a sort of veranda and looked at his magnificent view and then the Duke was taken to see Hitler and I was entertained by three or four of these men, one of them being Hess who stayed behind, and Schmidt, of course, went because he always had him . . . You were nearly two hours . . .

Edward had been annoyed that Hitler insisted their conversation take place through an interpreter. But the presence of Paul Schmidt, the only other person in the room when the two men spoke, offers an important record of what actually transpired, which agrees with the version Edward gave to Murphy. Schmidt's account was published in his 1951 memoir, *Hitler's Interpreter.*

[The Duke] expressed his admiration for the industrial welfare arrangements he had seen, especially at the Krupp works in Essen. Social progress in Germany was the principal subject of conversations between Hitler and the Windsors during the afternoon. Hitler was evidently making an effort to be as amiable as possible towards the Duke, whom he regarded as Germany's friend, having especially in mind a speech the Duke had made several years before, extending the hand of friendship to German ex-servicemen's associations. In these conversations there was, so far as I could see, nothing whatever to indicate whether or not the Duke of Windsor really sympathized with the ideology and practices of the Third Reich, as Hitler seemed to assume he did. Apart from some appreciative words for the measures taken in Germany in the field of social welfare, the Duke did not discuss political questions. He was frank and friendly with Hitler, and displayed the social charm for which he is known throughout the world . . .[21]

DUCHESS: . . . Then there was tea in this big room . . . and of course he [Hitler] did not speak any English so I could not really talk to him at all . . . so we had tea with him and he was very nice, and then he came and saw us off, at the steps and that is the picture when we just shook hands with him . . .

MURPHY: What was your impression of Hitler?

DUCHESS: Well, I thought . . . I think anyone that you see a whole country become absolutely fanatic about you are fascinated to meet him, and you begin to think they must have something because you have heard it so much. I thought he had the most extraordinary eyes. He was certainly not a good-looking man in any way, nor did I think he had any dignity or bearing, but he certainly had eyes . . .

MURPHY: They were piercing eyes?

DUCHESS: Yes, absolutely piercing, and intense, intense. I should think a bundle of nerves. And very long, slim hands, like musicians' hands . . . But as far as the visit was concerned . . . I think the Duke had vaguely in the back of his mind that he would do something with housing. He did not expect to get anything from the British Government, that had become very apparent, and he thought he might do something in a private capacity with housing as a job. There was nothing concrete worked out. And therefore I think he was interested in, as I told you, the two places to see probably the best housing . . . America and Germany . . . It was done in the most normal way, out of a real interest, thinking maybe that would be the sort of job he could have . . .

MURPHY: Was there any attempt to work on you concerning the British attitude?

DUCHESS: Absolutely none. Absolutely none. Not on me. I don't know what the German conversations were, but I am sure there wasn't.

DUKE: No.

According to Edward's detective, David Storrier, who accompanied the Windsors to Berlin, Edward was not impressed by the encounter. Storrier recalled their conversation in the car as they drove away from the Berghof. 'The Duke said he found them distasteful people and said, "Winston [Churchill] is right. He [Hitler] cannot be trusted."[22]

Speaking to Murphy, Wallis was clearly aware of the impact that the image of her outstretched hand to Hitler had on the public imagination. But as part of Bedaux's plan there should have been another picture of another tea-time meeting that Wallis could have described to Murphy. It would have communicated a very different political message. This photograph would have captured the American President Franklin D. Roosevelt welcoming Edward and Wallis to the White House. In a format similar to their visit to Berchtesgaden, the informal afternoon meeting was designed as an opportunity for Edward to discuss with Roosevelt the pressing issues he believed existed around housing and industrial conditions. In an added boost to his mission, the First Lady, Eleanor Roosevelt, who was scheduled to be away at the time of Edward's planned meeting with her husband, had agreed to escort him around the New Deal model housing settlement, which she had helped sponsor, in Greenbelt, Maryland. Both meetings, had they happened, might have reframed Edward's encounters in Hitler's Germany but on 5 November 1937, only hours before they were to set sail, Edward announced that due to the 'grave misconceptions and misstatements' that had arisen about his 'motives and purposes',[23] he was compelled to cancel their visit.

The Windsors had returned to Paris from Germany on 24 October. Almost immediately upon their arrival they realised the implications of their tour, particularly in the American press, which was on heightened alert. The couple's 'flirtation with Germany' and 'Edward as a Fascist propagandist'[24] made for uneasy headlines, as did the growing public disquiet around Bedaux. He had now taken centre-stage as the 'Duke's Guide'[25] and his track record, both business and personal, suddenly came under intense investigation. Bedaux's business links with Germany were highlighted, as was his efficiency system, which, as the Washington Post asserted, was 'liked' by employers but condemned by labour leaders, who believed it 'makes nervous wrecks of men'.[26]

Alert to the fact that his actions were being misinterpreted, Edward felt compelled to come to his own defence and clarify what his intentions were in making the trip to Germany and the forthcoming one to the United States. Having initially refused to address the Anglo-American Press Association, whose luncheon in Paris he had been invited to attend on 27 October, he changed his mind and agreed to speak. He insisted, he told the room of gathered journalists, that he had travelled to Germany 'as a completely independent observer without any political considerations of any sort or kind and entirely on my own initiative', and balked at the press 'speculation' and 'search for ulterior motives in regard to the Duchess's and my doings'. He urged the press to take him at his word and view his travels as the responsible actions of a man who did not want a 'purely inactive life of leisure' but through private initiative might offer solutions to help solve 'some of the vital problems that beset the world to-day'.[27]

Edward's speech was reported in the United States but his words had little impact on the impression being formed by his activities. And despite receiving a reassuring letter from Churchill on 28 October, congratulating him on the 'distinction and success' of his visit to Germany and wishing him a 'prosperous' American 'journey',[28] events quickly overtook the Windsors' plans as Bedaux, now in the United States, faced the full condemnation of press scrutiny. Powerful labour-union leaders took aim, citing his exploitation of the working man and his links to Fascist regimes. On 3 November the Baltimore Federation of Labor touched off a nation-wide campaign against the 'Bedaux system' and promised organised protests wherever the Windsors went. The drama played out in the headlines of American newspapers until Edward was finally forced to confront reality. 'My decision,' he wrote to Bedaux on 9 November, 'was the only one possible.'[29]

'In the elements that brought about the crash,' the British Ambassador to Washington, Sir Ronald Lindsay, advised Hardinge on 7 November, 'I give the first place to labour in general and to Bedaux in particular. It is certain that the Duke could hardly have chosen a more unsuitable man to act as his agent and organiser.'[30] Though Edward was bitterly disappointed at the outcome, his brother breathed a sigh of relief. While Buckingham Palace had viewed the Windsors' trip to Germany as a fait accompli, the King was agitated by the prospect of their American visit, which he and his advisers feared might garner the Windsors support at the expense of the new monarch. Such was George VI's and Queen Elizabeth's distress over the announcement of Edward's tour that Lindsay was summoned to Balmoral for an emergency conference with them. But the failure of Edward's enterprise, which, as he wrote to George VI, he 'never wished to be a triumphal progress',[31] still elicited Lindsay's sympathy. With striking prescience, he observed the heart of Edward's dilemma in his post-abdication life. He was a creature of negatives, neither a private individual nor a royal figure, and, if he continued to behave as a member of the Royal Family, he did so without the protections and protocols that would once have guarded him. Lindsay concluded to Hardinge:

> The Duke put himself in an entirely false and illogical position, for he purported to be a private person desiring as such to investigate for himself and to do some public good, and yet his tour was organised as a royal progress . . . The Duke is in fact neither the one thing nor the other, and tragic as it may be I could wish, for the sake of the future, that he may learn a lesson from the events of this week. Apart from blunders made . . . all the criticism arose . . . out of the essential falsity of his position.[32]

Like Lindsay, Wallis also laid the blame squarely on Bedaux, as she explained to Murphy. Why, she asked, had there not been some guidance, some warning offered to them about the risks? Though Edward had sometimes chafed at the corps of palace advisers that had guided his royal life, he had relied upon their discretion and judgement to steer him in the right direction. Cut off from that source of support, Bedaux's network filled the void their absence had left. And, as Wallis pointed out to Murphy, George VI had himself sanctioned the use of Candé as an appropriate site for their wedding. Trusting in this, but more importantly relying on the character reference from Herman Rogers and the friendship formed between Wallis and Fern during the spring of 1937, Edward stopped short of asking more difficult questions about his enthusiastic sponsor. It was a naive omission but, as Wallis had told Murphy on 5 December 1954, 'You have to trust some people sometimes.' With hindsight she also acknowledged a sadder reality: 'Everybody seems to have had a motive in our life, to use us at that time.'[33]

DUCHESS: . . . I think it is very important to realise that we really did not know anything about Charles Bedaux other than what Eddy Rogers [Herman Rogers's brother] wrote to Herman. I think it is very important to register that. It may sound a very stupid thing to say . . . But I had never heard of Charles Bedaux or anything about him . . . We took Herman Rogers's brother's word for it and never questioned it . . . The strange thing is . . . the British Government. You would have thought [they] would want to have kept the Duke out of the public eye; one of the things was to beat him as flat as a flounder, and keep him out of the public eye. Well, they knew if he went to Germany he would get into the public eye and they knew that Bedaux was a character under fire . . . then they should have sent out some minor official to France and said that this is the situation, because they ought not have wanted him to get into the public eye but evidently they wanted him to get in the public eye in an unfavorable light. Or someone could have done some long distance advising. Because you cannot throw a man out of a country, who has been advised by a government all his life, and then expect him to make wise decisions right off the bat.

After the very public breakdown of their trip to the United States in November 1937, the Windsors turned their attention to more domestic matters and set about making a home for themselves in France. Between 1937 and the outbreak of war they divided their time between Paris and Cap d'Antibes, and were at La Croë when hostilities broke out in Poland on 1 September 1939. War was declared in France and Britain on 3 September. After a brief visit to London, their first since 1936, the couple returned to their rented home in Paris, 24 boulevard Suchet, where Edward took up a post with the British Military Mission at

Vincennes. In May 1940, as the Germans advanced into France, Edward and Wallis, like many, fled the city for the south, hoping to escape the imminent Nazi occupation. After a brief stopover at Biarritz, where many British expatriates had gathered, they made their way to La Croë. But the respite was short-lived. On 10 June Italy declared war on France. With Italian troops marching on south-eastern France and German troops nearing Bordeaux, the Windsors were once more forced to flee. 'Did you hear from Winston [at this time]?' Murphy asked Edward, during an interview in 1954. 'Nothing . . . Nothing at all,' he replied. 'We were completely isolated.'[34] Unable to reach Bordeaux, where the remnants of the British Embassy were being evacuated, on 19 June they joined a convoy of vehicles led by the British Consul General at Nice, Major Hugh Dodds, headed for Spain, the only escape route now open to them. 'It was really like leaving a house on fire,'[35] Wallis told Murphy.

On 20 June they arrived at Perpignan, just ten miles from the Spanish border. 'Was any preparation made for your exit into Spain?' Murphy asked. 'None whatsoever,' Edward replied. It was the Spanish Ambassador to France, José de Lequerica, responding to Edward's cable from Perpignan, who eventually granted their entry into Spain. After two days in Barcelona, they made their way to Madrid. Unlike other visits to European capitals, the Windsors' presence was officially acknowledged, and they were greeted by the British Ambassador, Sir Samuel Hoare, who had been alerted by Lequerica to their arrival. Expecting to leave immediately for Lisbon, where Churchill had arranged for two flying boats to take them back to Britain, they were instead told to wait a further week. The Duke of Kent was on an official visit to Lisbon. Wanting to avoid an awkward encounter between the brothers that would necessarily include Wallis (whom no member of Edward's family had yet received), it was deemed best by all parties, including Edward, that he wait until his brother had departed. It was an unfortunate delay. Comfortably installed at the Ritz Hotel, Edward began to ruminate once more about his future and Wallis's position were they to return to Britain. 'Then,' as Wallis explained to Murphy, 'the Duke started to send Winston [Churchill] some cables because he wanted more or less to know what were the plans for us on arrival in England.

They mightn't have suited the Duke. Considering the way his family had treated me he wanted to be sure what was going to happen to me, arriving in the country. So he started some cables . . .'[36]

By the time the couple left for Lisbon on 2 July (the same day the Duke of Kent had departed), ostensibly to rendezvous with the two flying boats and return to Britain, tensions between Edward and the government had heightened. Edward had laid down a series of conditions for his return: a job and recognition by his family for his wife. Oblivious to the crisis Britain faced and engulfed by bitterness about his family's attitude, he bombarded Churchill with messages. As Philip Ziegler notes, Edward's 'sense of proportion, never his strongest quality, had failed him totally',[37] and he was consumed entirely by his own cause. 'I see now', he later admitted to Murphy of his demands, 'I may have well been right and wrong in my standing on a point of personal honor in the midst of war. But my hurt had embittered me, and I did not have the good sense to see that my wife, being the kind of woman she is, could manage very well with what we had.'[38]

Arriving in Lisbon, Edward and Wallis were met by a familiar face, the British Ambassador, Sir Walford Selby. Selby had been stationed in Vienna in 1937 and had been part of Edward's intimate circle in the months immediately following the abdication when he was at Enzesfeld. Though Selby had been warned by the British government to stay away, his wife had attended their wedding at Candé the following June. When advised of the Windsors' arrival in Portugal, Selby immediately took responsibility for finding them a suitable place to stay. He approached the manager at the Palácio Hotel in Estoril, a stylish resort town at the heart of the Portuguese Riviera, who suggested that the villa of the wealthy Portuguese banker, Ricardo Espírito Santo, would be a more suitable place to accommodate the couple. Selby secured the house and was on hand to meet the Windsors when they arrived on 3 July. Much to his surprise, the Espírito Santos were also standing by to greet their guests in their capacity as host and hostess, which had not been part of the initial arrangement. But Selby overlooked the change in plan. After all, he thought, the Windsors would be in Portugal for just a few days. But, as it transpired, it was a further four weeks before Edward and Wallis left. When they did it was aboard the American export liner *Excalibur*, bound for the Bahamas, where Edward was to serve the remainder of the war as Governor General.

As they settled into the Espírito Santos' home, the 'cabelise row', as Wallis called it, between Edward and Churchill continued. 'He wanted to have a guarantee,' Wallis told Murphy, 'that if I came to England I wasn't going to be put in the bottom drawer. We were up all night wording these messages,' she continued, 'the Duke and I pacing the floor in dressing-gowns . . . so another salvo could go off the next morning, and another one came in the next evening. And you can imagine,' she concluded, 'who won the war of words.' On 4 July Churchill cabled back with the offer for Edward of the governorship of the Bahamas. 'A third-class governorship',[39] Edward called it, of a colony deemed so unimportant that it was one of the few places in the British Empire that he had not visited as Prince of Wales.

As the Windsors lingered in Portugal, awaiting passage to the Bahamas, the Duke was again at leisure to air his increasingly pessimistic outlook about the war to whomever was around to listen. 'I know, my sweet, you have a way of telling too much to strangers,'[40] Wallis had warned Edward in February 1937 – when, alone and disgruntled, he spoke freely of his bitterness towards his family to anyone who passed through Enzesfeld. This time it was among the Lisbon nightlife that Edward began openly to air his grievances. He publicly expressed his disagreement with Churchill's position on the war and made no attempt to hide the fact that he still believed peace at any price was better than human slaughter. His views were no doubt exacerbated by resentments of the moment and by his and Wallis's uncomfortable flight from France where he had witnessed at first hand the impact of the country's capitulation. Among the people Edward spoke to during this period was Miguel Primo de Rivera, the Marquess of Estella, and son of the former Prime Minister of Spain, whom Edward had first met on a visit to Spain in 1927.

According to documents recovered in 1945 from the German Foreign Ministry and published in 1957, a series of conversations, facilitated by Ricardo Espírito Santo, took place between Primo de Rivera and Edward as he and Wallis prepared to leave for the Bahamas. The content of these meetings was reported back by Primo de Rivera to the Spanish Minister of the Interior, Ramón Serrano Súñer, who reported them to the German Ambassador in Spain, Eberhard von Stohrer, who reported them via cable to the German Foreign Minister, Joachim von Ribbentrop, as information obtained from an 'Agent of the Minister of Interior'. Edward's remarks recorded from the distance of a third-hand source form the basis of the allegation that he was a Nazi collaborator.

In these exchanges, Edward was, according to Primo de Rivera, supposedly 'toying with the idea of dissociating himself from present tendency of British policy by a public declaration and breaking with his brother'.[41] Rivera also reported that Edward might even go so far as to refuse his posting in the Bahamas and take up residence in southern Spain. On 25 July Stohrer reported to Ribbentrop that Primo de Rivera had allegedly advised Edward that he 'might yet be destined to play a large part in British politics and possibly ascend British throne'. Stohrer added that, according to Primo de Rivera, the Duke and Duchess 'appeared surprised', continuing, 'Both seem to be completely bound up in formalistic ways of thought . . . that according to British constitution this was not possible after abdication.' Stohrer's account of the meeting, which he reported third hand to Ribbentrop, concluded by noting, 'When agent [Primo de Rivera] then remarked that the course of the war may produce changes even in the British constitution, the Duchess in particular became thoughtful.'[42] Despite the flirtation with an alternative course of action Edward, according to Primo de Rivera (information filtered from Súñer to Stohrer), 'remained adamant that he would travel to the Bahamas. They,' the message continued, 'no longer feel themselves to be safe . . . Nevertheless Duke declared he wished to go to Bahamas; possibility of peace did not exist.' Though he was open to eventually fulfilling the 'role of intermediary' he remained firm in insisting that the 'situation in England was by no means hopeless'. Should that change, Edward supposedly said, 'he could, if necessary, also intervene from the Bahamas'.[43]

In his answer, given verbally to the agent, the Duke allegedly expressed his approval of the Führer's desire for peace, which was, he stated, in complete agreement with his own feelings. He was further convinced, the report continued, 'that if he had been King there would never have been a war. He would gladly respond to the appeal made to him to cooperate in the work of peace at the appropriate time,' but 'he must obey official instructions of his Government'.[44] Though their mission to keep Edward had failed, Stohrer softened the blow in his penultimate message to Ribbentrop, adding, 'Duke hesitated right up to the last moment. Ship was therefore obliged to delay her departure.'[45] In fact, as Wallis told Murphy in 1954, their delay had been caused by a last-minute summons from the Portuguese Prime Minister, António de Oliveira Salazar, whom they met with on their final afternoon in Lisbon. The meeting ran over and they arrived twenty minutes after *Excalibur* was scheduled to set sail. 'Well, at that time,' the Duchess remembered, 'everything that the Windsors did was done on purpose . . . Well you can't stand on the deck and say, "I'm very sorry but I'm seeing the dictator of Portugal, I didn't keep the boat waiting deliberately." But it was one of those terrible Windsor things . . .'[46]

Despite Edward's departure, one final salvo flew from Lisbon to Berlin. The German Ambassador to Portugal, Oswald von Hoyningen-Huene, who had, earlier in the month, reported to Ribbentrop the third-hand account of Edward's grim assessment that Britain could not withstand the military might of Germany and believed that 'continued severe bombing would make England ready for peace',[47] added a final postscript to the intrigue. His 'Agent' (Espírito Santo) had supposedly received a telegram from Edward, during his layover in Bermuda, reconfirming that he remained ready 'as soon as action is necessary on his part'.[48] This final missive, of which there is no primary evidence, was, as Philip Ziegler notes, the 'most suspect'.[49] Knowing that his cable, emanating from a British territory, would be intercepted by British intelligence, there seems no plausible explanation as to why Edward would have sent such a careless message confirming something that had ostensibly already been agreed to in person.

The Chinese whispers that passed to Ribbentrop argued that

Monckton, who arrived in Lisbon on 28 July, had been the decisive factor in persuading Edward to board the ship. Sent by Churchill, on what he later described as 'another very odd job',[50] Monckton found the Duke, as he told Murphy in August 1948, 'worried and apprehensive'. Alongside his more diplomatic efforts to entice Edward back to Spain, Ribbentrop had instructed his agents to convince the Windsors that they were at risk of being kidnapped or even assassinated by the British government. In fact, it was Ribbentrop who, in an almost comic subplot to the episode, contemplated their abduction, should all other means of keeping the Windsors in Europe fail. 'The plot,' Monckton advised Murphy, 'was Machiavellian in its simplicity. The Germans were confident that they could take England, and Ribbentrop had the insane belief that the Duke might be reinstalled as a kind of Quisling. Therefore, the British Government was anxious to remove him . . . before there was a danger of his yielding to temptation through a misguided sense of service or of being trapped in some way.'[51] The steadying hand of his old adviser no doubt assuaged the fears that he and Wallis felt about their safety, but there seems never to have been any real question that Edward would not take up his post. Despite his one foray into radicalism, the abdication, Edward had throughout his life operated along conventional lines, chafing at his royal role but usually agreeing to its demands.

Murphy first became aware of the existence of the cables in 1954 when, in an unrelated incident connected to Edward's wartime service in France, his name surfaced, for the first time, in the publication of the captured archives of the German Foreign Ministry. 'Yesterday,' Murphy wrote in his diary, on 10 November, after spending the day at the Windsors' Paris home working with Wallis on her memoir, 'the British government published another batch of captured German Foreign Office documents, among which were several letters by an obscure German diplomat [Count Julius von Zech-Burkersroda, German Ambassador to The Hague at the start of the Second World War]. One of those letters claimed that certain details concerning the Anglo-French plans in the event of a German invasion of Belgium had been divulged by the Duke's entourage in 1940.' The Duke, Murphy recorded, had known about the documents since last summer and 'decided they were of no consequence. In his customary frugality he filed them away in his iron box, telling no one. The Duke has publicly denied ever meeting the German diplomat. Actually the incident is of no particular consequence.'[52]

Murphy and Edward dismissed the importance of the revelations, as did Churchill, now back in Downing Street, who vigorously defended the Duke during Prime Minister's Questions in the House of Commons on 16 November. Edward, Churchill told the House, had no objection to the publication of the cables when he was informed of their exist-ence. 'He thought,' Churchill asserted, 'and I agreed with him, that they could be treated with contempt.'[53] Edward's official biographer Philip Ziegler shared Churchill's assessment, particularly as the leaked infor-mation Edward was accused of imparting was 'the exact opposite of what the Duke knew to be the truth about Allied intentions'.[54]

Edward, who was in London when the story broke, returned to Paris on 15 November. Tired after his journey, he left immediately with Wallis for the Mill, where Murphy found him thoroughly engrossed in gardening and preoccupied with the planting of 'horticultural samples he had brought back from London'.[55] But Edward knew, as Murphy was shortly to find out, that there was more about Germany to come.

Charles Murphy's Diary
Paris, 17 November 1954[56]

> . . . I went to the *Express* office on Fleet Street and exchanged trans-Atlantic telephone greetings with Lord Beaverbrook who is in New York . . . Both he and young Max [Aitken] mentioned that the captured German Foreign Office [documents] concerning the Duke's supposed pro-German inclinations go far beyond those published last week; that they involve, among others, their Lisbon host, Espírito Santo.

This view was supported by Sir Walter Monckton [now Minister of Labour and National Services] whom I saw with George Allen at the Ministry of Labour. Walter confirmed that more compromising material is in the possession of both the British and American Governments, that this material is to be kept indefinitely in the deep-freeze; and that Churchill informed the Duke, on the occasion of their meeting last week in London, of the existence of the material. Monckton, however, dismissed the material as of no real consequence. It was merely another example of the Duke's unworldliness and lack of judgement . . .

Other more illustrious individuals shared Murphy's assessment of the material, including the American President Dwight D. Eisenhower, who wrote to Churchill, on 2 July 1953,

I am completely astonished to learn that a microfilm was made of the documents to which you refer. At the time, in 1945, that the existence of these documents was called to my attention, I had them thoroughly examined by Ambassador Winant [American Ambassador to Britain 1941–6] and by a member of my own Intelligence Staff. They completely agreed that there was no possible value to them, that they were obviously concocted with some idea of promoting German propaganda and weakening Western resist-ance, and that they were totally unfair to the Duke. As a consequence, they were turned over upon capture to the American Ambassador.[57]

Eisenhower's revealing letter was in reply to Churchill's own lengthy plea for the President to step in and stop what appeared to be the imminent publication of the material related to Edward's time in Lisbon.

'All these telegrams,' Churchill wrote to Eisenhower on 27 June 1953, 'are from German sources and represent a Nazi-German intrigue to entangle and compromise a Royal Prince who had been driven out of France and had taken refuge in Portugal . . . The historical importance of the episode is negligible,' he argued, 'and the allegations rest only on the assertions of German and pro-German officials in making the most of anything they could pick up.'[58]

Churchill had been warned about the captured files as far back as August 1945 and from the outset was determined to suppress them. But his vigorous mission to 'destroy all traces of these German intrigues'[59] was counterbalanced by Edward's relative calm when warned of the material in July 1947 by George VI. According to Godfrey Thomas, he was undisturbed by the allegations, 'suggesting,' Thomas recorded, '(as had already occurred to us as a possibility) that the German Ambassador was making up a good story on the lines that he thought would please his chief, Ribbentrop'.[60] Churchill's futile efforts to prevent publication ultimately proved disastrous for Edward's reputation. Though it is clear from what he wrote that he believed the cables were an elaborate fiction, his intervention, once revealed, was construed as confirmation that Churchill too shared the view that Edward was a traitor.

When the inevitable occurred on 31 July 1957, it made headlines in Britain and the United States. The *New York Times* correspondent Russell Baker dubbed the revelations of 'dubious validity' but acknowledged they would add 'another controversial chapter'[61] to Edward's story. Backed by the British government, who asserted that he 'never wavered in his loyalty to the British cause',[62] Edward released a lengthy statement refuting the claim that he had ever knowingly conspired with the enemy. 'These communications,' he said, 'comprise in part complete fabrications and in part gross distortions of the truth . . . While I was in Lisbon certain people who I discovered to be pro-Nazi sympathizers did make definite efforts to persuade me to return to Spain . . . At no time did I ever entertain any thought of complying with such a suggestion, which I treated with the contempt it deserved.'[63]

Significantly, two of Britain's key diplomatic players in the episode spoke out immediately in defence of Edward. 'My first comment on these German allegations,' Samuel Hoare, by then Viscount Templewood, wrote in the *Daily Express*, 'is that they come from Nazi sources and that Nazi Ministers invariably reported only what Hitler wished to hear.' He concluded, 'The significant fact is that the Duke himself rejected the advances and patriotically accepted the Governorship of the Bahamas.'[64] Walford Selby was even more emphatic. He told the *Daily Telegraph* that the material was 'grossly slanderous' and 'one of the finest examples I have had of the way the Nazis were capable of lying'.[65] He made it clear in a lengthy interview that it had been at his behest that the Windsors found themselves at the mercy of Espírito Santo. And in what seems a shocking lack of judgement, Selby admitted being fully aware of Santo's pro-German leanings. 'In any case,' he wrote to Edward, on 24 September 1957, 'it is my hope that I may have contributed to silence the utterly absurd suggestions . . . which emerged from the German disclosures.'[66] In a letter to the journalist Collin Brooks, Selby added, 'Certainly I did not see eye to eye with the Duke about Germany, but to suggest that he was a traitor to his country is absurd.'[67]

Edward was appreciative of Selby's intervention and maintained that he knew nothing of Espírito Santo's intrigues. 'He was a pleasant enough host, with a fine collection of Lowestoft china,' Edward wrote to Selby, on 14 August 1957, 'and he certainly never gave me any cause to suspect his pro-Nazi sympathies.'[68] He was equally grateful to Hoare, who had not always been a firm supporter. Hoare had disagreed with much of what Edward said in *A King's Story* and argued publicly that he had misrepresented Baldwin's role in the crisis. But Hoare seems not to have hesitated when it came to defending Edward from these accusations. As with Selby, Edward took pains to express his gratitude, noting freely in his letter of 15 August 1958 that he had indeed met Primo de Rivera twice during his stay in Lisbon. Edward recorded that both times the man had tried to 'entice me back to Spain', although 'in due fairness to him his efforts were distinctly half-hearted . . . I suspect that he realized he was up against a "stone wall" from the outset of his mission.'[69]

At the end of 1962, Edward faced a final salvo from the captured German documents when reports were published that Edward, through his second cousin Charles, Duke of Saxe-Coburg and Gotha, had tried to forge an alliance with Nazi Germany in 1936 – a move far outside his prerogatives as a constitutional monarch. Though by no means as scandalous as the material published in 1957, it was an uncomfortable public reminder of Edward's past associations with Hitler's Germany, which for any new story were always accompanied by imagery from his ill-judged visit in 1937. In response, and as he had done before, Edward issued a statement to the press denouncing the documents as second-hand evidence that had been 'slanted to curry favor with Hitler', and denied he had meddled in political affairs. But in a dash of contro-versial honesty, he admitted that in the 1930s, along with many others 'who had the interests of Great Britain at heart', he had sought 'some understanding with Germany despite the fact that Hitler was in power, in order to prevent the calamity of a second World War'.[70]

Though the headlines were brief, it prompted Murphy's 'dismay'. 'Your answer,' he told Edward, on 2 January 1963, 'was forthright and convincing.' It chimed, Murphy noted, with others in American intelligence, including Allen Dulles, the first civilian director of the American Central Intelligence Agency. Dulles, Murphy advised Edward, 'recalled to me the other day that when the first batch of such documents was up for consideration, he and other members of the U.S. Government thought it was wrong to publish them, if only because the assertions concerning you were so patently ill-founded.' In conclusion, Murphy added, 'It was his impression at the time that the British Government, alas, was quite indifferent.'[71]

Aware that his reputation had been impacted by the successive bursts of allegations, in 1966 Edward made a final attempt at addressing the controversy in one of the six articles that were published in the *Chicago Daily Tribune*[72] to commemorate the thirtieth anniversary of the abdication. Addressing forthrightly his political alignment, he hoped to add a final and unequivocal postscript to a period that he increas-ingly worried might define his legacy. Though his words are now almost forgotten, they are an honest and self-critical appraisal of views that dictated his actions during this controversial period.

I let my admiration for the good side of [the] German character dim what was being done to it by the bad. I thought that the rest of us could be fence-sitters while the Nazis and the Reds slugged it out; and, in any event, the immediate task as I saw it then, for all Europe-minded people of my generation – the generation that had fought in the first World War – was to prevent another conflict between Germany and the West that could bring down our civilizations. Well, I was wrong about that. I suppose that what saddened and alarmed me most about the looming crisis was the dreadful recollection of the carnage I had gazed upon in France and Italy. World War II happened, after all . . . One evil thing (Nazism) was destroyed, another evil thing (Communism) was saved, and nothing particularly useful was demonstrated, except that men's cleverness in inventing devices for their own extinction continues to be inferior to their instincts for self-survival.

Epilogue

In writing *A King's Story* Edward had hoped to be the architect of his own legacy. He had persisted with the task in the face of almost constant disapproval, flagging only briefly when confronted with a crisis in his marriage – which mattered to him above everything else. He was determined to tell his story, not only the story of the abdication but also of other intertwining narratives: his quest for love, his wish to redefine the monarchy and his journey of self-realisation, one that highlighted his attempt at making a meaningful contribution to the world through leadership. And to ensure the reader did not miss the point that for the first forty-two years of his life he had occupied a central role in the last surviving imperial dynasty, he insisted, against the advice of his publishers, that a full listing of his travels as Prince of Wales and as King be included as an appendix. As the readers turned the page from his farewell at Portsmouth Harbour on 12 December 1936, they were reminded that for twenty-four years Edward had represented Britain with distinction around the globe. 'Many in England think I should not write this book,' he told Murphy, in the late autumn of 1950. They believe 'I should remain dead but unburied.' The book, he knew, 'was bound to give rise to criticism – a condition not unknown to me . . . But,' he added poignantly, 'I do not wish to be remembered only as a man who abdicated.'[1]

But his hope remains unfulfilled. Not only is Edward remembered for having forsaken kingship, but his integrity now stands compromised by the avalanche of accusations that have obscured any other perspectives of either his actions or his character. His activities in the lead-up to and during the Second World War have left him exposed to adverse judgements, and in the fifty-one years since his death, with no heirs to guard his reputation, sensationalism now dominates his biographical persona. The published version of *A King's Story* now feels an incomplete record, which skirts pressing questions around who Edward was and what he truly believed – most notably about Germany. In recovering his unpublished words, deemed too personal or too revealing for publication in his own lifetime, we are afforded a more direct approach to Edward as a person, which enables us to think again about the judgements we have made.

But certain facts are indisputable. He made no attempt to hide his inclination towards appeasement and isolationism in the 1930s. He believed in an outstretched hand to Germany, a country in which he had strong familial ties, and concurred with many others who felt that what happened in German domestic politics was none of Britain's (or America's) business. National Socialism was, he believed, a bulwark against the even greater international threat of Communism, which for Edward had distinctly personal roots. Old enough to remember meeting the Russian Tsar, Nicholas II, when he had visited England in 1909 with his family, Edward had been left in permanent terror of far-left politics by their ruthless murder at the hands of their Bolshevik captors.

His visit to Germany in 1937 was a public-relations nightmare. Yet at the time, convinced of his own independent mission, he saw nothing wrong in being photographed amid the panoply of the Third Reich, a country that then enjoyed full diplomatic relations with Britain. He was, after all, just one among numerous members of the British elite who travelled to survey Hitler's Germany and were seduced by what the appeasement historian Tim Bouverie calls 'its noxious glamour'.[2] Lloyd George, Britain's First World War Prime Minister, had met Hitler at the Berghof on 4 September 1936 as part of his own tour of the country and was, according to The Times, 'profoundly interested to hear from the Führer a detailed description of the schemes of economic reconstruction . . . now proceeding in Germany'.[3] Following him were Anthony Eden, Sir John Simon and Neville Chamberlain, all of whom felt able to speak with Hitler on a diplomatic footing.

Edward believed cooperation with Germany was the best means of avoiding war, a desire that superseded all other concerns. He remained resistant to any other perspective, just as he had in 1936 when his desire for Wallis blinded him to any other path but abdication. However misguided, his convictions were sincere, and he was convinced there could be no political justification for a repetition of the human suffering he had witnessed as a young man in France. In May 1938, rereading a selection of his correspondence from the opening days of the First World War, he reflected grimly:

It is . . . rather terrifying to read in the midst of the uncertainties and anxieties of the world today what an average boy of twenty wrote nearly a quarter of a century ago. How alarming that he, typical of his age and imbued with the natural eager inconsequence of youth, should describe his orders for the front as 'joyful news', and that he regarded participation in a world war almost in a holiday mood, and anyway as a glorious adventure. How disillusioned we all were at the end of it, and how many international political mistakes have been made . . . since the Armistice. One wonders if the generation of that age of today feel as we did, or are they convinced of the appalling consequences of another world war and its futility? No! Far worse than that how it would utterly destroy civilization.[4]

Though bitterness marred their relationship during the period, George VI shared his brother's commitment to appeasement in the late 1930s, and publicly endorsed the now controversial policy by appearing on the balcony of Buckingham Palace with Neville Chamberlain to celebrate the announcement that he and Hitler had secured: 'Peace for our time'.

A year later Edward broke what he called 'his self-imposed silence' and gave public voice to these private sentiments when he spoke from Verdun in a radio broadcast carried on the American network NBC on 8 May 1939. Ignored by the BBC out of loyalty to George VI, Edward's message was a simple but earnest appeal for peace, and a reflection of his abiding belief that a repetition of the human slaughter he had witnessed during the First World War must be prevented at all costs. He called for leaders to rise above 'jealousies and suspicions' and 'to save humanity from the terrible fate that threatens it today'.

He expressed no political sympathies and offered no concrete solutions. That, he said, must be 'left to those who have the power to guide the nations'. Instead, he spoke 'simply as a soldier of the last war whose most earnest prayer it is that such cruel and destructive madness shall never again overtake mankind'.[5] The address, his first since the abdication, had no impact, but it demonstrated that despite his exile, he still believed he was an international figure to be reckoned with. In the timeline of events, it is uncomfortably close to the point of no return and demonstrates a wilful disregard for the threat that Germany posed. Even on the eve of war he sent a last-minute appeal by cable to Hitler – a plea for peace at any price. That he carried this belief through to the fall of France is also probably true. His views make him wrong, but they do not make him a traitor. He certainly did not wish to remain in his home under Nazi occupation – and, like many, fled in fear of the incoming regime.

The supposedly damning allegations of Edward's time in Lisbon are all based on hearsay, and none record that he ever spoke directly with anyone who was a declared enemy of Britain. Residing in a neutral country, to which his brother the Duke of Kent had paid an official visit only weeks before, he was sheltering in the home and with hosts who had been selected for him by a British Ambassador with whom he had a long and trusting relationship. That he should have felt himself to be in safe quarters seems like common sense. That he should have been more circumspect in advertising his opinions is also clear, but that these lapses should constitute the basis for allegations of full-blown collaboration is a gross misrepresentation of the facts. In the absence of any credible primary material, we must judge him by the episode's conclusion: he complied with orders, left Portugal, and spent the next five years fulfilling his duty as Governor of the Bahamas.

It is important also to recognise that what we perceive as the decisive events of Edward's life and character were not, as evidenced by his writing, ones that Edward would have shared. Germany seems a footnote in comparison with the many and varied topics he chose to reflect upon in the years he spent compiling his memoir. If one is trying to pinpoint his political affiliations, his lengthy and adulatory reflections on the United States offer a better indication of the country, apart from Great Britain, to which he felt most drawn and whose culture and politics he admired and sought to incorporate in his own life. His informal and democratic style as Prince of Wales was a direct result of his early encounters with America in the 1920s and served him well during the 1930s when he faced ordinary Britons whose lives had been devastated by the international economic crisis that followed the stock-market crash of 1929. The challenges of the ensuing decade brought to the fore the very best in Edward's character, and his relaxed manner ensured that the British monarchy, still reeling from the dynastic upheavals of the First World War, was perceived as approachable and empathetic. He also endorsed, in the limited capacity he was allowed, the Rooseveltian call to arms that 'something must be done' to help men who, through no fault of their own, faced personal ruin. These views were just as controversial in his own day as his appeasement politics are now. But he echoed the philosophy that was driving the American New Deal, and his plea for the people of South Wales seems a direct reiteration of Roosevelt's own appeal made just five months earlier to the people of the United States as he exclaimed, 'Better the occasional faults of a government that lives in a spirit of charity than the consistent omissions of a government frozen in the ice of its own indifference.'[6]

Most believe that Edward failed unequivocally at his royal destiny. His mother certainly thought so. 'Looking back,' he admitted to Murphy, 'I realize that she was unable to bring herself to believe that I could even think of abdicating, let alone do it.'[7] Queen Mary never understood or forgave her son's decision to pursue self-fulfilment over the prescribed definitions of duty. In George VI's reign, kingship was increasingly defined around the framework of personal self-sacrifice, making Edward's failures seem all the more acute. But that characterisation, like so much of the scholarship that exists about his life, is too simple a conclusion. First, Edward's own attitude towards the abdication was neither embarrass-ment nor shame. He recognised his reign was unfulfilled, but he viewed with pride the position he had once held and believed that in renouncing the Crown he had performed the ultimate act of personal sacrifice.

He clung to the conviction that in refusing to risk the foundations of constitutional monarchy for his own personal ends, he had discharged the duty to which he had been born. And perhaps, more importantly, the current simplified account of his life discounts the two decades he spent as Prince of Wales, when through ingenuity and an extraordinary understanding of the changing landscape of media culture he transformed the very fabric of his role and established precedents that flourish in today's modern monarchy. He carried through this philosophy as King and championed a more relaxed approach to the discharge of royal duties. He believed the sovereign's function was analogous to that of a CEO and felt the excessive trappings of Court tradition were out of place in a twentieth-century setting.

The shock of his abdication arrested any immediate development of these modernising inclinations as his successor sought to re-establish the link to the more traditional regal domesticity of George V. Yet even as his family reviled him, they also sought to replicate his successes. It is difficult to imagine whether George VI's consort, Queen Elizabeth, would have summoned Cecil Beaton to Buckingham Palace in 1939 to help craft a new glamorous public image had she not seen the visual *tour de force* of Beaton's photographs of Edward and Wallis's wedding: their striking modernity made a powerful argument for a very different vision of British royal identity. The compelling sight of George VI surveying the burned-out rubble of London's East End might not have been thought an appropriate task for a monarch, had not his older brother broken the ice of royal protocol and made a public-relations triumph by going down into mines and walking through dockyards as a means of expressing the institution's solidarity with working-class hardship. Edward's success as a global ambassador for Britain has been copied repeatedly, most notably by Queen Elizabeth II when, in 1954, she undertook a five-month tour of the Commonwealth aimed at solidifying support for a still precarious alliance. But perhaps his most lasting contribution to the framework of modern monarchy is the precedent Edward set for a monarch to pursue personal fulfilment at the expense of royal convention. He was a pioneer in his attitude towards marriage and called publicly for adjustments to the traditional royal rulebook. He failed to win concessions for himself yet paved the way for his successors. Few have acknowledged his legacy in this or any other arena.

During his long exile Edward became all too aware of his erasure from the canon of twentieth-century royal history. It sat uneasily with him, as did the lasting feeling that he had, throughout his royal career, been thwarted, frustrated always by the limitations of a position at the fore of public life yet devoid of power. His portfolio as King was vast, but over the course of his short reign it became increasingly void of meaning. His personal preoccupations took over and he abandoned the only thing he could have achieved: the revitalisation of the style and character of kingship. Furthermore, as he admitted to Murphy in January 1950, he chafed at the idea that as King he would have been forced to support policies with which he disagreed. A man who, at the best of times, had difficulty concealing his opinions, he may have realised that he was ill-suited for the role of a constitutional monarch, who, as Walter Bagehot famously noted, had only three inalienable rights: 'the right to be consulted, the right to encourage, the right to warn'.[8] Plagued by self-doubt, Edward was forthright in acknowledging his complicated relationship with a system that, despite his exile, he remained bound to by deep ties. 'It is very hard,' he acknowledged to Murphy in 1950, 'to shake off one's past, especially a past as rigid and fixed as mine.'[9]

Yet despite his reservations, Edward clung to the belief that his service had in fact meant something to the country of his birth, at the same time acknowledging that he and kingship were decidedly ill-matched. 'I believe in all truth,' he told Murphy, in one of their final conversations before the publication of A King's Story, 'that I brought the monarchy closer to the people, but in the process of doing so I gradually lost faith myself in the institution.'[10] It is a powerful remark that points to the roots of Edward's failure. But it also makes a case for him as a truly modern monarch, one whose modernity enabled him to face the existential question of whether monarchy, in a contemporary context, is, after all, an oxymoron. Did he come to see that the closer the monarchy came to the people the more impossible it became as an institution – that in the end monarchy and democracy were incompatible? Edward was not able fully to answer this question and perhaps he was incapable of doing so, but when faced in December 1936 with a choice between personal happiness and the possession of what seemed a hollow crown, there was never any doubt about which he would choose.

Edward himself gives us this new perspective on the abdication. The authenticity of his voice, present throughout the volume of words he left behind, compels us to listen. He should continue to be heard as we reflect on the life and importance of a man who was once a king.

Acknowledgements

Writing this book has been a unique privilege. Not only did it fulfill a long-held ambition to write about Edward VIII but it also took me on an incredible journey – through material that had lain buried for more than seventy years – and gave me an experience that I never thought possible. For the last twelve months I have lived on a daily basis with Edward, Wallis and of course, Charles J. V. Murphy – without whom none of these stories would exist. All three came alive through their writing in ways I could never have imagined.

Early on in my work I had the extraordinary opportunity to meet with Charles Murphy's daughter and son-in-law, Edythe and John Holbrook. They welcomed me into their home and into their memories. I was astonished over the course of the more than four hours we spent together in early September 2022 to hear their stories, which they shared freely and enthusiastically. Murphy, or 'Gramps' as he became known in the family after grandchildren appeared, emerged vividly as did 'Windsor', who Edythe, even from the distance of more than seventy years, recalled with vividness and affection. The continued generosity of the Murphy family over the course of the last year has made all the difference to this project. Sara Guggenheim, Edythe's daughter, has played an enormous role by sharing numerous anecdotes about her grandfather which have enlivened my understanding of his character and shaped many of the book's passages. She has sent me a steady stream of incredible family pictures and been patient as we worked through the various copyright approvals. I quote from Murphy's writings through the generous permission of Edythe Holbrook but I am just as grateful for the kindness, support and encouragement she, John and Sara have given me over these many months. It is of great personal regret that I was not able to share the end result of my work with John, who passed away in February 2023. John was an astute and perceptive biographer of his father-in-law and it is a privilege to be able to quote from his words in my own text.

I am grateful for the assistance and permission of many others who have aided in my archival research over the course of my writing. Jane Parr at the Howard Gotlieb Archival Research Center (Boston University) has been immensely helpful and patient with my many requests over these months. She was invaluable in navigating the voluminous collection that is Murphy's archive. For permission to quote from material in the Royal Archives I acknowledge His Majesty Charles III. I would also like to thank Julie Crocker and her many colleagues for all their assistance throughout my several research visits to Windsor. I wish to express my gratitude to Eve Neiger at Boston Public Library for sending early on the digitised Amory files which really got this book started and for organising the logistics of my visits in 2023. Dr Bethany Hamblen at Balliol College has been incredible throughout my several trips to Oxford and assisted in numerous ways. I would also like to thank the staff at Columbia University Library, the Lincolnshire Archives, and the New York Historical Society. I am thankful for the help offered by the Pasteur Institute in Paris. I also wish to acknowledge the various individuals who have generously granted permission to quote from the following individuals: Sir David Thomas for Sir Godfrey Thomas, Octavian von Hofmannsthal for Raimund von Hofmannsthal, Topo and Jasmine Swope for John Swope, Lord Hardinge for Alexander Hardinge, the Churchill Archives Centre who hold the papers of Alan Lascelles and Anna Seagrim, and finally the Parliamentary Archives for Lord Beaverbrook.

In so many respects this book would not have happened without the guiding touch of Hugo Vickers, who has for almost twenty years been both a friend and a mentor. He has literally been at the start and the finish of this text – helping me lift mere ideas into a practicable subject and then at the end diligently reading and re-reading drafts of this text for both errors and insights. Without Hugo I would not have met Tom Perrin who took a chance on an aspiring writer and brought my idea of this new perspective on this most controversial king to Hodder and making my project a reality. He has been an editor par excellence throughout these many months. He gave me perspective when the strain of the work prevented it and offered heartening motivation when the timeline at various points felt an impossibility. His efforts on my behalf have been gargantuan and for that I remain indebted. To others at Hodder I would also like to share my thanks: Rebecca Mundy, Alice Cottrell, Janet Aspey, Christian Duck, Richard Peters and Kerri Logan. Hazel Orme undertook her copy-editing role with skill and precision. Jane Smith has been a diligent sleuth as she researched and cleared illustrations. Neil Spence trained his lens on a hesitant subject and created a beautiful author photograph – thank you!

Of paramount significance to the genesis of this project is Jonathan Cook, who has in one form or the other been working with me on Edward since 2021. His influence can be found on every page. He has forced me to think more critically about my subject than I would otherwise have done and remained patient throughout as I struggled with various sections – offering motivation and productive criticism that has shaped my writing. It is no exaggeration to say that I would not have been able to write this book without him. He is one of several, I know, who breathed a sigh of relief when this project was at last complete.

There are many others whose contribution and help I am immensely grateful for. Ted Powell, whose impressive and insightful work on Edward is the foundation stone of my own, has been an inspiration. He has patiently read this manuscript in various drafts and offered an often much-needed boost of enthusiasm when the demands of production became overwhelming. Michael Weatherburn generously shared his voluminous research on Charles Bedaux as well as his astute insights on the historiographic sensationalism that has overwhelmed the Windsors. Marianne Hinton has done so much throughout my research and writing both from the practical to the emotional. I am so thankful for our friendship. Cameron Thomson kindly read several chapters and caught several previously overlooked mistakes. Maria Vasquez kept our home running through the long months when my preoccupation was elsewhere and was a nurturing presence to all. To Ilana Miller, Mark

Anderson, Stephen Stephanou, Michael Nash, Brooke Michie, Jeanne Passante and Bob Neville – all good friends – thank you for remaining friends despite my absence of late. I am extremely grateful to Kewsong Lee and Zita Ezpeleta whose generous nature afforded me the flexibility over these last six months to complete my manuscript.

To my very much-loved niece Olivia and nephew Theodore – I hope you will both one day read this book for yourselves. Olivia, in particular, has patiently accepted my many absences and cancellations over the last year as the demands of Edward took precedence over everything – even our time together.

Though I spared them the minutiae of the text, it is impossible not to acknowledge the influence, support and love given to me by Dr Margaret Stetz and Mark Samuels Lasner. They have stepped in at various points in my life to steady the ship and given me throughout the confidence to continue pursuing my passions whatever the circumstances. This endeavour would not have been possible without them.

To my parents – their love and the opportunities they gave me growing up have given me the life I lead today. My mother – my best friend – inspired my love of British history and not only accepted but encouraged my very unique interests as a child. To my father, I stand in awe. A brilliant mathematician and true renaissance man, he has read every word of this book (in quadruplicate – if not more) – painstakingly editing its many errors but also bringing to the text a wisdom and understanding without which it would be a lesser product.

And last, but very much not least, I come to Martin. This is book is truly for him and because of him. He has been unfailing in his love and unwavering in his encouragement in this and in all things. He has endured the strain, exhaustion and irritation of the many months of writing and all the while responded in patience and quiet enthusiasm. His constancy is my bedrock and his love solidifies all things. Our life together with B means more than I can say. I love you – for always.

Bibliography

Archive Sources

The Churchill Papers, Churchill Archives Center, Cambridge

The Cleveland Amory Collection, Boston Public Library, Boston

The Beaverbrook Papers, Parliamentary Archives, London

The Family Papers of Cust and Brownlow Families, Lincolnshire Archives, Lincoln

The Papers of Sir Alan Lascelles, Churchill Archives Centre, University of Cambridge

The Daniel Longwell Papers, Columbia University Library, New York

The Papers of Walter Turner Monckton, Balliol College Archives, University of Oxford

Charles J. V. Murphy Collection, Boston University Libraries, Howard Gotlieb Archival Research Center

The Royal Archives, Windsor Castle

The Papers of Anna Seagrim, Churchill Archives Centre, University of Cambridge

The Archive of Sir Walford Selby, Bodleian Archives and Manuscripts, University of Oxford

The Templewood Papers, Cambridge University Library, University of Cambridge

Time Inc. Archive, New York Historical Society, New York

Life Magazines

Flanner, Janet, 'The Windsor Team', *Life*, 9 June 1941

Murphy, Charles J. V., Davenport, John, 'The Lives of Winston Churchill', *Life*, 21 May 1945

Windsor, Duke of, 'The Story of the Education of a Prince', *Life*, 8, 15, 22 December 1947

Windsor, Duke of, 'A King's Story', *Life*, 22, 29 May, 5, 12 June 1950

Printed Sources

Allen, Martin, *Hidden Agenda: How the Duke of Windsor Betrayed the Allies* (Macmillan, 2000)

Amory, Cleveland, *The Best Cat Ever* (Little Brown & Co., 1993)

Bagehot, Walter, *The English Constitution* (Oxford University Press, 2001)

Beaken, Robert, ed., *Faithful Witness: The Confidential Diaries of Alan Don, Chaplain to the King, the Archbishop and the Speaker, 1931–1946* (SPCK, 2020)

Beaken, Robert, *Cosmo Lang: Archbishop in War and Crisis* (I. B. Tauris, 2012)

Beaverbrook, Lord, *The Abdication of King Edward VIII* (Atheneum, 1966)

Birkenhead, Lord, *Walter Monckton: The Life of Viscount Monckton of Brenchley* (Weidenfeld & Nicolson, 1969)

Bloch, Michael, *Wallis and Edward: Letters 1931–1937* (Summit, 1982)

Bloch, Michael, *The Duke of Windsor's War* (Weidenfeld & Nicolson, 1982)

Bloch, Michael, *The Secret File of the Duke of Windsor* (Harper & Row, 1988)

Bouverie, Tim, *Appeasement: Chamberlain, Hitler, Churchill and the Road to War* (Duggan, 2019)

Bryan III, Joe, and Murphy, Charles J. V., *The Windsor Story: An Intimate Portrait of Edward VIII and Mrs Simpson by the authors who knew them best* (William Morrow, 1979)

Cadbury, Deborah, *Princes at War: The British Royal Family's Private Battle in the Second World War* (Bloomsbury, 2016)

'Duke and Duchess of Windsor visit their E.P. Ranch'. *Canadian Cattlemen*, May 1950.

Cannadine, David, 'Churchill and the British Monarchy', *Transactions of the Royal Historical Society*, 2001, Vol. 1, pp. 249–72

Churchill, Winston, *The Second World War, Vol. 1 The Gathering Storm* (Houghton Mifflin, 1948)

Clarke, Peter, *Mr. Churchill's Profession: The Statesman as Author* (Bloomsbury, 2012)

Colville, John, *The Fringes of Power: Downing Street Diaries 1939–1955* (Hodder & Stoughton, 1985)

Documents on German Foreign Policy, 1918–1945, Series D (1937–1945), Vol. X: The War Years 23 June – 31 August 1940, HMSO, 1957

Donaldson, Frances, *Edward VIII: The Road to Abdication* (J. B. Lippincott, 1947)

Elson, Robert, *The World of Time Inc.: The Intimate History of a Publishing Enterprise, Vol. II: 1941–1960* (Atheneum, 1973).

Flanner, Janet, 'Annals of Collaboration; Equivalism - I, II, III', *New Yorker*, September / October 1945

Godfrey, Rupert, *Letters from a Prince: Edward Prince of Wales to Mrs Freda Dudley Ward, March 1918–January 1921* (Warner, 1999)

Hardinge, Helen, *Loyal To Three Kings* (William Kimber, 1967)

Harris, Kenneth, 'Interview with Edward Duke of Windsor and Wallis Duchess of Windsor', 1970. https://www.youtube.com/watch?v=w8u7Ntic5fo

Hart Davis, Duff, ed., *A King's Counsellor: Abdication and War: The Diaries of Sir Alan Lascelles* (Weidenfeld & Nicolson, 2006)

Heffer, Simon, ed., *Henry 'Chips' Channon: The Diaries: 1918–1938* (Hutchinson, 2021)

Holbrook, John, 'Charles J. V. Murphy' (Private circulation only, 2022)

Inglis, Brian, *Abdication* (Macmillan, 1966)

King, Greg, *The Duchess of Windsor: The Uncommon Life of Wallis Simpson* (Citadel, 1999)

Lownie, Andrew, *Traitor King: The Scandalous Exile of the Duke and Duchess of Windsor* (Blink, 2021)

Mayhall, Laura E. Nym, 'The Prince of Wales Versus Clark Gable: Anglophone Celebrity and Citizenship Between the Wars', *Cultural and Social History*, Vol. 4, Issue 4, pp. 529–43.

McDowall, Duncan, 'A Game of Thrones, 1936-Style: How Three Canadians Shaped the Abdication of Edward VIII', *University of Toronto Quarterly*, Vol. 90, no.1, Winter 2021, pp. 1–20.

Menkes, Suzy, *The Windsor Style* (Grafton, 1987)

Morton, Andrew, *Wallis In Love: The Untold Life of the Duchess of Windsor* (Grand Central, 2018)

Mosley, Diana, *The Duchess of Windsor: An Illustrated Biography* (Pan Macmillan, 1980)

Nicolson, Harold, *The Later Years, 1945–1962* (Atheneum, 1968)

Norwich, John Julius, ed., *The Duff Cooper Diaries 1915–1951* (Weidenfeld & Nicolson, 2005)

Owens, Edward, *The Family Firm: Monarchy, Mass Media and the British Public 1932–1953* (University of London Press, 2020)

Phillips, Adrian, *The King Who Had To Go: Edward VIII, Mrs Simpson and the Hidden Politics of the Abdication Crisis* (Biteback, 2018)

Pope-Hennessy, James, *Queen Mary* (George Allen and Unwin, 1959)

Powell, Ted, *King Edward VIII: An American Life* (Oxford University Press, 2018)

Roosevelt, 'The Acceptance Speech for the Renomination for the Presidency, Philadelphia', 27 June 1936. Franklin D. Roosevelt Library.

Schmidt, Paul, *Hitler's Interpreter* (Fonthill Media, 2016)

Shawcross, William *The Queen Mother: The Official Biography* (Alfred A. Knopf, 2009)

Smith, Judith Haas, *Larger Than Life: The Legacy of Daniel Longwell and Mary Fraser Longwell* (AuthorHouse, 2015)

Trethewey, Rachel, *Before Wallis: Edward VIII's Other Women* (The History Press, 2018)

Urbach, Karina, *Go-Betweens for Hitler* (Oxford University Press, 2015)

Vickers, Hugo, *The Private World of the Duke and Duchess of Windsor* (Abbeville, 1996)

Vickers, Hugo, *Behind Closed Doors: The Tragic, Untold Story of Wallis Simpson* (Arrow, 2012)

Vickers, Hugo, *The Quest for Queen Mary* (Zuleika, 2018)

Weatherburn, Michael, 'Scientific Management at Work: The Bedaux System, Management Consulting, and Worker Efficiency in British Industry, 1914–1948,' thesis, University of Oxford, 2014

Williams, Susan, *The People's King: The True Story of the Abdication* (Allen Lane, 2003)

Williamson, Philip, and Baldwin, Edward, ed., *Baldwin Papers* (Cambridge University Press, 2004)

Windsor, Edward, Duke of, *A King's Story* (G. P. Putnam's, 1951)

Windsor, Wallis, *The Heart Has Its Reasons* (Michael Joseph, 1956)

Windsors: A Royal Family, 1994. Public Broadcasting Service (PBS).

Woolf, Virginia, *The Diary of Virginia Woolf* (Harcourt Brace, 1984)

Ziegler, Philip, *King Edward VIII* (Collins, 1990)

Ziegler, Philip, 'Churchill and the Monarchy', *History Today*, Vol. 43, March 1993

Endnotes

Introduction

1   Morton, *Wallis in Love*, p. 339.
2   Audio recording, 'Cannes, Canada & observations on British', Cleveland Amory Papers (MS.SC.0006), Boston Public Library.
3   'HRH's Description of Duchess', undated. From the Charles J. V. Murphy Collection, Boston University Libraries, Howard Gotlieb Archival Research Center (*hereafter: 'Murphy Collection').
4   'Diary', January 1950, Murphy Collection.
5   'Winston Churchill', *Life*, 21 May 1945.
6   Charles Murphy to Henry Luce, 20 February 1947, Daniel Longwell Papers, Rare Book & Manuscript Library, Columbia University, *hereafter: 'Daniel Longwell Papers'.
7   Holbrook, 'Charles John Vincent Murphy: A Biographical Sketch of My Father-In-Law', p. 6.
8   Ibid.
9   Edward, Duke of Windsor, to George VI, 10 April 1945, RA/GVI/PRIV/01/02/27.
10 Edward to Walter Monckton, 31 May 1946, RA/EDW/PRIV/6311.
11 Walter Monckton to Edward, Duke of Windsor, 7 June 1948, RA/EDW/PRIV/6312.
12 Charles Murphy to Hank Walter 8 November 1946, Murphy Collection.
13 'Tape Interview with Daniel Longwell,' 18 August 1957, Time Inc. Archive, New York Historical Society.
14 Ibid.
15 Charles Murphy to Daniel Longwell, 13 July 1947, Daniel Longwell Papers.
16 Ibid.
17 Ibid.
18 Monica Wyatt to Daniel Longwell, 30 May 1948, Daniel Longwell Papers.

19 'Notes', undated, Murphy Collection.
20 Edward, Duke of Windsor, to Daniel Longwell, 28 August 1948, Daniel Longwell Papers.

1. A Self-Made Monarch

1 Henry Luce to Edward, Duke of Windsor, 19 March 1947, Time Inc. Archive, New York Historical Society.
2 Edward, Duke of Windsor to Henry Luce, 24 March 1947, Time Inc. Archive, New York Historical Society.
3 Daniel Longwell to Henry Luce, 14 February 1947, Time Inc. Archive, New York Historical Society.
4 Charles Murphy to Henry Luce, 20 February 1947, Murphy Collection.
5 Edward, Duke of Windsor to Daniel Longwell, 10 May 1947, Daniel Longwell Papers.
6 *Canberra Times*, 27 May 1949, p. 1.
7 Ibid.
8 Edward, Duke of Windsor to Daniel Longwell, 19 June 1947, Daniel Longwell Papers.
9 Murphy and Bryan, *The Windsor Story*, p. 408.
10 Menkes, *Windsor Style*, p. 82.
11 Menkes, *Windsor Style*, p. 76.
12 'The New Riviera', *Life*, 10 November 1947.
13 Charles Murphy to Daniel Longwell, 13 July 1947, Daniel Longwell Papers.
14 Ibid.
15 Murphy, Bryan, *The Windsor Story*, p. 410.
16 Ibid.
17 Charles Murphy to Allen Grover, 30 July 1947. Time Inc. Archive, New York Historical Society.
18 Ibid.
19 'World War I', 17 July 1947, Murphy Collection.
20 Ibid.
21 'Position and Privilege', July 1947, Murphy Collection.
22 Ibid.

ENDNOTES

23 Charles Murphy to Allen Grover, 30 July 1947, Time Inc. Archive, New York Historical Society.
    Ibid.
24 Ibid.
25 Charles Murphy to Walter Monckton, 31 July 1947, Murphy Collection.
26 Daniel Longwell to Edward, Duke of Windsor, 30 July 1947, Daniel Longwell Papers.
27 Edward, Duke of Windsor, to Daniel Longwell, 15 September 1947, Daniel Longwell Papers.
28 Charles Murphy to Hank Walter, 24 September 1947, Murphy Collection.
29 Charles Murphy to Hank Walter, 3 October 1947, Murphy Collection.
30 Ibid.
31 Murphy to Longwell, 8 October 1947, Daniel Longwell Papers.
32 Longwell to Murphy, 8 October 1947, Daniel Longwell Papers.
33 Walter Graebner to Daniel Longwell, 1 November 1947, Daniel Longwell Papers.
34 'FYI' (Time Inc. Newsletter), 8 December 1947, Murphy Collection.
35 Ibid.
36 Daniel Longwell to Henry Luce, 28 November 1947, Daniel Longwell Papers.
37 Charles Murphy to Walter Graebner, 26 November 1947, Murphy Collection.
38 Charles Murphy to George Allen, 2 December 1947, Murphy Collection.
39 Daniel Longwell to Henry Luce, 19 December 1947, Daniel Longwell Papers.
40 Daniel Longwell to Edward, Duke of Windsor, 3 December 1947, Daniel Longwell Papers.
41 Daniel Longwell to Edward, Duke of Windsor, 11 December 1947, Daniel Longwell Papers.
42 Edward, Duke of Windsor to Henry Luce, 22 December 1947, Time Inc. Archive, New York Historical Society.
43 *Life*, 15 December 1947.
44 Daniel Longwell to Walter Graebner, 28 November 1947, Daniel Longwell Papers.
45 Walter Graebner to Charles Murphy, 13 December 1947, Murphy Collection.
46 Raimund von Hofmannsthal to Charles Murphy, 19 December 1947, Daniel Longwell Papers.

47 Edward, Duke of Windsor, to Charles Murphy, 30 December 1947, Murphy Collection.

48 Daniel Longwell to Edward, Duke of Windsor, 30 December 1947, Daniel Longwell Papers.

2. On Tour

1 George Allen to Charles Murphy, 31 December 1947, Murphy Collection.

2 Charles Murphy to George Allen, 5 January 1948, Murphy Collection.

3 Daniel Longwell to Edward, Duke of Windsor, 2 January 1948, Daniel Longwell Papers.

4 Edward, Duke of Windsor, to Daniel Longwell, 8 January 1948, Daniel Longwell Papers.

5 Charles Murphy to Daniel Longwell, 2 February 1948, Daniel Longwell Papers.

6 Charles Murphy to Edward, Duke of Windsor, 13 February 1948, Murphy Collection.

7 Charles Murphy to Edward, Duke of Windsor, 8 March 1948, Murphy Collection.

8 'Tours', undated, Murphy Collection.

9 RA/EDW/PRIV/BOOKS.

10 Quoted in *A King's Story*, p. 145.

11 Quoted in Powell, *An American Life*, from Amery, *My Political Life*, p. 197.

12 'Overseas Tour', undated, Murphy Collection.

13 Powell, *An American Life*, p. 50

14 'Canada-U.S.', 24–5 July 1947, Murphy Collection.

15 *A King's Story*, p. 134.

16 Powell, *An American Life*, p. 59.

17 'Conversations: His Royal Highness & Sir Godfrey Thomas', 6 June 1949. Murphy Collection.

18 'Trips', undated, Murphy Collection.

19 'Trips', undated, Murphy Collection.

20 'Travels', undated, Murphy Collection.

21 'British', undated, Murphy Collection.

22 Ziegler, *King Edward VIII*, p. 145.

23 'XI', undated, Murphy Collection.

24 Ibid.
25 'VI', undated, Murphy Collection.
26 RA/EDW/PRIV/BOOKS.
27 'XI', undated, Murphy Collection.
28 RA/EDW/PRIV/BOOKS
29 The Fort', undated, Murphy Collection.
30 'Chapter IX', undated, Murphy Collection.
31 'Fort', undated, Murphy Collection.
32 'The Fort', undated, Murphy Collection.
33 Daniel Longwell to Edward, Duke of Windsor, 14 April 1948, Daniel
    Longwell Papers.
34 'General', 3 May 1948, Murphy Collection.
35 Godfrey, *Letters from a Prince*, p. 286.
36 Godfrey, *Letters from a Prince*, p. 286–7.
37 Godfrey, *Letters from a Prince*, p. 483.
38 'South America', 5 May 1948, Murphy Collection.
39 *New York Times*, 31 March 1931, p. 1.
40 *The Times*, 12 June 1935.
41 Ibid.
42 Clive Wigram to George V, 12 June 1935, RA/PS/PSO/GVI/C/19/281.
43 George V to Clive Wigram, 12 June 1935, RA/PS/PSO/GVI/C/19/282.
44 RA/EDW/PRIV/BOOKS.
45 Draft 'IV', undated, Murphy Collection.
46 'Lack of Power', undated, Murphy Collection.
47 'Middle Years', undated, Murphy Collection.
48 'VII', undated, Murphy Collection.
49 'Hunting', 12 May 1948, Murphy Collection.
50 'Royal Warrants', 12 May 1948, Murphy Collection.
51 'Diary', 15 May 1948, Murphy Collection.

3. Operation Belvedere

1 Max Aitken, Lord Beaverbrook, to Edward, Duke of Windsor, 24 July 1948.
   BBK/G/6/15, Parliamentary Archives.
2 Ibid.

3 Charles Murphy to Daniel Longwell, 30 July 1948, Murphy Collection.
4 Ibid.
5 Ibid.
6 Charles Murphy to Daniel Longwell, 3 August 1948, Daniel Longwell Papers.
7 Daniel Longwell to Edward, Duke of Windsor, 12 August 1948, Daniel Longwell Papers.
8 Charles Murphy to Daniel Longwell, 22 August 1948, Daniel Longwell Papers.
9 Charles Murphy to Daniel Longwell, 3 August 1948, Daniel Longwell Papers.
10 'Duchess – Montecatini', 22 September 1949, Murphy Collection.
11 'Interview with Mrs Merryman', February 1950, Murphy Collection.
12 'Interview with Rickatson-Hatt', July 1949, Murphy Collection.
13 'Chapter IX', undated, Murphy Collection.
14 'L-II', undated, George Allen to Edward, Duke of Windsor, 20 April 1950, Monckton Trustees 20, Balliol College.
15 'HRH's Description of Duchess', undated, Murphy Collection.
16 Charles Murphy to Daniel Longwell, 22 August 1948, Daniel Longwell Papers.
17 Ibid.
18 Ibid.
19 Ibid.
20 Untitled draft, 26 August 1948, Murphy Collection.
21 Ibid.
22 Edward, Duke of Windsor, to Daniel Longwell, 28 August 1948, Daniel Longwell Papers.
23 Daniel Longwell to Edward, Duke of Windsor, 10 September 1948, Monckton Trustees 20, Balliol College.
24 Daniel Longwell to Charles Murphy, 10 September 1948, Daniel Longwell Papers.
25 Walter Monckton to George Allen, 1 September 1948, Monckton Trustees 20, Balliol College.
26 Edward, Duke of Windsor, to Walter Monckton, 11 September 1948, Monckton Trustees 20, Balliol College.
27 Walter Monckton to George VI, RA/GVI/OUT/MONCKTON 2.
28 Edward, Duke of Windsor, to Daniel Longwell, 28 August 1948, Daniel Longwell Papers.

29 Edward, Duke of Windsor, to Monckton, 2 October 1948, Monckton Trustees 20, Balliol College.

30 Ibid.

31 Ibid.

32 'Memos from conversation between HRH and Lord Beaverbrook', 24 September 1948, Murphy Collection.

33 Charles Murphy to Daniel Longwell, 25 October 1948, Murphy Collection.

34 Charles Murphy to Ken Rawson, 28 November 1948, Murphy Collection.

35 '1936/Source – George Allen', November 1948, Murphy Collection

36 Charles Murphy to Daniel Longwell, 5 November 1948, Daniel Longwell Papers.

37 Ibid.

38 Godfrey, *Letters from a Prince*, p. 292.

39 'First Post-War', undated, Murphy Collection.

40 'Chapter XXII', undated, Murphy Collection.

41 Charles Murphy to Edward, Duke of Windsor, 10 November 1948, Murphy Collection.

42 Godfrey Thomas untitled notes, 4 November 1948, Murphy Collection.

43 Charles Murphy to Ken Rawson, 11 November 1948, Murphy Collection.

44 Quoted in *A King's Story*, p. 263.

45 'Diary', January 1949, Murphy Collection.

46 'King George V's Funeral', undated, Murphy Collection.

47 Cooper, Diaries, p.227.

48 RA/EDW/PRIV/BOOKS.

49 Edward, Duke of Windsor, to Walter Monckton, 8 December 1948, Monckton Trustees 20, Balliol College.

50 Monckton to Gray Phillips, 17 December 1948, Monckton Trustees 20, Balliol College.

51 Charles Murphy to Daniel Longwell, 25 December 1948, Daniel Longwell Papers.

52 *New York Times*, 14 December 1936.

53 Edward, Duke of Windsor, to Max Aitken, Lord Beaverbrook, 29 December 1948, BBK/G/6/15, Parliamentary Archives.

54 Charles Murphy to Max Aitken, 26 December 1948, Murphy Collection.

55 Monica Wyatt to Charles Murphy, 31 December 1948, Murphy Collection.

4. Kingship

1   Charles Murphy to George Allen, 3 January 1949, Murphy Collection.
2   'Chapter VI', undated, Murphy Collection.
3   'Middle Years', undated, Murphy Collection.
4   'VI Tours', undated, Murphy Collection.
5   'Chapter VI Middle Years', undated, Murphy Collection.
6   Untitled note, undated, Murphy Collection.
7   'HRH Windsor', undated, Murphy Collection.
8   'HRH 1936, Source – Sir Walter Monckton', undated, Murphy Collection.
9   Ibid.
10 'IX Last Years as Prince of Wales', undated, Murphy Collection.
11 '1st D.', 3 January 1949, Murphy Collection.
12 RA/EDW/PRIV/BOOKS.
13 Ibid.
14 'IX', Undated, Murphy Collection.
15 'My Family', 4 May 1948, Murphy Collection.
16 'First Post-War', undated, Murphy Collection.
17 'Chapter XIV, Nahlin Cruise', undated, Murphy Collection.
18 Ziegler, King Edward VIII, p. 282.
19 'Men Friends', 18 August 1948, Murphy Collection.
20 'Draft', 21 January 1949, Murphy Collection.
21 Quoted in Ziegler, King Edward VIII, p. 287.
22 'Note on the Hypocritical British Attitude towards Divorce', undated, Murphy Collection.
23 Mosley, The Duchess of Windsor, p. 89.
24 'Note on the Hypocritical British Attitude towards Divorce', undated, Murphy Collection.
25 'Fort Belvedere', undated, Murphy Collection.
26 'Fort Belvedere, W.W. Paris', 1954, Murphy Collection.
27 'Diary', January 1949, Murphy Collection.
28 'Diary', February 1949, Murphy Collection.
29 'Windsor Notes, Sir John Aird', November 1973, Murphy Collection.
30 'Notes from Conversations between HRH and Sir John Aird', 8 February 1949, Murphy Collection.
31 'Diary', February 1949, Murphy Collection.

32 Charles Murphy to Henry Walter, 26 March 1949, Murphy Collection.
33 'Diary,' April 1949, Murphy Collection.

5. The Crisis Unfolds

1 Nicolson, *Later Years*, pp. 98–9.
2 'Diary', Spring 1949, Murphy Collection
3 Charles Murphy to Henry Walter, 26 March 1949, Murphy Collection.
4 Charles Murphy to Daniel Longwell, 24 April 1949, Murphy Collection.
5 Daniel Longwell to Charles Murphy, 3 May 1949, Daniel Longwell Papers.
6 'Fort Belvedere – W.W. Paris', 1954, Murphy Collection.
7 'Interview with Mrs Merryman', February 1950, Murphy Collection.
8 'Chapter XV', 14 July 1949, BBK/G/6/27, Parliamentary Archives.
9 'Interview with Lord Beaverbrook – Cap d'Ail', 14 July 1949, Murphy Collection.
10 'Chapter XV', 14 July 1949, BBK/G/6/27, Parliamentary Archives.
11 'Chapter XV', 15 July 1949, BBK/G/6/27, Parliamentary Archives.
12 Charles Murphy to Daniel Longwell, 29 August 1949, Daniel Longwell Papers.
13 'Chapter XV', 20 July 1949, BBK/G/6/27, Parliamentary Archives.
14 'Conversation with Lord Beaverbrook, Cap d'Ail', 25 July 1949, Murphy Collection.
15 Alexander Hardinge to Edward, Duke of Windsor, 13 November 1936, quoted from 'Chapter XVI', 20 July 1949, BBK/G/6/27, Parliamentary Archives.
16 'Hardinge', undated, Murphy Collection.
17 'October to December 1936', Monckton Trustees 22, Balliol College.
18 Ibid.
19 Windsor, *A King's Story*, p. 331.
20 Ibid.
21 'Chapter XV', 25 July 1949, BBK/G/6/27, Parliamentary Archives.
22 Untitled draft, 26 August 1948, Murphy Collection.
23 'Chapter XV', 25 July 1949, BBK/G/6/27, Parliamentary Archives.
24 Pope-Hennessey, *Queen Mary*, p. 574.
25 Untitled notes, undated, Murphy Collection.

26 'VII Prince of Wales', undated, Murphy Collection.
27 '1929', 3 May 1948, Murphy Collection.
28 'VIII Unemployment', undated, Murphy Collection.
29 Untitled notes, undated, Murphy Collection.
30 'Interview with Lord Beaverbrook – Cap d'Ail', 14 July 1949, Murphy Collection.
31 *The Times*, 20 November 1936.
32 Ziegler, *King Edward VIII*, p. 301.
33 Untitled note, undated, Murphy Collection.
34 'HRH La Croë', 1947, Murphy Collection.
35 'VI-Travels', undated, Murphy Collection.
36 'Second Meeting with Max Beaverbrook', 16 July 1949, Murphy Collection.
37 'Chapter XVII', 2 May 1949, BBK/G/6/27, Parliamentary Archives.
38 Ibid.
39 'Chapter XVII', 2 May 1949, BBK/G/6/27, Parliamentary Archives.
40 'Chapter XV Duff Cooper Episode', undated. Murphy Collection.
41 'Chapter XVII', 2 May 1949, BBK/G/6/27, Parliamentary Archives.
42 'Chapter XV', undated, Murphy Collection.
43 Ibid.
44 Windsor, *A King's Story*, p. 341
45 'Chapter XVII', 3 May 1949, BBK/G/6/27, Parliamentary Archives.
46 '1936, Duchess', undated, Murphy Collection.
47 Ibid.
48 'Chapter XVII', 4 May 1949, BBK/G/6/27, Parliamentary Archives.
49 'Second Meeting with Max Beaverbrook', 16 July 1949, Murphy Collection.
50 Abdication – HRH', undated, Murphy Collection.
51 'Chapter XVII', 4 May 1949, BBK/G/6/27, Parliamentary Archives.
52 'Second Meeting with Max Beaverbrook,' 16 July 1949. Murphy Collection.
53 Ibid.
54 Ibid.
55 'October to December 1936', Monckton Trustees 22, Balliol College.
56 Ibid.
57 'Interview with Lord Beaverbrook – Cap d'Ail', 14 July 1949, Murphy Collection.

6. The Story Breaks

1 'Diary', 1949, Murphy Collection.
2 'Chapter XVII', 9 May 1949, BBK/G/6/27, Parliamentary Archives.
3 'Second Meeting with Max Beaverbrook', 16 July 1949, Murphy Collection.
4 Chapter XVII', 12 May 1949, BBK/G/6/27, Parliamentary Archives.
5 Beaverbrook, *The Abdication of King Edward VIII*, p. 65.
6 'Interview with Lord Beaverbrook – Cap d'Ail', 14 July 1949, Murphy Collection.
7 'Interview with Rickatson-Hatt', July 1949, Murphy Collection.
8 Ibid.
9 'Chapter XVII', 28 April 1949, BBK/G/6/27, Parliamentary Archives.
10 Windsor, *A King's Story*, p. 355.
11 Ibid.
12 'Interview with Rickatson-Hatt', July 1949, Murphy Collection.
13 'Chapter XIX Source: Monckton', 23 October 1949, Murphy Collection.
14 'Interview 47 Upper Brook Street, (HRH), Lord Brownlow, George Allen', 8 December 1949, Murphy Collection.
15 'Interview 47 Upper Brook Street, (HRH), Lord Brownlow, George Allen' 8 December 1949. Murphy Collection.
16 Ibid.
17 'Abdication (Belvedere) – W.W.', undated, Murphy Collection.
18 'Abdication', undated, Murphy Collection.
19 'Interview with Mrs Merryman', February 1950, Murphy Collection.
20 'HRH 1936, Source – Sir Walter Monckton', undated, Murphy Collection.
21 *Daily Mail*, 23 November 1936.
22 Spender, *New York Times*, 'The King Who Would Not Be King', 15 April 1951.
23 Draft broadcast, 1936. Monckton Trustees 14, Balliol College Library.
24 'Men Friends', 18 August 1948, Murphy Collection.
25 'Winston', undated, Murphy Collection.
26 Cannadine, 'Churchill and the British Monarchy', p. 259.
27 Quoted in Cannadine, p. 258.
28 'Chapter XIII Churchill's Entrance', undated, Murphy Collection.
29 'Interview with Lord Beaverbrook – Cap d'Ail', 14 July 1949, Murphy Collection.

30 'Source: Lord Beaverbrook', 25 July 1949, Murphy Collection.
31 'Second Meeting with Beaverbrook', 16 July 1949, Murphy Collection.
32 'XVII King's Party', undated, Murphy Collection.
33 'Chapter XVII', 20 May 1949, BBK/G/6/27, Parliamentary Archives.
34 'Chapter XIX Source: Monckton', 23 October 1949, Murphy Collection.
35 Ibid.
36 'King's Party – HRH', undated, Murphy Collection.
37 'Chapter XVII', 25 May 1949, BBK/G/6/27, Parliamentary Archives.
38 'H.R.H. Fort Belvedere, Source Walter Monckton', undated, Murphy Collection.

7. The King's Party

1 'King's Party – HRH', undated, Murphy Collection.
2 'XI', undated, Murphy Collection.
3 Quoted in 'Chapter XIX', 15 August 1949, BBK/G/6/27, Parliamentary Archives.
4 'Draft', 22 May 1949, RA/EDW/PRIV/BOOKS.
5 'Chapter XIX', 15 August 1949, BBK/G/6/27, Parliamentary Archives.
6 'Two Interviews with Lord Beaverbrook', 16 August 1949, Murphy Collection.
7 'Chapter XIX'. 15 August 1949, BBK/G/6/27, Parliamentary Archives.
8 'October to December 1936', Monckton Trustees 22, Balliol College.
9 'Chapter XIX', 15 August 1949, BBK/G/6/27, Parliamentary Archives.
10 'XIX', undated, Murphy Collection.
11 'Churchill', undated, Murphy Collection.
12 'Interview, 47 Upper Brook Street, (HRH), Lord Brownlow, George Allen', 8 December 1949, Murphy Collection.
13 Quoted in Williams, *The People's King*, p. 173.
14 'Source – Lord Beaverbrook', 25 July 1949, Murphy Collection.
15 'King's Party', undated, Murphy Collection.
16 Channon, *The Diaries*, p. 603.
17 Channon, *The Diaries*, p. 605.
18 'King's Party', undated, Murphy Collection.
19 Ibid.

20 'Second Meeting with Beaverbrook', 16 July 1949, Murphy Collection. Ibid.

21 Ziegler, 'Churchill and the Monarchy', p. 4.

22 Winston Churchill to Edward, Duke of Windsor, 5 December 1936, quoted in 'Chapter XIX', 15 August 1949, BBK/G/6/27, Parliamentary Archives.

23 Colville, *The Fringes of Power*, p. 716.

24 Churchill, *The Gathering Storm*, p. 197.

25 'Diary Windsor', 15 May 1948, Murphy Collection.

26 'Source – Monckton', 23 October 1949, Murphy Collection.

27 'HRH, 1936, Source – Sir Walter Monckton', undated, Murphy Collection.

28 'Interview with Lord Beaverbrook – Cap d'Ail', 14 July 1949, Murphy Collection.

29 Ibid.

30 'XVII', undated, Murphy Collection.

31 'HRH –King's Party', undated, Murphy Collection.

32 H.R.H. Fort Belvedere Source Walter Monckton', undated, Murphy Collection.

33 'Abdication W.W.', undated, Murphy Collection.

34 Monckton to Alan Lascelles, 27 May 1949, Monckton Trustees 20, Balliol College.

35 Ibid.

36 Copy of Winston Churchill statement, 5 December 1936, BBK/G/6/6, Parliamentary Archives.

37 'Chapter XIX', 15 August 1949, BBK/G/6/27, Parliamentary Archives.

38 Charles Murphy to Max Aitken, Lord Beaverbrook, 11 August 1949, BBK/G/6/23, Parliamentary Archives.

39 'Chapter XIX', 15 August 1949, BBK/G/6/27, Parliamentary Archives.

40 'Chapter XX', Source: Monckton, 23 October 1949, Murphy Collection.

41 'Source: Monckton', 23 October 1949, Murphy Collection.

42 'Chapter XVI, Meeting with Walter Monckton, London', July 1949, Murphy Collection.

43 'Draft', 31 May 1949, RA/EDW/PRIV/BOOKS.

44 'Chapter XIX', 15 August 1949, BBK/G/6/27, Parliamentary Archives.

45 'XVII', undated, Murphy Collection.

46 'Second Interview with Goddard, Walter Monckton, A. G. Allen', 8 December 1949, Murphy Collection.

47 'Source: Monckton', 23 October 1949, Murphy Collection.

48 'Chapter XXI', 15 June 1949, BBK/G/6/27, Parliamentary Archives.

49 'Interview, 47 Upper Brook Street, (HRH), Lord Brownlow, George Allen', 8 December 1949. Murphy Collection.

50 'Draft', 31 May 1949, RA/EDW/PRIV/BOOKS.

51 'Beaverbrook-Brownlow Plot', 13 May 1949. Lord Brownlow, George Allen', 8 December 1949, Murphy Collection.

52 Brownlow statement, 9 December 1936, BNLW 4/4/9/4, Lincolnshire Archives.

53 'Draft', 11 June 1949, RA/EDW/PRIV/BOOKS.

8. Abdication

1 Windsor, *A King's Story*, p. 398.

2 'H.R.H. Fort Belvedere, Source Walter Monckton', undated, Murphy Collection.

3 'Draft', 10 June 1949, RA/EDW/PRIV/BOOKS.

4 Chapter XIX', 15 June 1949, BBK/G/6/27, Parliamentary Archives.

5 '1936, Source – George Allen, London', November 1948, Murphy Collection.

6 'XX', undated, Murphy Collection.

7 Williamson and Baldwin (eds), *Baldwin Papers*, p. 418.

8 'Baldwin's Attitude – Geo. Allen', 13 May 1949, Murphy Collection.

9 'Chapter XIX, Source Monckton', 23 October 1949, Murphy Collection.

10 RA/EDW/PRIV/BOOKS.

11 'Draft', 31 May 1949, RA/EDW/PRIV/BOOKS.

12 'Mrs Simpson's Position – HRH', undated, Murphy Collection.

13 'HRH 1936, Source – Sir Walter Monckton', undated, Murphy Collection.

14 Abdication (Belvedere) – W.W.', undated, 'HRH 1936, Source – Sir Walter Monckton', undated, Murphy Collection.

15 'Fort Belvedere', undated, Murphy Collection.

16 'Chapter XIX', 15 June 1949, BBK/G/6/27, Parliamentary Archives.

17 'Chapter XIX', 24 June 1949, BBK/G/6/27, Parliamentary Archives.

18 Edward to George VI, 11 February 1936, quoted in Bloch, *The Secret File of the Duke of Windsor*, p. 50.

19 'Chapter XIX', 24 June 1949, BBK/G/6/27, Parliamentary Archives.

20 'October to December 1936', Monckton Trustees 22, Balliol College.
21 'Chapter XIX', 24 June 1949, BBK/G/6/27, Parliamentary Archives.
22 Abdication timeline compiled by Charles Murphy, undated, Murphy Collection.
23 'Chapter XXI', 15 June 1949, BBK/G/6/27, Parliamentary Archives.
24 'Chapter XIX', 24 June 1949, BBK/G/6/27, Parliamentary Archives.
25 'Chapter XIX', 24 June 1949, BBK/G/6/27, Parliamentary Archives.
26 'Chapter XVI, Meeting with Walter Monckton, London', July 1949, Murphy Collection.
27 'October to December 1936', Monckton Trustees 22, Balliol College.
28 Inglis, *Abdication*, p. 368.
29 'October to December 1936', Monckton Trustees 22, Balliol College.
30 Woolf, *Diaries*, Vol. 5, p. 41.
31 Harris, 'Interview with the Duke of Windsor', https://www.youtube.com/watch?v=w8u7Ntic5fo.
32 Hardinge, *Loyal To Three Kings*, p. 174.
33 *The Windsors: A Royal Family*, episode 2, 'Brothers at War', 1994. Public Broadcasting Service (PBS)
34 'Chapter XXI', 15 June 1949, BBK/G/6/27, Parliamentary Archives.
35 'The Duke of Connaught', undated, Murphy Collection.
36 'Abdication', undated, Murphy Collection.
37 'Chapter XIX', 24 June 1949, BBK/G/6/27, Parliamentary Archives.
38 'Windsor – Abdication', undated, Murphy Collection.

9. The Finish Line

1 Edward, Duke of Windsor, to Walter Monckton, 13 August 1949, Monckton Trustees 20, Balliol College.
2 Charles Murphy to Edward, Duke of Windsor, 23 November 1949, Murphy Collection.
3 Godfrey Thomas to Walter Monckton, 19 June 1949, Monckton Trustees 20, Balliol College.
4 Walter Monckton to Charles Murphy, 8 July 1949, Murphy Collection.
5 Walter Monckton to Charles Murphy, 8 July 1949, Murphy Collection.
6 Walter Monckton to Gray Phillips, 17 December 1948, Monckton Trustees 20, Balliol College.

7   Walter Monckton to Alan Lascelles, 8 July 1949, Monckton Trustees 20, Balliol College.

8   Davis, *King's Counsellor*, p. xiii.

9   Alan Lascelles to Joan Lascelles, 26 July 1936, GBR/0014/LASL II/1/15B

10 'Chapter XVII', 27 May 1949, BBK/G/6/27, Parliamentary Archives.

11 Alan Lascelles to Nigel Nicolson, 5 August 1965, GBR/0014/LASL8/8

12 Charles Murphy to Daniel Longwell, 11 July 1949, Murphy Collection.

13 Walter Monckton to Alan Lascelles, 8 July 1949, Monckton Trustees 20, Balliol College.

14 Charles Murphy to Walter Monckton, 15 July 1949, Murphy Collection.

15 Charles Murphy to Max Aitken, 1 August 1949, Murphy Collection.

16 Max Aitken, Lord Beaverbrook, to Charles Murphy, 3 August 1949, BBK/G/6/23, Parliamentary Archives.

17 Charles Murphy to Max Aitken, Lord Beaverbrook, 11 August 1949, BBK/G/6/23, Parliamentary Archives.

18 Max Aitken, Lord Beaverbrook to Edward Duke of Windsor, 22 August 1949, BBK/G/6/15, Parliamentary Archives.

19 Charles Murphy to Ken Rawson, 29 August 1949, Murphy Collection.

20 Colville, *The Fringes of Power*, p. 509.

21 Charles Murphy to Ken Rawson, 24 August 1949, Murphy Collection.

22 Ibid.

23 Charles Murphy to Daniel Longwell, 23 August 1949, Daniel Longwell Papers.

24 'Diary', 18 September 1949, Murphy Collection.

25 Henry Luce to Max Beaverbrook, 23 September 1949, BBK/G/6/28, Parliamentary Archives.

26 Walter Monckton to George Allen, 4 October 1949, Monckton Trustees 20, Balliol College.

27 'Chapter 19, 20, 21 and 22. A.G.A.'s Notes', 21 October 1949, Murphy Collection.

28 Charles Murphy to Walter Monckton, 5 October 1949, Monckton Trustees 20, Balliol College.

29 Charles Murphy to Daniel Longwell, 13 October 1949, Daniel Longwell Papers.

30 Walter Monckton to Charles Murphy, 14 October 1949, Monckton Trustees 20, Balliol College.

31 Charles Murphy to Walter Monckton, 17 October 1949, Monckton Trustees 20, Balliol College.

32 Edward, Duke of Windsor, to Walter Monckton, 24 October 1949, Monckton Trustees 20, Balliol College.

33 Charles Murphy to George Allen, 28 October 1949, Murphy Collection.

34 Ibid.

35 Daniel Longwell to Edward, Duke of Windsor, 2 December 1949, Daniel Longwell Papers.

36 Edward, Duke of Windsor, to Daniel Longwell, 6 December 1949, Daniel Longwell Papers.

37 Daniel Longwell to Edward, Duke of Windsor, 29 December 1949, Daniel Longwell Papers.

38 Charles Murphy to George Allen, 30 December 1949, Murphy Collection.

39 Charles Murphy to Edward, Duke of Windsor, 23 November 1949, Murphy Collection.

40 Untitled, undated note, Murphy Collection.

41 'Diary', January 1950, Murphy Collection.

42 Charles Murphy to George Allen, 6 March 1950, Murphy Collection.

43 Daniel Longwell to Edward, Duke of Windsor, 8 March 1950, Daniel Longwell Papers.

44 Charles Murphy to Michael Wardell, 28 February 1950, Murphy Collection.

45 Edward, Duke of Windsor, to George Allen, 19 March 1950, Murphy Collection.

46 Charles Murphy to George Allen, 4 April 1950, Murphy Collection.

47 Ibid.

48 Ibid.

49 'Diary', March 1950, Murphy Collection.

50 'Duke and Duchess of Windsor visit their E.P. Ranch'. *Canadian Cattlemen*, May 1950.

51 Charles Murphy to George Allen, 4 April 1950, Murphy Collection.

52 Charles Murphy to Walter Monckton, 6 April 1950, Monckton Trustees 20, Balliol College.

53 Ibid

54 'L-II: D-1', 5 April 1950, Monckton Trustees 21, Balliol College.

55 Ibid.

56 Quoted in George Allen to Daniel Longwell, 20 April 1950, Murphy Collection.

57 Alan Lascelles to Walter Monckton, 18 April 1950, Monckton Trustees 20, Balliol College.
58 George Allen to Edward, Duke of Windsor, 20 April 1950, Monckton Trustees 20, Balliol College.
59 George Allen to Daniel Longwell, 20 April 1950, Daniel Longwell Papers.
60 Ibid.
61 Max Aitken, Lord Beaverbrook, to Charles Murphy 14 April 1950, BBK/G/6/23, Parliamentary Archives.
62 Charles Murphy to George Allen, 28 April 1950, Murphy Collection.
63 Henry Luce to Edward, Duke of Windsor, 28 April 1950, Murphy Collection.
64 Charles Murphy to Henry Luce, 28 April 1950, Murphy Collection.
65 Walter Monckton to Alan Lascelles, 5 May 1950, Monckton Trustees 20, Balliol College.
66 Alan Lascelles to Walter Monckton, 10 May 1950, Monckton Trustees 20, Balliol College.
67 Daniel Longwell to Charles Murphy, 14 June 1950, Murphy Collection.
68 Hank Walter to George Allen, 15 June 1950. Murphy Archive
69 Charles Murphy to Hank Walter, 26 June 1950, Murphy Collection.
70 Owen Morshead, 28 July 1950, RA/EDW/PRIV/BOOKS.
71 Alexander Hardinge to Owen Morshead, 28 July 1950, RA/EDW/PRIV/BOOKS.
72 Daniel Longwell to Edward, Duke of Windsor, 10 July 1950, Daniel Longwell Papers.
73 Charles Murphy to Hank Walter, 26 June 1950, Murphy Collection.
74 Charles Murphy to Edward, Duke of Windsor, 1 September 1950, Murphy Collection.
75 Ibid.
76 Charles Murphy to Hank Walter, 11 November 1950, Murphy Collection.
77 Murphy to Phyllis Westberg, 23 January 1973, Murphy Collection.
78 Charles Murphy to George Allen, 23 February 1951, Murphy Collection.

10. The Duchess Speaks

1 Daniel Longwell to Edward, Duke of Windsor, 13 April 1951, Daniel Longwell Papers.
2 Spender, New York Times, 'The King who Would Not Be King', 15 April 1951.

3   Seagrim, Anna, 19 April 1956, GBR/0014/SEAG/1/1, Churchill Archives.

4   Edward, Duke of Windsor, to Eric, Earl of Dudley, 3 May 1951, RA/EDW/
    PRIV/MAIN/A/7950.

5   Edward, Duke of Windsor, to Otto, Archduke of Austria, 26 April 1951,
    RA/EDW/MAIN/PRIV/7933.

6   Charles Murphy to Edward, Duke of Windsor, 23 November 1951, RA/
    EDW/PRIV/MAIN/A/8063.

7   Edward, Duke of Windsor, to Murphy, 25 July 1954, Murphy Collection.

8   Daniel Longwell to Wallis, Duchess of Windsor, 19 August 1949, Daniel
    Longwell Papers.

9   Daniel Longwell to Roy Larsen, 22 November 1950, Daniel Longwell Papers.

10 Daniel Longwell to Charles Murphy, 31 July 1952, Daniel Longwell Papers.

11 'Diary', 8 January 1954, Murphy Collection.

12 'Interview with Edward, Duke of Windsor', c. 1962, Murphy Collection.

13 'Diary', 16 February 1954, Murphy Collection.

14 Interview with Edward, Duke of Windsor, c. 1962, Murphy Collection.

15 Charles Murphy to Wallis, Duchess of Windsor, 31 October 1953, Murphy
    Collection.

16 Charles Murphy to Wallis, Duchess of Windsor, 5 August 1954, Murphy
    Collection.

17 'Diary', 19 October 1954, Murphy Collection

18 Charles Murphy to Hildegarde Maynard, 2 November 1954, Murphy Collection.

19 'The Abdication', 28 October 1954, Murphy Collection.

20 'Diary', 30 October 1954, Murphy Collection.

21 'Diary', 6 November 1954, Murphy Collection.

22 'Interview with Wallis, Duchess of Windsor', 6 November 1954, Murphy
    Collection.

23 Ibid.

24 Ibid.

25 Monckton memorandum, undated, Monckton Trustees 22, Balliol College.

26 Quoted in Ziegler, *King Edward VIII*, p. 346.

27 Edward, Duke of Windsor, to Queen Mary, 27 May 1937, RA/EDW/PRIV/
    MAIN/A/405.

28 'Diary', 7 November 1954, Murphy Collection.

29 Audio recording, 'Cannes, Canada & observations on British', Cleveland
    Amory Papers, MS.SC.0006, Boston Public Library.

30 Monckton memorandum, undated, Monckton Trustees 22, Balliol College.
31 Duke of Windsor Draft Statement (May–June 1937), Monckton Trustees 15, Balliol College.
32 Monckton memorandum, undated, Monckton Trustees 22, Balliol College.
33 Walter Monckton to George Allen, 9 June 1937, Monckton Trustees 15, Balliol College.
34 Edward, Duke of Windsor, to George VI, 2 June 1937, quoted in Bloch, *The Secret File of the Duke of Windsor*, p. 77.
35 Interview with Edward, Duke of Windsor, c. 1962, Murphy Collection.
36 'Diary', 21 November 1954, Murphy Collection.
37 'Diary', 28 November 1954, Murphy Collection.
38 'Diary', 5 December 1954, Murphy Collection.
39 Audio recording, 'Cannes, Canada & observations on British', Cleveland Amory Papers, MS.SC.0006, Boston Public Library.
40 Ibid.
41 Wallis, Duchess of Windsor, to Edward, Duke of Windsor, 14 December 1946, quoted in Bloch, *Wallis and Edward*, p. 276.
42 'Diary', 12 February 1955, Murphy Collection.
43 'Diary', 20 February 1955, Murphy Collection.
44 'Diary', 5 April 1955, Murphy Collection.
45 Edward, Duke of Windsor, to Charles Murphy, 27 April 1954, Murphy Collection.
46 Wallis, Duchess of Windsor, to Charles Murphy, 27 April 1955, Murphy Collection.
47 'Diary', 18 August 1955, Murphy Collection.
48 'Diary', 6 September 1955, Murphy Collection.
49 Edward, Duke of Windsor, to Charles Murphy, 14 October 1955, Murphy Collection.
50 Transcript of interview with Cleveland Amory on *Today*, 1 October 1956, Murphy Collection.
51 'Diary', 26 September 1955, Murphy Collection.
52 'Diary', 20 October 1955, Murphy Collection.
53 Charles Murphy to Max Aitken Lord Beaverbrook, 12 April 1956, Murphy Collection.

11. The German Question

1   *New York Times*, 4 June 1972, p. 77.
2   Edward, Duke of Windsor, to Charles Murphy, 17 January 1972, Murphy Collection.
3   Charles Murphy to Wallis, Duchess of Windsor, 17 April 1972, Murphy Collection.
4   Charles Murphy to Wallis, Duchess of Windsor, 9 June 1972, Murphy Collection.
5   Charles Murphy to Max Aitken Lord Beaverbrook, 12 April 1956, Murphy Collection.
6   Lownie, *Traitor King*.
7   Ziegler, *King Edward VIII*, p. 552.
8   *New York Times*, 29 May 1972.
9   *The Times*, 4 October 1937, p. 14.
10 *New York Times*, 23 October 1937.
11 Audio recording, 'Cannes, Canada & observations on British', Cleveland Amory Papers, MS.SC.0006, Boston Public Library.
12 Ibid.
13 Weatherburn, *Scientific Management at Work*, p. 75.
14 Powell, *An American Life*, p. 202
15 Oscar Solbert to Edward, Duke of Windsor, 27 April 1937, Private Collection.
16 *New York Times*, 2 July 1937.
17 Flanner, 'Annals of Collaboration', *New Yorker*, p. 32.
18 Eric Phipps to O. C. Harvey (Foreign Office), 4 October 1937, RA/PS/PSO/GVI/C/042/053a.
19 Walford Selby to Collin Brooks, 5 September 1937, Bodleian Library.
20 'Interview with Wallis, Duchess of Windsor', 6 November 1954, Murphy Collection.
21 Schmidt, *Hitler's Interpreter*, pp.85–6.
22 David Storrier diary, quoted in *The Sunday Times*, 16 August 1998.
23 *New York Times*, 6 November 1937.
24 *Chicago Tribune*, 25 October 1937.
25 *New York Times*, 24 October 1937.
26 *Washington Post*, 24 October 1937.
27 Speech to the Anglo-American Press Association, 27 October 1937, RA/EDW/PRIV/3472.

28 Winston Churchill to Edward, Duke of Windsor, 28 October 1937, CHAR 2/300, Churchill Archive Trust.

29 Edward, Duke of Windsor, to Charles Bedaux, 9 November 1937 Sworders Auction House, April 2021, *Books and Maps* catalogue.

30 Ronald Lindsay to Alexander Hardinge, 7 November 1937, RA/PS/PSO/GVI/C/042/099a.

31 Ronald Lindsay to George VI, 6 November 1937, RA/PS/PSO/GVI/C/19/281.

32 Ibid.

33 'Interview with Wallis, Duchess of Windsor', 6 November 1954, Murphy Collection.

34 Audio recording, 'Cannes, Canada & observations on British', Cleveland Amory Papers, MS.SC.0006, Boston Public Library.

35 Ibid.

36 Ibid.

37 Ziegler, *King Edward VIII*, p. 423

38 Interview with Edward, Duke of Windsor, c. 1962, Murphy Collection.

39 Audio recording, 'Cannes, Canada & observations on British', Cleveland Amory Papers, MS.SC.0006, Boston Public Library.

40 Wallis, Duchess of Windsor, to Edward, Duke of Windsor, 6 February 1937, quoted in Bloch, *Wallis and Edward*, p. 304

41 Eberhard von Stohrer to Joachim von Ribbentrop, 23 July 1940, BBK/G/6/20, Parliamentary Archives.

42 Eberhard von Stohrer to Joachim von Ribbentrop, 25 July 1940, BBK/G/6/20, Parliamentary Archives.

43 Eberhard von Stohrer to Joachim von Ribbentrop, 31 July 1940, BBK/G/6/20, Parliamentary Archives.

44 Oswald von Hoyningen-Heune to Joachim von Ribbentrop, 2 August 1940. BBK/G/6/20, Parliamentary Archives.

45 Eberhard von Stohrer to Joachim von Ribbentrop, 3 August 1940, BBK/G/6/20, Parliamentary Archives.

46 Audio recording, 'Cannes, Canada & observations on British', Cleveland Amory Papers, MS.SC.0006, Boston Public Library.

47 Oswald von Hoyningen-Heune to Joachim von Ribbentrop, 10 July 1940, quoted in Ziegler from *Documents on German Foreign Policy*. Series D, Vol. X, p. 425.

48 Eberhard von Stohrer to Joachim von Ribbentrop, 15 August 1940, BBK/G/6/20, Parliamentary Archives.

49 Ziegler, *King Edward VIII*, p. 435.
50 Monckton memorandum, undated, Monckton Trustees 22, Balliol College.
51 'Diary, H.R.H World War 2, Sir Walter Monckton', 5 November 1948, Murphy Collection.
52 'Diary', 11 November 1954, Murphy Collection.
53 *The Times*, 17 November 1954.
54 Ziegler, *King Edward VIII*, p. 415.
55 'Diary', 17 November 1954, Murphy Collection.
56 Ibid.
57 Dwight D. Eisenhower to Winston Churchill, 2 July 1953, BBK/G/6/20, Parliamentary Archives.
58 Winston Churchill to Dwight D. Eisenhower, 27 June 1953, BBK/G/6/20, Parliamentary Archives.
59 Winston Churchill to Clement Attlee, 26 August 1945, quoted in Cabinet Minutes August 1953, BBK/G/6/20, Parliamentary Archives.
60 Quoted in Ziegler, *King Edward VIII*, p.550.
61 *New York Times*, 31 July 1957.
62 *The Times*, 1 August 1957.
63 *The Times*, 2 August 1957.
64 *Daily Express*, 2 August 1957.
65 *Daily Telegraph*, 1 August 1957.
66 Walford Selby to Edward, Duke of Windsor, 2 September 1957, Selby Archive, Bodleian Library.
67 Walford Selby to Collin Brooks, 5 September 1937, Selby Archive, Bodleian Library.
68 Edward, Duke of Windsor, to Walford Selby, 14 August 1957, Selby Archive, Bodleian Library.
69 Edward, Duke of Windsor, to Samuel Hoare Viscount Templewood, 15 August 1958, GBR/0012/MS Templewood, Cambridge University Library.
70 *The Times*, 29 December 1962.
71 Charles Murphy to Edward, Duke of Windsor, 2 January 1963, Murphy Collection.
72 *Chicago Tribune*, 13 December 1966.

Epilogue

1 'Introduction HRH', 1950, Murphy Collection.
2 Bouverie, *Appeasement*, p. 108.
3 *The Times*, 5 September 1936.
4 Edward, Duke of Windsor, to Sir George Arthur, 12 May 1938, RA/EDW/ PRIV/3622.
5 *New York Times*, 9 May 1939.
6 Roosevelt, 'The Acceptance Speech for the Renomination for the Presidency, Philadelphia', 27 June 1936. Franklin D. Roosevelt Library.
7 'Nineteen Twenties', undated, Murphy Collection.
8 Bagehot, *The English Constitution*, p. 85.
9 'HRH Paris', 1950, Murphy Collection.
10 'The Nineteen Twenties', 1950, Murphy Collection.

Picture credits

Plate section 1

Page 1: Hulton-Deutsch Collection/CORBIS/Corbis via Getty Images; Page 2 top left: Spencer Arnold Collection/Hulton Archive/Getty Images; Page 2 middle left: Spencer Arnold Collection/Hulton Archive/Getty Images; Page 2 bottom right: Ernest Brooks/Central Press/Hulton Royals Collection/Getty Images; Page 3 top right: Martin Munkacsi/ullstein bild via Getty Images; Page 3 top left: Central Press/Hulton Royals Collection/Getty Images; Page 3 bottom: Robert Sennecke/ullstein bild via Getty Images; Page 4 top: Universal History Archive/ Universal Images Group via Getty Images; Page 4 middle left: PA Images/Alamy Stock Photo; Page 4 bottom right: Popperfoto via Getty Images/Getty Images; Page 5 top left: Central Press/Hulton Royals Collection/Getty Images; Page 5 middle right: The Print Collector/Getty Images; Page 5 bottom left: Universal History Archive/Universal Images Group via Getty Images; Page 6 top left: Universal History Archive/Universal Images Group via Getty Images; Page 6 middle left: Central Press/Hulton Royals Collection/Getty Images; Page 6 middle right: Popperfoto via Getty Images/Getty Images; Page 6 bottom left: SuperStock/Alamy Stock Photo; Page 7 top: Bentley Archive/Popperfoto via Getty Images/Getty Images; Page 7 bottom: Popperfoto via Getty Images/ Getty Images; Page 8 top: Popperfoto via Getty Images/Getty Images; Page 8 bottom: Keystone-France/Gamma-Keystone via Getty Images

Plate section 2

Page 1: Lady Alexandra Metcalfe/Cahrlie Metcalfe/Balliol College Historic Collections, Monckton Trustees 16, folio 52b verso; Page 2 top: Keystone/ Hulton Royals Collection/Getty Images; Page 2 bottom: Bettmann/Getty Images; Page 3 top left: Universal History Archive/Universal Images Group via Getty Images; Page 3 bottom: Keystone/Hulton Archive/Getty Images; Page 4 top left: John Swope/Getty Images; Page 4 middle right: John Swope/Getty Images; Page 4 bottom left: Keystone Press/Alamy Stock Photo; Page 5 top: Hulton-Deutsch Collection/CORBIS/Corbis via Getty Images; Page 5 middle:

David Savill/Topical Press Agency/Hulton Archive/Getty Images; Page 5 bottom: Hulton Archive/Getty Images; Page 6 top left: Philippe Halsman/Magnum Images; Page 6 middle right: Keystone-France/Gamma-Keystone via Getty Images; Page 6 bottom left: Express/Express/Getty Images; Page 6 bottom right: Illustrated London News Ltd/Mary Evans; Page 7 top left: Taken by Murphy Family photographer unknown; Page 7 middle right: Taken by Murphy Family photographer unknown; Page 7 middle left: Courtesy of Joey Vars/Belleview Inn/George Spencer; Page 7 bottom right: Associated Press/Alamy Stock Photo; Page 8 top left: John Swope/Getty Images Page 8 bottom right: Courtesy of Joey Vars/Belleview Inn/George Spencer

Index